Croatian

lonely planet

phrasebooks
and
Gordana & Ivan Ivet

Croatian phrasebook
1st edition – March 2005

Published by
Lonely Planet Publications Pty Ltd ABN 36 005 607 983
90 Maribyrnong St, Footscray, Victoria 3011, Australia

Lonely Planet Offices
Australia Locked Bag 1, Footscray, Victoria 3011
USA 150 Linden St, Oakland CA 94607
UK 72-82 Rosebery Ave, London, EC1R 4RW

Cover illustration
Adriatic Sunseeker by Daniel New

ISBN 1 74059 996 9

text © Lonely Planet Publications Pty Ltd 2005
cover illustration © Lonely Planet Publications Pty Ltd 2005

  10 9 8 7 6 5 4 3 1

Printed through the Bookmaker International Ltd
Printed in China

acknowledgments

Editor Francesca Coles would like to acknowledge the following for their contributions to this phrasebook:

Gordana and Ivan Ivetac for their polished translations and linguistic and cultural expertise. Both Gordana and Ivan are NAATI accredited Croatian to English translators and interpreters with extensive experience in the field. Gordana also teaches a course on the cultural and ethical aspects of interpreting at RMIT. Ivan (a native of the town of Pula in coastal Croatia) has a BA in Italian and Philosophy and is completing a PhD in Molecular Biology at Monash University.

Editors Quentin Frayne, Piers Kelly and Annelies Mertens for advice, feedback and companionship along the way.

In-house Croatian speakers Zeljko Basic and Jack Gavran for help with the transliteration system and queries generally.

Freelance editor Adrienne Costanzo for her eagle-eyed proofing.

Wendy Wright for the inside illustrations and Daniel New for the cover.

Paul Piaia for assistance with the map.

Lonely Planet Language Products

Publishing Manager: Karin Vidstrup Monk
Commissioning Editors: Karina Coates/Ben Handicott
Editors: Francesca Coles, Meladel Mistica and Jodie Martire
Layout Designer: David Kemp
Project Manager: Fabrice Rocher
Managing Editors: Karin Vidstrup Monk/Annelies Mertens
Layout Manager: Adriana Mammarella
Series Designers: Yukiyoshi Kamimura/Brendan Dempsey
Cartographer: Wayne Murphy

make the most of this phrasebook ...

Anyone can speak another language! It's all about confidence. Don't worry if you can't remember your school language lessons or if you've never learnt a language before. Even if you learn the very basics (on the inside covers of this book), your travel experience will be the better for it. You have nothing to lose and everything to gain when the locals hear you making an effort.

finding things in this book

For easy navigation, this book is in sections. The Tools chapters are the ones you'll thumb through time and again. The Practical section covers basic travel situations like catching transport and finding a bed. The Social section gives you conversational phrases, pick-up lines, the ability to express opinions – so you can get to know people. Food has a section all of its own: gourmets and vegetarians are covered and local dishes feature. Safe Travel equips you with health and police phrases, just in case. Remember the colours of each section and you'll find everything easily; or use the comprehensive Index. Otherwise, check the two-way traveller's Dictionary for the word you need.

being understood

Throughout this book you'll see coloured phrases on each page. They're phonetic guides to help you pronounce the language. You don't even need to look at the language itself, but you'll get used to the way we've represented particular sounds. The pronunciation chapter in Tools will explain more, but you can feel confident that if you read the coloured phrase slowly, you'll be understood.

communication tips

Body language, ways of doing things, sense of humour – all have a role to play in every culture. 'Local talk' boxes show you common ways of saying things, or everyday language to drop into conversation. 'Listen for ...' boxes supply the phrases you may hear. They start with the phonetic guide (because you'll hear it before you know what's being said) and then lead in to the language and the English translation.

croatian

Romania

Bulgaria

Hungary

Greece

Skopje
Macedonia

Belgrade

Serbia

Albania

Strait of Otranto

Montenegro

Sarajevo

Bosnia and Hercegovina

Austria

Zagreb

Croatia

Adriatic Sea

Ljubljana
Slovenia

Italy

Gulf of Venice

Italy

Tyrrhenian Sea

official language
widely understood
generally understood

For more details, see the **introduction**.

Croatian is the language of one of the world's newest countries. Like the country itself, Croatian has an intriguing, cosmopolitan, and at times fraught, history.

Croatian's linguistic ancestor was brought to the region in the sixth and seventh centuries AD by the South Slavs who may have crossed the Danube from the region now known as Poland. This ancestral language split off into two branches: East South Slavic, which later evolved into Bulgarian and Macedonian, and West South Slavic, of which Slovene, Serbian and Croatian are all descendants.

Croatia may be a peaceful country today but the Balkan region to which it belongs has a long history of invasion and conflict. These upheavals have enriched and politicised the language. The invasion by Charlemagne's armies and forced conversion to the Roman Church in AD 803 left its mark on Croatian in the form of words borrowed from Latin and the adoption of the Latin alphabet rather than the Cyrillic alphabet (with which Serbian is written). Subsequent invasions by the Hapsburg, Ottoman and Venetian empires added vibrancy to the language through the influx of German, Turkish and Venetian dialect loan words. Many words from the standard Italian of Croatia's neighbour Italy have also added colour.

Croatian is not really a separate language from Serbian or Bosnian. Linguists

---

at a glance ...

language name:
Croatian

name in language:
hrvatski jezik
hr·vat·skee je·zeek

language family: Slavic

approximate number of speakers: 5 million

close relatives:
Bosnian, Macedonian, Serbian and Slovenian

donations to English:
cravat, dalmatian

---

commonly refer to the language spoken in Croatia, Serbia and Bosnia-Hercegovina under the umbrella term Serbo-Croatian while acknowledging dialectical difference. Croats, Serbs and Bosnians themselves generally maintain that they speak different languages, however. This polarisation of language identities reflects the desire to retain separate ethnic identities.

The good news is that, if you venture into Serbia or Montenegro, you'll be able to enrich your travel experience there by using this phrasebook. Croatian is also a handy lingua franca in any of the other states that made up part of the former Yugoslavia, as it's an official language in Bosnia-Hercegovina. People in Macedonia and Slovenia, who speak closely related languages, generally understand Croatian.

Croatian has plenty of appeal. As well as its rich vocabulary, it has a lovely repertoire of soft lisping sounds such as *sh*, *zh* and *ch* and a lilting musical rhythm due to its use of high and low pitches. It also has an intriguing grammar, quite different from English. It is, however, readily understandable.

Take this phrasebook with you to help make your trip hassle free. It's packed with all the practical language information you'll need and it will also open up a world of possibilities for social interaction and cultural exchange with the locals. Need more encouragement? Remember, the contact you make through using Croatian will make your travel experience unique. Local knowledge, new relationships and a sense of satisfaction are on the tip of your tongue, so don't just stand there – say something!

abbreviations used in this book

m	masculine	pol	polite
f	feminine	inf	informal
n	neuter	imp	imperfective
sg	singular	perf	perfective
pl	plural	lit	literally

Croatian pronunciation is quite straightforward for English speakers as many of the sounds are similar to English sounds. Some claim, in fact, that for English speakers, Croatian pronunciation is the easiest to master among the European languages.

vowel sounds

There are seven vowel sounds in Croatian. In the written language, vowels that appear next to each other don't run together to form diphthongs (vowel sound combinations) as in English. When you see two or more vowels written next to each other in a Croatian word, pronounce each vowel separately.

symbol	english equivalent	croatian example	transliteration
a	father	*zdravo*	zdra·vaw
ai	aisle	*ajvar*	ai·var
aw	raw	*brod*	brawd
e	let	*pet*	pet
ee	bee	*sidro*	see·draw
oo	book	*skupo*	skoo·paw
oy	boy	*tvoj*	tvoy

consonant sounds

Croatian consonant sounds all have equivalents, or close equivalents, in English. The rolled r sound can be pronounced in combination with another consonant (or more than one consonant) as a separate syllable, as in the word *Hrvat* hr·vat 'Croatian'. If these syllables without vowels look a bit intimidating, try inserting a slight 'uh' sound before the r to help them run off your tongue more easily. The sound s can appear as a syllable on its own.

symbol	english equivalent	croatian example	transliteration
b	big	glazba	glaz·ba
ch	chilli	četiri, ćuk	che·tee·ree, chuk
d	din	doručak	daw·roo·chak
f	fun	fotograf	faw·taw·graf
g	go	jagoda	ya·gaw·da
h	hit	hodnik	hawd·neek
j	jam	džep, đak	jep, jak
k	kick	krov	krawv
l	loud	lutka	loot·ka
l'	million	kašalj	kash·al'
m	man	mozak	maw·zak
n	no	nafta	naf·ta
n'	canyon	siječanj	see·ye·chan'
r	rag (but 'rolled')	radnik	rad·neek
s	salt	sastanak	sas·ta·nak
sh	show	košta	kawsh·ta
t	tin	sat	sat
ts	hits	prosinac	pro·see·nats
v	very	viza	vee·za
y	yes	svjetlost	svyet·lawst
z	zoo	zec	zets
zh	pleasure	koža	kaw·zha

When y comes after another consonant and before a vowel (as in the word djeca dye·tsa) it runs together with the preceding consonant and vowel. The preceding consonant is then pronounced with the tongue rising up towards the roof of the mouth. Something similar happens in English when you say 'and you' quickly. You don't need to be too conscious of this feature as it should happen more or less automatically as you follow the pronunciation guides.

stress & pitch accent

Certain syllables in Croatian have stress, which means you emphasise one syllable over another. As a general rule, in two-syllable words stress usually falls on the first syllable. In words of three or more syllables, stress may fall on any syllable except the last. In our pronunciation guides, the stressed syllable is italicised.

Croatian also has what's known as pitch accent. A stressed vowel may have either a rising or a falling pitch and be long or short. The combination of stress, pitch and vowel length in a given syllable can affect the meaning of a word. The word *sam* pronounced with a short vowel and falling pitch means 'alone' and sounds like 'sum'. When it's pronounced with a long vowel with falling pitch however, it means 'I am' and sounds like 'sarm'.

You don't need to worry about reproducing this feature of Croatian and we haven't indicated it in this book, as it only distinguishes meaning in a very few cases. In such cases it should be clear from the context what is meant. You may notice though that the speech of native speakers has an appealing musical lilt to it. You may also notice marks over the vowels in some dictionaries and grammar books to indicate vowel length and pitch.

reading & writing

Croatian is so closely related to Serbian that many people describe them as two dialects of the same language. However, religion and historical circumstances dictated that Croatian be written in the Latin alphabet, like English, rather than the Cyrillic alphabet, like Serbian. The Croatian alphabet has 30 letters, of which three are digraphs (single sounds made up of a combination of two letters). The accents above letters change the pronunciation of letters. The letter *c* for example is pronounced like the 'ts' in 'cats', while the letter č is pronounced like the 'ch' in 'cheese'.

Croatian spelling is absolutely phonetic – there's a fixed regular correspondence between letters and the way they're pronounced even when they're combined into words. What you see is what you say!

letter for letter

The table below shows the correspondences between the Croatian alphabet and the Serbian Cyrillic alphabet. This could come in handy if you venture beyond the confines of Croatia and want to try to read and understand written Serbian.

croatian		serbian		croatian		serbian	
A a	a	A a	a	L l	el	Л л	el
B b	be	Б б	be	Lj lj	l'	Љ љ	l'
C c	tse	Ц ц	tse	M m	em	М м	em
Č č	tch	Ч ч	tch	N n	en	Н н	en
Ć ć	ch	Ћ ћ	ch	Nj nj	n'	Њ њ	n'
D d	de	Д д	de	O o	aw	О о	aw
Dž dž	dzh	Џ џ	dzh	P p	pe	П п	pe
Đ đ	j	ђ ђ	j	R r	er	Р р	er
E e	e	E e	e	S s	es	С с	es
F f	ef	Ф ф	ef	Š š	sh	Ш ш	sh
G g	ge	Г г	ge	T t	te	Т т	te
H h	ha	X x	ha	U u	oo	У у	oo
I i	ee	И и	ee	V v	ve	В в	ve
J j	y	J j	y	Z z	zed	З з	zed
K k	ka	К к	ka	Ž ž	zh	Ж ж	zh

This chapter is arranged alphabetically for ease of navigation and is designed to help you go beyond the phrases in this book to create your own sentences. Don't worry too much about the rules of grammar. A couple of well-chosen words and gestures and a desire to communicate will generally help you get your message across.

All illustrations of points shown in the tables (other than examples of verbs) are given in the nominative case unless otherwise stated (for an explanation of case see **me, myself & I**). We haven't given you all the different case forms and endings, but if you want to delve into them there are many good basic textbook grammars of Croatian available, a useful one being *Colloquial Croatian and Serbian* by Celia Hawkesworth (Routledge, 1998).

a/an & the

There are no equivalents of the English articles 'a/an' and 'the'. In Croatian the context indicates whether something is meant to be indefinite (corresponding to 'a/an') or definite (corresponding to 'the').

adjectives see describing things

articles see a/an & the

be

Below are the present tense forms of the verb *biti* 'be'. The pronouns are in brackets because they're mostly not used in Croatian as the verb endings tell you who's doing the action of the verb, ie who's the subject.

I am	*(ja) sam*	(ya) sam
you are sg inf	*(ti) si*	(tee) see
you are sg pol	*(vi) ste*	(vee) ste
he/she/it is	*(on/ona/ono) je* m/f/n	(awn/*aw*·na/*aw*·naw) ye
we are	*(mi) smo*	(mee) smaw
you are pl	*(vi) ste*	(vee) ste
they are m/f/n	*(oni/one/ona) su*	(*aw*·nee/*aw*·ne/*aw*·na) soo

I'm Australian.
Ja sam Australac/   ya sam a·oo·*stra*·lats/
Australka. m/f   a·oo·*stral*·ka
(lit: I am Australian)

If you want to form a negative sentence with 'be' to express 'I'm/You're not' etc, just add the prefix *ni-* to the forms of *biti* above, eg *nisam, nisi*, etc.

I'm not Croatian.
Ja nisam Hrvat/Hrvatica. m/f   ya *nee*·sam hr·vat/hr·*va*·tee·tsa
(lit: I not-am Croat)

case see **me, myself & I**

describing things

Adjectives take different endings depending on the gender of the noun described, whether it's singular or plural and according to case (see **me, myself & I**).

gender/number	adjective ending
masculine singular	ends in a consonant or -*i*
masculine plural	ends in -*i*
feminine singular	ends in -*a*
feminine plural	ends in -*e*
neuter singular	ends in -*o*
neuter plural	ends in -*a*

He's a good man. (masculine noun and adjective)
 On je dobar čovjek.   awn ye *daw*·bar *chaw*·vyek
 (lit: he is good man)

She's a good woman. (feminine noun and adjective)
 Ona je dobra žena.   *aw*·na ye *daw*·bra *zhe*·na
 (lit: she is good woman)

doing things

In Croatian each verb has two forms. This is because Croatian makes the distinction between 'action as process' and 'action as completion' and calls the former the imperfective aspect and the latter the perfective aspect.

 The imperfective aspect is used for actions that are thought of as continuing, habitual, ongoing or incomplete, while the perfective aspect is for actions that are thought of as complete or limited. Note that verbs in the perfective aspect can't refer to present events because actions in the present are, by nature, unfinished. Both forms of the verb are provided in the dictionary.

past

Talking about the past in Croatian isn't hard. You just take the present tense of the verb *biti* (see **be**) and follow it with a verb form known as the active past participle. Forming the active past participle of most verbs is quite straightforward. The majority of verbs in Croatian end in -*ti* and to turn these verbs into the active past participle you just remove the -*ti* ending and add the endings shown in the table on the next page. The endings agree in gender and number with the subject of a sentence.

gender/number of subject	active past participle ending
masculine singular	-o
masculine plural	-li
feminine singular	-la
feminine plural	-le
neuter singular	-lo
neuter plural	-la

Here's an example with the verb *imati* 'have':

I had a ticket.

Ja sam imao/imala	ya sam ee·*ma*·aw/ee·*ma*·la
kartu. m/f	*kar*·too
(lit: I am had ticket)	

present

There are a few intricacies to forming the present tense of verbs in Croatian, more than is possible to outline here. A rule of thumb though, which works for many verbs, is to remove the -*ti* from the infinitive (dictionary form) of a verb and to add the following endings as shown here for the verb *čitati* 'read':

person		ending	present tense form	
I	*ja*	-m	*čitam*	*chee*·tam
you sg inf	*ti*	-š	*čitaš*	*chee*·tash
he/she/it	*on/ona/ ono* m/f/n	no ending	*čita*	*chee*·ta
we	*mi*	-mo	*čitamo*	chee·*ta*·maw
you sg pol & pl	*vi*	-te	*čitate*	chee·*ta*·te
they m/f/n	*oni/one/ ona*	-ju	*čitaju*	chee·*ta*·yoo

You'll find the present tense forms of the useful verbs 'be' and 'have' under those headings in this phrasebuilder.

future

To talk about future events you use a form of the verb *htjeti* (lit: 'want' but equivalent to 'will' in English) followed by the infinitive (dictionary) form of a verb.

I will	*(ja) ću*	(ja) choo
you will sg inf	*(ti) ćeš*	(tee) chesh
you will sg pol	*(vi) ćete*	(vee) *che*·te
he/she/it will	*(on/ona/ono) će*	(awn/aw·na/aw·ne) che
we will	*(mi) ćemo*	(mee) *che*·maw
you will pl	*(vi) ćete*	(vee) *che*·te
they will m/f/n	*(oni/one/ona) će*	(aw·nee/aw·ne/aw·na) che

I will read.
   Ja ću čitati.   ya choo *chee*·ta·tee
   (lit: I will read)

gender

In Croatian, all nouns – words that denote a person, thing or idea – have one of three genders: masculine, feminine or neuter. Gender is assigned to words more or less arbitrarily, though masculine and feminine persons and animals mostly carry masculine and feminine gender, respectively.

The gender of nouns is indicated where relevant in this phrasebook and for all nouns in the dictionary. Here are some handy generalisations to help you identify what gender a noun in the singular might be:

- masculine nouns mostly end in a consonant, eg, *muž* 'husband'
- feminine nouns often end in *-a*, eg *žena* 'woman'
- neuter nouns end in *-o* or *-e*, eg *vino* 'wine' and *dijete* 'child'

Verbs can take different endings according to gender too. They reflect the gender of the subject (the doer of the action). One expression that you'll come across frequently in this phrasebook is 'I'd like …' which translates as *Želio/Željela bih* … **m/f**. The gender markers indicate that if you're a man you select the first option, while if you're a woman you select the second.

I'd like to withdraw money. (man speaking)
| *Želio bih* | zhe·lee·aw beeh |
| *podignuti novac.* | paw·deeg·noo·tee naw·vats |

(lit: I-want-**m** would change money)

I'd like to withdraw money. (woman speaking)
| *Željela bih* | zhe·lye·la beeh |
| *podignuti novac.* | paw·deeg·noo·tee naw·vats |

(lit: I-want-**f** would change money)

gender in this book

Throughout this book we've used the abbreviations **m**, **f** and **n** to indicate gender. The order of presentation is masculine, feminine and then neuter.

If a letter or letters have been added to a masculine form to denote a feminine or neuter form these will appear in parentheses, eg *Židov(ka)* 'Jew' which has the masculine form *Žid* and the feminine form *Židovka*. Where the change involves more than the addition of a letter, different words are given separated by a slash. Sometimes, it's just a case of substituting the final letter of a word to make feminine or neuter forms as in this example: *mladi/a* mla·dee/a 'young' which has the masculine form *mladi* and the feminine form *mlada*.

have

To say that you have something you just use a form of the verb *imati* 'have' followed by the noun. As the direct object of the sentence, the nouns possessed should be in the accusative case, but you're sure to be understood if you just use the nominative case (dictionary form) of a noun (see **me, myself & I** for an explanation of the word case).

I have	(ja) imam	(ja) *ee*·mam
you have sg inf	(ti) imaš	(tee) *ee*·mash
you have sg pol	(vi) imate	(vee) ee·*ma*·te
he/she/it has	(on/ona/ono) ima m/f/n	(awn/*aw*·na/ aw·naw) *ee*·ma
we have	(mi) imamo	(mee) ee·*ma*·maw
you have pl	(vi) imate	(vee) ee·*ma*·te
they have m/f/n	(oni/one/ona) imaju	(*aw*·nee/*aw*·ne/ aw·na) ee·*ma*·yoo

I have a car.

Imam auto. *ee*·mam *a*·oo·taw
(lit: I-have car)

me, myself & I

In Croatian, the endings of nouns, adjectives and pronouns may change depending on their 'case'. The case of a word conveys grammatical information. Case can indicate whether a word is the subject (doer of the action), object (undergoer of the action) or indirect object (recipient of an action) of a sentence. These roles are signified by the nominative, accusative and dative cases respectively. It can also indicate possession, location, motion or the means with which something is done. There are seven cases in Croatian. Most of these have equivalents in English prepositions such as 'with', 'into', 'in', 'of' and so on. Other cases have no equivalents in English because English uses a fixed word order to signify basic grammatical relations. Croatian case endings are too numerous to list here but if you really want to learn the language, try to get hold of a comprehensive grammar guide to get you started.

All the nouns, pronouns and adjectives in the phrases in this book are, of course, in the appropriate case so you don't need to worry about this feature of Croatian. It does explain though, why you may see one word in several different guises. The town *Pula* can become *Pulu* or *Puli* when used with prepositions, for example. It also explains why word order in Croatian might sometimes seem muddled up (see **word order**).

more than one

There are a few tricks to forming the plural of nouns in Croatian. In the case of masculine nouns there's a distinction between animate nouns (those referring to living beings, animals etc) and inanimate nouns (those referring to objects).

animate masculine nouns of one syllable	*-ovi or -evi*
animate masculine nouns of more than one syllable	*-i*
inanimate masculine nouns	*-ovi or -evi*
feminine nouns ending in –a	*-e*
feminine nouns ending in a consonant	*-i*
neuter nouns	*-a*

my & your

A common way of indicating possession is to use what are known as possessive pronouns ('my, your, his, her' etc in English). These agree in gender (masculine or feminine), number (singular or plural) and case (see **me, myself & I**) with the person or thing possessed.

	masculine singular		feminine singular	
my	*moj*	moy	*moja*	moy·a
your	*tvoj*	tvoy	*tvoja*	tvoy·a
his	*njegov*	nye·gawv	*njegova*	nye·gaw·va
her	*njen*	nyen	*njena*	nye·na
our	*naš*	nash	*naša*	na·sha
your	*vaš*	vash	*vaša*	va·sha
their	*njihov*	nyee·hawv	*njihova*	nyee·haw·va

	neuter singular		plural (all genders)	
my	moje	moy·e	moji	moy·ee
your	tvoje	tvoy·e	tvoji	tvoy·ee
his	njegovo	nye·gaw·vaw	njegovi	nye·gaw·vee
her	njeno	nye·naw	njeni	nye·nee
our	naše	na·she	naši	na·shee
your	vaše	va·she	vaši	va·shee
their	njihovo	nye·haw·vaw	njihovi	nyee·haw·vee

That's my brother and that's my sister.
 To je moj brat a to je taw ye moy brat a taw ye
 moja sestra. moy·a ses·tra
 (lit: that is my brother and that is my sister)

negative

Croatian negatives are easy. Just add the word *ne* 'not' before
the verb.

I (don't) speak Croatian.
 Ja (ne) govorim hrvatski. ya (ne) gaw·vaw·reem hr·vat·skee
 (lit: I (not) speak Croatian)

Ne is used with all negative forms like *nikada* 'never' and *nitko*
'nobody' etc.

I never drink spirits.
 Ja nikada ne pijem ya nee·ka·da ne pee·yem
 žestoka alkoholna pića. zhe·staw·ka al·kaw·hawl·na pee·cha
 (lit: I never not drink strong alcoholic drinks)

personal pronouns

Personal pronouns are not usually necessary in the subject position (for the doer, eg 'I'), unless you want to emphasise who the doer is. This is because the doer is indicated with a verb ending. As for the direct object (undergoer of the action) pronouns, they have long and short forms indicated by the brackets. The short forms are neutral while the long forms are for emphasis. The short forms are generally much more common.

subject (nominative case) pronouns					
I	*ja*	ya	we	*mi*	mee
you sg inf	*ti*	tee	you pl	*vi*	vee
you sg pol	*vi*	vee			
he	*on*	awn	they m/f/n	*oni/ one/ ona*	*aw*-nee/ *aw*-ne/ *aw*-na
she	*ona*	*aw*-na			
it	*ono*	*aw*-naw			

direct object (accusative case) pronouns					
me	*me(ne)*	*me*(·ne)	us	*nas*	nas
you sg inf	*te(be)*	*te*(·be)	you pl	*vas*	vas
you sg pol	*vas*	vas			
him	*(nje)ga*	(nye·)ga	them m/f/n	*(nj)ih*	(ny)eeh
her	*nju/je**	nyoo/ye			
it	*(nje)ga*	(nye·)ga			

* long form *nju* and short form *je*.

The polite form of 'you', *vi*, can be used when addressing strangers, older people or people in positions of authority. When talking to family, friends or peers you can use the informal form *ti*. In this phrasebook we've generally given phrases in the polite form but where you see the abbreviation inf you have an informal option to use where appropriate.

plural see more than one

pointing things out

To point things out in Croatian you use the words *evo/eno* 'here/there is' or 'here/there are' before the thing that you're drawing attention to.

There's my sister.
  Eno moje sestre.   e·naw *moy·e se·stre*
  (lit: there-is my sister)

If you want to indicate that there's an absence of something, you use the word *nema* 'there is not'.

There's no-one home.
  Nema nikoga doma.   ne·ma *nee·kaw·ga daw·ma*
  (lit: there-is-not nobody home)

Another way to or point out a person or object is to use one of the following words for 'this/these' or 'that/those' and 'that over there' (ie, referring to a thing further away) before the noun.

this		that		that over there	
ovaj m	aw·vai	*taj* m	tai	*onaj* m	aw·nai
ova f	aw·va	*ta* f	ta	*ona* f	aw·na
ovo n	aw·vaw	*to* n	taw	*ono* n	aw·naw

This island is beautiful.
  Ovaj otok je predivan.   aw·vai aw·tawk ye *pre·dee·van*
  (lit: this island is beautiful)

polite & informal see personal pronouns

possession see **my & your** and **have**

questions

Questions may be introduced by the use of question words as in English. These are the most common ones:

what	*što*	shtaw
What are you doing?	*Što radite?*	shtaw *ra*·dee·te
who	*tko*	tkaw
Who are you?	*Tko ste vi?*	tkaw ste vee
where	*gdje*	gdye
Where do you live?	*Gdje živite?*	gdye *zhee*·vee·te
where to	*kamo*	*ka*·maw
Where are you going to?	*Kamo idete?*	*ka*·maw *ee*·de·te
why	*zašto*	*za*·shtaw
Why are you visiting Croatia?	*Zašto posjećujete Hrvatsku?*	*za*·shtaw paw·*sye*·choo·ye·te *hr*·vat·skoo
how	*kako*	*ka*·kaw
How are you?	*Kako ste?*	*ka*·kaw ste
when/ at what time	*kada*	*ka*·da
When do you leave?	*Kada krećete?*	*ka*·da *kre*·che·te
how much	*koliko*	kaw·*lee*·kaw
How much is a ticket?	*Koliko je jedna karta?*	kaw·*lee*·kaw ye *yed*·na *kar*·ta

To form a yes-no type question you insert the word *li* (a question particle) immediately after the main verb in the question. The verb must always come first in the question sentence.

Have you been to Croatia before?
> *Jesi li bio/bila ikada*   ye·see lee *bee*·aw/*bee*·la *ee*·ka·da
> *u Hrvatskoj?* m/f   oo hr·*vat*·skoy
> (lit: are-you *li* been ever in Croatia)

The simplest way to form questions is to keep the structure of a statement but raise your intonation (making your voice rise in pitch) towards the end of the sentence.

You can also form questions by adding the expression *zar ne* 'isn't it' to the end of a statement, which usually implies that you'll get a positive response.

Beautiful day, isn't it?
> *Predivan dan, zar ne?*   *pre*·dee·van dan zar ne
> (lit: beautiful day isn't it)

You can just use *zar* on its own at the start of a question but this gives a tone of surprise to the question.

You're studying Croatian?
> *Zar učiš Hrvatski?*   zar oo·cheesh hr·vat·skee
> (lit: really you-are-studying Croatian)

talking about location

You can specify the location of something by using a preposition (like 'in') in front of the place, just as you do in English. In Croatian, prepositions change the case (see **me, myself & I**) of the nouns that they come before. You don't need to worry about this as people will understand you if you just pick nouns referring to a place out of a dictionary. English and Croatian prepositions don't necessarily translate one-for-one so that, for example, you may see 'at' translated as *kod*, *pri*, *na* or *u* in different contexts.

I'd like to get off at Pula.
> *Želim izaći u Puli.*   zhe·leem ee·*za*·chee oo *poo*·lee
> (lit: I-want get-off at Pula)

verbs see doing things

word order

Generally, basic sentences in Croatian follow the same word order as in English (subject first, followed by the verb, followed by the object). However, because Croatian has case (see **me, myself & I**) to indicate who did what to whom, sentences do not have to be limited to this fixed order for their meaning to be clear.

People describe Croatian as having 'free word order' but this doesn't mean that it's totally random. Word order in Croatian can vary to emphasise different elements in a sentence, for example to highlight information that's new or particularly informative. So remember if you're trying to decipher or form a Croatian sentence, that word order in Croatian can be quite flexible.

say what?

Croatian is not uniform all over the country but has many dialectical variations. It's typically divided into three major dialects: Cakavian, Kajkavian and Stokavian.

The three major dialects draw their names from the different ways that each dialect has of saying the word 'what': *ča*, *kaj* and *što*. *Čakavski cha·kav·skee* is spoken on the Adriatic Coast. *Kajkavski kai·kav·skee* is spoken in the Zagreb and Zagorje regions. *Štokavski shtaw·kav·skee* is centred around Hercegovina and Slavonia. *Štokavski* has three subdialects, Ekavian (the basis of Serbian), Ikavian and Iekavian. The Iekavian dialect has special status as the literary standard and is the form of Croatian used in the mass media. This phrasebook also uses the *Štokavski* standard.

Do you speak (English)?
Govorite/   gaw·vaw·ree·te/
Govoriš li   gaw·vaw·reesh lee
(engleski)? **pol/inf**   (en·gle·skee)

Does anyone speak (English)?
Da li itko govori   da lee eet·kaw gaw·vaw·ree
(engleski)?   (en·gle·skee)

Do you understand?
Da li razumijete/   da lee ra·zoo·mee·ye·te/
razumiješ? **pol/inf**   ra·zoo·mee·yesh

Yes, I understand.
Da, razumijem.   da, ra·zoo·mee·yem

No, I don't understand.
Ne, ja ne razumijem.   ne, ya ne ra·zoo·mee·yem

I (don't) understand.
Ja (ne) razumijem.   ya (ne) ra·zoo·mee·yem

I speak (English).
Ja govorim   ya gaw·vaw·reem
(engleski).   (en·gle·skee)

I don't speak (Croatian).
Ja ne govorim   ya ne gaw·vaw·reem
(hrvatski).   (hr·vat·skee)

I speak a little.
Ja govorim malo.   ya gaw·vaw·reem ma·law

What does 'dobro' mean?
Što znači 'dobro'?   shtaw zna·chee daw·braw

How do you …?	Kako se …?	ka·kaw se …
pronounce this	izgovara	eez·gaw·va·ra
write 'dobro'	piše 'dobro'	pee·she daw·braw
Could you	Možete li	maw·zhe·te lee
please …?	molim vas …? pol	maw·leem vas …
	Možeš li	maw·zhesh lee
	molim te …? inf	maw·leem te …
repeat that	to	taw
	ponoviti	paw·naw·vee·tee
speak more	govoriti	gaw·vaw·ree·tee
slowly	sporije	spaw·ree·ye
write it down	to napisati	taw na·pee·sa·tee

---

tongue torture

Tongue twisters are called *jezikolomke* ye·zee·kaw·lawm·ke (lit: tongue breakers) in Croatian. You should have fun exercising your tongue with these little numbers, particularly as they're laced with 'r's between and before consonants. If you're having trouble negotiating these tricky syllables, refer to **pronunciation**, page 11.

Na vrh brda vrba mrda.
na vrh br·da vr·ba mr·da
(High on the hilltop, the willow sways.)

Cvrči cvrči cvrčak na čvoru crne smrče.
tsvr·chee tsvr·chee tsvr·chak na chvaw·roo tsr·ne smr·che
(A cricket chirps and chirps on the knotted branch of a black spruce.)

Crni jarac crnom trnu crn vrh grize.
Ne grizi mi crni jarče, crnom trnu crn vrh!
tsr·nee ya·rats tsr·nawm tr·noo tsrn vrh gree·ze
ne gree·zee mee tsr·nee yar·che, tsr·nawm tr·noo tsrn vrh
(A black billy goat is chewing the black tip of a black thorny shrub. Don't you chew the top of my black thorny shrub off, you black billy goat!)

cardinal numbers

osnovni brojevi

0	*nula*	noo·la
1	*jedan/jedna/*	ye·dan/yed·na/
	jedno m/f/n	yed·naw
2	*dva/dvije* m&n/f	dva/dvee·ye
3	*tri*	tree
4	*četiri*	che·tee·ree
5	*pet*	pet
6	*šest*	shest
7	*sedam*	se·dam
8	*osam*	aw·sam
9	*devet*	de·vet
10	*deset*	de·set
11	*jedanaest*	ye·da·na·est
12	*dvanaest*	dva·na·est
13	*trinaest*	tree·na·est
14	*četrnaest*	che·tr·na·est
15	*petnaest*	pet·na·est
16	*šesnaest*	shes·na·est
17	*sedamnaest*	se·dam·na·est
18	*osamnaest*	aw·sam·na·est
19	*devetnaest*	de·vet·na·est
20	*dvadeset*	dva·de·set
21	*dvadesetjedan/*	dva·de·set·ye·dan/
	dvadesetjedna/	dva·de·set·yed·na/
	dvadesetjedno m/f/n	dva·de·set·yed·naw
30	*trideset*	tree·de·set
40	*četrdeset*	che·tr·de·set
50	*pedeset*	pe·de·set
60	*šezdeset*	shez·de·set
70	*sedamdeset*	se·dam·de·set
80	*osamdeset*	aw·sam·de·set
90	*devedeset*	de·ve·de·set
100	*sto*	staw
1,000	*tisuću*	tee·soo·choo
1,000,000	*jedan milijun*	ye·dan mee·lee·yoon

ordinal numbers

redni brojevi

1st	*prvi/a/o* m/f/n	pr·vee/a/aw
2nd	*drugi/a/o* m/f/n	droo·gee/a/aw
3rd	*treći/a/e* m/f/n	tre·chee/a/e
4th	*četvrti/a/o* m/f/n	chet·vr·tee/a/aw
5th	*peti/a/o* m/f/n	pe·tee/a/aw

fractions

razlomci

a quarter	*četvrtina*	chet·vr·*tee*·na
a third	*trećina*	tre·*chee*·na
a half	*polovina*	paw·law·*vee*·na
three-quarters	*tri četvrtine*	tree chet·vr·*tee*·ne
all	*sve*	sve
none	*ništa*	neesh·ta

useful amounts

korisne količine

How much/many?	*Koliko?*	kaw·*lee*·kaw
Please give me ...	*Molim dajte mi ...*	*maw*·leem *dai*·te mee ...
a few	*nekoliko*	ne·kaw·lee·kaw
less	*manje*	*ma*·nye
(just) a little	*(samo) malo*	(*sa*·maw) *ma*·law
a lot	*puno*	*poo*·naw
many	*mnogo*	*mnaw*·gaw
more	*više*	*vee*·she
some	*malo*	*ma*·law

For more amounts, see **self-catering**, page 158.

telling the time

Official times are given according to the 24-hour clock. In conversation, though, Croatians mainly use the 12-hour clock.

What time is it?	*Koliko je sati?*	kaw·*lee*·kaw ye *sa*·tee
It's one o'clock.	*Jedan je sat.*	*ye*·dan ye sat
It's (ten) o'clock.	*(Deset) je sati.*	(*de*·set) ye *sa*·tee
Five past (ten).	*(Deset) i pet.*	(*de*·set) ee pet
Quarter past (ten).	*(Deset) i petnaest.*	(*de*·set) ee pet·na·est
Half-past (ten).	*(Deset) i po.*	(*de*·set) ee paw
Quarter to (ten).	*Petnaest do (deset).*	pet·na·est daw (*de*·set)
Twenty to (ten).	*Dvadeset do (deset).*	*dva*·de·set daw (*de*·set)
At what time?	*U koliko sati?*	oo kaw·*lee*·kaw *sa*·tee
am	*prijepodne*	*pree*·ye·*pawd*·ne
pm	*popodne*	paw·*pawd*·ne

the calendar

days

Monday	*ponedjeljak*	paw·*ne*·dye·lyak
Tuesday	*utorak*	oo·*taw*·rak
Wednesday	*srijeda*	sree·*ye*·da
Thursday	*četvrtak*	chet·*vr*·tak
Friday	*petak*	*pe*·tak
Saturday	*subota*	soo·*baw*·ta
Sunday	*nedjelja*	*ne*·dye·lya

months

January	siječanj	see·ye·chan'
February	veljača	ve·lya·cha
March	ožujak	aw·zhoo·yak
April	travanj	tra·van'
May	svibanj	svee·ban'
June	lipanj	lee·pan'
July	srpanj	sr·pan'
August	kolovoz	kaw·law·vawz
September	rujan	roo·yan
October	listopad	lee·staw·pad
November	studeni	stoo·de·nee
December	prosinac	praw·see·nats

nature's seasons

The names of the months look unrecognisable because, unlike the English months, they're not based on the Roman calendar. Instead they draw their meanings from ancient Slavic roots depicting the evolution of the seasons in the natural world. Some of these meanings are now obscure to Croatian speakers themselves but others retain delightfully poetic meanings. Here are a few of them:

January	siječanj	timber-cutting time
April	travanj	the season of growing grass
June	lipanj	linden-blossom time
July	srpanj	the time of the sickle (harvest time)
October	listopad	literally: leaf-fall

dates

What date is it today?
Koji je danas datum?   kaw·yee ye da·nas da·toom

It's (18 October).
(Osamnaesti   (aw·sam·na·e·stee
listopad).   lee·staw·pad)

seasons

spring	*proljeće* n	*praw*·lye·che
summer	*ljeto* n	*lye*·taw
autumn/fall	*jesen* f	*ye*·sen
winter	*zima* f	*zee*·ma

present

sadašnjost

now	*sada*	*sa*·da
this ...		
afternoon	*ovog*	*aw*·vawg
	popodneva	paw·*pawd*·ne·va
month	*ovog mjeseca*	*aw*·vawg *mye*·se·tsa
morning	*ovog jutra*	*aw*·vawg *yoo*·tra
week	*ovog tjedna*	*aw*·vawg *tyed*·na
year	*ove godine*	*aw*·ve *gaw*·dee·ne
today	*danas*	*da*·nas
tonight	*večeras*	ve·*che*·ras

past

prošlost

(three days) ago	*prije (tri dana)*	*pree*·ye (tree *da*·na)
day before yesterday	*prekjučer*	prek·*yoo*·cher
last ...		
month	*prošlog mjeseca*	*prawsh*·lawg *mye*·se·tsa
week	*prošlog tjedna*	*prawsh*·lawg *tyed*·na
year	*prošle godine*	*prawsh*·le *gaw*·dee·ne
last night	*sinoć*	*see*·nawch
since (May)	*od (svibnja)*	awd (*sveeb*·nya)

yesterday ...	jučer ...	yoo·cher ...
afternoon	popodne	paw·pawd·ne
evening	uvečer	oo·ve·cher
morning	ujutro	oo·yoo·traw

future

budućnost

day after tomorrow	prekosutra	pre·kaw·soo·tra
in (six days)	za (šest dana)	za (shest da·na)
next ...		
month	idućeg mjeseca	ee·doo·cheg mye·se·tsa
week	idućeg tjedna	ee·doo·cheg tyed·na
year	iduće godine	ee·doo·che gaw·dee·ne
tomorrow ...	sutra ...	soo·tra ...
afternoon	popodne	paw·pawd·ne
evening	uvečer	oo·ve·cher
morning	ujutro	oo·yoo·traw
until (June)	do (lipnja)	daw (leep·nya)

during the day

tokom dana

afternoon	poslijepodne n	paw·slee·ye·pawd·ne
dawn	zora f	zaw·ra
day	dan m	dan
evening	večer f	ve·cher
midday	podne n	pawd·ne
midnight	ponoć f	paw·nawch
morning	jutro n	yoo·traw
night	noć f	nawch
sunrise	izlazak sunca m	eez·la·zak soon·tsa
sunset	zalazak sunca m	za·la·zak soon·tsa

How much is it?
Koliko stoji?   kaw·*lee*·kaw *stoy*·ee

Can you write down the price?
Možete li napisati   *maw*·zhe·te lee na·*pee*·sa·tee
cijenu?   tsee·*ye*·noo

Do you accept …?	*Da li prihvaćate …?*	da lee *pree*·hva·cha·te …
credit cards	*kreditne kartice*	*kre*·deet·ne *kar*·tee·tse
debit cards	*debitne kartice*	*de*·beet·ne *kar*·tee·tse
travellers cheques	*putničke čekove*	*poot*·neech·ke *che*·kaw·ve
Where can I …?	*Gdje mogu …?*	gdye *maw*·goo …
I'd like to …	*Želio/Željela bih …* m/f	*zhe*·lee·aw/*zhe*·lye·la beeh …
cash a cheque	*unovčiti ček*	oo·*nawv*·chee·tee chek
change a travellers cheque	*zamijeniti putnički ček*	za·mee·*ye*·nee·tee *poot*·neech·kee chek
change money	*zamijeniti novac*	za·mee·*ye*·nee·tee *naw*·vats
get a cash advance	*uzeti predujam u gotovini*	oo·ze·tee *pre*·doo·yam oo gaw·taw·*vee*·nee
withdraw money	*podignuti novac*	*paw*·deeg·noo·tee *naw*·vats

What's the charge for that?

Kolika je pristojba	kaw·*lee*·ka ye *pree*·stoy·ba
za to?	za taw

What's the exchange rate?

Koji je tečaj razmjene?	*koy*·ee ye *te*·chai raz·mye·ne

Could I have a receipt, please?

Mogu li dobiti račun,	*maw*·goo lee *daw*·bee·tee ra·choon
molim?	*maw*·leem

Where's …?	*Gdje se nalazi …?*	gdye se *na*·la·zee …
an automated	*bankovni*	*ban*·kawv·nee
teller machine	*automat*	a·oo·*taw*·mat
a foreign	*mjenjačnica za*	mye·*nyach*·nee·tsa za
exchange office	*strane valute*	*stra*·ne va·*loo*·te

I'd like …, please.	*Želio/Željela*	zhe·lee·aw/zhe·lye·la
	bih … m/f	beeh …
my change	*moj ostatak*	moy aw·*sta*·tak
	novca	*nawv*·tsa
a refund	*povrat novca*	*pawv*·rat *nawv*·tsa

---

the colour of money

The currency in Croatia is the *kuna* (*koo*·na), which is divided into 100 *lipa* (*lee*·pa). Interestingly, the currency takes its name from the marten, a ferret-like animal whose pelt was used as a means of exchange in the Middle Ages. The word *lipa* means 'linden tree'. Though it has no obvious association with trade, the linden tree has a sacred significance in Slavic mythology as, among other things, a symbol of good luck and prosperity.

getting around

Which ... goes to (Dubrovnik)?	Koji ... ide za (Dubrovnik)?	koy·ee ... ee·de za (doo·brawv·neek)
boat	brod	brawd
bus	autobus	a·oo·taw·boos
plane	zrakoplov	zra·kaw·plawv
tram	tramvaj	tram·vai
train	vlak	vlak

When's the ... (bus)?	Kada ide ... (autobus)?	ka·da ee·de ... (a·oo·taw·boos)
first	prvi	pr·vee
last	zadnji	zad·nyee
next	slijedeći	slee·ye·de·chee

What time does it leave?
U koliko sati kreće?   oo kaw·lee·kaw sa·tee kre·che

What time does it get to (Pula)?
U koliko sati stiže u (Pulu)?   oo kaw·lee·kaw sa·tee stee·zhe oo (poo·loo)

Is this seat free?
Da li je ovo sjedište slobodno?   da lee ye aw·vaw sye·deesh·te slaw·bawd·naw

That's my seat.
Ovo je moje sjedište.   aw·vaw ye moy·e sye·deesh·te

Please tell me when we get to (Pula).
Molim vas recite mi kada stignemo u (Pulu).   maw·leem vas re·tsee·te mee ka·da steeg·ne·maw oo (poo·loo)

Please stop here.
Molim vas stanite ovdje.   maw·leem vas sta·nee·te awv·dye

tickets

Where do I buy a ticket?
Gdje mogu kupiti kartu? — gdye *maw*·goo *koo*·pee·tee *kar*·too

Do I need to book?
Trebam li rezervirati? — tre·bam lee re·zer·*vee*·ra·tee

A ... ticket (to Split).	*Jednu ... kartu (do Splita).*	*yed*·noo ... *kar*·too (daw *splee*·ta)
1st-class	*prvorazrednu*	pr·*vaw*·raz·red·noo
2nd-class	*drugorazrednu*	droo·gaw·*raz*·red·noo
child's	*dječju*	*dyech*·yoo
one-way	*jednosmjernu*	*yed*·naw·smyer·noo
return	*povratnu*	*paw*·vrat·noo
student's	*studentsku*	*stoo*·dent·skoo

I'd like a ... seat.	*Želio/Željela bih ... sjedište.* m/f	*zhe*·lee·aw/*zhe*·lye·la beeh ... *sye*·deesh·te
nonsmoking	*nepušačko*	ne·poo·*shach*·kaw
smoking	*pušačko*	poo·*shach*·kaw

I'd like a/an ... seat.	*Želio/Željela bih sjedište ...* m/f	*zhe*·lee·aw/*zhe*·lye·la beeh *sye*·deesh·te ...
aisle	*u sredini*	oo sre·*dee*·nee
window	*do prozora*	daw *praw*·zaw·ra

I'd like to ... my ticket, please.	*Želio/Željela bih ... svoju kartu, molim.* m/f	*zhe*·lee·aw/*zhe*·lye·la beeh ... *svoy*·oo *kar*·too *maw*·leem
cancel	*poništiti*	*paw*·nee·shtee·tee
change	*promijeniti*	praw·mee·*ye*·nee·tee
confirm	*potvrditi*	pawt·*vr*·dee·tee

Is there (a) ...?	*Imate li ...?*	ee·*ma*·te lee ...
air-conditioning	*klima-uređaj*	klee·ma·*oo*·re·jai
blanket	*deku*	*de*·koo
toilet	*zahod*	*za*·hawd

How much is it?
Koliko stoji? — kaw·*lee*·kaw *stoy*·ee

How long does the trip take?
Koliko traje putovanje? — kaw·*lee*·kaw *trai*·e poo·taw·*va*·nye

Is it a direct route?
Je li to direktan pravac? — ye lee taw dee·*rek*·tan *pra*·vats

What time should I check in?
U koliko se sati — oo kaw·*lee*·kaw se *sa*·tee
trebam prijaviti? — *tre*·bam pree·*ya*·vee·tee

Can I get a sleeping berth?
Mogu li dobiti — *maw*·goo lee *daw*·bee·tee
kabinu s ležajem? — ka·*bee*·noo s *le*·zhai·em

luggage

prtljaga

Where can I find ...?	*Gdje se nalazi ...?*	gdye se *na*·la·zee ...
the baggage claim	*šalter za podizanje prtljage*	*shal*·ter za paw·*dee*·za·nye prt·*lya*·ge
a luggage locker	*pretinac za odlaganje prtljage*	*pre*·tee·nats za awd·*la*·ga·nye prt·*lya*·ge

My luggage	*Moja prtljaga*	moy·a prt·lya·ga
has been …	*je …*	ye …
damaged	*oštećena*	awsh·te·che·na
lost	*izgubljena*	eez·goob·lye·na
stolen	*ukradena*	oo·kra·de·na

That is/isn't mine.
To je/nije moje. taw ye/*nee*·ye *moy*·e

Can I have some coins/tokens?
Mogu li dobiti *maw*·goo lee *daw*·bee·tee
nekoliko kovanica/ ne·kaw·lee·kaw kaw·*va*·nee·tsa/
žetona? zhe·*taw*·na

bus & coach

How often do buses come?
Koliko često kaw·*lee*·kaw *che*·staw
dolaze autobusi? *daw*·la·ze a·oo·*taw*·boo·see

Does it stop at (Split)?
Da li staje u (Splitu)? da lee *stai*·e oo (*splee*·too)

What's the next stop?
Koja je slijedeća stanica? *koy*·a ye slee·*ye*·de·cha *sta*·nee·tsa

I'd like to get off at (Split).
Želim izaći u (Splitu). *zhe*·leem ee·*za*·chee oo (*splee*·too)

How long do we stop here?
Koliko dugo kaw·*lee*·kaw *doo*·gaw
ostajemo ovdje? *aw*·stai·e·maw *awv*·dye

city	*gradski*	*grad*·skee
inter-city	*međugradski*	me·joo·*grad*·skee
local	*mjesni*	*mye*·snee

train

What station is this?
Koja stanica je ovo?   koy·a sta·nee·tsa ye aw·vaw

What's the next station?
Koja je slijedeća stanica?   koy·a ye slee·ye·de·cha sta·nee·tsa

Does it stop at (Pula)?
Da li staje u (Puli)?   da lee stai·e oo (poo·lee)

Do I need to change?
Trebam li presjedati?   tre·bam lee pre·sye·da·tee

Which carriage is (for) ...?	*Koja kola su za ...?*	koy·a kaw·la soo za ...
(Dubrovnik)	*(Dubrovnik)*	(doo·brawv·neek)
1st class	*prvi razred*	prvee raz·red
dining	*ručavanje*	roo·cha·va·nye

Is it ...?	*Da li je ...?*	da lee ye ...
direct	*direktan*	dee·rek·tan
express	*brzi*	br·zee

you might read ...

brzi vlak	br·zee vlak	**fast train**
dolasci	daw·las·tsee	**arrivals**
lokalni vlak	law·kal·nee vlak	**local train**
ne vozi	ne vaw·zee	**no service Sundays**
nedjeljom	ne·dye·lyawm	**and public holidays**
i blagdanima	ee blag·da·nee·ma	
obvezatno	awb·ve·zat·naw	**compulsory seat**
rezerviranje	re·zer·vee·ra·nye	**reservation**
sjedišta	sye·deesh·ta	
odlasci	awd·las·tsee	**departures**
poslovni	paw·slawv·nee	**executive train**
vlak	vlak	**(1st class only)**
presjedanje	pre·sye·da·nye	**change of trains**
svakodnevno	sva·kawd·nev·naw	**daily**

tram

tramvaj

Is this the tram to (Arena)?
Je li ovo tramvaj ye lee *aw*·vaw *tram*·vai
koji ide do (Arene)? *koy*·ee *ee*·de daw (a·*re*·ne)

Could you tell me when we get to (Arena)?
Možete li mi reći kada *maw*·zhe·te lee mee *re*·chee *ka*·da
stignemo kod (Arene)? *steeg*·ne·maw kawd (a·*re*·ne)

boat

brod/čamac

The word *brod* (brawd) is generally used for a ship, whereas the word *čamac* (*cha*·mats) usually refers to a smaller private boat.

What's the sea like today?
Kakvo je danas more? *kak*·vaw ye *da*·nas *maw*·re

Are there life jackets?
Postoje li prsluci *paw*·stoy·e lee *pr*·sloo·tsee
za spašavanje? za spa·*sha*·va·nye

What island is this?
Koji otok je ovo? *koy*·ee *aw*·tawk ye *aw*·vaw

What beach is this?
Koja plaža je ovo? *koy*·a *pla*·zha ye *aw*·vaw

I feel seasick.
Osjećam morsku bolest. *aws*·ye·cham *mawr*·skoo *baw*·lest

anchor	*sidro* n	*see*·draw
anchorage	*sidrarina* f	see·*dra*·ree·na
cabin	*kabina* f	ka·*bee*·na
captain	*kapetan* m	ka·*pe*·tan
car deck	*platforma za*	plat·*fawr*·ma za
	vozila na brodu f	*vaw*·zee·la na *braw*·doo
car ferry	*trajekt za*	*trai*·ekt za
	prijevoz vozila m	pree·*ye*·vawz *vaw*·zee·la

charter yacht	*zakupljena jahta* f	*za*·koop·lye·na *yah*·ta
deck	*paluba* f	*pa*·loo·ba
ferry	*trajekt* m	*trai*·ekt
oar	*veslo* n	*ve*·slaw
port	*luka* f	*loo*·ka
sail	*jedro* n	*ye*·draw
speedboat	*gliser* m	*glee*·ser
yacht	*jahta* f	*yah*·ta

How much is the daily hire of your charter boats?
Koliki stoji dnevni kaw·*lee*·kee stoy·ee *dnev*·nee
zakup vaših čamaca? za·koop va·sheeh cha·ma·tsa

Is the skipper included?
Da li je u to uključen da lee ye oo taw ook·lyoo·chen
i skipper? ee *skee*·per

Where can I anchor a boat like this?
Gdje smijem usidriti gdye *smee*·yem oo·*seed*·ree·tee
ovakav čamac? aw·*va*·kav *cha*·mats

Which navigational devices is it equipped with?
Kojim navigacionim *koy*·eem *na*·vee·ga·tsee·aw·neem
uređajima je opremljen? oo·re·jai·ee·ma ye *aw*·prem·lyen

taxi

I'd like a taxi ...	*Trebam taksi ...*	*tre*·bam *tak*·see ...
at (9am)	*u (devet*	oo (*de*·vet
	prijepodne)	pree·ye·*pawd*·ne)
now	*sada*	*sa*·da
tomorrow	*sutra*	*soo*·tra

Where's the taxi rank?
Gdje je taksi stanica? gdye ye *tak*·see *sta*·nee·tsa

Is this taxi free?
Da li je ovaj taksi da lee ye *aw*·vai *tak*·see
slobodan? *slaw*·baw·dan

Please put the meter on.
Molim uključite   maw·leem ook·*lyoo*·chee·te
taksimetar.   tak·see·me·tar

How much is it to ...?
Koliko stoji prijevoz   kaw·*lee*·kaw *stoy*·ee pree·*ye*·vawz
do ...?   daw ...

Please take me to (this address).
Molim da me odvezete   maw·leem da me *awd*·ve·ze·te
na (ovu adresu).   na (*aw*·voo a·*dre*·soo)

How much is it?
Koliko to stoji?   kaw·*lee*·kaw taw *stoy*·ee

Please ...	*Molim vas ...*	maw·leem vas ...
slow down	*usporite*	oo·*spaw*·ree·te
stop here	*stanite ovdje*	sta·nee·te *awv*·dye
wait here	*pričekajte ovdje*	pree·che·kai·te *awv*·dye

car & motorbike

car & motorbike hire

I'd like to hire a/an ...	*Želio/Željela bih iznajmiti ...* m/f	zhe·lee·aw/*zhe*·lye·la beeh eez·*nai*·mee·tee ...
4WD	*automobil sa pogonom na sva četiri kotača*	a·oo·taw·*maw*·beel sa *paw*·gaw·nawm na sva *che*·tee·ree kaw·*ta*·cha
automatic	*automobil sa automatskim mjenjačem*	a·oo·taw·*maw*·beel sa a·oo·*taw*·mat·skeem mye·*nya*·chem
manual	*automobil sa ručnim mjenjačem*	a·oo·taw·*maw*·beel sa *rooch*·neem mye·*nya*·chem
motorbike	*motocikl*	maw·taw·*tsee*·kl

With ...	*Sa ...*	sa ...
air-conditioning	*klima-uređajem*	*klee·ma·oo·re·jai·em*
a driver	*vozačem*	vaw·*za*·chem

How much for	*Koliko stoji*	kaw·*lee*·kaw *stoy*·ee
... hire?	*... najam?*	... *nai*·am
daily	*dnevni*	*dnev*·nee
weekly	*tjedni*	*tyed*·nee

Does that include insurance/mileage?
Da li to uključuje i   da lee taw ook·*lyoo*·choo·ye ee
osiguranje/   aw·see·goo·*ra*·nye/
kilometražu?   kee·law·me·*tra*·zhoo

on the road

What's the speed limit?
Koja je dozvoljena   *koy*·a ye *dawz*·vaw·lye·na
brzina?   *br*·zee·na

Is this the road to (Pazin)?
Je li ovo cesta za (Pazin)?   ye lee *aw*·vaw *tse*·sta za (*pa*·zeen)?

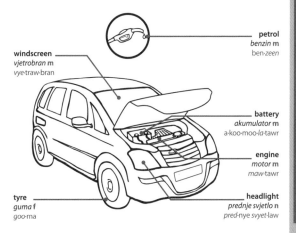

petrol
benzin m
ben·*zeen*

windscreen
vjetrobran m
vye·traw·bran

battery
akumulator m
a·koo·moo·*la*·tawr

engine
motor m
maw·tawr

tyre
guma f
goo·ma

headlight
prednje svjetlo n
pred·nye *svyet*·law

Is it a tollway?
Da li se na ovom   da lee se na *aw*·vawm
putu plaća cestarina?   *poo*·too *pla*·cha tse·*sta*·ree·na

(How long) Can I park here?
(Koliko dugo) Mogu   (kaw·*lee*·kaw *doo*·gaw) *maw*·goo
ovdje parkirati?   *awv*·dye par·*kee*·ra·tee

Where's a petrol station?
Gdje je benzinska   gdye ye *ben*·zeen·ska
stanica?   *sta*·nee·tsa

Please fill it up.
Pun rezervoar molim.   poon re·zer·*vaw*·ar *maw*·leem

I'd like … litres.
Trebam … litara.   *tre*·bam … *lee*·ta·ra

Can you check	*Možete li*	*maw*·zhe·te lee
the …?	*provjeriti …?*	*praw*·vye·ree·tee …
oil	*ulje*	*oo*·lye
tyre pressure	*tlak zraka u*	tlak *zra*·ka oo
	gumama	*goo*·ma·ma
water	*vodu*	*vaw*·doo

diesel	*dizel gorivo* n	*dee*·zel *gaw*·ree·vaw
leaded	*olovni benzin* m	*aw*·lawv·nee ben·*zeen*
LPG	*tekući plin* m	te·*koo*·chee pleen
regular	*normalni*	*nawr*·mal·nee
	benzin m	ben·*zeen*
unleaded	*bezolovni*	be·*zaw*·lawv·nee
	benzin m	ben·*zeen*

road signs

Izlaz	*eez*·laz	**Exit**
Jednosmjerno	*yed*·naw·smyer·naw	**One-Way**
Stop	stawp	**Stop**
Ulaz	*oo*·laz	**Entrance**
Ustupite	oo·*stoo*·pee·te	**Give Way**
Pravo Prednosti	*pra*·vaw *pred*·naw·stee	

problems

I need a mechanic.

Trebam	*tre*·bam
automehaničara.	a·oo·taw·me·*ha*·nee·cha·ra

The car/motorbike has broken down (at Pazin).

Automobil/Motocikl	a·oo·taw·*maw*·beel/maw·taw·*tsee*·kl
se pokvario (u Pazinu).	se pawk·*va*·ree·aw (oo *pa*·zee·noo)

I've had an accident.

Imao/Imala sam	*ee*·ma·aw/*ee*·ma·la sam
prometnu nezgodu. m/f	*praw*·met·noo *nez*·gaw·doo

The car/motorbike won't start.

Automobil/Motocikl	a·oo·taw·*maw*·beel/maw·taw·*tsee*·kl
neće upaliti.	ne·che oo·*pa*·lee·tee

I have a flat tyre.

Imam probušenu	*ee*·mam *praw*·boo·she·noo
gumu.	*goo*·moo

I've lost my car keys.
Izgubio/Izgubila   eez·goo·bee·aw/eez·goo·bee·la
sam ključeve od   sam klyoo·che·ve awd
automobila. m/f   a·oo·taw·maw·bee·la

I've locked the keys inside.
Zaključao/Zaključala   zak·lyoo·cha·aw/zak·lyoo·cha·la
sam ključeve unutra. m/f   sam klyoo·che·ve oo·noo·tra

I've run out of petrol.
Nestalo mi je benzina.   ne·sta·law mee ye ben·zee·na

Can you fix it (today)?
Možete li ga   maw·zhe·te lee ga
popraviti (danas)?   paw·pra·vee·tee (da·nas)

How long will it take?
Koliko dugo će trebati?   kaw·lee·kaw doo·gaw che tre·ba·tee

bicycle

bicikl

I'd like …	*Želio/Željela bih …* m/f	zhe·lee·aw/zhe·lye·la beeh …
my bicycle repaired	*popravak svoga bicikla*	paw·pra·vak svaw·ga bee·tsee·kla
to buy a bicycle	*kupiti bicikl*	koo·pee·tee bee·tsee·kl
to hire a bicycle	*iznajmiti bicikl*	eez·nai·mee·tee bee·tsee·kl

I'd like a … bike.	*Želio/Željela bih … bicikl.* m/f	zhe·lee·aw/zhe·lye·la beeh … bee·tsee·kl
mountain	*brdski*	brd·skee
racing	*trkaći*	tr·ka·chee
second-hand	*polovni*	paw·lawv·nee

Do I need a helmet?
Treba li mi kaciga?   tre·ba lee mee ka·tsee·ga

Is there a bicycle-path map?
Da li postoji karta   da lee paw·stoy·ee kar·ta
biciklističkih staza?   bee·tsee·klee·steech·keeh sta·za

I'm ... | *Ja sam ovdje ...* | ya sam *awv*·dye ...
in transit | *u prolazu* | oo *praw*·la·zoo
on business | *poslovno* | *paw*·slawv·naw
on holiday | *na odmoru* | na *awd*·maw·roo

I'm here for | *Ostajem ovdje* | aw·sta·yem *awv*·dye
(three) ... | *na (tri) ...* | na (tree) ...
days | *dana* | *da*·na
months | *mjeseca* | *mye*·se·tsa
weeks | *tjedna* | *tyed*·na

I'm going to (Zagreb).
Ja idem u (Zagreb).   ya *ee*·dem oo (*za*·greb)

I'm staying at (the Intercontinental).
Odsjesti ću u   awd·sye·stee choo oo
(Interkontinentalu).   (*een*·ter·kawn·tee·nen·*ta*·loo)

The children are on this passport.
Djeca su na   dye·tsa soo na
ovoj putovnici.   aw·voy poo·*tawv*·nee·tsee

border crossing

51

I have nothing to declare.
    Nemam ništa za   ne·mam neesh·ta za
    prijaviti.   pree·ya·vee·tee

I have something to declare.
    Imam nešto za   ee·mam nesh·taw za
    prijaviti.   pree·ya·vee·tee

Do I have to declare this?
    Trebam li ovo   tre·bam lee aw·vaw
    prijaviti?   pree·ya·vee·tee

That's (not) mine.
    To (nije) moje.   taw (nee·ye) moy·e

I didn't know I had to declare it.
    Nisam znao/znala da   nee·sam zna·aw/zna·la da
    to treba prijaviti. **m/f**   taw tre·ba pree·ya·vee·tee

signs

Carinarnica	tsa·ree·nar·nee·tsa	**Customs**
Karantena	ka·ran·te·na	**Quarantine**
Oslobođeno	aw·slaw·baw·je·naw	**Duty-Free**
od Carine	awd tsa·ree·ne	
Pregled	pre·gled	**Passport Control**
Putovnica	poo·tawv·nee·tsa	
Ulazak	oo·la·zak	**Immigration**
u Zemlju	oo zem·lyoo	

Where's (the market)?
Gdje je (tržnica)? gdye ye (*tr*·zhnee·tsa)

How do I get there?
Kako mogu tamo stići? ka·kaw *maw*·goo ta·maw *stee*·chee

How far is it?
Koliko je udaljeno? kaw·*lee*·kaw ye oo·da·lye·naw

Can you show me (on the map)?
Možete li mi to *maw*·zhe·te lee mee taw
pokazati (na karti)? paw·*ka*·za·tee (na *kar*·tee)

It's ...	*Nalazi se ...*	*na*·la·zee se ...
behind ...	*iza ...*	*ee*·za ...
close	*nedaleko*	*ne*·da·le·kaw
here	*ovdje*	*aww*·dye
in front of ...	*ispred ...*	*ee*·spred ...
near ...	*blizu ...*	*blee*·zoo ...
next to ...	*pored ...*	*paw*·red ...
on the corner	*na uglu*	na *oo*·gloo
opposite ...	*nasuprot ...*	*na*·soo·prawt ...
straight ahead	*ravno naprijed*	*rav*·naw *na*·pree·yed
there	*tamo*	*ta*·maw

Turn ...	*Skrenite ...*	*skre*·nee·te ...
at the corner	*na uglu*	na *oo*·gloo
at the traffic lights	*na semaforu*	na *se*·ma·faw·roo
left	*lijevo*	*lee*·ye·vaw
right	*desno*	*de*·snaw

north	sjever	sye·ver
south	jug	yoog
east	istok	ees·tawk
west	zapad	za·pad

By ...		
bus	autobusom	a·oo·taw·boo·sawm
foot	pješke	pyesh·ke
taxi	taksijem	tak·see·yem
train	vlakom	vla·kawm
tram	tramvajem	tram·vai·em

typical addresses

What's the address?
Koja je adresa?   koy·a ye a·dre·sa

avenue	avenija f	a·ve·nee·ya
lane	prolaz m	praw·laz
street	ulica f	oo·lee·tsa

traffic lights
semafor m
se·ma·fawr

bus
autobus m
a·oo·taw·boos

shop
prodavaonica f
praw·da·va·aw·nee·tsa

pedestrian
crossing
pješački prijelaz m
pye·shach·kee
pree·ye·laz

intersection
raskrižje n
ras·kreezh·ye

corner
ugao m
oo·ga·aw

taxi
taksi m
tak·see

finding accommodation

Where's a ...?	*Gdje se nalazi ...?*	gdye se·*na*·la·zee ...
bed and	*konačište i*	*kaw*·na·cheesh·te ee
breakfast	*doručak*	*daw*·roo·chak
camping ground	*kamp*	kamp
guesthouse	*privatni*	*pree*·vat·nee
	smještaj	smyesh·tai
	za najam	za *nai*·am
hotel	*hotel*	*haw*·tel
nudist camping	*nudistički*	noo·*dee*·steech·kee
ground	*kamp*	kamp
pension	*pansion*	pan·*see*·awn
room for rent	*najmljena soba*	nai·mlye·na *saw*·ba
youth hostel	*prenoćište za*	pre·naw·cheesh·te za
	mladež	*mla*·dezh
Can you	*Možete li*	*maw*·zhe·te lee
recommend	*preporučiti*	pre·paw·*roo*·chee·tee
somewhere ...?	*negdje ...?*	*neg*·dye ...
cheap	*jeftino*	*yef*·tee·naw
good	*dobro*	*daw*·braw
luxurious	*luksuzno*	*look*·sooz·naw
nearby	*blizu*	*blee*·zoo
romantic	*romantično*	raw·*man*·teech·naw

What's the address?
Koja je adresa? koy·a ye a·*dre*·sa

local talk		
dive	*ozloglašena*	aw·*zlaw*·gla·she·na
	gostionica f	gaw·stee·*aw*·nee·tsa
rat-infested	*ušljivo*	*oosh*·lyee·vaw
top spot	*odlično mjesto* n	*awd*·leech·naw *mye*·staw

booking ahead & checking in

I'd like to book a ..., please.	Želio/Željela bih rezervirati ..., molim. m/f	zhe·lee·aw/zhe·lye·la beeh re·zer·vee·ra·tee ... maw·leem
campsite	mjesto za kampiranje	mye·staw za kam·pee·ra·nye
room	sobu	saw·boo

I have a reservation.
Imam rezervaciju.   ee·mam re·zer·va·tsee·yoo

My name's ...
Moje ime je ...   moy·e ee·me ye ...

For (three) nights/weeks.
Na (tri) noći/tjedna.   na (tree) naw·chee/tyed·na

From (2 July) to (6 July).
Od (2. srpnja) do (6. srpnja).   awd (droo·gawg srp·nya) daw (she·stawg srp·nya)

Do I need to pay upfront?
Trebam li platiti unaprijed?   tre·bam lee pla·tee·tee oo·na·pree·yed

Is breakfast included?
Da li je doručak uključen?   da lee ye daw·roo·chak ook·lyoo·chen

Do you offer half-board?
Da li nudite polu-pansion?   da lee noo·dee·te paw·loo·pan·see·awn

Do you have a swimming pool?
Imate li bazen za plivanje?   ee·ma·te lee ba·zen za plee·va·nye

listen for ...

kaw·lee·kaw naw·chee	Koliko noći?	How many nights?
paw·poo·nye·naw	popunjeno	full
poo·tawv·nee·tsa	putovnica	passport

How much is it per ...?	*Koliko je po ...?*	kaw·*lee*·kaw ye paw ...
night	*noći*	*naw*·chee
person	*osobi*	*aw*·saw·bee
week	*tjednu*	*tyed*·noo
Can I pay by ...?	*Mogu li platiti sa ...?*	*maw*·goo lee *pla*·tee·tee sa ...
credit card	*kreditnom karticom*	*kre*·deet·nawm *kar*·tee·tsawm
debit card	*debitnom karticom*	*de*·beet·nawm *kar*·tee·tsawm
travellers cheque	*putničkim čekom*	*poot*·neech·keem *che*·kawm

For other methods of payment, see **money**, page 37.

room at the inn

These local room classifications will come in handy if you're booking a room in a private home. This is one of the best accommodation options in Croatia. Not only is it cheaper than a hotel but interacting with your hosts will give you an opportunity to experience local culture.

jedna zvjezdica   *yed*·na zvye·zdee·tsa
one-star (room with a bathroom shared between two rooms or with the owner)

dvije zvjezdice   *dvee*·ye zvye·zdee·tse
two-star (room with a bathroom shared with one other room)

tri zvjezdice   tree zvye·zdee·tse
three-star (room with a private bathroom)

Be sure to check when booking whether the price is per person or per room by asking:

Is this the price per ...?	*Da li je ovo cijena po ...?*	da lee ye *aw*·vaw tsee·*ye*·na paw ...
person	*osobi*	*aw*·saw·bee
room	*sobi*	*saw*·bee

Do you have a … room?	Imate li … sobu?	ee·ma·te lee … saw·boo
double	*dvokrevetnu*	*dvaw·kre·vet·noo*
single	*jednokrevetnu*	*yed·naw·kre·vet·noo*

Do you have a twin room?

Imate li jednokrevetnu sobu sa francuskim ležajem?

ee·ma·te lee yed·naw·kre·vet·noo saw·boo sa fran·tsoo·skeem le·zhai·em

Can I see it?

Mogu li je vidjeti?

maw·goo lee ye vee·dye·tee

I'll take it.

Uzet ću ovu.

oo·zet choo aw·voo

requests & queries

When/Where is breakfast served?

Kada/Gdje služite doručak?

ka·da/gdye sloo·zhee·te daw·roo·chak

Please wake me at (seven).

Probudite me u (sedam) molim.

praw·boo·dee·te me oo (se·dam) maw·leem

Do you have a/an …?	Imate li …?	ee·ma·te lee …
elevator/lift	*dizalo*	*dee·za·law*
laundry service	*usluge pranja rublja*	*oo·sloo·ge pra·nya roob·lya*
safe	*sef*	*sef*
swimming pool	*bazen za plivanje*	*ba·zen za plee·va·nye*

Can I use the …?	Mogu li koristiti …?	maw·goo lee kaw·ree·stee·tee …
kitchen	*kuhinju*	*koo·hee·nyoo*
laundry	*praonicu*	*pra·aw·nee·tsoo*
telephone	*telefon*	*te·le·fawn*

Do you … here?	Da li … ovdje?	da lee … awv·dye
arrange tours	organizirate	awr·ga·nee·zee·ra·te
	turistička	too·ree·steech·ka
	putovanja	poo·taw·va·nya
change money	mijenjate	mee·ye·nya·te
	novac	naw·vats

Could I have …,	Mogu li dobiti	maw·goo lee daw·bee·tee
please?	… molim?	… maw·leem
an extra	jednu dodatnu	yed·noo daw·dat·noo
blanket	deku	de·koo
a mosquito net	mrežu za	mre·zhoo za
	komarce	kaw·mar·tse
a receipt	račun	ra·choon
my key	moj ključ	moy klyooch

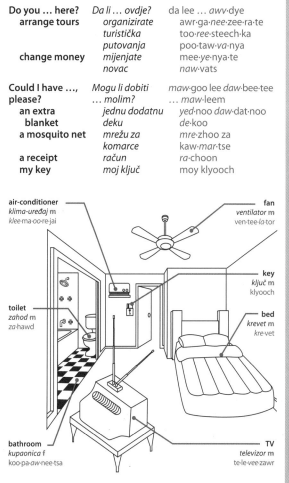

air-conditioner
klima-uređaj m
klee·ma·oo·re·jai

toilet
zahod m
za·hawd

bathroom
kupaonica f
koo·pa·aw·nee·tsa

fan
ventilator m
ven·tee·la·tor

key
ključ m
klyooch

bed
krevet m
kre·vet

TV
televizor m
te·le·vee·zawr

Is there a message for me?

Ima li koja poruka	ee·ma lee *koy*·a *paw*·roo·ka
za mene?	za *me*·ne

Can I leave a message for someone?

Mogu li ostaviti	*maw*·goo lee *aw*·sta·vee·tee
poruku za nekoga?	*paw*·roo·koo za *ne*·kaw·ga

I'm locked out of my room.

Zaključao/Zaključala	zak·lyoo·cha·aw/zak·lyoo·cha·la
sam svoju sobu iznutra. m/f	sam *svoy*·oo *saw*·boo eez·*noo*·tra

complaints

It's too ...	Suviše je ...	soo·vee·she ye ...
bright	*osvijetljeno*	aw·svee·*yet*·lye·naw
cold	*hladno*	*hlad*·naw
dark	*tamno*	*tam*·naw
expensive	*skupo*	*skoo*·paw
noisy	*bučno*	*booch*·naw
small	*malo*	*ma*·law

The ... doesn't work.	... je neispravan.	... ye *ne*·ee·spra·van
air-conditioning	*Klima-uređaj*	*klee*·ma·oo·re·jai
fan	*Ventilator*	ven·tee·*la*·tawr
toilet	*Zahod*	*za*·hawd

Can I get another ...?

Mogu li dobiti još	*maw*·goo lee *daw*·bee·tee yawsh
jedan/jednu/jedno ...? m/f/n	ye·dan/*yed*·noo/*yed*·naw ...

This ... isn't clean.

Ovaj/Ova/Ovo ...	aw·vai/*aw*·va/*aw*·vaw ...
nije čist/čista/čisto. m/f/n	*nee*·ye cheest/*chees*·ta/*chees*·taw

blanket	*deka* f	*de*·ka
sheet	*plahta* f	*plah*·ta
towel	*ručnik* m	*rooch*·neek

checking out

odlazak

What time is checkout?
U koliko sati   oo kaw·lee·kaw sa·tee
treba napustiti sobu?   tre·ba na·poo·stee·tee saw·boo

Can I have a late checkout?
Smijem li sobu   smee·yem lee saw·boo
napustiti kasnije od   na·poo·stee·tee ka·snee·ye awd
navedenog vremena?   na·ve·de·nawg vre·me·na

Can you call a taxi for me (for 11 o'clock)?
Možete li mi pozvati   maw·zhe·te lee mee paw·zva·tee
taksi (za 11 sati)?   tak·see (za ye·da·na·est sa·tee)

I'm leaving now.
Ja sada odlazim.   ya sa·da awd·la·zeem

Can I leave my bags here?
Mogu li ovdje   maw·goo lee awv·dye
ostaviti svoje torbe?   aw·sta·vee·tee svoy·e tawr·be

There's a mistake in the bill.
Ima jedna greška   ee·ma yed·na gresh·ka
na računu.   na ra·choo·noo

Could I have my ..., please?	*Mogu li dobiti ..., molim?*	maw·goo lee daw·bee·tee ... maw·leem
deposit	*svoj depozit*	svoy de·paw·zeet
passport	*svoju putovnicu*	svoy·oo poo·tawv·nee·tsoo
valuables	*svoje dragocjenosti*	svoy·e dra·gaw·tsye·naw·stee

I had a great stay, thank you.
Moj boravak je bio — moy *baw*·ra·vak ye *bee*·aw
ugodan, hvala vam. — oo·*gaw*·dan *hva*·la vam

I'll recommend it to my friends.
Preporučit ću vas — pre·paw·*roo*·cheet choo vas
svojim prijateljima. — *svoy*·eem *pree*·ya·te·lyee·ma

I'll be back ...	*Vraćam se natrag ...*	*vra*·cham se *na*·trag ...
in (three) days	*za (tri) dana*	za (tree) *da*·na
on (Tuesday)	*u (utorak)*	oo (*oo*·taw·rak)

camping

kampiranje

Do you have ...?	*Imate li ...?*	ee·*ma*·te lee ...
electricity	*struju*	*stroo*·yoo
a laundry	*praonicu*	pra·*aw*·nee·tsoo
shower facilities	*tuševe*	*too*·she·ve
a site	*mjesto za kampiranje*	*mye*·staw za kam·*pee*·ra·nye
tents for hire	*šatore za najam*	*sha*·taw·re za *nai*·am

How much is it per ...?	*Koliko stoji po ...?*	kaw·*lee*·kaw *stoy*·ee paw ...
caravan	*kamp kućici*	kamp *koo*·chee·tsee
person	*osobi*	*aw*·saw·bee
tent	*šatoru*	*sha*·taw·roo
vehicle	*vozilu*	*vaw*·zee·loo

Can I ...? *Mogu li ...?* maw·goo lee ...
  camp here *ovdje kampirati* awv·dye kam·pee·ra·tee
  park next *parkirati pored* par·kee·ra·tee paw·red
  to my tent *svoga šatora* svaw·ga sha·taw·ra

Is it coin-operated?
Treba li ubaciti tre·ba lee oo·ba·tsee·tee
kovanice? kaw·va·nee·tse

Is the water drinkable?
Da li je ova voda pitka? da lee ye aw·va vaw·da peet·ka

Who do I ask to stay here?
Koga trebam pitati kaw·ga tre·bam pee·ta·tee
da li mogu ostati ovdje? da lee maw·goo aw·sta·tee awv·dye

Could I borrow ...?
Da li bih mogao/mogla da lee beeh maw·ga·aw/maw·gla
posuditi ...? **m/f** paw·soo·dee·tee ...

renting

I'm here to *Ja sam došao/* ya sam daw·sha·aw/
see the ... *došla vidjeti* daw·shla vee·dye·tee
for rent. *... za najam.* **m/f** ... za nai·am
Do you have *Imate li ...* ee·ma·te lee ...
a/an ... *za najam?* za nai·am
for rent?
  apartment *stan* stan
  cabin *kabinu* ka·bee·noo
  house *kuću* koo·choo
  room *sobu* saw·boo
  villa *vilu* vee·loo

furnished *namješteno* nam·yesh·te·naw
partly *djelomično* dye·law·meech·naw
  furnished *namješteno* nam·yesh·te·naw
unfurnished *nenamješteno* ne·nam·yesh·te·naw

staying with locals

Can I stay at your place?
Mogu li ostati kod vas?   maw·goo lee *aw*·sta·tee kawd vas

Is there anything I can do to help?
Mogu li vam pomoći   maw·goo lee vam *paw*·maw·chee
na bilo koji način?   na *bee*·law *koy*·ee na·cheen

Thanks for your hospitality.
Hvala vam na   hva·la vam na
gostoprimstvu.   gaw·staw·*preems*·tvoo

I have a (sleeping bag).
Ja imam (svoju vreću   ya ee·mam (*svoy*·oo vre·choo
za spavanje).   za *spa*·va·nye)

Can I …?	*Mogu li …?*	maw·goo lee …
bring anything	*donijeti neku*	daw·nee·*ye*·tee ne·koo
for the meal	*hranu za naš*	hra·noo za nash
	obrok	*awb*·rawk
do the dishes	*oprati suđe*	aw·pra·tee soo·je
set/clear	*namjestiti/*	na·mye·stee·tee/
the table	*raščistiti stol*	rash·*chee*·stee·tee stawl

the host with the most

Croatian hosts delight in regaling visitors with homemade delicacies and drinks. If you're fortunate enough to be invited to share a meal you can express your appreciation of your host's culinary prowess in the following manner:

Kako je ovo dobro i ukusno!
   ka·kaw ye *aw*·vaw   This is so good and tasty!
   daw·braw ee oo·koo·snaw

For their part, your hosts will implore you to eat to excess, possibly by saying:

Jedi sinko/kćeri, samo udri!
   ye·dee seen·kaw/k·che·ree   Eat, my son/daughter. Let it rip!
   sa·maw oo·dree

looking for ...

Where's ...?	Gdje je ...?	gdye ye ...
a department store	robna kuća	rawb·na koo·cha
the market	tržnica	tr·zhnee·tsa
a supermarket	supermarket	soo·per·mar·ket

Where can I buy (a padlock)?
Gdje mogu kupiti (lokot)?
gdye *maw*·goo koo·pee·tee (*law*·kawt)

For phrases on directions, see **directions**, page 53, and for additional shops and services, see the **dictionary**.

making a purchase

I'm just looking.
Ja samo razgledam.
ya sa·maw raz·gle·dam

I'd like to buy (an adaptor plug).
Želim kupiti (utikač za konverter).
zhe·leem koo·pee·tee (oo·tee·kach za kawn·ver·ter)

How much is it?
Koliko stoji?
kaw·lee·kaw stoy·ee

Can you write down the price?
Možete li napisati cijenu?
maw·zhe·te lee na·pee·sa·tee tsee·ye·noo

Do you have any others?
Imate li bilo kakve druge?
ee·ma·te lee bee·law kak·ve droo·ge

Can I look at it?
Mogu li to pogledati?
maw·goo lee taw paw·gle·da·tee

Could I have it wrapped?
Možete li mi to   *maw*·zhe·te lee mee taw
zamotati?   za·*maw*·ta·tee

Does it have a guarantee?
Ima li ovo garanciju?   *ee*·ma lee *aw*·vaw ga·*ran*·tsee·yoo

Can I have it sent abroad?
Možete li mi to   *maw*·zhe·te lee mee taw
poslati u inozemstvo?   *paw*·sla·tee oo ee·naw·*zemst*·vaw

Can you order it for me?
Možete li to naručiti   *maw*·zhe·te lee taw na·*roo*·chee·tee
za mene?   za *me*·ne

Can I pick it up later?
Mogu li doći   *maw*·goo lee *daw*·chee
po to kasnije?   paw taw *ka*·snee·ye

It's faulty.
Neispravno je.   ne·ees·prav·naw ye

Do you accept ...?	*Da li prihvaćate ...?*	da lee *pree*·hva·cha·te ...
credit cards	*kreditne kartice*	*kre*·deet·ne *kar*·tee·tse
debit cards	*debitne kartice*	*de*·beet·ne *kar*·tee·tse
travellers cheques	*putničke čekove*	*poot*·neech·ke *che*·kaw·ve

Could I have a ..., please?	*Mogu li dobiti ..., molim?*	*maw*·goo lee *daw*·bee·tee ... *maw*·leem
bag	*vrećicu*	*vre*·chee·tsoo
receipt	*račun*	*ra*·choon

I'd like ..., please.	*Želio/Željela bih ... m/f*	*zhe*·lee·aw/*zhe*·lye·la beeh ...
my change	*moj ostatak novca*	moy aw·*sta*·tak *nawv*·tsa
a refund	*povrat novca*	*pawv*·rat *nawv*·tsa
to return this	*ovo vratiti*	*aw*·vaw *vra*·tee·tee

PRACTICAL

66

bargaining

Prices in shops are generally fixed but you could try bargaining at a market, *tržnica* (*tr*·zhnee·tsa).

That's too expensive.
To je preskupo. — taw ye *pre*·skoo·paw

Do you have something cheaper?
Imate li nešto jeftinije? — ee·ma·te lee *nesh*·taw yef·*tee*·nee·ye

I'll give you (five kuna).
Dati ću vam (pet kuna). — *da*·tee choo vam (pet *koo*·na)

local talk		
bargain	*prigodna cijena* f	*pree*·gawd·na tsee·*ye*·na
rip-off	*prekomjerna cijena* f	*pre*·kaw·myer·na tsee·*ye*·na
sale	*rasprodaja* f	*ra*·spraw·da·ya
specials	*posebne ponude* f pl	*paw*·seb·ne *paw*·noo·de

clothes

My size is ... — *Moja veličina je ...* — *moy*·a ve·lee·*chee*·na ye ...
  (40) — *(četrdeset)* — (che·tr·*de*·set)
  large — *krupna* — *kroop*·na
  medium — *srednja* — *sred*·nya
  small — *sitna* — *seet*·na

Can I try it on?
Mogu li to probati? — *maw*·goo lee taw *praw*·ba·tee

It doesn't fit.
Ne odgovara mi to. — ne awd·*gaw*·va·ra mee taw

For sizes, see **numbers & amounts,** page 31. For clothing items, see the **dictionary.**

Though it might relate to an outmoded item of apparel, the word 'cravat' has interesting origins. It's thought to stem from the word *Hrvat* (hr·vat) meaning 'a Croat'. These neck scarves were purportedly so named because they were worn by Croatian mercenaries serving in the French army during the Thirty Year's War of the early 17th century.

The black-and-white spotted dogs known as Dalmatians meanwhile, are thought not to have originated in the coastal province of Dalmatia but to have been brought there by Roma people for use as guard dogs.

repairs

Can I have my ... repaired here?

Mogu li popraviti	maw·goo lee paw·pra·vee·tee
svoj/svoju/svoje ...	svoy/svoy·oo/svoy·e ...
ovdje? m/f/n	awv·dye

When will	*Kada će biti*	ka·da che bee·tee
my ... be ready?	*gotov/*	gaw·tawv/
	gotove ...? sg/pl	gaw·taw·ve ...
backpack	*moj ranac* sg	moy *ra*·nats
camera	*moj*	moy
	foto-aparat sg	faw·taw·a·pa·rat
(sun)glasses	*moje naočale*	moy·e na·aw·cha·le
	(za sunce) pl	(za soon·tse)
shoes	*moje cipele* pl	moy·e tsee·pe·le
watch	*sat* sg	sat

hairdressing

I'd like (a) …	Želio/Željela bih … m/f	zhe·lee·aw/zhe·lye·la beeh …
blow wave	feniranje	fe·nee·ra·nye
colour	bojenje kose	boy·e·nye kaw·se
haircut	šišanje	shee·sha·nye
my beard trimmed	podrezivanje brade	paw·dre·zee·va·nye bra·de
shave	brijanje	bree·ya·nye
trim	skraćivanje	skra·chee·va·nye

Don't cut it too short.
Nemojte me ošišati prekratko.
ne·moy·te me aw·shee·sha·tee pre·krat·kaw

Please use a new blade.
Molim vas koristite novi žilet.
maw·leem vas kaw·ree·stee·te naw·vee zhee·let

Shave it all off!
Obrijte sve potpuno!
aw·breey·te sve pawt·poo·naw

I should never have let you near me!
Nisam vam nikada trebao ni dozvoliti blizu!
nee·sam vam nee·ka·da tre·ba·aw nee dawz·vaw·lee·tee blee·zoo

For colours, see the **dictionary**.

books & reading

Do you have …?	Imate li …?	ee·ma·te lee …
a book by (August Senoa)	knjigu (Augusta Šenoe)	knyee·goo (a·oo·goo·sta she·naw·e)
an entertainment guide	vodič o zbivanjima u svijetu razonode	vaw·deech aw zbee·va·nye·ma oo svee·ye·too ra·zaw·naw·de

Is there an English-language ...?	Postoji li ... za engleski jezik?	paw·stoy·ee lee ... za en·gle·skee ye·zeek
bookshop	knjižara	knyee·zha·ra
section	odjel	awd·yel
I'd like (a) ...	Želio/Željela bih ... m/f	zhe·lee·aw/zhe·lye·la beeh ...
dictionary	rječnik	ryech·neek
newspaper (in English)	novine (na engleskom)	naw·vee·ne (na en·gles·kawm)
notepad	bilježnicu	bee·lyezh·nee·tsoo

Can you recommend a book for me?

| Možete li mi preporučiti jednu knjigu? | maw·zhe·te lee mee pre·paw·roo·chee·tee yed·noo knyee·goo |

Do you have Lonely Planet guidebooks?

| Imate li Lonely Planet priručnike? | ee·ma·te lee lawn·lee ple·net pree·rooch·nee·ke |

music

glazba

I'd like a ...	Želio/Željela bih... m/f	zhe·lee·aw/zhe·lye·la beeh ...
blank tape	jednu praznu kazetu	yed·noo praz·noo ka·ze·too
CD	jedan CD	ye·dan tse de
DVD	jedan DVD	ye·dan de·ve·de

I'm looking for something by (Oliver Dragojevic).
Tražim nešto od   *tra*-zheem *nesh*-taw awd
(Olivera Dragojevića).   (*aw*-lee-ve-ra dra-*goy*-e-vee-cha)

What's their best recording?
Koji je njegov   *koy*-ee ye *nye*-gawv
najbolji album?   nai-baw-lyee *al*-boom

Can I listen to this?
Mogu li ovo   *maw*-goo lee *aw*-vaw
poslušati?   *paw*-sloo-sha-tee

photography

I need … film	*Trebam … film*	*tre*-bam … feelm
for this	*za ovaj*	za *aw*-vai
camera.	*foto-aparat.*	*faw*-taw-a-*pa*-rat
APS	*APS*	a pe es
B&W	*crno-bijeli*	*tsr*-naw-bee-*ye*-lee
colour	*kolor*	*kaw*-lawr

I need … film	*Trebam film …*	*tre*-bam feelm …
for this	*za ovaj*	za *aw*-vai
camera.	*foto-aparat.*	*faw*-taw-a-*pa*-rat
slide	*za dijapozitive*	za dee-ya-*paw*-zee-tee-ve
(200) speed	*brzine (dvijesto)*	br-*zee*-ne (*dvee*-ye-staw)

Can you …?	*Možete li …?*	*maw*-zhe-te lee …
develop this	*razviti ovaj*	*raz*-vee-tee *aw*-vai
film	*film*	feelm
load my film	*staviti moj film*	*sta*-vee-tee moy feelm
	u foto-aparat	oo *faw*-taw-a-*pa*-rat

When will it be ready?
Kada će to biti   *ka*-da che taw *bee*-tee
gotovo?   *gaw*-taw-vaw

How much is it?
Koliko to stoji?   kaw-*lee*-kaw taw *stoy*-ee

I need a passport photo taken.

Trebam se slikati   tre·bam se slee·ka·tee
za putovnicu.   za poo·tawv·nee·tsoo

I'm not happy with these photos.

Nisam zadovoljan/   nee·sam za·daw·vaw·lyan/
zadovoljna sa ovim   za·daw·vawl'·na sa aw·veem
fotografijama. m/f   faw·taw·gra·fee·ya·ma

I don't want to pay the full price.

Ne želim platiti   ne zhe·leem pla·tee·tee
punu cijenu.   poo·noo tsee·ye·noo

souvenirs

embroidery	*vez* m	vez
folklore items	*folklorni*	fawl·klawr·nee
	predmeti m pl	pred·me·tee
handicrafts	*ručni rad* m	rooch·nee rad
lace	*čipka* f	cheep·ka
paintings	*slike* f pl	slee·ke
pottery	*grnčarija* f	grn·cha·ree·ya
silver jewellery	*srebrni nakit* m	sre·br·nee na·keet
sculptures	*skulpture* f pl	skoolp·too·re
stone carvings	*Bračanske*	bra·chan·ske
from Brač	*rezbarije*	rez·ba·ree·ye
	u kamenu f pl	oo ka·me·noo
woodcarvings	*drvorezi* m pl	dr·vaw·re·zee

books on historical and cultural heritage

knjige o povjesnoj   knyee·ge aw paw·vye·snoy
i kulturnoj baštini f pl   ee kool·toor·noy bash·tee·nee

jewellery and souvenirs made of shells, sea urchins etc

ukrasi iz mora m pl   oo·kra·see eez maw·ra

traditional folk costumes

tradicionalne narodne   tra·dee·tsee·aw·nal·ne na·rawd·ne
nošnje f pl   nawsh·nye

post office

Postal services are catered for by HTP Hrvatska. If you just want to send a few postcards you can avoid going to the post office by buying stamps, *poštanske marke* (*pawsh*·tan·ske *mar*·ke), from any kiosk newsagent and dropping your mail into a yellow mailbox, *poštanski sandučić* (*pawsh*·tan·ske san·*doo*·cheech).

I want to send a …	*Želim poslati …*	*zhe*·leem *paw*·sla·tee …
fax	*telefaks*	*te*·le·faks
letter	*pismo*	*pee*·smaw
parcel	*paket*	*pa*·ket
postcard	*dopisnicu*	*daw*·pee·snee·tsoo

I want to buy a/an …	*Želim kupiti …*	*zhe*·leem *koo*·pee·tee …
aerogram	*avionski*	a·*vee*·awn·skee
	telegram	*te*·le·gram
envelope	*omotnicu*	*aw*·mawt·nee·tsoo
stamp	*jednu poštansku marku*	*yed*·noo *pawsh*·tan·skoo *mar*·koo

customs declaration	*prijava robe na carini* f	*pree*·ya·va *raw*·be na *tsa*·ree·nee
domestic	*domaće*	*daw*·ma·che
fragile	*lomljivo*	*lawm*·lyee·vaw
international	*međunarodno*	me·joo·*na*·rawd·naw
mail	*pošta* f	*pawsh*·ta
mailbox	*poštanski sandučić* m	*pawsh*·tan·skee san·*doo*·cheech
postcode	*poštanski broj* m	*pawsh*·tan·skee broy
post office	*poštanski ured* m	*pawsh*·tan·skee oo·red

snail mail		
airmail	*zračna pošta* f	zrach·na pawsh·ta
express mail	*ekspres pošta* f	eks·pres pawsh·ta
registered mail	*preporučena pošta* f	pre·paw·roo·che·na pawsh·ta
sea mail	*prekomorska pošta* f	pre·kaw·mawr·ska pawsh·ta
surface mail	*obična pošta* f	aw·beech·na pawsh·ta

Please send it by air/surface mail to (Australia).
Molim da pošaljete to   maw·leem da paw·sha·lye·te taw
zračnom/običnom   zrach·nawm/aw·beech·nawm
poštom u (Australiju).   pawsh·tawm oo (a·oo·stra·lee·yoo)

It contains (souvenirs).
Ovo sadrži (suvenire).   aw·vaw sa·dr·zhee (soo·ve·nee·re)

Where's the poste restante section?
Gdje se nalazi post restant   gdye se na·la·zee pawst re·stant
odjel?   awd·yel

Is there any mail for me?
Ima li bilo kakve   ee·ma lee bee·law kak·ve
pošte za mene?   pawsh·te za me·ne

phone

What's your phone number?
Koji je vaš/tvoj   koy·ee ye vash/tvoy
broj telefona? pol/inf   broy te·le·faw·na

Where's the nearest public phone?
Gdje je najbliži javni   gdye ye nai·blee·zhee yav·nee
telefon?   te·le·fawn

I want to ...	Želim ...	zhe·leem ...
buy a phonecard	kupiti telefonsku karticu	koo·pee·tee te·le·fawn·skoo kar·tee·tsoo
call (Singapore)	nazvati (Singapur)	naz·va·tee (seen·ga·poor)
make a (local) call	obaviti (lokalni) poziv	aw·ba·vee·tee (law·kal·nee) paw·zeev
reverse the charges	obaviti poziv na račun pozvanog	aw·ba·vee·tee paw·zeev na ra·choon pawz·va·nawg
speak for (three) minutes	govoriti (tri) minute	gaw·vaw·ree·tee (tree) mee·noo·te

How much does ... cost?	Koliko košta ...?	kaw·lee·kaw kawsh·ta ...
a (three)-minute call	poziv od (tri) minute	paw·zeev awd (tree) mee·noo·te
each extra minute	svaka naknadna minuta	sva·ka nak·nad·na mee·noo·ta

Can I look at a phone book?
Mogu li pogledati u imenik?
maw·goo lee paw·gle·da·tee oo ee·me·neek

The number is ...
Broj je ...
broy ye ...

What's the area/country code for (New Zealand)?
Koji je područni/ državni pozivni broj za (Novi Zeland)?
koy·ee ye paw·drooch·nee/ dr·zhav·nee paw·zeev·nee broy za (naw·vee ze·land)

Hello.	Halo.	ha·*law*
It's …	Ovdje …	*awv*·dye …
Is … there?	Da li je … tamo?	da lee ye … *ta*·maw
Can I speak to …?	Mogu li dobiti …?	*maw*·goo lee *daw*·bee·tee …
It's engaged.	Zauzeto je.	za·oo·ze·taw ye
I've been cut off.	Prekinuli su me.	*pre*·kee·noo·lee soo me
The connection is bad.	Veza je loša.	ve·za ye *law*·sha

listen for …

kree·vee broy
Krivi broj. Wrong number.

tkaw *zaw*·ve
Tko zove? Who's calling?

s keem *zhe*·lee·te *raz*·gaw·va·ra·tee
S kim želite razgovarati? Who do you want to speak to?

sa·maw tre·*noo*·tak
Samo trenutak. One moment.

awn/*aw*·na *nee*·ye *awv*·dye
On/Ona nije ovdje. He/She is not here.

Please tell (him/her) I called.
Molim da (mu/joj) kažete — maw·leem da moo/yoy *ka*·zhe·te
da sam zvao. m — da sam *zva*·aw
Molim da (mu/joj) kažete — maw·leem da moo/yoy *ka*·zhe·te
da sam zvala. f — da sam *zva*·la

Can I leave a message?
Mogu li ostaviti — maw·goo lee *aw*·sta·vee·tee
poruku? — *paw*·roo·koo

My number is …
Moj broj je … — moy broy ye …

I don't have a contact number.
Nemam broj na koji — ne·mam broy na *koy*·ee
me možete dobiti. — me maw·zhe·te *daw*·bee·tee

I'll call back later.
Nazvati ću kasnije. — naz·va·tee choo *ka*·snee·ye

mobile phone/cellphone

I'd like a …	Trebao/Trebala bih … m/f	tre·ba·aw/tre·ba·la beeh …
charger for my phone	punjač za moj telefon	poo·nyach za moy te·le·fawn
mobile phone/ cellphone for hire	iznajmiti mobilni telefon	eez·nai·mee·tee maw·beel·nee te·le·fawn
prepaid mobile phone/ cellphone	unaprijed plaćeni mobilni telefon	oo·na·pree·yed pla·che·nee maw·beel·nee te·le·fawn
SIM card	SIM karticu	seem kar·tee·tsoo

What are the rates?
Koje su cijene telefoniranja?
koy·ee soo tsee·ye·ne te·le·faw·nee·ra·nya

(3 kuna) per (30) seconds.
(3 kune) po (30) sekundi.
(tree koo·ne) paw (tree·de·set) se·koon·dee

the internet

Where's the local Internet café?
Gdje je mjesni internet kafić?
gdye ye mye·snee een·ter·net ka·feech

How do I log on?
Kako mogu pristupiti mreži?
ka·kaw maw·goo pree·stoo·pee·tee mre·zhee

Please change it to English-language setting.
Molim vas da promijenite jezičnu opciju na engleski jezik.
maw·leem vas da praw·mee·ye·nee·te ye·zeech·noo awp·tsee·yoo na en·gle·skee

I'd like to …	Želio/Željela bih … m/f	zhe·lee·aw/zhe·lye·la beeh …
check my email	provjeriti svoj email	praw·vye·ree·tee svoy ee·ma·eel
get Internet access	pristup internetu	pree·stoop een·ter·ne·too
use a printer	koristiti pisač	kaw·ree·stee·tee pee·sach
use a scanner	koristiti skener	kaw·ree·stee·tee ske·ner

Do you have …?	Imate li …?	ee·ma·te lee …
Macs	Macintosh računala	me·keen·tawsh ra·choo·na·la
PCs	PC-e	pe tse e
a Zip drive	pogon za Zip diskete	paw·gawn za zeep dee·ske·te

How much per …?	Koja je cijena po …?	koy·a ye tsee·ye·na paw …
hour	satu	sa·too
(five) minutes	(pet) minuta	(pet) mee·noo·ta
page	stranici	stra·nee·tsee

It's crashed.

Došlo je do prestanka rada računala.   *dawsh·law ye daw pre·stan·ka ra·da ra·choo·na·la*

I've finished.

Završio/Završila sam. m/f   *za·vr·shee·aw/za·vr·shee·la sam*

---

say I!

When you see a phrase containing the word 'I' in English, you'll notice that the Croatian translation often has two options to choose from. These are separated by a slash and are followed by the gender markers m/f, as in the phrase: Želio/Željela bih … m/f 'I'd like …'.

The two alternatives are masculine and feminine verb forms. Making the right selection is simple as it's based on the gender of the speaker – the person saying 'I'. If you're a man, you choose the first option and say Želio bih. If you're a woman, you say Željela bih. See the **a–z phrasebuilder**, page 19 for more on gender in Croatian.

banking
bankovno poslovanje

Where can I ...?	Gdje mogu ...?	gdye *maw*·goo ...
I'd like to ...	Želio/Željela bih ... m/f	*zhe*·lee·aw/*zhe*·lye·la beeh ...
cash a cheque	unovčiti ček	oo·*navv*·chee·tee chek
change a travellers cheque	zamijeniti putnički ček	za·mee·*ye*·nee·tee poot·neech·kee chek
change money	zamijeniti novac	za·mee·*ye*·nee·tee *naw*·vats
get a cash advance	uzeti predujam u gotovini	oo·ze·tee *pre*·doo·yam oo gaw·taw·*vee*·nee
withdraw money	podignuti novac	*paw*·deeg·noo·tee *naw*·vats
Where's ...?	Gdje se nalazi ...?	gdye se *na*·la·zee ...
an ATM	bankovni automat	*ban*·kawv·nee a·oo·*taw*·mat
a foreign exchange office	mjenjačnica za strane valute	*mye*·nyach·nee·tsa za *stra*·ne va·*loo*·te

What time does the bank open?

U koliko sati se otvara banka?
oo kaw·*lee*·kaw *sa*·tee se *awt*·va·ra *ban*·ka

The ATM took my card.

Bankovni automat mi je oduzeo karticu.
ban·kawv·nee a·oo·*taw*·mat mee ye *aw*·doo·ze·aw *kar*·tee·tsoo

I've forgotten my PIN.

Zaboravio/Zaboravila sam svoj osobni tajni broj. m/f
za·*baw*·ra·vee·aw/za·*baw*·ra·vee·la sam svoy *aw*·sawb·nee *tai*·nee broy

Can I use my credit card to withdraw money?

Mogu li koristiti svoju kreditnu karticu za podizanje novca?
maw·goo lee kaw·ree·*stee*·tee svoy·oo *kre*·deet·noo *kar*·tee·tsoo za *paw*·dee·za·nye *nawv*·tsa

What's the ...?	Koji/Kolika	koy·ee/kaw·lee·ka
	je ...? m/f	ye ...
charge for that	pristojba za to f	pree·stoy·ba za taw
exchange rate	tečaj razmjene m	te·chai raz·mye·ne

Has my money arrived yet?

| Da li je moj novac | da lee ye moy naw·vats |
| stigao? | stee·ga·aw |

How long will it take to arrive?

| Koliko će trebati | kaw·lee·kaw che tre·ba·tee |
| da stigne? | da steeg·ne |

For other useful phrases, see **money**, page 37.

For other useful phrases, see **money**, page 37.

---

listen for ...

| ee·den·tee·fee·ka·tsee·ya | identifikacija | **identification** |
| poo·tawv·nee·tsa | putovnica | **passport** |

ee·ma·maw ye·dan praw·blem
Imamo jedan problem.   **There's a problem.**

mee taw ne maw·zhe·maw oo·ra·dee·tee
Mi to ne možemo uraditi.   **We can't do that.**

nee·ye vam aw·sta·law neesh·ta nawv·tsa
Nije vam ostalo ništa novca.   **You have no funds left.**

pawt·pee·shee·te awv·dye
Potpišite ovdje.   **Sign here.**

I'd like a/an ...	Želio/Željela bih ... m/f	zhe·lee·aw/zhe·lye·la beeh ...
audio set	set slušalica	set sloo·sha·lee·tsa
catalogue	katalog	ka·ta·log
guidebook in English	turistički vodič na engleskom	too·ree·steech·kee vaw·deech na en·gles·kawm
(local) map	kartu (mjesta)	kar·too (mye·sta)

Do you have information on ... sights?	Da li imate informacije o ... znamenitostima?	da lee ee·ma·te een·fawr·ma·tsee·ye aw ... zna·me·nee·taw·stee·ma
cultural	kulturnim	kool·toor·neem
historical	povijesnim	paw·vee·ye·sneem
religious	vjerskim	vyer·skeem

I need a guide.
Trebam vodiča.   tre·bam vaw·dee·cha

I'd like to see ...
Želio/Željela bih vidjeti ... m/f   zhe·lee·aw/zhe·lye·la beeh vee·dye·tee ...

Could you take a photo of me?
Možete/Možeš li me slikati? pol/inf   maw·zhe·te/maw·zhesh lee me slee·ka·tee

Can I take a photo (of you)?
Mogu li ja slikati (vas/tebe)? pol/inf   maw·goo lee ya slee·ka·tee (vas/te·be)

I'll send you the photo.
Poslati ću vam/tebi tu fotografiju. pol/inf   paw·sla·tee choo vam/te·bee too faw·taw·gra·fee·yoo

Who made it?
Tko je to napravio?   tkaw ye taw *na*·pra·vee·aw

How old is it?
Koliko je to staro?   kaw·*lee*·kaw ye taw *sta*·raw

behold the grb!

On a sojourn in Croatia one thing that becomes imprinted upon your subconscious is the ubiquitous red-and-white checked emblem in the shape of a shield. It's known as the *Hrvatski grb* (hr·vat·skee grb) 'the Croatian coat of arms' or simply as *grb*. It's been around for hundreds of years and is about as potent a symbol of nationalism as you can find.

The origins of the *grb* are obscure but legend has it that a Croatian king defeated a Venetian prince at chess to maintain Croatia's freedom and so the chessboard was symbolically enshrined as a symbol of this freedom. Today, following the breakaway from the former Yugoslavia, the *grb* is proudly displayed everywhere to celebrate independence for which the Croats have yearned for over a millenium.

getting in

What time does it open/close?
U koliko sati se   oo kaw·*lee*·kaw *sa*·tee se
otvara/zatvara?   *awt*·va·ra/*zat*·va·ra

What's the admission charge?
Koliko stoji ulaznica?   kaw·*lee*·kaw *stoy*·ee oo·laz·nee·tsa

Is there a	Imate li	ee·ma·te lee
discount for …?	*popust za …?*	*paw*·poost za …
children	*djecu*	*dye*·tsoo
families	*obitelji*	aw·*bee*·te·lyee
groups	*grupe*	*groo*·pe
seniors	*starije ljude*	*sta*·ree·ye *lyoo*·de
pensioners	*umirovljenike*	oo·mee·rawv·lye·*nee*·ke
students	*studente*	*stoo*·den·te

tours

Can you recommend a ...?	*Možete li mi preporučiti ...?*	maw·zhe·te lee mee pre·paw·*roo*·chee·tee ...
When's the next ...?	*Kada je idući/ iduća ...?* m/f	*ka*·da ye ee·*doo*·chee/ ee·doo·cha ...
boat trip	*izlet brodom* m	*eez*·let *braw*·dawm
day trip	*dnevni izlet* m	*dnev*·nee *eez*·let
tour	*turistička ekskurzija* f	too·*ree*·steech·ka ek·*skoor*·zee·ya
Is ... included?	*Da li je ... uključen/ uključena?* m/f	da lee ye ... ook·lyoo·chen/ ook·lyoo·che·na
accommodation	*smještaj* m	*smye*·shtai
food	*hrana* f	*hra*·na
transport	*prijevoz* m	pree·*ye*·vawz

The guide will pay.
 Vodič će platiti.   *vaw*·deech che *pla*·tee·tee

The guide has paid.
 Vodič je platio/platila. m/f *vaw*·deech ye *pla*·tee·aw/*pla*·tee·la

How long is the tour?
 Koliko traje ekskurzija? kaw·*lee*·kaw *trai*·e ek·*skoor*·zee·ya

What time should we be back?
 U koje bi se vrijeme oo *koy*·e bee se vree·*ye*·me
 trebali vratiti? *tre*·ba·lee *vra*·tee·tee

I'm with them.
 Ja sam s njima. ya sam s *nyee*·ma

signs

Besplatan Ulaz	be·spla·tan oo·laz	**Free Admission**
Informacije	een·fawr·*ma*·tsee·ye	**Information**
Izlaz	*eez*·laz	**Exit**
Misa u Toku	*mee*·sa oo *taw*·koo	**Service (Mass) in Progress**
Muški	*moosh*·kee	**Men**
Ne Diraj	ne *dee*·rai	**Do Not Touch**
Otvoren	*awt* vawr·en	**Open**
Ulaz	*oo*·laz	**Entrance**
WC	ve·*tse*	**Toilets**
Zabranjen Ulaz	za·bra·nyen oo·laz	**No Entry**
Zabranjene Blic Kameri	za·bra·nye·ne bleets ka·me·ree	**No Flash Photography**
Zabranjeno Fotografirati	za·bra·nye·naw faw·taw·gra·*fee*·ra·tee	**No Photography**
Zabranjeno Pušenje	za·bra·nye·naw poo·she·nye	**No Smoking**
Zatvoren	zat vawr·en	**Closed**
Ženski	*zhen*·skee	**Women**

I'm attending a …	*Ja idem na …*	ya *ee*·dem na …
conference	*konferenciju*	kon·fe·*ren*·tsee·yoo
course	*tečaj*	*te*·chai
meeting	*sastanak*	*sa*·sta·nak
trade fair	*sajam*	*sai*·am

Where's the …?	*Gdje je …?*	gdye ye …
business centre	*poslovni*	*paw*·slawv·nee
(eg in hotel)	*centar*	*tsen*·tar
conference	*konferencija*	kon·fe·*ren*·tsee·ya
meeting	*sastanak*	*sa*·sta·nak

I'm with …	*Ovdje sam sa …*	*awv*·dye sam sa …
(Kras)	*(Krašem)*	(kra·shem)
my colleague(s)	*svojim kolegom/*	*svoy*·eem kaw·*le*·gawm/
	kolegama sg/pl	kaw·*le*·ga·ma
(two) others	*(dvoje) drugih*	(dvoy·e) droo·geeh

I'm alone.
Ja sam sam/sama. m/f   ya sam sam/*sa*·ma

---

home alone

There's a little trick to the pronunciation of the above phrase *Ja sam sam*. It might look like simple repetition, but to be understood you'll need to say the first *sam* shorter than the second. You'll also need to pitch your voice a bit lower for the second *sam*. This aspect of Croatian is called pitch accent. See **pronunciation**, page 13, for an explanation of how it works if you're curious.

I have an appointment with …
Ja imam sastanak sa …   ya *ee*·mam *sa*·sta·nak sa …

I'm staying at …, room …
Ostajem u …, soba …   *aw*·stai·em oo … *saw*·ba …

I need ...	*Treba mi ...*	*tre*·ba mee ...
a computer	*računalo*	ra·*choo*·na·law
an Internet connection	*priključak na internet*	*pree*·klyoo·chak na *een*·ter·net
an interpreter	*tumač*	*too*·mach
more business cards	*još posjetnica*	yosh *paw*·syet·nee·tsa
to send a fax	*da pošaljem telefaks*	da *paw*·sha·lyem te·le·faks

Here's my business card.
Evo vam moja posjetnica. e·vaw vam *moy*·a paw·syet·nee·tsa

That went very well.
To je odlično prošlo. taw ye *awd*·leech·naw *prawsh*·law

Thank you for your time.
Zahvaljujem na vašem vremenu. za·hva·lyoo·yem na *va*·shem *vre*·me·noo

Shall we go for a drink/meal?
Hoćemo li na piće/ večeru? *haw*·che·maw lee na *pee*·che/ *ve*·che·roo

It's on me.
Ja častim. ya *cha*·steem

down to business

Croatian business etiquette doesn't present any real peculiarities. One thing to be conscious of, though, is that Croatians in coastal areas have a more relaxed and flexible attitude to time than their Anglo-Saxon counterparts. Agitation about deadlines or punctuality might meet with the standard response:

Relax, we still have time.
Stani malo, imamo još vremena. *sta*·nee *ma*·law ee·ma·maw yosh *vre*·me·na

Away from the coastal areas, Croatians see themselves as hard-working and efficient go-getters in the Central European mould. They tend to be more bureacratic and punctual in their business dealings than their Latin-influenced compatriots.

senior & disabled travellers
stariji i onesposobljeni putnici

Because of the number of wounded war veterans, more attention is being paid to the needs of disabled travellers. In Zagreb, ZET Electric Tram Company (*Zagrebački Električni Tramvaj*) offers a service for disabled people.

I have a disability.

Ja sam onesposobljen/	ya sam aw·ne·*spaw*·sawb·lyen/
onesposobljena. **m/f**	aw·ne·*spaw*·sawb·lye·na

I need assistance.

Ja trebam pomoć.	ya *tre*·bam *paw*·mawch

What services do you have for people with a disability?

Koje usluge nudite	*koy*·e oo·sloo·ge *noo*·dee·te
za onesposobljene?	za aw·ne·*spaw*·sawb·lye·ne

Are there disabled toilets?

Imate li zahod	*ee*·ma·te lee *za*·hawd
za onesposobljene?	za aw·ne·*spaw*·sawb·lye·ne

Are there disabled parking spaces?

Postoji li parkiralište	*paw*·stoy·ee lee par·*kee*·ra·leesh·te
za onesposobljene?	za aw·ne·*spaw*·sawb·lye·ne

Is there wheelchair access?

Imate li pristup za	*ee*·ma·te lee *pree*·stoop za
invalidska kolica?	een·*va*·leed·ska kaw·*lee*·tsa

How wide is the entrance?

Koje širine je ulaz?	*koy*·e shee·*ree*·ne ye *oo*·laz

I'm deaf.

Ja sam gluh/gluha. **m/f**	ya sam glooh/*gloo*·ha

I have a hearing aid.

Ja nosim slušni aparat.	ya *naw*·seem *sloosh*·nee a·*pa*·rat

Are guide dogs permitted?

Da li je dozvoljen	da lee ye *dawz*·vaw·lyen
pristup psima	*pree*·stoop *psee*·ma
vodičima?	vaw·*dee*·chee·ma

How many steps are there?

Koliko stepenica ima?   kaw·*lee*·kaw ste·pe·nee·tsa ee·ma

Is there a lift?

Da li postoji dizalo?   da lee *paw*·stoy·ee *dee*·za·law

Are there rails in the bathroom?

Imate li ručke za   ee·ma·te lee *rooch*·ke za
oslanjanje u kupaonici?   aw·sla·nya·nye oo koo·pa·*aw*·nee·tsee

Could you call me a disabled taxi?

Da li biste mi mogli   da lee *bee*·ste mee *maw*·glee
pozvati taksi za   pawz·va·tee *tak*·see za
onesposobljene?   aw·ne·*spaw*·sawb·lye·ne

Could you help me cross the street safely?

Da li biste mi mogli   da lee *bee*·ste mee *maw*·glee
pomoći sigurno   paw·maw·chee see·goor·naw
prijeći ulicu?   pree·*ye*·chee oo·lee·tsoo

Is there somewhere I can sit down?

Ima li negdje gdje   ee·ma lee *ne*·gdye gdye
mogu sjesti?   *maw*·goo sye·stee

guide dog	*pas vodič* m	pas *vaw*·deech
older person	*starija osoba* f	sta·ree·ya *aw*·saw·ba
person with a disability	*onesposobljena osoba* f	aw·ne·*spaw*·sawb·lye·na *aw*·saw·ba
ramp	*kosina za pristup kolicima* f	kaw·*see*·na za *pree*·stoop kaw·*lee*·tsee·ma
walking frame	*metalno pomagalo za hodanje* n	*me*·tal·naw paw·*ma*·ga·law za *haw*·da·nye
walking stick	*štap za hodanje* m	shtap za *haw*·da·nye
wheelchair	*invalidska kolica* f pl	een·*va*·leed·ska kaw·*lee*·tsa

travelling with children

Is there a …?	*Imate li …?*	*ee·ma·te lee …*
baby change room	*sobu za previjanjebeba*	*saw·boo za pre·vee·ya·nye be·ba*
child-minding service	*usluge čuvanja djece*	*oo·sloo·ge choo·va·nya dye·tse*
child-sized portion	*dječju porciju*	*dyech·yoo pawr·tsee·yoo*
children's menu	*dječji jelovnik*	*dyech·yee ye·lawv·neek*
crèche	*jaslice*	*ya·slee·tse*
discount for children	*popust za djecu*	*paw·poost za dye·tsoo*
family ticket	*kartu za cijelu obitelj*	*kar·too za tsee·ye·loo aw·bee·tel'*
I need a/an …	*Treba mi …*	*tre·ba mee …*
baby seat	*sjedalo za dijete*	*sye·da·law za dee·ye·te*
(English-speaking) baby-sitter	*dadilja (koja govori engleski)*	*da·dee·lya (koy·a gaw·vaw·ree en·gle·skee)*
booster seat	*potporno dječje sjedalo*	*pawt·pawr·naw dyech·ye sye·da·law*
cot	*dječji krevet*	*dyech·yee kre·vet*
highchair	*visoka stolica za bebe*	*vee·saw·ka staw·lee·tsa za be·be*
plastic bag	*plastična vrećica*	*pla·steech·na vre·chee·tsa*
potty	*tuta*	*too·ta*
sick bag	*vrećica za povraćanje*	*vre·chee·tsa za paw·vra·cha·nye*
stroller	*dječja hodalica*	*dyech·ya haw·da·lee·tsa*

Where's the nearest …?	Gdje je najbliži/a/e …? m/f/n	gdye ye nai·blee·zhee/a/e …
drinking fountain	izvor pitke vode m	eez·vawr peet·ke vaw·de
park	park m	park
playground	igralište n	ee·gra·leesh·te
swimming pool	bazen za plivanje m	ba·zen za plee·va·nye
tap	slavina f	sla·vee·na
theme park	tematski luna-park m	te·mat·skee loo·na·park
toy shop	prodavaonica igračaka f	praw·da·va·aw·nee·tsa ee·gra·cha·ka

Do you sell …?	Da li prodajete …?	da lee praw·dai·e·te …
baby wipes	vlažne maramice za bebe	vlazh·ne ma·ra·mee·tse za be·be
painkillers for babies	dječje tablete protiv bolova	dyech·ye ta·ble·te praw·teev baw·law·va
disposable diapers/ nappies	pelene za jednokratnu upotrebu	pe·le·ne za yed·naw·krat·noo oo·paw·tre·boo
tissues	papirnate rupčiće	pa·peer·na·te roop·chee·che

Do you hire out …?	Da li iznajmljujete …?	da lee eez·naim·lyoo·ye·te …
prams	dječja kolica	dyech·ya kaw·lee·tsa
strollers	dječje hodalice	dyech·ye haw·da·lee·tse

I need a pram.
Trebaju mi dječja kolica. tre·bai·oo mee dyech·ya kaw·lee·tsa

Is there space for a pram?
Ima li mjesta za kolica? ee·ma lee mye·sta za kaw·lee·tsa

Are there any good places to take children around here?
Ima li u okolini dobrih mjesta za djecu? ee·ma lee oo aw·kaw·lee·nee daw·breeh mye·sta za dye·tsoo

Are children allowed?
Da li je dozvoljen   da lee ye *dawz*·vaw·lyen
pristup djeci?   *pree*·stoop dye·tsee

Where can I change a nappy?
Gdje mogu   gdye *maw*·goo
promijeniti pelene?   praw·mee·ye·nee·tee *pe*·le·ne

Do you mind if I breast-feed here?
Da li vam smeta   da lee vam *sme*·ta
ako ovdje dojim?   *a*·kaw *awv*·dye doy·eem

Could I have some paper and pencils, please?
Mogu li dobiti malo   *maw*·goo lee *daw*·bee·tee *ma*·law
papira i olovku molim?   pa·*pee*·ra ee *aw*·lawv·koo *maw*·leem

Is this suitable for (three)-year old children?
Da li je ovo pogodno   da lee ye *aw*·vaw *paw*·gawd·naw
za (tri) godine   za (tree) *gaw*·dee·ne
staru djecu?   *sta*·roo dye·tsoo

Do you know a dentist/doctor who is good with children?
Da li znate zubara/   da lee *zna*·te zoo·*ba*·ra/
liječnika koji je dobar   lee·*yech*·nee·ka koy·ee ye *daw*·bar
sa djecom?   sa *dye*·tsawm

For health issues, see **health**, page 177.

talking with children

When's your birthday?
Kada je tvoj rođendan?   *ka*·da ye tvoy *raw*·jen·dan

When's your name day?
Kada je tvoj imendan?   *ka*·da ye tvoy *ee*·men·dan

Do you go to school/kindergarten?
Ideš li u školu/   *ee*·desh lee oo *shkaw*·loo/
vrtić?   *vr*·teech

What grade are you in?
U kojem si razredu?   oo *koy*·em see *raz*·re·doo

Do you like ...?	*Voliš li ...?*	*vaw*·leesh lee ...
school	*školu*	*shkaw*·loo
sport	*sport*	spawrt
your teacher	*svog nastavnika*	svawg *na*·stav·nee·ka

What do you do after school?
Čime se baviš nakon   *chee*·me se *ba*·veesh *na*·kawn
nastave?   *na*·sta·ve

Do you learn English?
Učiš li engleski?   *oo*·cheesh lee *en*·gle·skee

I come from very far away.
Ja dolazim iz   ya *daw*·la·zeem eez
jako daleke zemlje.   ya·kaw *da*·le·ke *zem*·lye

Are you lost?
Da li si se izgubio/   da lee see se eez·*goo*·bee·aw/
izgubila? m/f   eez·*goo*·bee·la

---

gender reminder

Throughout this book we've used the abbreviations m, f and n to indicate gender. The order of presentation is masculine, feminine and then neuter.

If a letter or letters have been added to a masculine form to denote a feminine or neuter form, these will appear in parentheses. Where the change involves more than the addition of a letter, different words are given separated by a slash. Sometimes, it's just a case of substituting the final letter of a word to make feminine or neuter forms as in this example: *mladi/a* (mla·dee/a) 'young' which has the masculine form *mladi* and the feminine form *mlada*.

Gender marking mostly applies to nouns and adjectives but it can apply to verb forms also. See gender in the **a–z phrasebuilder**, page 19 for more on gender in Croatian.

basics

osnove

Yes.	*Da.*	da
No.	*Ne.*	ne
Please.	*Molim.*	*maw*·leem
Thank you	*Hvala vam/ti*	*hva*·la vam/tee
(very much).	*(puno).* **pol/inf**	*(poo*·no)
You're welcome.	*Nema na čemu.*	*ne*·ma na *che*·moo
Excuse me. (to get attention)	*Oprostite.*	aw·*praw*·stee·te
Excuse me. (to get past)	*Ispričavam se.*	ee·spree·*cha*·vam se
Sorry.	*Žao mi je.*	*zha*·aw mee ye

greetings & goodbyes

pozdravi dobrodošlice i oproštaja

It's usual for both men and women to shake hands when meeting for the first time and often on subsequent encounters too. Greeting someone with a kiss on each cheek is reserved for close friends.

Hello.	*Bog.*	bawg
Hi.	*Ćao.*	*cha*·aw
Good morning.	*Dobro jutro.*	*daw*·braw *yoo*·traw
Good afternoon/day.	*Dobar dan.*	*daw*·bar dan
Good evening.	*Dobra večer.*	*daw*·bra *ve*·cher

How are you?
Kako ste/si? pol/inf ka·kaw ste/see

Fine. And you?
Dobro. A vi/ti? pol/inf daw·braw, a vee/tee

What's your name?
Kako se zovete/zoveš? pol/inf ka·kaw se zaw·ve·te/zaw·vesh

My name is …
Zovem se … zaw·vem se …

I'd like to introduce you to …
Želim vas/te zhe·leem vas/te
upoznati sa … pol/inf oo·pawz·na·tee sa …

I'm pleased to meet you.
Drago mi je da dra·gaw mee ye da
smo se upoznali. smaw se oo·pawz·na·lee

This is my …	*Ovo je moj/moja/*	aw·vaw ye moy/moy·a/
	moje … m/f/n	moy·e …
child	*dijete n*	dee·ye·te
colleague	*kolega/*	kaw·le·ga/
	kolegica m/f	kaw·le·gee·tsa
friend	*prijatelj/*	pree·ya·tel'/
	prijateljica m/f	pree·ya·te·lyee·tsa
husband	*muž m*	moozh
partner	*suprug/*	soo·proog/
(intimate)	*supruga m/f*	soo·proo·ga
wife	*žena f*	zhe·na

For other family members, see **family**, page 101.

Bye.	*Ćao.*	cha·aw
Goodbye.	*Zbogom.*	zbaw·gawm
Good night.	*Laku noć.*	la·koo nawch
See you later.	*Doviđenja.*	daw·vee·je·nya

Croatian has two forms for the singular 'you', *ti* (tee) and *vi* (vee) though the pronouns themselves are not often used because verbs carry endings that indicate whether *ti* or *vi* is being referred to. With family, friends, children or peers, use the informal *ti* forms of the verb. The polite *vi* forms should be used when addressing strangers or people you've just met. Also use the polite forms to address a person considerably older than you, as to use *ti* forms could be seen as very disrespectful.

Phrases in this book are mostly given in the polite form but where you see inf you have a casual option to use where appropiate. If you feel (or someone else feels) that you're on a familiar-enough footing to use *ti* forms, the following phrase can be used:

You don't have to address me politely – we can use *ti*.

Nemorate mi persirati,	ne·maw·ra·te mee per·see·ra·tee
možemo prijeći na ti.	maw·zhe·maw pree·ye·chee na tee

addressing people

obraćanje ljudima

Croatians use a person's proper title when addressing an older person, an unfamiliar person, a someone in a position of authority or in other more formal contexts. The proper use of titles is seen as reflecting an individual's good upbringing. The convention is to write titles with an exclamation mark following them.

Mr/Sir	*Gospodine!*	gaw·*spaw*·dee·ne
Mrs/Madam	*Gospođo!*	gaw·spaw·jaw
Ms	*G'đo!*	g·jaw
Miss	*Gospođice!*	gaw·spaw·jee·tse
Doctor	*Doktore!*	dawk·taw·re
Professor	*Profesore!*	praw·fe·saw·re

In addition to these generic titles, you can address people by using one of the forms below, as appropriate. Some of these might seem a little odd or abrupt to English speakers but they're quite usual in Croatian. Again these titles are generally reserved for more formal contexts, including official situations or when a service is being rendered, such as in a shop or restaurant.

Boy	*Dečko!*	dech·kaw
Friend	*Prijatelju!*	pree·ya·te·lyoo
Girl	*Djevojčice!*	dye·voy·chee·tse
Young man	*Momče!*	mawm·che
Young woman	*Djevojko!*	dye·voy·kaw
An older female (lit: aunt)	*Teta!*	te·ta
An older male (lit: uncle)	*Čiko!*	chee·kaw

making conversation

Croatians are generally open and outgoing people so you shouldn't find it too hard to strike up a conversation. Good conversation topics to break the ice include football (soccer) and sports in general, food and wine and world events. Tread very lightly when discussing religion (in what is a profoundly Catholic country), politics and, most importantly, the war in the former Yugoslavia.

What a beautiful day!
Kakav predivan dan!   ka·kav pre·dee·van dan

It's so nice here.
Predivno je ovdje.   pre·deev·naw ye awv·dye

What are you up to?
Što se radi?   shtaw se ra·dee

What's up?
Što ima?   shtaw ee·ma

Nice/Awful weather, isn't it?
   Lijepo/Užasno   lee·*ye*·paw/*oo*·zha·snaw ye
   vrijeme, zar ne?   vree·*ye*·me zar ne

How are things?
   Kako stoje stvari?   ka·kaw *stoy*·e stva·ree

Everything OK?
   Sve u redu?   sve oo *re*·doo

Do you live here?
   Vi živite ovdje? pol   vee *zhee*·vee·te *awv*·dye
   Ti živiš ovdje? inf   tee *zhee*·veesh *awv*·dye

Where are you going?
   Gdje idete/ideš? pol/inf   gdye ee·de·te/*ee*·desh

What are you doing?
   Što radite/radiš? pol/inf   shtaw *ra*·dee·te/*ra*·deesh

Do you like it here?
   Da li vam/ti se   da lee vam/tee se
   sviđa ovdje? pol/inf   *svee*·ja *awv*·dye

I love it here.
   Obožavam ovo mjesto.   aw·*baw*·zha·vam *aw*·vaw *mye*·staw

What's this called?
   Kako se ovo zove?   ka·kaw se *aw*·vaw *zaw*·ve

Can I take a photo (of you)?
   Mogu li (vas/te)   *maw*·goo lee (vas/te)
   slikati? pol/inf   *slee*·ka·tee

That's (beautiful), isn't it?
   To je (predivno), zar ne?   taw ye (*pre*·deev·naw) zar ne

Just joking.
   Samo se šalim.   *sa*·maw se *sha*·leem

Are you here on holiday?
   Jeste/Jesi li ovdje   *ye*·ste/*ye*·see lee *awv*·dye
   na odmoru? pol/inf   na *awd*·maw·roo

I'm here ...	*Ja sam ovdje ...*	ya sam *awv*·dye ...
for a holiday	*na odmoru*	na *awd*·maw·roo
on business	*poslovno*	*paw*·slawv·naw
to study	*kao student*	*ka*·aw *stoo*·dent

How long are you here for?
Koliko dugo   kaw·*lee*·kaw *doo*·gaw
ste/si ovdje? pol/inf   ste/see *awv*·dye

I'm here for (four) weeks/days.
Ja sam ovdje na   ya sam *awv*·dye na
(četiri) tjedna/dana.   (*che*·tee·ree) tyed·na/*da*·na

nationalities

nacionalnosti

Where are you from?
Odakle ste/si? pol/inf   aw·*da*·kle ste/see

I'm from …	*Ja sam iz …*	ya sam eez …
Australia	*Australije*	a·oo·*stra*·lee·ye
England	*Engleske*	*en*·gles·ke
the USA	*Amerike*	a·*me*·ree·ke

For more nationalities, see the **dictionary**.

age

godište

How old …?	*Koliko …*	kaw·*lee*·kaw …
	godina?	*gaw*·dee·na
are you	*imate/imaš* pol/inf	ee·ma·te/ee·mash
is your son	*vaš/tvoj* pol/inf	vash/tvoy
	sin ima	seen ee·ma
is your daughter	*vaša/tvoja* pol/inf	va·sha/tvoy·a
	kći ima	k·*chee* ee·ma

SOCIAL

I'm … years old.
Imam … godina.   ee·mam … gaw·dee·na

He/She is … years old.
On/Ona ima … godina.   awn/aw·na ee·ma … gaw·dee·na

Too old!
Prestar/Prestara! m/f   pre·star/pre·sta·ra

I'm younger than I look.
Mlađi/Mlađa sam nego   mla·jee/mla·ja sam ne·gaw
što izgledam. m/f   shtaw eez·gle·dam

For your age, see **numbers & amounts**, page 31.

occupations & studies

What's your occupation?
Čime se bavite/   chee·me se ba·vee·te/
baviš? pol/inf   ba·veesh

I'm a …	*Ja sam …*	ya sam …
chef	*šef kuhinje/*	shef koo·hee·nye/
	šefica kuhinje m/f	shef·ee·tsa koo·hee·nye
journalist	*novinar/*	naw·vee·nar/
	novinarka m/f	naw·vee·nar·ka
manual	*fizički radnik/*	fee·zeech·kee rad·neek/
labourer	*fizička*	fee·zeech·ka
	radnica m/f	rad·nee·tsa
mechanical	*inženjer*	een·zhe·nyer
engineer	*strojarstva* m&f	stroy·ar·stvaw
musician	*muzičar/*	moo·zee·char/
	muzičarka m/f	moo·zee·char·ka
public servant	*službenik/*	sloozh·be·neek/
	službenica m/f	sloozh·be·nee·tsa
teacher	*nastavnik/*	na·stav·neek/
	nastavnica m/f	na·stav·nee·tsa
trades person	*zanatlija/*	za·nat·lee·ya/
	obrtnica m/f	aw·brt·nee·tsa

local talk

Come in/Sit down.	*Izvolite.*	eez·*vaw*·lee·te
Come on then!	*Daj ajde više!*	dai *ai*·de vee·she
Great!	*Super!*	*soo*·per
Hey!	*Hej!*	hey
It's OK.	*U redu je.*	oo *re*·doo ye
Just a minute.	*Trenutak.*	tre·*noo*·tak
Maybe.	*Možda*	*mawzh*·da
No problem.	*Nema problema.*	*ne*·ma praw·*ble*·ma
No way!	*Nema šanse!*	*ne*·ma *shan*·se
See you.	*Vidimo se.*	*vee*·dee·maw se
Sure.	*Svakako!*	*sva*·ka·kaw
Watch out!	*Pazite/Pazi!* pol/inf	*pa*·zee·te/*pa*·zee

I work in ...	*Ja sam zaposlen/*	ya sam *za*·paw·slen/
	zaposlena u ... m/f	*za*·paw·sle·na oo ...
administration	*upravi*	oo·*pra*·vee
health	*zdravstvu*	*zdrav*·stvoo
retail	*trgovini*	tr·*gaw*·vee·nee
	na malo	na *ma*·law

I'm ...	*Ja sam ...*	ya sam ...
retired	*umirovljen/*	oo·*mee*·rawv·lyen/
	umirovljena m/f	oo·*mee*·rawv·lye·na
self-employed	*samostalno*	sa·maw·stal·naw
	zaposlen/	*za*·paw·slen/
	zaposlena m/f	*za*·paw·sle·na
unemployed	*nezaposlen/*	ne·*za*·paw·slen/
	nezaposlena m/f	ne·*za*·paw·sle·na

I'm studying ...	*Ja studiram ...*	ya *stoo*·dee·ram ...
humanities	*društvene*	*droosht*·ve·ne
	znanosti	*zna*·naw·stee
Croatian	*hrvatski*	*hr*·vat·skee
science	*znanost*	*zna*·nawst

What are you studying?

Što vi studirate? pol	shtaw vee *stoo*·dee·ra·te
Što ti studiraš? inf	shtaw tee *stoo*·dee·rash

family

In Croatia, family is sacred and people you meet may well ask you about yours. It'll be appreciated if you reciprocate. Take care not to offend, however, by expressing surprise about aspects of family life that may seem unusual by the standards of your own culture (such as adult children still living at home).

Do you have a ...?	*Imate/Imaš li ...?* pol/inf	ee·ma·te/ee·mash lee ...
I have a ...	*Ja imam ...*	ya ee·mam ...
I don't have a ...	*Ja nemam ...*	ya ne·mam ...
brother	*brata*	bra·ta
daughter	*ćerku*	cher·koo
family	*obitelj*	aw·bee·tel'
father	*oca*	aw·tsa
granddaughter	*unuku*	oo·noo·koo·
grandfather	*djeda*	dye·da
grandmother	*baku*	ba·koo
grandson	*unuka*	oo·noo·ka
husband	*muža*	moo·zha
mother	*majku*	mai·koo
partner (intimate)	*supružnika*	soo·proozh·nee·ka
sister	*sestru*	ses·troo
son	*sina*	see·na
wife	*ženu*	zhe·noo
I'm ...	*Ja sam ...*	ya sam ...
married	*u braku*	oo bra·koo
separated	*rastavljen/ rastavljena* m/f	ra·stav·lyen/ ra·stav·lye·na
single	*neoženjen/ neudata* m/f	ne·aw·zhe·nyen/ ne·oo·da·ta

Are you married?

Jeste li vi vjenčani? pol — ye·ste lee vee vyen·cha·nee

Jesi li ti vjenčan/ vjenčana? inf m/f — ye·see lee tee vyen·chan/ vyen·cha·na

farewells

Tomorrow is my last day here.

Sutra mi je zadnji	soo·tra mee ye *zad*·nye
dan ovdje.	dan *awv*·dye

If you come to (Scotland) you can visit me.

Ako ikad dođete	a·kaw ee·kad *daw*·je·te
u (Škotsku), možete	oo (*shkawt*·skoo) *maw*·zhe·te
me posjetiti. pol	me *paw*·sye·tee·tee
Ako ikad dođeš	a·kaw ee·kad *daw*·jesh
u (Škotsku), možeš	oo (*shkawt*·skoo) *maw*·zhesh
me posjetiti. inf	me *paw*·sye·tee·tee

Keep in touch!

Ostanimo u vezi!	aw·sta·nee·maw oo ve·zee

It's been great meeting you.

Bilo je lijepo	bee·law ye lee·ye·paw
upoznati vas/te. pol/inf	oo·pawz·na·tee vas/te

Here's my ...	*Ovo je moj ...* m	aw·vaw ye moy ...
	Ovo je moja ... f	aw·vaw ye moy·a ...
What's your ...?	*Koji je tvoj ...?* m	koy·ee ye tvoy ...
	Koja je tvoja ...? f	koy·a ye tvoy·a ...
address	*adresa* f	a·dre·sa
email address	*email adresa* f	ee·ma·eel a·dre·sa
phone number	*broj telefona* m	broy te·le·faw·na

well wishing

Bless you!	*Nazdravlje!*	naz·drav·lye
Bon voyage!	*Sretan put!*	sre·tan poot
Congratulations!	*Čestitke!*	che·steet·ke
Good luck!	*Sretno!*	sret·naw
Happy birthday!	*Sretan rođendan!*	sre·tan raw·jen·dan
Merry Christmas!	*Sretan božić!*	sre·tan baw·zheech

In this chapter phrases are given in the informal *ti* forms. If you're not sure what this means, see the **a-z phrasebuilder**, page 24.

common interests

česte zanimacije

What do you do in your spare time?
Što radiš u   shtaw *ra*·deesh oo
slobodno vrijeme?   *slaw*·bawd·naw vree·*ye*·me

Do you like …?	*Voliš li …?*	*vaw*·leesh lee …
I (don't) like …	*Ja (ne) volim …*	ya (ne) *vaw*·leem …
card games	*kartanje*	*kar*·ta·nye
computer games	*kompjuterske igre*	kawm·*pyoo*·ter·ske *ee*·gre
cooking	*kuhanje*	*koo*·ha·nye
dancing	*ples*	ples
drawing	*crtanje*	*tsr*·ta·nye
films	*filmove*	*feel*·maw·ve
gardening	*vrtlarstvo*	vrt·*lars*·tvaw
hiking	*rekreaciono*	re·kre·a·*tsee*·aw·naw
	pješačenje	pye·*sha*·che·nye
music	*glazbu*	*glaz*·boo
painting	*slikanje*	*slee*·ka·nye
photography	*fotografiju*	faw·taw·*gra*·fee·yoo
reading	*čitanje*	*chee*·ta·nye
shopping	*kupovanje*	koo·*paw*·va·nye
socialising	*druženje*	*droo*·zhe·nye
sport	*sport*	spawrt
travelling	*putovanja*	poo·taw·*va*·nya

For more sporting activities, see **sport**, page 129.

interests

103

music

What music do you like?
Koju vrstu glazbe voliš?   koy·oo vr·stoo *glaz*·be *vaw*·leesh

What bands do you like?
Koje grupe voliš?   koy·e *groo*·pe *vaw*·leesh

Do you …?	*Da li …?*	da lee …
dance	*plešeš*	*ple*·shesh
go to concerts	*ideš na*	*ee*·desh na
	koncerte	*kawn*·tser·te
listen to music	*slušaš glazbu*	*sloo*·shash *glaz*·boo
play an	*sviraš neki*	*svee*·rash *ne*·kee
instrument	*instrument*	een·stroo·*ment*
sing	*pjevaš*	*pye*·vash

blues	*bluz* m	blooz
classical music	*klasična glazba* f	*kla*·seech·na *glaz*·ba
electronic music	*elektronska*	e·*lek*·trawn·ska
	glazba f	*glaz*·ba
folk music	*folk glazba* f	fawlk *glaz*·ba
jazz	*džez* m	jez
opera	*opera* f	*aw*·pe·ra
operetta	*opereta* f	aw·pe·*re*·ta
pop	*pop* m	pawp
rock	*rock* m	rawk
traditional music	*tradicionalna*	tra·dee·tsee·aw·nal·na
	glazba f	*glaz*·ba
world music	*etno glazba* f	*et*·naw *glaz*·ba

Planning to go to a concert? See **going out**, page 113.

cinema & theatre

I feel like	Htio/Htjela bih	htee·aw/htye·la beeh
going to a …	otići na … m/f	aw·tee·chee na …
Did you like	Da li ti se	da lee tee se
the …?	dopao …?	daw·pa·aw …
ballet	balet	ba·let
film	film	feelm

I feel like going to a play.
Htio/Htjela bih otići htee·aw/htye·la beeh aw·tee·chee
na predstavu. m/f na pred·sta·voo

Did you like the play?
Da li ti se dopala da lee tee se daw·pa·la
predstava? pred·sta·va

What's showing at the cinema/theatre tonight?
Što se prikazuje u shtaw se pree·ka·zoo·ye oo
kinu/kazalištu kee·noo/ka·za·leesh·too
večeras? ve·che·ras

Is it in English?
Da li je na engleskom? da lee ye na en·gles·kawm

Does it have (English) subtitles?
Da li je film titlovan da lee ye feelm teet·law·van
(na engleski)? (na en·gle·skee)

Is this seat taken?
Je li ovo mjesto ye lee aw·vaw mye·staw
zauzeto? za·oo·ze·taw

This is my seat.
Ovo je moje mjesto. aw·vaw ye moy·e mye·staw

Have you seen …?
Da li si pogledao/ da lee see paw·gle·da·aw/
pogledala …? m/f paw·gle·da·la …

Who's in it?
Tko glumi u tome? tkaw gloo·mee oo taw·me

It stars …
Glavnu ulogu igra … glav·noo oo·law·goo ee·gra …

I thought it was ...	Ja mislim	ya *mee*·sleem
	da je bio ...	da ye *bee*·aw ...
excellent	odličan	*awd*·lee·chan
long	dugačak	*doo*·ga·chak
OK	OK	*aw*·key

I (don't) like ...	Ja (ne) volim ...	ya (ne) *vaw*·leem ...
action movies	akcione	*ak*·tsee·aw·ne
	filmove	*feel*·maw·ve
animated films	animirane	a·nee·*mee*·ra·ne
	filomove	*feel*·maw·ve
(Croatian) cinema	(hrvatski) film	(*hr*·vat·skee) feelm
comedies	komedije	*kaw*·me·dee·ye
documentaries	dokumentarce	daw·koo·men·*tar*·tse
drama	drame	*dra*·me
horror movies	filmove strave	*feel*·maw·ve *stra*·ve
	i užasa	ee *oo*·zha·sa
sci-fi	filmove	*feel*·maw·ve
	naučne	*na*·ooch·ne
	fantastike	fan·*ta*·stee·ke
short films	kratkometražne	krat·kaw·*me*·trazh·ne
	filmove	*feel*·maw·ve
thrillers	trilere	*tree*·le·re
war movies	ratne filmove	*rat*·ne *feel*·maw·ve

---

lost in translation

Croatians are proud of their rich literary heritage. It's a heritage that has absorbed the crosscurrents of Central European and Latin influence. Unfortunately though, little of Croatia's literary output is available in English translation.

The country's towering literary figure is undoubtedly the 20th-century novelist and playwright Miroslav Krleža. Always politcally active, Krleža broke with Tito in 1967 over the writer's campaign for equality between the Serbian and Croatian literary languages. He famously stated: 'Serbian and Croatian are one and the same language, which Croats call Croatian and Serbs Serbian'. His popular novel *The Return of Philip Latinovicz* which depicts the concerns of a changing Yugoslavia has been translated into English.

feelings

osjećaji

I'm (not) …	Ja (ni)sam …	ya (nee·)sam …
annoyed	uznemiren/	ooz·ne·mee·ren/
	uznemirena m/f	ooz·ne·mee·re·na
disappointed	razočaran/	ra·zaw·cha·ran
	razočarana m/f	ra·zaw·cha·ra·na
embarrassed	posramljen/	paw·sram·lyen/
	posramljena m/f	paw·sram·lye·na
happy	sretan/sretna m/f	sre·tan/sret·na
hungry	gladan/gladna m/f	gla·dan/glad·na
sad	tužan/tužna m/f	too·zhan/toozh·na
surprised	iznenađen/	eez·ne·na·jen/
	iznenađena m/f	eez·ne·na·je·na
thirsty	žedan/žedna m/f	zhe·dan/zhed·na
tired	umoran/	oo·maw·ran/
	umorna m/f	oo·mawr·na
worried	zabrinut/	za·bree·noot/
	zabrinuta m/f	za·bree·noo·ta

Are you hot/cold?
   Je li vam toplo/hladno? pol   ye lee vam *taw·plaw/hlad·naw*
   Je li ti toplo/hladno? inf   ye lee tee *taw·plaw/hlad·naw*

I'm (not) hot/cold.
   Meni (ni)je toplo/hladno.   me·nee (nee·)ye *taw·plaw/hlad·naw*

And how are you?
   A kako ste vi? pol   a *ka·*kaw ste vee
   A kako si ti? inf   a *ka·*kaw see tee

If feeling unwell, see **health**, page 177.

mixed emotions		
a little	*malo*	*ma·law*
I'm a little sad.	*Malo sam tužan/ tužna.* m/f	*ma·law sam too·zhan/ toozh·na*
extremely	*krajnje*	*krai·nye*
I'm extremely sorry.	*Krajnje mi je žao.*	*krai·nye mee ye zha·aw*
very	*vrlo*	*vr·law*
I feel very lucky.	*Osjećam se vrlo sretno.*	*aw·sye·cham se vr·law sret·naw*

opinions

Did you like it?
  Da li vam/ti se svidjelo? pol/inf da lee vam/tee se svee·dye·law

I thought it was …	*Mislio/Mislila sam da je bilo …* m/f	*mee·slee·aw/mee·slee·la sam da ye bee·law …*
It's …	*Ovo je …*	*aw·vaw ye …*
awful	*užasno*	*oo·zha·snaw*
beautiful	*lijepo*	*lee·ye·paw*
boring	*dosadno*	*daw·sad·naw*
great	*odlično*	*awd·leech·naw*
interesting	*zanimljivo*	*za·neem·lyee·vaw*
OK	*OK*	*aw·key*
original	*originalno*	*aw·ree·gee·nal·naw*
strange	*neobično*	*ne·aw·beech·naw*

politics & social issues

You should anticipate being drawn into animated discussions on aspects of the recent conflict in the former Yugoslavia as the horrors of war are still very much alive in people's minds. Locals will seize the opportunity of converting you to the Croatian cause. Unless you enjoy very heated debates, you're best advised to stay in the role of nonjudgmental listener.

Who do you vote for?

Za koga glasate/	za *kaw*·ga *gla*·sa·te/	
glasaš? pol/inf	*gla*·sash	

I support the	*Ja sam pristaša*	ya sam *pree*·sta·sha
... party.	*... stranke.*	... *stran*·ke
I'm a member	*Ja sam član*	ya sam chlan
of the ... party.	*... stranke.*	... *stran*·ke
communist	*komunističke*	kaw·moo·*nee*·steech·ke
conservative	*konzervativne*	*kawn*·zer·va·teev·ne
democratic	*demokratske*	de·*maw*·krat·ske
farmers'	*seljačke*	se·lyach·ke
green	*zelene*	ze·le·ne
Istrian	*istarske*	ee·star·ske
regionalist	*regionalističke*	re·gee·aw·na·*lee*·steech·ke
liberal	*liberalne*	*lee*·be·ral·ne
(progressive)		
social	*socijal-*	saw·tsee·*yal*·
democratic	*demokratske*	de·*maw*·krat·ske
socialist	*socijalističke*	saw·tsee·ya·*lee*·steech·ke

Did you hear about ...?

Jeste li čuli za ...? pol	*ye*·ste lee *choo*·lee za ...	
Jesi li čuo/čula za ...? inf m/f	*ye*·see lee *choo*·aw/*choo*·la za ...	

Do you agree with it?

Da li podržavate/	da lee paw·*dr*·zha·va·te/	
podržavaš to? pol/inf	paw·*dr*·zha·vash taw	

I (don't) agree with ...

Ja (ne) podržavam ...	ya (ne) paw·*dr*·zha·vam ...	

How do people feel about …?	Kako ljudi gledaju na …?	ka·kaw lyoo·dee gle·dai·oo na …
abortion	indicirani abortus	een·dee·tsee·ra·nee a·bawr·toos
admission into the EU	primanje u Europsku uniju	pree·ma·nye oo e·oo·rawp·skoo oo·nee·yoo
animal rights	prava životinja	pra·va zhee·vaw·tee·nya
crime	kriminal	kree·mee·nal
the economy	privredu	preev·re·doo
education	obrazovanje	aw·bra·zaw·va·nye
equal opportunity	jednake mogućnosti	yed·na·ke maw·gooch·naw·stee
euthanasia	eutanaziju	e·oo·ta·na·zee·yoo
globalisation	globalizaciju	glaw·ba·lee·za·tsee·yoo
human rights	ljudska prava	lyood·ska pra·va
immigration	imigraciju	ee·mee·gra·tsee·yoo
racism	rasnu netrpeljivost	ra·snoo ne·tr·pe·lyee·vawst
the return of war refugees	povratak ratnih izbjeglica	paw·vra·tak rat·neeh eez·bye·glee·tsa
sexism	spolnu diskriminaciju	spawl·noo dee·skree·mee·na·tsee·yoo
unemployment	nezaposlenost	ne·za·paw·sle·nawst

hot topics

If you really have a burning curiosity to learn more about Croatian attitudes to the recent conflict in the former Yugoslavia and its aftermath, you could try out the phrase below. Best not to trot it out in a slivovitz-fuelled context as the passions aroused could be strong enough on their own.

How do people feel about the extradition of generals to the international war-crimes tribunal in the Hague?

Kako ljudi gledaju na isporuku generala međunarodnom sudu za ratne zločine u Hagu?	ka·kaw lyoo·dee gle·dai·oo na ee·spaw·roo·koo ge·ne·ra·la me·joo·na·rawd·nawm soo·doo za rat·ne zlaw·chee·ne oo ha·goo

the environment

Is there a … problem here?
Postoji li ovdje problem …?	paw·stoy·ee lee awv·dye praw·blem …	

What should be done about …?
Što bi trebalo učiniti u vezi …?	shtaw bee tre·ba·law oo·chee·nee·tee oo ve·zee …	

acid rain	*kisele kiše* f pl	kee·se·le kee·she
conservation	*zaštita okoliša* f	zash·tee·ta aw·kaw·lee·sha
drought	*suša* f	soo·sha
ecosystem	*ekosustav* m	e·kaw·soo·stav
endangered species	*ugrožene vrste* n	oo·graw·zhe·ne vr·ste
hunting	*lov na životinje* m	lawv na zhee·vaw·tee·nye
hydroelectricity	*hidroelektrane* n	hee·draw·e·lek·tra·ne
irrigation	*navodnjavanje* n	na·vawd·nya·va·nye
nuclear energy/ testing	*nuklearna energija/ testiranja* f	noo·kle·ar·na e·ner·gee·ya/ te·stee·ra·nya
ozone layer	*ozonski omotač* m	aw·zawn·skee aw·maw·tach
pesticides	*pesticidi* m pl	pe·stee·tsee·dee
marine algae	*pošast morskih algi* m	paw·shast mawr·skeeh al·gee
pollution	*zagađenje* n	za·ga·je·nye
protection of marine flora and fauna	*zaštita morske flore i faune* f	zash·tee·ta mawr·ske flaw·re ee fa·oo·ne
recycling program	*plan za preradu otpadaka* m	plan za pre·ra·doo awt·pa·da·ka
subterranean waterways	*podzemne vode* f pl	pawd·zem·ne vaw·de
toxic waste	*toksični otpad* m	tawk·seech·nee awt·pad
water supply	*vodovod* m	vaw·daw·vawd
timber industry	*djelatnosti drvne industrije* f pl	dye·lat·naw·stee drv·ne een·doo·stree·ye

Is this a protected …?	*Je li ovo …?*	ye lee *aw*·vaw …
forest	*zaštićena šuma*	zash·tee·che·na *shoo*·ma
park	*zaštićen park*	zash·tee·chen park
species	*zaštićena vrsta*	zash·tee·che·na *vr*·sta

colourful Croatian

Croatian speakers can draw on a rich variety of swear words and obscene expressions to make their feelings plainly felt. Most swearing involves liberal use of the verb 'fuck' *jebati* (*ye*·ba·tee), which is often juxtaposed with references to the two sacred cows of Croatian society: religion and family. These unholy alliances give it impressive expressive force.

Swearing in any language tends to be very idiomatic and difficult to translate, but even the most hardened Anglophone might blanch at the graphic nature of Croatian swearing. However, what might sound like a string of unbelievable obscenities to an English speaker is not quite as bad as it sounds to Croatian speakers for whom colourful swearing is an intrinsic part of the language.

If you're exposed to some colourful Croatian you may even find it quite amusing and it's best not to take offence, as this may not be the swearer's intention. Here are a couple of expressions to give you a little of the flavour of Croatian swearing:

Jebo te patak!
  ye·baw te *pa*·tak — Can you believe it?
                         (lit: may a he-duck fuck you)

Jebem ti sve po spisku!
  ye·bem tee sve paw — Fuck everyone on the list
  spee·skoo — of your nearest and dearest!

In this chapter phrases are given in the informal *ti* forms. If you're not sure what this means, see the **a-z phrasebuilder**, page 24.

where to go

gdje izaći

What's there to do in the evenings?
Što se može raditi   shtaw se *maw*·zhe ra·dee·tee
uvečer?   oo·ve·cher

What's on …?	*Što se događa …?*	shtaw se *daw*·ga·ja …
locally	*u ovom mjestu*	oo *aw*·vawm mye·stoo
this weekend	*ovoga vikenda*	*aw*·vaw·ga vee·ken·da
today	*danas*	*da*·nas
tonight	*večeras*	ve·*che*·ras

Where can I find …?	*Gdje mogu pronaći …?*	gdye *maw*·goo praw·*na*·chee …
clubs	*noćne klubove*	*nawch*·ne *kloo*·baw·ve
gay venues	*'gay' lokale*	gey law·*ka*·le
places to eat	*ugostiteljske lokale*	oo·*gaw*·stee·tel'·ske law·*ka*·le
pubs	*gostionice*	gaw·stee·*aw*·nee·tse

Is there a local … guide?	*Postoji li mjesni vodič kroz …?*	paw·*stoy*·ee lee mye·snee *vaw*·deech krawz …
entertainment	*zbivanja u svijetu razonode*	*zbee*·va·nya oo svee·*ye*·too ra·*zaw*·naw·de
event	*predstojeća zbivanja*	pred·*stoy*·e·cha *zbee*·va·nya
film	*filmske novosti*	*feelm*·ske *naw*·vaw·stee
gay	*'gay' aktivnosti*	gey ak·*teev*·naw·stee
music	*glazbu*	*glaz*·boo

I feel like going to a ...	Želim otići ...	zhe·leem aw·tee·chee ...
ballet	na balet	na ba·let
bar	u bar	oo bar
café	u kafić	oo ka·feech
concert	na koncert	na kawn·tsert
disco	u disko	oo dee·skaw
festival	na festival	na fe·stee·val
film	na prikazivanje filma	na pree·ka·zee·va·nye feel·ma
hotel for	u hotel sa	oo haw·tel sa
terrace	plesnom	ple·snawm
dancing	terasom	te·ra·sawm
karaoke bar	u karaoke bar	oo ka·ra·aw·ke bar
nightclub	u noćni klub	oo nawch·nee kloob
party	na zabavu	na za·ba·voo
performance	na priredbu	na pree·red·boo
play	na predstavu	na pred·sta·voo
pub	u gostionicu	oo gaw·stee·aw·nee·tsoo
restaurant	u restoran	oo re·staw·ran

For more on eateries, bars and drinks, see **eating out**, page 145.

invitations

pozivanje nekoga na nešto

Would you like to go (for a/an) ...?	Da li bi htio/ htjela otići na ...? m/f	da lee bee htee·aw/ htye·la aw·tee·chee na ...
I feel like going (for a/an) ...	Ja želim otići na ...	ya zhe·leem aw·tee·chee na ...
coffee	kavu	ka·voo
dancing	ples	ples
drink	piće	pee·che
ice cream	sladoled	sla·daw·led
meal	ručak	roo·chak

What are you doing …?	Što radiš …?	shtaw *ra*·deesh …
now	*trenutno*	*tre*·noot·naw
this weekend	*ovoga vikenda*	*aw*·vaw·ga vee·ken·da
tonight	*večeras*	ve·*che*·ras

I feel like going out somewhere.
*Ja želim ići
negdje vani.*
ya *zhe*·leem *ee*·chee
ne·gdye *va*·nee

I feel like going for a walk.
Ja želim ići u šetnju.
ya *zhe*·leem *ee*·chee oo *shet*·nyoo

Do you know a good restaurant?
*Da li znaš dobar
restoran?*
da lee znash *daw*·bar
re·*staw*·ran

Do you want to come to the concert with me?
*Da li bi htio/htjela ići
samnom na koncert.* **m/f**
da lee bee *htee*·aw/*htye*·la *ee*·chee
sam·nawm na *kawn*·tsert

We're having a party.
*Planiramo napraviti
zabavu.*
pla·nee·ra·maw *na*·pra·vee·tee
za·ba·voo

You should come.
Ti si pozvan/pozvana. **m/f** tee see *pawz*·van/*pawz*·va·na

responding to invitations

Sure!
Svakako! *sva*·ka·kaw

Yes, I'd love to.
Da, volio/voljela bih. **m/f** da, *vaw*·lee·aw/*vaw*·lye·la beeh

That's very kind of you.
To je baš lijepo od tebe. taw ye bash lee·*ye*·paw awd *te*·be

Where shall we go?
*Gdje bismo mogli
otići?*
gdye *bee*·smaw *maw*·glee
aw·tee·chee

No, I'm afraid I can't.
Ne, nažalost ne mogu.   ne, *na*·zha·lawst ne *maw*·goo

What about tomorrow?
A kako bi bilo sutra?   a *ka*·kaw bee *bee*·law *soo*·tra

Sorry, I can't sing/dance.
Oprosti, ali ja ne   aw·*praw*·stee, *a*·lee ya ne
znam pjevati/plesati.   znam *pye*·va·tee/*ple*·sa·tee

arranging to meet

What time will we meet?
U koje vrijeme ćemo   oo *koy*·e vree·*ye*·me *che*·maw
se naći?   se *na*·chee

Where will we meet?
Gdje ćemo se naći?   gdye *che*·maw se *na*·chee

Let's meet …   *Hajde da*   *hai*·de da
    se nađemo …   se *na*·je·maw …
  at (eight) o'clock   *u (osam) sati*   oo (*aw*·sam) *sa*·tee
  at (the entrance)   *na (ulazu)*   na (*oo*·la·zoo)

I'll pick you up.
Ja ću te pokupiti.   ya choo te *paw*·koo·pee·tee

Are you ready?
Jesi li spreman/spremna? m/f   *ye*·see lee *spre*·man/*sprem*·na

I'm ready.
Ja sam spreman/   ya sam *spre*·man/
spremna. m/f   *sprem*·na

I'll be coming later.
Ja ću ti se   ya choo tee se
pridružiti kasnije.   pree·*droo*·zhee·tee *ka*·snee·ye

Croatian rhythms

dalmatinska a   dal·*ma*·teen·ska a
cappella klapa   ka·*pe*·la *kla*·pa

male a cappella choral singing from the Dalmatian coast whose main motifs are love, wine and love of homeland. *Klapa* is still very much a living tradition and is often sung in company over food and wine.

diple i mih   *dee*·ple ee meeh

traditional Istrian triangular bagpipes with a less piercing sound than Scottish bagpipes

kolo   *kaw*·law

lively Slavic dance in which men and/or women hold hands in either a circle or line and dance to the accompaniment of an accordion, violins or the *tamburica*

roženice/sopile   raw·zhe·*nee*·tse/saw·*pee*·le

traditional Istrian two-stem reed pipe with a very penetrating oboe-like sound

tamburica   *tam*·boo·ree·tsa

type of three-string or five-string mandolin popular in inland Croatia which has also given its name to a musical style centred around idyllic themes of love and village life

zagorske i   *za*·gawr·ske ee
međimurske popevke   me·jee·moor·ske paw·*pev*·ke

traditional melancholic folk songs from the regions of Zagorje and Međimurje, with alternating monophonic and polyphonic segments

Where will you be?
Gdje ćeš ti biti?   gdye chesh tee *bee*·tee

If I'm not there by (nine), don't wait for me.
Ako ne budem tamo do   *a*·kaw ne *boo*·dem *ta*·maw daw
(devet), nemoj me čekati.   (*de*·vet) *ne*·moy me *che*·ka·tee

OK!
OK!   aw·*key*

I'll see you then.
Vidimo se tada.   *vee*·dee·maw se *ta*·da

going out

117

See you later/tomorrow.
   Vidimo se kasnije/   *vee·dee·maw se ka·snee·ye/*
   sutra.   *soo·tra*

I'm looking forward to it.
   Jedva čekam.   *ye·dva che·kam*

Sorry I'm late.
   Oprosti što kasnim.   *aw·praw·stee shtaw ka·sneem*

Never mind.
   Nije važno.   *nee·ye vazh·naw*

drugs

droge

I don't take drugs.
   Ja ne koristim droge.   ya ne *kaw·ree·steem draw·ge*

I take … occasionally.
   Ja koristim … ponekad.   ya *kaw·ree·steem* … *paw·ne·kad*

Do you want to have a smoke?
   Hoćeš zapaliti?   *haw·chesh za·pa·lee·tee*

Do you have a light?
   Imaš li vatre?   *ee·mash lee va·tre*

I'm high.
   Ja sam napljugan/   ya sam nap·*lyoo·*gan/
   napljugana. m/f   nap·*lyoo·*ga·na

In this chapter phrases are given in the informal *ti* forms. If you're not sure what this means, see the **a–z phrasebuilder**, page 24.

asking someone out

kako nekoga pitati da sa vama izađe

Where would you like to go (tonight)?
Gdje bi htio/htjela   gdye bee *htee*·aw/*htye*·la
izaći (večeras)? m/f   ee·*za*·chee (ve·*che*·ras)

Would you like to do something (tomorrow)?
Da li bi htio/htjela   da lee bee *htee*·aw/*htye*·la
samnom nešto raditi   *sam*·nawm *nesh*·taw *ra*·dee·tee
(sutra)? m/f   (*soo*·tra)

Yes, I'd love to.
Da, to bih baš volio/   da, taw beeh bash *vaw*·lee·aw/
voljela. m/f   *vaw*·lye·la

Sorry, I can't.
Žao mi je, ali ne mogu.   *zha*·aw mee ye *a*·lee ne *maw*·goo

pick-up lines

fraze udvaranja

Would you like a drink?
Mogu li ti kupiti   *maw*·goo lee tee *koo*·pee·tee
piće?   *pee*·che

You look like someone I know.
Ličiš na nekoga   *lee*·cheesh na *ne*·kaw·ga
koga znam.   *kaw*·ga znam

You're a fantastic dancer.
Krasno plešeš.   *kra*·snaw *ple*·shesh

You were made for me.
   Stvoren/Stvorena   stvaw·ren/stvaw·re·na
   si za mene. m/f   see za *me*·ne

You blow me away.
   Obaraš me s nogu.   aw·ba·rash me s *naw*·goo

Can I …?	*Mogu li …?*	*maw*·goo lee …
dance with you	*dobiti ovaj ples*	*daw*·bee·tee *aw*·vai ples
sit here	*ovdje sjesti*	*awv*·dye *sye*·stee
take you home	*te ispratiti*	te ee·spra·tee·tee
	kući	*koo*·chee

rejections

nepoželjno udvaranje

I'm here with my boyfriend.
   Ovdje sam sa   *awv*·dye sam sa
   svojom curom.   *svoy*·awm *tsoo*·rawm

I'm here with my girlfriend.
   Ovdje sam sa   *awv*·dye sam sa
   svojim dečkom.   *svoy*·eem *dech*·kawm

Excuse me, I have to go now.
   Oprosti, ali sada   aw·*praw*·stee *a*·lee *sa*·da
   stvarno žurim.   *stvar*·naw *zhoo*·reem

---

giving someone the flick

Leave me alone!
   Ostavi me na miru!   aw·sta·vee me na *mee*·roo

Don't touch me!
   Ne dodiruj me!   ne daw·*dee*·rooy me

Please control yourself.
   Molim te obuzdaj se.   *maw*·leem te aw·*booz*·dai se

Piss off!
   Odjebi!   aw·*dye*·bee

He's a babe.
  On je super frajer.   awn ye *soo*·per *frai*·er

She's a babe.
  Ona je super frajerica.   *aw*·na ye *soo*·per *frai*·e·ree·tsa

He's hot.
  On je privlačan.   awn ye *preev*·lach·an

She's hot.
  Ona je privlačna.   *aw*·na ye *preev*·lach·na

He's a bastard.
  On je nitkov.   awn ye *neet*·kawv

She's a bitch.
  Ona je pokvarena.   *aw*·na ye *pawk*·va·re·na

He gets around.
  On je kurver.   awn ye *koor*·ver

She gets around.
  Ona je drolja.   *aw*·na ye *draw*·lya

I'd rather not.
  Radije nebih.   *ra*·dee·ye *ne*·beeh

No, thank you.
  Ne, hvala ti.   ne, *hva*·la tee

Who do you think you are?
  Što si ti umišljaš?   shtaw see tee oo·*meesh*·lyash

getting closer

zbližavanje

I like you very much.
  Jako mi se sviđaš.   *ya*·kaw mee se *svee*·jash

You're great.
  Super si.   *soo*·per see

Can I kiss you?
  Smijem li te poljubiti?   *smee*·yem lee te paw·*lyoo*·bee·tee

Do you want to come inside for a while?
Da li želiš ući   da lee *zhe*·leesh *oo*·chee
na kratko?   na *krat*·kaw

Do you want a massage?
Hoćeš masažu?   *haw*·chesh ma·*sa*·zhoo

Can I stay over?
Mogu li ostati kod   *maw*·goo lee *aw*·sta·tee kawd
tebe večeras?   te·be ve·*che*·ras

sex

Kiss me.
Poljubi me.   paw·*lyoo*·bee me

I want you.
Želim te.   *zhe*·leem te

Let's go to bed.
Idemo u krevet.   ee·de·maw oo *kre*·vet

Touch me here.
Dodirni me tu.   daw·*deer*·nee me too

Do you like this?
Da li ti se to sviđa?   da lee tee se taw *svee*·ja

I (don't) like that.
(Ne) sviđa mi se to.   (ne) *svee*·ja mee se taw

I think we should stop now.
Mislim da bi sada   *mee*·sleem da bee *sa*·da
trebali stati.   *tre*·ba·lee *sta*·tee

Do you have a (condom)?
Imaš li (prezervativ)?   ee·mash lee (pre·zer·va·*teev*)

Let's use a (condom).
Hajde da stavimo   *hai*·de da *sta*·vee·maw
(prezervativ).   (pre·zer·va·*teev*)

I won't do it without protection.
Ne želim dalje bez zaštite.   ne *zhe*·leem *da*·lye bez *zash*·tee·te

It's my first time.
Ovo mi je prvi put.   aw·vaw mee ye pr·vee poot

Don't worry, I'll do it myself.
Ne brini, sam/   ne bree·nee, sam/
sama ću. m/f   sa·ma choo

It helps to have a sense of humour.
Smisao za humor   smee·sa·aw za hoo·mawr
pomaže.   paw·ma·zhe

Oh my god!
O bože!   aw baw·zhe

That's great.
To je predivno.   taw ye pre·deev·naw

Easy tiger!
Lakše malo mačore!   lak·she ma·law ma·chaw·re

faster	*brže*	br·zhe
harder	*jače*	ya·che
slower	*sporije*	spaw·ree·ye
softer	*nježnije*	nyezh·nee·ye

That was …	*Bilo je …*	bee·law ye …
amazing	*prekrasno*	pre·kra·snaw
romantic	*romantično*	raw·man·teech·naw
wild	*strastveno*	strast·ve·naw

pillow talk

Whisper sweet nothings to your love with these terms of endearment. The words 'my fawn' and 'my little kitten' are usually reserved for women.

my candy	*slatkišu*	slat·kee·shoo
my dear	*dragi/draga* m/f	dra·gee/dra·ga
my fawn	*lane moje*	la·ne moy·e
my joy	*srećo moja*	sre·chaw moy·a
my little kitten	*mače moje malo*	ma·che moy·e ma·law
my love	*ljubavi moja*	lyoo·ba·vee moy·a
my soul	*dušo moja*	doo·shaw moy·a
my treasure	*zlato moje*	zla·taw moy·e

love

I love you.
   Volim te.   *vaw*·leem te

I think we're good together.
   Mislim da smo dobar par.   *mee*·sleem da smaw *daw*·bar par

Will you …?	*Da li hoćeš …?*	da lee *haw*·chesh …
go out with me	*samnom*	*sam*·nawm
	izlaziti	*eez*·la·zee·tee
marry me	*udati se*	*oo*·da·tee se
	za mene	za *me*·ne
meet my	*upoznati*	oo·*pawz*·na·tee
parents	*moje roditelje*	*moy*·e *raw*·dee·te·lye

problems

Are you seeing someone else?
   Viđaš li nekoga drugog?   *vee*·jash lee *ne*·kaw·ga *droo*·gawg

You're just using me for sex.
   Ti me samo koristiš   tee me *sa*·maw *kaw*·ree·steesh
   za seks.   za seks

I don't think it's working out.
   Mislim da nam ne ide.   *mee*·sleem da nam ne *ee*·de

We'll work it out.
   Riješit ćemo probleme.   ree·*ye*·sheet *che*·maw praw·*ble*·me

I never want to see you again.
   Ne želim te više   ne *zhe*·leem te *vee*·she
   nikada vidjeti.   *nee*·ka·da *vee*·dye·tee

religion

vjera

What's your religion?
Koje ste/si vjere? pol/inf   *kaw*·ye ste/see *vye*·re

I'm …	*Ja sam …*	ya sam …
agnostic	*agnostik* m&f	ag·*naw*·steek
Buddhist	*budist(kinja)* m/f	boo·*deest*(·kee·nya)
Catholic	*katolik/*	ka·*taw*·leek/
	katolkinja m/f	ka·tawl·kee·nya
Christian	*kršćanin/*	krsh·cha·neen/
	kršćanka m/f	krsh·chan·ka
Hindu	*hindu* m&f	heen·*doo*
Jewish	*Židov(ka)* m/f	zhee·*dawv*(·ka)
Muslim	*musliman(ka)* m/f	moo·*slee*·man(·ka)
Orthodox	*pravoslavac/*	pra·vaw·*sla*·vats/
	pravoslavka m/f	pra·vaw·*slav*·ka
Protestant	*protestant(kinja)* m/f	praw·te·*stant*(·kee·nya)
Roman	*rimski katolik/*	*reem*·skee ka·*taw*·leek/
Catholic	*rimska katolkinja* m/f	*reem*·ska ka·tawl·kee·nya
Greek	*grko-katolik/*	*gr*·kaw·ka·*taw*·leek/
Catholic	*grko-katolkinja* m/f	*gr*·kaw·ka·tawl·kee·nya

I (don't) believe in …	*Ja (ne) vjerujem u …*	ya (ne) *vye*·roo·yem oo …
astrology	*astrologiju*	a·*straw*·*law*·gee·yoo
fate	*sudbinu*	*sood*·bee·noo
God	*boga*	*baw*·ga

Where can I attend …?	*Gdje mogu otići …?*	gdye *maw*·goo aw·*tee*·che …
mass	*na misu*	na *mee*·soo
a service	*na obred*	na *aw*·bred

Where can I pray/worship?
Gdje se mogu moliti?   gdye se *maw*·goo *maw*·lee·tee

Can I pray/worship here?
Da li se mogu   da lee se *maw*·goo
ovdje pomoliti?   *awv*·dye paw·*maw*·lee·tee

I didn't mean to do anything wrong.
Nisam htio/htjela   *nee*·sam *htee*·aw/*htye*·la
uraditi ništa krivo. m/f   oo·*ra*·dee·tee *neesh*·ta *kree*·vaw

cultural differences

Is this a local or national custom?
Je li ovo mjesni ili   ye lee *aw*·vaw *mye*·snee ee·lee
nacionalni običaj?   na·tsee·aw·*nal*·nee *aw*·bee·chai

I don't want to offend you.
Ne želim vas/te   ne *zhe*·leem vas/te
uvrijediti. pol/inf   oo·vree·*ye*·dee·tee

I'm not used to this.
Nisam na ovo   *nee*·sam na *aw*·vaw
navikao/navikla. m/f   na·*vee*·ka·aw/na·*vee*·kla

I'd rather not join in.
Ja radije nebih   ya *ra*·dee·ye *ne*·beeh
sudjelovao/   soo·dye·law·va·aw/
sudjelovala. m/f   soo·dye·law·va·la

I'll try it.
Ja ću to probati.   ya choo taw *praw*·ba·tee

I'm sorry, it's against my beliefs.
Žao mi je, ali to   *zha*·aw mee ye *a*·lee taw
je protivno mojim   ye *praw*·teev·naw *moy*·eem
vjerovanjima.   vye·*raw*·va·nyee·ma

This is …	*Ovo je …*	*aw*·vaw ye …
different	*neobično*	*ne*·aw·beech·naw
fun	*zabavno*	*za*·bav·naw
interesting	*zanimljivo*	za·*neem*·lyee·vaw

When's the … open?	Kada je … otvoren/ otvorena? m/f	ka·da ye … aw·tvaw·ren/ aw·tvaw·re·na
church	crkva f	tsr·kva
gallery	galerija f	ga·le·ree·ya
museum	muzej m	moo·zey

What kind of art are you interested in?

Koja vrsta umjetnosti vas/te zanima? pol/inf	kaw·ya vr·sta oo·myet·naw·stee vas/te za·nee·ma

What do you think of …?

Kako doživljavate/ doživljavaš …? pol/inf	ka·kaw daw·zheev·lya·va·te/ daw·zheev·lya·vash …

What's in the collection?

Što sadrži ta zbirka?	shtaw sa·dr·zhee ta zbeer·ka

It's an exhibition of …

Ova izložba je za …	aw·va eez·lawzh·ba ye za …

I'm interested in …

Zainteresiran/ Zainteresirana sam za … m/f	za·een·te·re·see·ran/ za·een·te·re·see·ra·na sam za …

I like the works of …

Sviđaju mi se djela koja spadaju pod …	svee·ja·yoo mee se dye·la kaw·ya spa·dai·oo pawd …

architecture	arhitektura f	ar·hee·tek·too·ra
artwork	umjetničko djelo n	oo·myet·neech·kaw dye·law
curator	kurator m	koo·ra·tawr
design	dizajn m	dee·zain
etching	gravura f	gra·voo·ra
exhibit	izložak predmet m	eez·law·zhak pred·met
exhibition hall	izložna dvorana f	eez·lawzh·na dvaw·ra·na

installation	*instalacija* f	een·sta·*la*·tsee·ya
opening	*otvaranje* n	awt·*va*·ra·nye
painter	*slikar* m	*slee*·kar
painting (the art)	*slika* f	*slee*·ka
painting (canvas)	*slikanje* n	*slee*·ka·nye
period	*razdoblje* n	*raz*·dawb·lye
permanent collection	*stalna zbirka* f	*stal*·na *zbeer*·ka
print	*kopija* f	*kaw*·pee·ya
sculptor	*kipar* m	*kee*·par
sculpture	*skulptura* f	skoolp·*too*·ra
statue	*kip* m	keep
studio	*atelje* m	a·te·*lye*
style	*stil* m	steel
technique	*tehnika* f	*teh*·nee·ka

… art	… *umjetnost*	… oo·myet·nawst
baroque	*barokna*	ba·*rawk*·na
Byzantine	*bizantinska*	bee·*zan*·teen·ska
expressionist	*ekspresionistička*	eks·pre·see·aw·*nee*·steech·ka
Gothic	*gotička*	*gaw*·teech·ka
graphic	*grafička*	*gra*·feech·ka
impressionist	*impresionistička*	eem·pre·see·aw·*nee*·steech·ka
minimalist	*minimalistička*	mee·nee·ma·*lee*·steech·ka
modern	*moderna*	*maw*·der·na
naive	*naivna*	*na*·eev·na
performance	*kazališna*	ka·za·*leesh*·na
pre-Romanesque	*pred-Romanička*	pred·raw·*ma*·neech·ka
Renaissance	*Renesansna*	re·ne·*san*·sna
Roman	*Rimska*	*reem*·ska
Romanesque	*Romanička*	raw·*ma*·neech·ka

In this chapter phrases are given in the informal *ti* forms. If you're not sure what this means, see the **a–z phrasebuilder**, page 24.

sporting interests

sportske zanimacije

What sport do you play?
Koji sport ti igraš?   koy·ee spawrt tee *ee*·grash

What sport do you follow?
Koji sport ti pratiš?   koy·ee spawrt tee *pra*·teesh

I play/do …	*Ja igram/ treniram …*	ya *ee*·gram/ *tre*·nee·ram …
I follow …	*Ja pratim …*	ya *pra*·teem …
athletics	*atletiku*	at·*le*·tee·koo
basketball	*košarku*	*kaw*·shar·koo
football (soccer)	*nogomet*	*naw*·gaw·met
handball	*rukomet*	*roo*·kaw·met
scuba diving	*ronjenje sa bocama*	*raw*·nye·nye sa *baw*·tsa·ma
tennis	*tenis*	*te*·nees
volleyball	*odbojku*	*awd*·boy·koo
water polo	*vaterpolo*	*va*·ter·paw·law
I …	*Ja …*	ya …
cycle	*vozim bicikl*	*vaw*·zeem bee·*tsee*·kl
run	*trčim*	*tr*·cheem
walk	*hodam*	*haw*·dam

For more sports, see the **dictionary**.

Who's your favourite team?
Koja je tvoja   koy·a ye tvoy·a
omiljena ekipa?   aw·mee·lye·na e·*kee*·pa

Who's your favourite sportsman?
Koji je tvoj omiljeni sportaš? koy·ee ye tvoy aw·mee·lye·nee spawr·tash

Who's your favourite sportswoman?
Koja je tvoja omiljena sportašica ? koy·a ye tvoy·a aw·mee·lye·na spawr·ta·shee·tsa

Do you like (basketball)?
Voliš li (košarku)? vaw·leesh lee (kaw·shar·koo)

Yes, very much.
Da, vrlo. da, vr·law

Not really.
Ne baš. ne bash

I like watching it.
Ja ga volim gledati. ya ga vaw·leem gle·da·tee

going to a game

Would you like to go to a game?
Da li bi išao/išla na utakmicu? m/f da lee bee ee·sha·aw/eesh·la na oo·tak·mee·tsoo

Who are you supporting?
Za koga navijaš? za kaw·ga na·vee·yash

Who's playing/winning?
Tko igra/pobjeđuje? tkaw ee·gra/paw·bye·joo·ye

scoring		
What's the score?		
Koji je rezultat?	koy·ee ye re·zool·tat	
draw/even	*neodlučeno/ ner="iješeno*	ne·awd·loo·che·naw/ ne·ree·ye·she·naw
match-point	*odlučujući poen* m	awd·loo·choo·yoo·chee paw·en
nil (zero)	*nula* f	noo·la

SOCIAL

130

That was a …	Bila je to …	*bee*·la ye taw …
game!	utakmica!	oo·tak·mee·tsa
bad	loša	*law*·sha
boring	dosadna	*daw*·sad·na
great	sjajna	*syai*·na

sports talk

What a …!	Kakav …!	*ka*·kav …
goal	gol	gawl
hit	pogodak	*paw*·gaw·dak
kick	šut	shoot
pass	dobačaj	d*aw*·ba·chai
performance	nastup	*na*·stoop

playing sport

igranje sporta

Do you want to play?
Hoćeš igrati? · *haw*·ches *ee*·gra·te

Can I join in?
Mogu li se pridružiti? · *maw*·goo lee se pree·*droo*·zhee·tee

That would be great.
To bi bilo super. · taw bee *bee*·law *soo*·per

I can't.
Ja ne mogu. · ya ne *maw*·goo

My/Your point.
Mo/Tvoj poen. · moy/tvoy paw·*en*

Kick/Pass it to me!
Šutni/Dodaj meni! · *shoot*·nee/*daw*·dai *me*·nee

You're a good player.
Ti si dobar igrač. m · tee see *daw*·bar *ee*·grach
Ti si dobra igračica. f · tee see *daw*·bra ee·*gra*·chee·tsa

Thanks for the game.
Hvala na igri. · *hva*·la na *ee*·gree

Where's a good place to go ...?	Gdje je dobro mjesto za ...?	gdye ye daw·braw mye·staw za ...
fishing	ribolov	ree·baw·lawv
horse riding	jahanje konja	ya·ha·nye kaw·nya
running	trčanje	tr·cha·nye
skiing	skijanje	skee·ya·nye
snorkeling	ronjenje s disalicom	raw·nye·nye s dee·sa·lee·tsawm
surfing	daskanje na valovima	da·ska·nye na va·law·vee·ma

Where's the nearest ...?	Gdje je ...	gdye ye ...
golf course	najbliži teren za golf	nai·blee·zhe te·ren za gawlf
gym	najbliža teretana	nai·blee·zha te·re·ta·na
swimming pool	najbliži bazen za plivanje	nai·blee·zhe ba·zen za plee·va·nye
tennis court	najbliže tenisko igralište	nai·blee·zhe te·nee·skaw ee·gra·leesh·te

What's the charge per ...?	Koja je cijena po ...?	koy·a ye tsee·ye·na paw ...
day	danu	da·noo
game	utakmici	oo·tak·mee·tsee
hour	satu	sa·too
visit	posjeti	paw·sye·tee

Can I hire a ...?	Mogu li iznajmiti ...?	maw·goo lee eez·nai·mee·tee ...
ball	loptu	lawp·too
bicycle	bicikl	bee·tsee·kl
court	igralište	ee·gra·leesh·te
racquet	reket	re·ket

Do I have to be a member to attend?

Da li moram biti član da bih prisustvovao/ prisustvovala? m/f	da lee maw·ram bee·tee chlan da beeh pree·soost·vaw·va·aw/ pree·soost·vaw·va·la

Is there a women-only session?
Postoji li termin   paw·stoy·ee lee ter·meen
samo za žene?   sa·maw za zhe·ne

Where are the changing rooms?
Gdje su svlačionice?   gdye soo svla·chee·aw·nee·tse

diving

Is the visibility good?
Da li je dobra vidljivost?   da lee ye daw·bra veed·lyee·vawst

How deep is the dive?
Na koju se dubinu   na koy·oo se doo·bee·noo
roni?   raw·nee

Is it a boat/shore dive?
Da li je zaron sa   da lee ye za·rawn sa
čamca/obale?   cham·tsa/aw·ba·le

I'd like to	*Želio/Željela*	zhe·lee·aw/zhe·lye·la
explore ...	*bih ... istražiti* m/f	beeh ... ee·stra·zhee·tee
archaeological	*podvodna*	pawd·vawd·na
sites	*arheološka*	ar·he·aw·lawsh·ka
	nalazišta	na·la·zeesh·ta
caves/	*podvodne*	pawd·vawd·ne
wrecks	*spilje/olupine*	spee·lye/aw·loo·pee·ne
	brodova	braw·daw·va

I'd like to go ...	*Želio/Željela*	zhe·lee·aw/zhe·lye·la
	bih ići ... m/f	beeh ee·chee ...
night	*na noćno*	na nawch·naw
diving	*ronjenje*	raw·nye·nye
scuba	*na ronjenje*	na raw·nye·nye
diving	*sa bocama*	sa baw·tsa·ma
snorkelling	*na ronjenje*	na raw·nye·nye
	sa disalicom	sa dee·sa·lee·tsawm
on a diving	*na ronilački*	na raw·nee·lach·kee
tour	*izlet*	eez·let

I'd like to …	Želio/Željela bih … m/f	zhe·lee·aw/zhe·lye·la beeh …
learn to dive	naučiti roniti	na·oo·chee·tee raw·nee·tee
see sea walls	vidjeti morske nasipe	vee·dye·tee mawr·ske na·see·pe

I want to hire (a) …	Želim iznajmiti …	zhe·leem eez·nai·mee·tee …
buoyancy vest	prsluk za spasavanje	pr·slook za spa·sa·va·nye
diving equipment	ronilačku opremu	raw·nee·lach·koo aw·pre·moo
flippers	peraje	pe·rai·e
mask	masku	ma·skoo
regulator	regulator	re·goo·la·tawr
snorkel	disalicu	dee·sa·lee·tsoo
tank	bocu	baw·tsoo
weight belt	olovni pojas	aw·lawv·nee poy·as
wetsuit	nepromočivo ronilačko odijelo	ne·praw·maw·chee·vaw raw·nee·lach·kaw aw·dee·ye·law

air fill	punjenje boca zrakom n	poo·nye·nye baw·tsa zra·kawm
dive (noun)	zaron m	za·rawn
dive (verb)	roniti	raw·nee·tee
diving boat	ronilački čamac m	raw·nee·lach·kee cha·mats
diving course	tečaj ronjenja m	te·chai raw·nye·nya

basketball

košarka

Who plays for (Cibona)?
Tko igra za (Cibonu)?   tkaw *ee*·gra za (tsee·*baw*·noo)

He's a great (player).
On je odličan (igrač).   awn ye *awd*·lee·chan (*ee*·grach)

Which team is the at the top of the league?
Koji je tim na čelu tablice?   *koy*·ee ye teem na *che*·loo ta·blee·tse

back (position)	*bek* m	bek
ball	*lopta* f	*lawp*·ta
basket (structure)	*koš* m	kawsh
coach	*trener* m	*tre*·ner
double fault	*dupla greška* f	*doo*·pla *gresh*·ka
expulsion	*isključenje* n	ees·klyoo·*che*·nye
fan	*navijač* m	na·*vee*·yach
foul	*prekršaj* m	*pre*·kr·shai
free throw	*slobodno bacanje* n	*slaw*·bawd·naw *ba*·tsa·nye
jump-shot	*skok šut* m	skawk shoot
out	*aut* m	*a*·oot
player	*igrač* m	ee·*grach*
rebound	*odbitak* m	awd·*bee*·tak
referee	*sudac* m	*soo*·dats
skyhook shot	*horok* m	*haw*·rawk
slam-dunk	*zakucavanje* n	za·koo·*tsa*·va·nye
time-out	*pauza* f	*pa*·oo·za
travel	*koraci* m pl	*kaw*·ra·tsee

football/soccer

Who plays for (Dinamo)?
Tko igra za (Dinamo)?   tkaw ee·gra za (*dee*·na·maw)

He's a great (goalkeeper).
On je odličan (vratar).   awn ye *awd*·lee·chan (*vra*·tar)

He played brilliantly in the match against (Italy).
On je sjajno odigrao   awn ye *syai*·naw *aw*·dee·gra·aw
utakmicu protiv   oo·tak·mee·tsoo *praw*·teev
(Italije).   (ee·*ta*·lee·ye)

What a great/terrible team!
   Kakav sjajan/užasan tim!   ka·kav *syai*·an/*oo*·zha·san teem

ball	*lopta* f	*lawp*·ta
coach	*trener* m	*tre*·ner
corner (kick)	*korner* m	*kawr*·ner
expulsion	*isključenje* f	ees·klyoo·*che*·nye
fan	*navijač* m	na·*vee*·yach
foul	*prekršaj* m	*pre*·kr·shai
free kick	*slobodni udarac* m	*slaw*·bawd·nee *oo*·da·rats
goal	*gol* m	gawl
goalkeeper	*vratar* m	*vra*·tar
offside	*ofsaid* m	*awf*·sa·eed
penalty	*penal* m	*pe*·nal
player	*igrač* m	*ee*·grach
red card	*crveni karton* m	*tsr*·ve·nee *kar*·tawn
referee	*sudac* m	*soo*·dats
striker	*napadač* m	na·*pa*·dach
yellow card	*žuti karton* m	*zhoo*·tee *kar*·tawn

tennis

I'd like to play tennis.
   Želim igrati tenis.   zhe·leem ee·gra·tee te·nees

Can we play at night?
   Možemo li igrati   maw·zhe·maw lee ee·gra·tee
   noću?   naw·choo

I need my racquet restrung.
   Trebam promjenu   tre·bam praw·mye·noo
   struna na mom reketu.   stroo·na na mawm re·ke·too

ace	*as* m	as
advantage	*prednost* f	*pred*·nawst
clay	*zemljana podloga* f	*zem*·lya·na *pawd*·law·ga
fault	*greška* f	*gresh*·ka
game, set, match	*gejm, set, meč* m	geym set mech
grass	*travnata podloga* f	*trav*·na·ta *pawd*·law·ga
hard court	*teniski teren sa tvrdom podlogom* m	*te*·nee·skee *te*·ren sa *tvr*·dawm *pawd*·law·gawm
net	*mreža* f	*mre*·zha
play doubles	*igrati u parovima*	ee·gra·tee oo pa·raw·vee·ma
racquet	*reket* m	*re*·ket
serve	*servis* m	*ser*·vees
set	*set* m	set
tennis ball	*teniska loptica* f	*te*·nee·ska *lawp*·tee·tsa

water sports

Can I book a lesson?
Mogu li zakazati sat obuke?　　maw·goo lee za·*ka*·za·tee sat *aw*·boo·ke

Can I hire (a) …?	*Mogu li iznajmiti …?*	maw·goo lee eez·*nai*·mee·tee …
boat	*čamac*	*cha*·mats
canoe	*kanu*	ka·*noo*
kayak	*kajak*	*kai*·ak
life jacket	*prsluk za spasavanje*	*pr*·slook za spa·*sa*·va·nye
sea kayak	*morski kajak*	*mawr*·skee *kai*·ak
snorkelling gear	*ronilačku masku i disalicu*	*raw*·nee·lach·koo *ma*·skoo ee dee·sa·lee·tsoo
water-skis	*skije za vodu*	*skee*·ye za *vaw*·doo
wetsuit	*nepromočivo podvodno odijelo*	ne·praw·*maw*·chee·vaw *pawd*·vawd·naw aw·dee·*ye*·law

Are there any …?	Da li ima kakvih …?	da lee *ee*·ma *kak*·veeh …
reefs	morskih grebenova	mawr·skeeh *gre*·be·naw·va
rips	jakih podvodnih struja	*ya*·keeh *pawd*·vawd·neeh *stroo*·ya
water hazards	opasnosti u vodi	aw·*pa*·snaw·stee oo *vaw*·dee

canoeing	kanuistika f	ka·noo·*ee*·stee·ka
guide	vodič m	*vaw*·deech
harbour master	lučki kapetan m	*looch*·kee ka·*pe*·tan
kayaking	kajakarenje n	kai·a·*ka*·re·nye
marina	marina f	ma·*ree*·na
motorboat	motorni čamac m	*maw*·tawr·nee *cha*·mats
oars	vesla n pl	*ve*·sla
port	luka f	*loo*·ka
sailing	jedrenje n	*ye*·dre·nye
sailing boat	jedrilica f	ye·*dree*·lee·tsa
surfboard	daska za surfanje f	*da*·ska za *soor*·fa·nye
surfing	daskanje na valovima n	*da*·ska·nye na *va*·law·vee·ma
swimming	plivanje n	*plee*·va·nye
wave	val m	val
water-skiing	skijanje na vodi n	*skee*·ya·nye na *vaw*·dee
windsurfing	jedrenje na dasci n	*ye*·dre·nye na *das*·tsee
yachting	krstarenje jahtom n	kr·*sta*·re·nye *yah*·tawm

For phrases about diving, see the **diving section**, page 133.
For phrases about hiking, see **outdoors**, page 139.

hiking

pješačenje

Where can I …?	*Gdje mogu …?*	gdye *maw*·goo …
buy supplies	*kupiti*	koo·pee·tee
	namirnice	na·meer·nee·tse
find someone	*naći nekoga*	na·chee ne·kaw·ga
who knows	*tko zna ovo*	tkaw zna *aw*·vaw
this area	*područje*	paw·drooch·ye
get a map	*nabaviti kartu*	na·ba·vee·tee *kar*·too
hire hiking gear	*iznajmiti*	eez·*nai*·mee·tee
	opremu	*aw*·pre·moo
	za pješačenje	za pye·*sha*·che·nye

Do we need	*Trebamo li*	tre·ba·maw lee
to take …?	*ponijeti …?*	*paw*·nee·ye·tee …
bedding	*krevetninu*	kre·vet·*nee*·noo
food	*hranu*	*hra*·noo
water	*vodu*	*vaw*·doo

How …?	*Koliko …?*	kaw·lee·kaw …
high is the climb	*je visok uspon*	ye *vee*·sawk *oo*·spawn
long is the trail	*dugačka staza*	*doo*·gach·ka *sta*·za

Is there a hut?
Da li postoji   da lee paw·*stoy*·ee
planinarska koliba?   pla·*nee*·nar·ska *kaw*·lee·ba

When does it get dark?
Kada obično padne noć?   ka·da *aw*·beech·naw *pad*·ne nawch

Do we need a guide?
Treba li nam vodič?   tre·ba lee nam *vaw*·deech

Are there land mines in this area?
Da li ima mina   da lee *ee*·ma *mee*·na
na ovom području?   na *aw*·vawm paw·drooch·yoo

watch your step

An unfortunate consequence of the recent war in the former Yugoslavia is the presence of land mines. Most mined areas are marked with warning signs which might have these words on them:

| *mine* | mee·ne | **mines** |
| *minirano* | mee·nee·ra·naw | **mined** |

Warning signs can be in the form of a red triangle with a black dot in the middle or depict a white skull and cross-bones against a red background. Unfortunately, warning signs are sometimes souvenired and mined areas may just be cordoned off with coloured plastic tape.

Less common improvised signs that you'll want to take close heed of if you venture off the beaten track include crossed tree branches or rock heaps by the road. Always be sure to check with the locals about the presence of land mines in their area and steer away from suspiciously deserted areas.

Is the track …?	*Je li staza …?*	ye lee *sta*·za …
dangerous	*opasna*	aw·pa·sna
marked	*označena*	aw·zna·che·na
open	*otvorena*	awt·vaw·re·na
scenic	*panoramska*	pa·naw·*ram*·ska
Which is the … route?	*Koji put je …?*	*koy*·ee poot ye …
easiest	*najlakši*	nai·lak·shee
shortest	*najkraći*	nai·kra·chee
Where can I find (a/the) …?	*Gdje se …?*	gdye se …
campsite	*nalazi kamp*	na·la·zee kamp
nearest	*nalazi najbliže*	na·la·zee nai·blee·zhe
village	*selo*	se·law
showers	*nalaze tuševi*	na·la·ze *too*·she·vee
toilets	*nalaze zahodi*	na·la·ze za·haw·dee

Where have you come from?

Odakle dolazite/	aw·*da*·kle *daw*·la·zee·te/
dolaziš? **pol/inf**	*daw*·la·zeesh

How long did it take?

Koliko dugo je trebalo?	kaw·*lee*·kaw *doo*·gaw ye *tre*·ba·law

Does this path go to ...?

Da li ovaj put vodi do ...?	da lee aw·vai poot *vaw*·dee daw ...

Is the water OK to drink?

Je li ova voda pitka?	ye lee aw·va *vaw*·da *peet*·ka

I'm lost.

Ja sam izgubljen/	ya sam eez·goob·lyen/
izgubljena. **m/f**	eez·goob·lye·na

beach

You may see a beach referred to as a *žal* (zhal) but the most common word is *plaža* (*pla*·zha). Beaches are an important focus for social life both day and night during the warmer months. Terrace dancing, *ples na terasama* (ples na te·*ra*·sa·ma), at beachside hotels is also a favourite summer pastime.

Where's the	*Gdje se nalazi*	gdye se *na*·la·zee
... beach?	*... plaža?*	... *pla*·zha
best	*najbolja*	*nai*·baw·lya
nearest	*najbliža*	*nai*·blee·zha
nudist	*nudistička*	noo·*dee*·steech·ka
public	*javna*	*yav*·na

---

signs

Zabranjen Ribolov	
za·bra·nyen *ree*·baw·lawv	**No Fishing**
Zabranjeno Plivanje	
za·bra·nye·naw *plee*·va·nye	**No Swimming**

bay	*uvala* f	oo·va·la
beach	*žal/plaža* f/m	zhal/*pla*·zha
cave	*spilja* f	*spee*·lya
channel	*kanal* m	*ka*·nal
cove	*dražica* f	*dra*·zhee·tsa
inlet	*draga* f	*dra*·ga
island	*otok* m	*aw*·tawk
lake	*jezero* n	*ye*·ze·raw
promontory	*rt* m	rt
reef	*morski greben* m	*mawr*·skee gre·ben

Is it safe to dive/swim here?
Da li je bezopasno — da lee ye *bez*·aw·pa·snaw
skakati/plivati ovdje? — *ska*·ka·tee/*plee*·va·tee *awv*·dye

What time is high/low tide?
U koliko sati je — oo kaw·*lee*·kaw *sa*·tee ye
plima/oseka? — *plee*·ma/*aw*·se·ka

Do we have to pay?
Trebamo li platiti? — *tre*·ba·maw lee *pla*·tee·tee

Could you put some sunscreen on my back, please?
Možete/Možeš li mi — *maw*·zhe·te/*maw*·zhesh lee mee
staviti kremu protiv — *sta*·vee·tee *kre*·moo *praw*·teev
sunca na leđa, molim? pol/inf — *soon*·tsa na *le*·ja *maw*·leem

How much for a/an …?	*Koliko stoji …?*	kaw·*lee*·kaw *stoy*·ee …
chair	*jedna stolica*	*yed*·na *staw*·lee·tsa
	za sklapanje	za *skla*·pa·nye
hut	*jedna kućica*	*yed*·na *koo*·chee·tsa
umbrella	*jedan suncobran*	*ye*·dan *soon*·tsaw·bran

SOCIAL

142

weather

What's the weather like?
Kakvo je vrijeme?   kak·vaw ye vree·ye·me

What will the weather be like tomorrow?
Kakvo će vrijeme   kak·vaw che vree·ye·me
biti sutra?   bee·tee soo·tra

It's ...	... je.	... ye
cloudy	*Oblačno*	aw·blach·naw
cold	*Hladno*	hlad·naw
fine	*Vedro*	ve·draw
freezing	*Ledeno*	le·de·naw
hot	*Vruće*	vroo·che
raining	*Kišovito*	kee·shaw·vee·taw
snowing	*Snjegovito*	snye·gaw·vee·taw
sunny	*Sunčano*	soon·cha·naw
warm	*Toplo*	taw·plaw
windy	*Vjetrovito*	vye·traw·vee·taw

flora & fauna

What ... is that?	... je to?	... ye taw
animal	Koja životinja	koy·a zhee·vaw·tee·nya
flower	Koji cvijet	koy·ee ts·vee·yet
plant	Koja biljka	koy·a beel'·ka
tree	Koje stablo	koy·e sta·blaw

Is it ...?	Je li ...?	ye lee ...
common	često	che·staw
dangerous	opasno	aw·pa·snaw
endangered	ugroženo	oo·graw·zhe·naw
poisonous	otrovno	aw·trawv·naw
protected	zaštićeno	zash·tee·che·naw

What is it used for?

Zašto se koristi? zash·taw se kaw·ree·stee

local plants & animals

almond tree	badem m	ba·dem
black bear	mrki medvjed m	mr·kee med·vyed
rosehip shrub	šipkov grm m	sheep·kawv grm
stone/pine marten	kuna bijelica/ zlatica f	koo·na bee·ye·lee·tsa/ zla·tee·tsa
white-headed vulture	bjeloglavi sup m	bye·law·gla·vee soop
wild goat	divokoza f	dee·vaw·kaw·za

Breakfast, *doručak* (*daw*·roo·chak), typically consists of toast with butter and rosehip jam, ham or prosciutto omelettes or bread rolls with a choice of toppings. Lunch, *ručak* (*roo*·chak), is usually taken between midday and 1pm, and in coastal regions in the summer months, is often followed by a siesta. Dinner, *večera* (*ve*·che·ra), is the main meal of the day and the time it's taken varies between 6 and 9pm.

breakfast	*doručak* m	*daw*·roo·chak
lunch	*ručak* m	*roo*·chak
dinner	*večera* f	*ve*·che·ra
snack	*užina* f	*oo*·zhee·na
eat	*jesti*	*ye*·stee
drink	*piti*	*pee*·tee
I'd like ...	*Želim ...*	*zhe*·leem ...
I'm starving!	*Gladan/Gladna*	*gla*·dan/*glad*·na
	sam kao vuk. m/f	sam *ka*·aw vook

finding a place to eat

pronalaženje mjesta za jelo

The word for café is both *kafić* (*ka*·feech) and *kavana* (ka·*va*·na), though *kafić* is much more commonly used. As restaurants don't usually display their menus outside you may need to go in and ask to have a look at the *jelovnik* (ye·*lawv*·neek).

Can you	*Možete/Možeš*	*maw*·zhe·te/*maw*·zhesh
recommend	*li preporučiti*	lee pre·paw·*roo*·chee·te
a ...	*neki ...* pol/inf	*ne*·kee ...
bar	*bar*	bar
café	*kafić*	*ka*·feech
restaurant	*restoran*	re·*staw*·ran

bistro   bee·*straw*

lively venue catering mainly to a young crowd and serving a variety of alcoholic drinks as well as a limited range of food – popular in beachside areas

buffet   bee·*fe*

small café – often with a lounge-style ambience including a TV – serving snacks and buffet-style foods, alcoholic and nonalcoholic beverages

gostionica   gaw·stee·*aw*·nee·tsa

inn or pub that also operates as a no-frills, cheap restaurant

kafić/kavana   *ka*·feech/ka·*va*·na

café – popular, usually licensed, social haunt that sometimes provides music and dancing in addition to a limited selection of dishes

konoba   kaw·*naw*·ba

rustic establishment that serves wine and local peasant-style specialities

menza/kantina   *men*·za/kan·*tee*·na

canteen usually for students or employees – for cheap eats as close to a home-cooked meal as one could hope

pekara   pe·*ka*·ra

bakery and pastry shop serving the full range of delectable Croatian pastries and bread

pivnica   *peev*·nee·tsa

pub or brewery-pub (pub attached to a brewery), often with an outdoor seating area during the warmer months, that sells a variety of draught and bottled beers and a limited selection of light meals

pizzeria   pee·tse·*ree*·a

restaurant that specialises in delicious, often wood-fired, pizzas that rival their Italian cousins as cheap and tasty fare

restoran   re·*staw*·ran

restaurant – serving a wide variety of dishes but often with a house speciality and usually licensed to sell alcohol

restoran sa   re·*staw*·ran sa
samoposluživanjem   sa·maw·paw·sloo·*zhee*·va·nyem
   quick and inexpensive self-service cafeteria with reasonably priced food of variable quality

slastičarnica   sla·stee·*char*·nee·tsa
   cake shop that serves ice cream, coffee, milk-based and other nonalcoholic drinks

taverna/birc   ta·*ver*·na/beerts
   tavern serving basic food as well as alcohol

Where would you go for ...?	*Gdje se može otići na ...?*	gdye se *maw*·zhe aw·*tee*·chee na ...
a celebration	*proslavu*	*praw*·sla·voo
a cheap meal	*jeftini obrok*	*yef*·tee·nee aw·brawk
local specialities	*mjesne specijalitete*	*mye*·sne spe·tsee·ya·lee·*te*·te
I'd like to reserve a table for ...	*Želim rezervirati stol za ...*	zhe·leem re·zer·*vee*·ra·tee stawl za ...
(two) people	*(dvoje) ljudi*	*(dvoy*·e) *lyoo*·dee
(eight) o'clock	*(osam) sati*	*(aw*·sam) *sa*·tee
I'd like ..., please.	*Mogu li dobiti ..., molim.*	*maw*·goo lee *daw*·bee·tee ... *maw*·leem
a children's menu	*dječji jelovnik*	*dyech*·yee ye·*lawv*·neek
the drink list	*cjenik pića*	*tsye*·neek *pee*·cha
a half portion	*pola obroka*	*paw*·la aw·*braw*·ka
the menu	*jelovnik*	ye·*lawv*·neek
a menu in English	*jelovnik na engleskom*	ye·*lawv*·neek na *en*·gle·skawm
nonsmoking	*nepušačko mjesto*	ne·poo·*shach*·kaw *mye*·staw
smoking	*pušačko mjesto*	poo·*shach*·kaw *mye*·staw
a table for (five)	*stol za (petoro)*	stawl za (*pe*·taw·raw)

Are you still serving food?
    Da li još servirate hranu?   da lee yawsh *ser*·vee·ra·te *hra*·noo

How long is the wait?
    Koliko dugo se čeka?   kaw·lee·kaw *doo*·gaw se *che*·ka

at the restaurant

u restoranu

What would you recommend?
    Što biste nam   shtaw *bee*·ste nam
    preporučili?   pre·paw·roo·chee·lee

What's in that dish?
    Od čega se   awd *che*·ga se
    sastoji ovo jelo?   sa·stoy·ee *aw*·vaw *ye*·law

What's that called?
    Kako se ono zove?   *ka*·kaw se *aw*·naw *zaw*·ve

I'll have that.
    Ja bih to naručio/   ya beeh taw na·*roo*·chee·aw/
    naručila. **m/f**   na·*roo*·chee·la

---

listen for ...

zat·vaw·re·naw ye
    Zatvoreno je.   **We're closed.**
poo·nee smaw
    Puni smo.   **We're full.**
sam·aw tre·*noo*·tak
    Samo trenutak.   **One moment.**
gdye *zhe*·lee·te *sye*·stee
    Gdje želite sjesti?   **Where would you like to sit?**
shtaw vam *maw*·goo paw·noo·dee·tee
    Što vam mogu ponuditi?   **What can I get for you?**
eez·*vaw*·lee·te
    Izvolite!   **Here you go!**
pree·yat·naw/*daw*·bar tek
    Prijatno/Dobar tek.   **Enjoy your meal.**

Does it take long to prepare?

	Da li priprema	da lee *pree*-pre-ma
	ovoga traje dugo?	*aw*-vaw-ga *trai*-e *doo*-gaw

Is it self-serve?

	Da li je ovdje	da lee ye *awv*-dye
	samoposluživanje?	sa-maw-paw-sloo-*zhee*-va-nye

Is service included in the bill?

	Da li je posluga	da lee ye *paw*-sloo-ga
	uključena	oo-klyoo-che-na
	u iznos na računu?	oo *eez*-naws na ra-*choo*-noo

Are these complimentary?

	Da li su ovi	da lee soo *aw*-vee
	besplatni?	be-splat-nee

I'd like …	*Želim …*	*zhe*-leem …
a local	*neki mjesni*	*ne*-kee *mye*-snee
speciality	*specijalitet*	spe-tsee-ya-*lee*-tet
a meal fit	*kraljevski*	*kra*-lyev-skee
for a king	*obrok*	*aw*-brawk
the menu	*jelovnik*	ye-*lawv*-neek
that dish	*ono jelo*	*aw*-naw ye-law

I'd like it with …	*Želim to sa …*	*zhe*-leem taw sa …
pepper	*paprom*	*pa*-prawm
salt	*soli*	*saw*-lee
tomato sauce/	*ketchupom*	*ke*-cha-pawm
ketchup		
vinegar	*ocatom*	*aw*-tsa-tawm

I'd like it	*Želim to bez …*	*zhe*-leem taw bez …
without …		
cheese	*sira*	*see*-ra
chilli	*čilija*	*chee*-lee-ya
garlic	*češnjaka*	chesh-*nya*-ka
nuts	*raznih oraha*	*raz*-neeh *aw*-ra-ha
oil	*ulja*	*oo*-lya

For other specific meal requests, see **vegetarian & special meals**, page 161.

predjela	*pre*·dye·la	appetisers
juhe	*yoo*·he	soups
salate	sa·*la*·te	salads
glavna jela	*glav*·na ye·la	main courses
prilozi	*pree*·law·zee	side dishes
poslastice	*paw*·sla·stee·tse	desserts
laki obroci	*la*·kee aw·braw·tsee	light meals
aperitivi	a·pe·ree·*tee*·vee	apéritifs
pića	*pee*·cha	drinks
bezalkoholna pića	be·zal·kaw·hawl·na *pee*·cha	soft drinks
topli napitci	*taw*·plee *na*·peet·tsee	hot drinks
žestoka pića	zhe·*staw*·ka *pee*·cha	spirits
piva	*pee*·va	beers
vinjaci	*vee*·nya·tsee	brandies
domaća vina	*daw*·ma·cha *vee*·na	local wines
pjenušava vina	pye·*noo*·sha·va *vee*·na	sparkling wines
bijela vina	bee·*ye*·la *vee*·na	white wines
crna vina	*tsr*·na *vee*·na	red wines
desertna vina	de·*sert*·na *vee*·na	dessert wines

For more words you might see on a menu, see the **culinary reader**, page 163.

talking food

razgovor o hrani

I love this dish.
 Obožavam ovo jelo.   aw·*baw*·zha·vam *aw*·vaw *ye*·law

I love the local cuisine.
 Obožavam kuhinju   aw·*baw*·zha·vam *koo*·hee·nyoo
 ovoga područja.   *aw*·vaw·ga *paw*·drooch·ya

That was delicious!
 To je bilo izvrsno!   taw ye *bee*·law *eez*·vr·snaw

My compliments to the chef.
Komplimenti   kawm·plee·*men*·tee
šefu kuhinje.   *she*·foo koo·hee·nye

I'm full.
Sit/Sita sam. m/f   seet/*see*·ta sam

This is …	*Ovo je …*	*aw*·vaw ye …
(too) cold	*(pre)hladno*	(pre·)*hlad*·naw
spicy	*pikantno*	pee·*kant*·naw
superb	*odlično*	awd·leech·naw

at the table

Please bring …	*Molim vas donesite …*	*maw*·leem vas daw·*ne*·see·te …
the bill	*račun*	ra·choon
a cloth	*stolnjak*	stawl·nyak
a menu	*jelovnik*	ye·*lawv*·neek
a serviette	*ubrus*	oo·broos

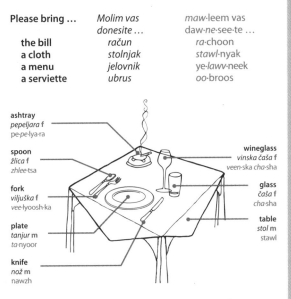

ashtray
pepeljara f
pe·*pe*·lya·ra

spoon
žlica f
zhlee·tsa

fork
viljuška f
vee·lyoosh·ka

plate
tanjur m
ta·nyoor

knife
nož m
nawzh

wineglass
vinska čaša f
veen·ska cha·sha

glass
čaša f
cha·sha

table
stol m
stawl

eating out

151

methods of preparation

I'd like it …	*Želim da bude …*	*zhe*·leem da *boo*·de …
I don't want it …	*Ne želim*	ne *zhe*·leem
	da bude …	da *boo*·de …
boiled	*obareno*	aw·*ba*·re·naw
deep-fried	*prženo u*	pr·zhe·naw oo
	dubokom ulju	doo·baw·kawm oo·lyoo
fried	*prženo*	pr·zhe·naw
grilled/broiled	*pečeno na*	pe·che·naw na
	roštilju	raw·shtee·lyoo
mashed	*zdrobljeno*	zdraw·blye·naw
	u kašu	oo ka·shoo
medium	*srednje pečeno*	sred·nye pe·che·naw
rare	*nepotpuno*	ne·pawt·poo·naw
	pečeno	pe·che·naw
reheated	*podgrijano*	pawd·gree·ya·naw
steamed	*kuhano na pari*	koo·ha·naw na *pa*·ree
well done	*dobro pečeno*	daw·braw pe·che·naw
with the dressing	*sa začinima sa*	sa za·chee·nee·ma sa
on the side	*strane*	stra·ne
without …	*bez …*	bez …

in the bar

Excuse me!
  Oprostite!   aw·*praw*·stee·te
I'm next.
  Ja sam slijedeći/a. **m/f**   ya sam slee·*ye*·de·chee/a
I'll have …
  Želim naručiti …   *zhe*·leem na·*roo*·chee·tee …
Same again, please.
  Opet isto, molim.   aw·pet *ee*·staw *maw*·leem

No ice, thanks.
Bez leda, hvala.   bez *le*·da *hva*·la

I'll buy you a drink.
Častim vas/te pićem. **pol/inf**   *cha*·steem vas/te *pee*·chem

What would you like?
Što želite/želiš? **pol/inf**   shtaw *zhe*·lee·te/*zhe*·leesh

It's my round.
Moj je red za čašćenje.   moy ye red za *chash*·che·nye

How much is that?
Koliko to stoji?   kaw·*lee*·kaw taw *stoy*·ee

Do you serve meals here?
Da li ovdje   da lee *awv*·dye
poslužujete obroke?   paw·*sloo*·zhoo·ye·te *aw*·braw·ke

nonalcoholic drinks

bezalkoholna pića

... (mineral) water	... (mineralna) voda f	... (*mee*·ne·ral·na) *vaw*·da
sparkling	gazirana	ga·*zee*·ra·na
still	obična	*aw*·beech·na
apricot juice with whipped cream	sok od marelice sa šlagom m	sawk awd ma·*re*·lee·tse sa *shla*·gawm
fizzy rosehip drink	pašareta f	pa·sha·*re*·ta
fresh lemonade	slatka limunada f	*slat*·ka lee·moo·*na*·da
(hot) water	(topla) voda f	(*taw*·pla) *vaw*·da
orange juice	sok od naranče m	sawk awd *na*·ran·che
rosehip and hibiscus tea	čaj od šipka i hibiscusa	chai awd *sheep*·ka ee hee·*bee*·skoo·sa
soft drink	bezalkoholno piće m	be·zal·kaw·*hawl*·naw *pee*·che
(cup of) tea ...	(šalica) čaja f ...	(*sha*·lee·tsa) *chai*·a ...
(cup of) coffee ...	(šalica) kave f ...	(*sha*·lee·tsa) *ka*·ve ...
with (milk)	sa (mlijekom)	sa (mlee·*ye*·kawm)
without (sugar)	bez (šećera)	bez (*she*·che·ra)

Croatians love their *kava* (*ka*·va), and you'll find coffee bars aplenty in towns and cities. Round tables are usually intended for those satisfied with just their daily fix, while rectangular tables are for those intending to eat as well.

black coffee	*crna kava* f	*tsr*·na *ka*·va
decaffeinated coffee	*kava bez kafeina* f	*ka*·va bez ka·fe·*ee*·na
iced coffee	*ledena kava* f	*le*·de·na *ka*·va
strong coffee	*jaka kava* f	*ya*·ka *ka*·va
Turkish coffee	*Turska kava*	*toor*·ska *ka*·va
weak coffee	*slaba kava* f	*sla*·ba *ka*·va
white coffee	*bijela kava* f	bee·*ye*·la *ka*·va

alcoholic drinks

alkoholna pića

beer	*pivo* n	*pee*·vaw
brandy	*rakija* f	ra·*kee*·ya
champagne	*šampanjac* m	sham·*pa*·nyats
cocktail	*koktel* m	kawk·*tel*
slivovitz (plum brandy)	*šljivovica* f	shlyee·vaw·*vee*·tsa

a shot of ...	*jedna čašica ...*	*yed*·na *cha*·shee·tsa ...
gin	*džina*	*jee*·na
rum	*ruma*	*roo*·ma
tequila	*tekile*	te·*kee*·le
vodka	*vodke*	*vawd*·ke
whisky	*viskija*	*vee*·skee·ya

a bottle/glass	boca/čaša	baw·tsa/cha·sha
of … wine	… vina	… vee·na
dessert	desertnog	de·sert·nawg
red	crnog	tsr·nawg
rosé	rosea	raw·se·a
sparkling	pjenušavog	pye·noo·sha·vawg
white	bijelog	bee·ye·lawg
a … of beer	jedna … piva	yed·na … pee·va
glass	čaša	cha·sha
large bottle	velika boca	ve·lee·ka baw·tsa
pint (500 ml)	krigla	kree·gla
small bottle	mala boca	ma·la baw·tsa

drinking up

If you're drinking in a threesome, don't at any price raise your thumb, index and middle finger all at once to signal another round. This is a Serbian gesture connected to Serbian nationalism and might see you swiftly ejected from your cosy bar-side nook.

Cheers!
Živjeli!   zhee·vye·lee

This is hitting the spot.
Ovo mi baš prija.   aw·vaw mee bash pree·ya

I feel fantastic!
Osjećam se fantastično!   aw·sye·cham se fan·ta·steech·naw

I think I've had one too many.
Mislim da sam   mee·sleem da sam
popio/popila   paw·pee·aw/paw·pee·la
previše. m/f   pre·vee·she

I'm feeling drunk.
Osjećam se pijano.   aw·sye·cham se pee·ya·naw

I'm pissed.
Pijan/Pijana sam. m/f   pee·yan/pee·ya·na sam

I feel ill.
   Muka mi je.   moo·ka mee ye

Where's the toilet?
   Gdje je zahod?   gdye ye *za*·hawd

Can you call a taxi for me?
   Možete/Možeš li mi   *maw*·zhe·te/*maw*·zhesh lee mee
   pozvati taksi? pol/inf   *pawz*·va·tee *tak*·see

I don't think you should drive.
   Mislim da nebi trebali   *mee*·sleem da *ne*·bee tre·ba·lee
   voziti. pol   *vaw*·zee·tee
   Mislim da nebi trebao/   *mee*·sleem da *ne*·bee tre·ba·aw/
   trebala voziti. m/f inf   tre·ba·la *vaw*·zee·tee

---

brandy reader

Croatia produces a great variety of wines but dearest to the hearts of most Croatians are the home-made brandies collectively known as *rakije* (ra·kee·ye) that come in a profusion of herbal and fruit flavours.

kruškovac	*kroosh*·ko·vats	pear-flavoured brandy
lozovača	*law*·zhaw·va·cha	herb-flavoured wine brandy
maraskino	ma·ra·*skee*·naw	sour-cherry brandy
orahovac	*aw*·ra·haw·vats	walnut brandy
pelinkovac	pe·*leen*·kaw·vats	herbal digestif brandy
šljivovica	*shlyee*·vaw·vee·tsa	plum brandy
travarica	*tra*·va·ree·tsa	bitter herbal brandy
vinjak	*vee*·nyak	wine brandy

buying food

kupovina hrane

What's the local speciality?
Što je ovdje
područni specijalitet?
shtaw ye *awv*·dye
paw·drooch·nee spe·tsee·ya·*lee*·tet

What's that?
Što je to?
shtaw ye taw

Can I taste it?
Mogu li to probati?
maw·goo lee taw *praw*·ba·tee

Can I have a bag, please?
Mogu li dobiti
vrećicu toga, molim?
maw·goo lee *daw*·bee·tee
vre·chee·tsoo *taw*·ga *maw*·leem

How much is (a kilo of cheese)?
Koliko stoji (kila sira)?
kaw·*lee*·kaw *stoy*·ee (*kee*·la *see*·ra)

How much?
Koliko?
kaw·*lee*·kaw

how would you like that?		
cooked	*kuhano*	*koo*·ha·naw
cured	*prerađeno*	*pre*·ra·je·naw
dried	*sušeno*	*soo*·she·naw
fresh	*svježe*	*svye*·zhe
frozen	*zaleđeno*	*za*·le·je·naw
raw	*sirovo*	*see*·raw·vaw
smoked	*dimljeno*	*deem*·lye·naw

	Želim …	zhe·leem …
(...) grams	(dvijesto) grama	(dvee·ye·staw) gra·ma
...lf a dozen	pola tuceta	paw·la too·tse·ta
a dozen	tucet	too·tset
half a kilo	pola kile	paw·la kee·le
a kilo	kilu	kee·loo
(two) kilos	(dvije) kile	(dvee·ye) kee·le
a bottle	bocu	baw·tsoo
a jar	staklenku	sta·klen·koo
a packet	kutiju	koo·tee·yoo
a piece	komad	kaw·mad
(three) pieces	(tri) komada	(tree) kaw·ma·da
a slice	krišku	kreesh·koo
(six) slices	(šest) krišaka	(shest) kree·sha·ka
a tin	limenku	lee·men·koo
(just) a little	(samo) malo	(sa·maw) ma·law
more	više	vee·she
some …	malo …	ma·law …
that one	onaj/onu/	aw·nai/aw·noo/
	ono m/f/n	aw·naw
this one	ovaj/ovu/	aw·vai/aw·voo/
	ovo m/f/n	aw·vaw

Less.	Manje.	ma·nye
A bit more.	Malo više.	ma·law vee·she
Enough.	Dosta.	daw·sta

listen for …

maw·goo lee vam paw·maw·chee	
Mogu li vam pomoći?	**Can I help you?**
shtaw zhe·lee·te	
Što želite?	**What would you like?**
nesh·taw droo·gaw	
Nešto drugo?	**Anything else?**
ne·ma taw·ga	
Nema toga.	**There isn't any.**
taw ye (pet) koo·na	
To je (pet) kuna.	**That's (five) kuna.**

Do you have …?	Da li imate …?	da lee *ee*·ma·te …
anything	nešto	*nesh*·taw
cheaper	jeftinije?	yef·*tee*·nee·ye
other kinds	druge vrste	*droo*·ge vr·ste
Where can I find the … section?	Gdje se nalazi dio prodavaonice za …?	gdye se *na*·la·zee *dee*·aw praw·da·va·*aw*·nee·tse za …
dairy	mliječne proizvode	mlee·*yech*·ne praw·*eez*·vaw·de
fish	ribu	*ree*·boo
frozen goods	zaleđenu hranu	za·le·je·noo *hra*·noo
fruit and vegetable	voće i povrće	*vaw*·che ee *paw*·vr·che
meat	meso	*me*·saw
poultry	meso od peradi	*me*·saw awd *pe*·ra·dee

pekara f	*pe*·ka·ra	bakery
prodavaonica	praw·da·va·*aw*·nee·tsa	bottle shop/
alkohola f	*al*·kaw·haw·la	liquor store
mesnica f	*me*·snee·tsa	butcher's shop
delikatese f pl	de·lee·ka·*te*·se	delicatessen
trgovac	*tr*·gaw·vats	greengrocer
povrćem m	*paw*·vr·chem	
tržnica f	*trzh*·nee·tsa	market
supermarket m	soo·per·*mar*·ket	supermarket

cooking utensils

pribor i posuđe za kuhanje

Could I please borrow a ...?	*Mogu li posuditi jedan/ jednu ... molim?* m/f	*maw*·goo lee paw·*soo*·dee·tee ye·dan/ *yed*·noo ... *maw*·leem
I need a ...	*Trebam jedan/ jednu ...* m/f	*tre*·bam ye·dan/ *yed*·noo ...
chopping board	*dasku za rezanje* f	*da*·skoo za re·za·nye
frying pan	*tavu* f	*ta*·voo
knife	*nož* m	nawzh
saucepan	*lonac* m	*law*·nats

For more cooking implements, see the **dictionary**.

ordering food

Is there a …	Da li znate za …	da lee *zna*·te za …
restaurant near here?	restoran ovdje blizu?	re·*staw*·ran *awv*·dye *blee*·zoo
Do you have … food?	Da li imate … obrok?	da lee *ee*·ma·te … *aw*·brawk
halal	halal	*ha*·lal
kosher	košer	*kaw*·sher
vegetarian	vegetarijanski	ve·ge·ta·*ree*·yan·skee

| I don't eat … | | |
| *Ja ne jedem …* | | ya ne *ye*·dem … |

| Is it cooked in/with …? | | |
| *Je li to kuhano u/sa …?* | | ye lee taw *koo*·ha·naw oo/sa … |

Could you prepare a meal without …?	Možete li prirediti obrok koji ne sadrži …?	*maw*·zhe·te lee pree·re·*dee*·tee *aw*·brawk *koy*·ee ne *sa*·dr·zhee …
butter	maslac	*ma*·slats
eggs	jaja	*yai*·a
fish	ribu	*ree*·boo
fish stock	riblji bujon	*reeb*·lyee *boo*·yawn
meat stock	mesni bujon	*mes*·nee *boo*·yawn
oil	ulje	*oo*·lye
pork	svinjetinu	*svee*·nye·tee·noo
poultry	meso od peradi	*me*·saw awd *pe*·ra·dee
red meat	crveno meso	*tsr*·ve·naw *me*·saw

Is this …?	Da li je ovo …?	da lee ye *aw*·vaw …
decaffeinated	*bez kafeina*	bez ka·fe·*ee*·na
free of	*bez*	bez
animal	*životinjskih*	zhee·*vaw*·teen'·skeeh
produce	*sastojaka*	sa·stoy·a·ka
free range	*domaće*	*daw*·ma·che
genetically	*genetski*	*ge*·net·skee
modified	*modificirano*	maw·dee·*fee*·tsee·ra·naw
gluten free	*bez glutena*	bez *gloo*·te·na
low fat	*s malo masnoće*	s *ma*·law ma·*snaw*·che
low in sugar	*s malo šećera*	s *ma*·law *she*·che·ra
organic	*organski*	*awr*·gan·skee
	proizvedeno	praw·eez·*ve*·de·naw
salt free	*bez soli*	bez *saw*·lee

special diets & allergies

posebna ishrana i alergije

I'm on a special diet.
Ja sam na posebnoj dijeti.   ya sam na *paw*·seb·noy dee·*ye*·tee

I'm allergic	*Ja sam alergičan/*	ya sam a·*ler*·gee·chan/
to …	*alergična na …* **m/f**	a·*ler*·geech·na na …
dairy	*mliječne*	mlee·*yech*·ne
produce	*proizvode*	praw·*eez*·vaw·de
eggs	*jaja*	*yai*·a
gelatine	*želatinu*	zhe·la·*tee*·noo
gluten	*gluten*	*gloo*·ten
honey	*med*	med
MSG	*glutaminat*	gloo·ta·mee·*nat*
nuts	*razne orahe*	*raz*·ne *aw*·ra·he
peanuts	*kikiriki*	*kee*·kee·*ree*·kee
seafood	*morske plodove*	*mawr*·ske *plaw*·daw·ve
shellfish	*školjke i rakove*	*shkawl'*·ke ee *ra*·kaw·ve

To explain your dietary restrictions with reference to religious beliefs, see **beliefs & cultural differences**, page 125.

culinary reader
kulinarski leksikon

This miniguide to Croatian cuisine lists dishes and ingredients in alphabetical order in Croatian. It's designed to help you get the most out of your gastronomic experience by providing you with food terms that you may see on menus etc. Adjectives on their own are given in the masculine form only. For an explanation of how to form feminine and neuter adjectives see the **a–z phrasebuilder**, page 16.

A

ajvar ⓜ *ai*-var *relish made from minced roast eggplant & capsicum & flavoured with lemon juice, garlic, olive oil & parsley*

ananas ⓜ *a*-na-nas *pineapple*

arambašići ⓜ pl *a*-ram-ba-shee-chee *mincemeat parcels rolled in vine or silver beet leaves (also called **japraci**)*

artičoka ⓕ ar-tee-*chaw*-ka *artichoke*

artičoke na dalmatinski način ⓕ pl ar-tee-*chaw*-ke na dal-*ma*-teen-skee *na*-cheen *artichokes stuffed with bread-crumbs soaked in milk & lemon juice, seasoned with parsley & garlic then drizzled with olive oil & oven baked*

B

bakalar ⓜ ba-ka-*lar* *dried salted cod that is reconstituted in water before cooking*
— **s krumpirom** s kroom-*pee*-rawm *dried salted cod simmered with oil, bay leaves & lemon slices – served with diced boiled potatoes & parsley*

baklava ⓕ ba-*kla*-va *filo pastry squares stuffed with chopped nuts, sugar & cinnamon & drenched in melted butter & rose-water flavoured syrup*

banana ⓕ ba-*na*-na *banana*

bečki odrezak ⓜ *bech*-kee *aw*-dre-zak *Wiener schnitzel*

bijeli mekani sir ⓜ bee-ye-lee *me*-ka-nee seer *cottage cheese*

blatina ⓕ *bla*-tee-na *well-known red wine*

blitva ⓕ *bleet*-va *silver beet • Swiss chard – green leafy vegetable indigenous to Croatia*

— **s krumpirom** s kroom-*pee*-rawm *boiled potatoes served with silver beet fried in garlic & drizzled with olive oil*

bola ⓕ *baw*-la *refreshing chilled drink made from sugar & fruit or herbs soaked in white wine*

borgonja ⓕ bawr-*gaw*-nya *Istrian red wine*

borovnica ⓕ baw-*rawv*-nee-tsa *blueberry*

brancin ⓜ bran-*tseen* *sea bass*

breskva ⓕ *bres*-kva *peach*

brodet ⓜ braw-*det* *tasty fish stew often served with polenta*
— **na dalmatinski način** na dal-*ma*-teen-skee *na*-cheen *Dalmatian-style mixed fish stew with rice*

bubreg ⓜ *boo*-breg *kidney*

bučice ⓕ pl boo-*chee*-tse *courgette • zucchini*

burek ⓜ *boo*-rek *oily flaky pastry stuffed with cheese or minced meat – popular breakfast food or snack of Turkish origin*
— **s mesom** s *me*-sawm *fried minced beef & onion layered between filo pastry sheets then topped with beaten eggs & milk & baked*
— **sa sirom** sa *see*-rawm *filo pastry layered with a mixture of beaten eggs, cottage cheese, sour cream & dill then oven baked*

burgundac ⓜ boor-*goon*-dats *premium red wine*

C

celer ⓜ *tse*-ler *celery*

cikla ⓕ *tsee*-kla *beetroot*

crna maslina ⓕ tsr-na *ma*-slee-na *black olive*

crni rižoto ⓜ *tsr-nee ree-zhaw-taw* 'black risotto' – highly prized risotto containing cuttlefish, squid, olive oil, onion, garlic, parsley & red wine & given its black colour by the addition of squid ink

crvena paprika ⓕ *tsr-ve-na pa-pree-ka* red capsicum • red bell pepper

cvjetača ⓕ *tsvye-ta-cha* cauliflower
— **s kiselim vrhnjem** *s kee-se-leem vrh-nyem* boiled cauliflower topped with sour cream, melted butter, cheese & breadcrumbs then oven baked

Č

čajno pecivo ⓝ *chai-naw pe-tsee-vaw* cookie • sweet biscuit

češnjak ⓜ *chesh-nyak* garlic

čevapčići ⓜ pl *che-vap-chee-chee* skinless minced beef & lamb sausages flavoured with garlic, parsley, pepper & salt – served grilled

čokoladna krema ⓕ *chaw-kaw-lad-na kre-ma* chocolate cream dessert

D

dagnja ⓕ *dag-nya* mussel

Dalmatinska salata od hobotnice ⓕ *dal-ma-teen-ska sa-la-ta awd haw-bawt-nee-tse* octopus salad – a Dalmatian speciality

dimljen *deem-lyen* smoked

dimljena riba ⓕ *deem-lye-na ree-ba* smoked fish

dimljeni losos ⓜ *deem-lye-nee law-saws* smoked salmon

dimljeni sir ⓜ *deem-lye-nee seer* smoked cheese

dingač ⓜ *deen-gach* Dalmatian red wine

dinja ⓕ *dee-nya* honeydew melon

divlji *deev-lyee* wild

divlja šparoga ⓕ *deev-lya shpa-raw-ga* wild asparagus

dnevni meni ⓜ *dnev-nee me-nee* daily special

doboš torta ⓕ *do-bosh tawr-ta* rich layered cake of Hungarian origin garnished with coffee cream & caramel

dobro pečen *daw-braw pe-chen* well done

domaći *daw-ma-chee* home-made • home-style

domaći rezanci ⓜ pl *daw-ma-chee re-zan-tsee* home-style egg noodles – often served in soups

dunja ⓕ *doo-nya* quince

Dž

džem ⓜ *jem* jam

džuveč ⓜ *joo-vech* casserole made from mixed vegetables pork cutlets & rice – flavoured with parsley, celery leaves, chilli & tomato paste

F

fazan ⓜ *fa-zan* pheasant

fileki ⓜ pl *fee-le-kee* tripe

francuska salata ⓕ *fran-tsoo-ska sa-la-ta* salad of diced potato, carrot & peas smothered in a lemony mayonnaise sauce

fuži ⓜ pl *foo-zhee* pasta twirls

G

gljiva ⓕ *glyee-va* mushroom

golub ⓜ *gaw-loob* pigeon

govedina ⓕ *gaw-ve-dee-na* beef

goveđa juha ⓕ *gaw-ve-ja yoo-ha* beef bouillon

goveđi gulaš ⓜ *gaw-ve-jee goo-lash* diced beef & pork braised with onion, sauerkraut, sour cream & paprika

grah ⓜ *grah* dried beans

graševina ⓕ *gra-she-vee-na* white riesling-style wine

grožđe ⓝ *grawzh-je* grape

gulaš od divljači ⓜ *goo-lash od deev-lya-chee* game goulash

gulaš-juha ⓕ *goo-lash-yoo-ha* 'goulash soup' – thick hearty soup containing red pepper, potatoes, diced beef flavoured with red wine, bay leaf, tomato paste, caraway seed, chilli, onion & garlic

guska ⓕ *goo-ska* goose

H

heljda ⓕ *hel'-da* buckwheat

hladetina ⓕ *hla-de-tee-na* brawn prepared from boiled pigs' hocks or trotters & cubed pork shoulder with the addition of

vegetables, boiled eggs, garlic, parsley &
paprika – a special-occasion treat

hladni pladanj ⓜ hlad·nee pla·dan' **cold
cuts** – might include thin slices of delicious Istrian or Dalmatian pršut & goat's
cheese, all garnished with olives

hobotnica ⓕ haw·bawt·nee·tsa **octopus**

hrenovka ⓕ hre·nawv·ka **frankfurter**

I

inćun ⓜ een·choon **anchovy**

Istarska jota ⓕ ee·star·ska yaw·ta **Istrian
stew** prepared from sauerkraut, beans,
potatoes & smoked dried meats –
seasoned with garlic & bay leaves

Istarski kaneloni ⓜ pl ee·star·skee
ka·ne·law·nee **pancakes** filled with
a mixture of fried cubed prosciutto &
ham, cottage cheese & mushrooms then
dipped in beaten egg & breadcrumbs,
fried & topped with a tomato sauce

Istarski lonac ⓜ ee·star·skee law·nats
Istrian hotpot of diced lamb, carrot, cab-
bage, garlic, tomato, onion & olive oil – flavoured with bay leaves &
sometimes white wine

J

jabuka ⓕ ya·boo·ka **apple**

jagoda ⓕ ya·gaw·da **strawberry**

jaje ⓝ yai·e **egg**
— **na oko** na aw·kaw **fried egg**

janjeća čorba ⓕ ya·nye·cha chawr·ba
lamb stew of parsley root, celeriac,
Brussels sprouts & carrot – flavoured with
tomato paste, sour cream, paprika, bay
leaves, lemon juice & parsley

janjeća juha ⓕ ya·nye·cha yoo·ha **soup**
made from lamb, root vegetables, rice,
cabbage, egg yolk, garlic, onion, bay
leaf, peppercorns, lemon juice, sour
cream, parsley & spices

janjetina ⓕ ya·nye·tee·na **lamb**
— **na ražnju** na razh·nyoo **lamb** cooked
on a spit

japraci ⓜ pl ya·pra·tsee **mincemeat**
parcels rolled in vine or silver beet leaves
(also called **arambašići**)

jastog ⓜ ya·stawg **lobster**

ječam ⓜ ye·cham **barley**

jegulja ⓕ ye·goo·lya **eel**

jetrena pašteta ⓕ ye·tre·na pash·te·ta
liverwurst (pâté)

jogurt ⓜ yaw·goort **yoghurt**

juha ⓕ yoo·ha **soup**
— **od bujače** awd boo·ya·che **pumpkin
soup**
— **od cvjetače** awd tsvye·ta·che
cauliflower soup with sour cream & egg
yolk – thickened with a roux
— **od gljiva s heljdinom kašom** awd
glyee·va s hel'·dee·nawm ka·shawm
rich **buckwheat & mushroom soup**
containing beef stock & sour cream &
seasoned with cloves & parsley
— **od graha** awd gra·ha **soup** made
from dried kidney or borlotti beans,
smoked bacon bones (or smoked pork
hock), onion, carrot, bay leaf & garlic
— **od graška** awd grash·ka **pea soup**
— **od heljdine kaše i krumpira** awd
hel'·dee·ne ka·she ee kroom·pee·ra
buckwheat & potato soup containing
sour cream, onion & minced parsley
— **od kisele repe i graha** awd kee·se·le
re·pe ee gra·ha **sour turnip & bean soup**
— **od kiselog kupusa i graha** awd
kee·se·lawg koo·poo·sa ee gra·ha
sauerkraut & bean soup
— **od krastavca** awd kra·stav·tsa
cucumber soup
— **od krumpira** awd kroom·pee·ra
potato soup containing smoked bacon,
garlic, sour cream, spices, marjoram, bay
leaves, parsley, vinegar & paprika
— **od krumpira na Zagorski način**
awd kroom·pee·ra na za·gawr·skee
na·cheen **Zagorje potato soup** containing smoked bacon & onion – flavoured
with marjoram, bay leaves, paprika,
parsley & vinegar
— **od mahuna** awd ma·hoo·na
runner-bean soup
— **od piletine i povrća** awd
pee·le·tee·ne ee paw·vr·cha **chicken
& vegetable soup** with carrot, celery,
parsnip & peas – served with **noklice**
(dumplings)
— **od povrća** awd paw·vr·cha
vegetable soup
— **od rajčica** awd rai·chee·tsa
tomato soup
— **od repe i kupusa** awd re·pe ee
koo·poo·sa **turnip & cabbage soup**

juha od špinata i krumpira yoo·ha awd shpee·na·ta ee kroom·pee·ra spinach & potato soup containing puréed spinach, diced potatoes & beef bouillon – thickened with a sour cream & egg yolk roux

K

kajgana ① kai·ga·na scrambled eggs
kalamari ⓜ pl ka·la·ma·ree calamari • squid
kapar ⓜ ka·par caper
kaša ① ka·sha gruel • porridge
— **od zobi** awd zaw·bee oatmeal porridge
kaštradina ① kash·tra·dee·na dried mutton soup with vegetables
kavijar ⓜ ka·vee·yar caviar
kesten ⓜ ke·sten chestnut
— **pire** pee·re dessert prepared from chestnut purée, sugar, vanilla, rum & cream & garnished with chocolate shavings
kiflice ① pl kee·flee·tse delicate crescent-shaped biscuits that come in a variety of flavours including vanilla
— **od badema** awd ba·de·ma almond biscuits dusted with icing sugar made from butter, flour, ground almonds & vanilla sugar
— **od oraha** awd aw·ra·ha biscuits made from a dough of butter, egg yolks, cream cheese, flour & sugar – stuffed with an egg white, sugar & ground-walnut filling
kiseli kupus ① kee·se·lee koo·poos sauerkraut – dear to the hearts of Croatians, sauerkraut is prepared from whole cored cabbage heads layered with horseradish, bay leaves, garlic, dried red pepper & salt
klinčić ⓜ kleen·cheech clove
knedle ① pl kned·le dumplings made from butter, semolina flour, eggs & milk – often served in soups
kobasica ① kaw·ba·see·tsa sausage
kolač ⓜ kaw·lach cake
komorač ⓜ kaw·maw·rach fennel
kompot ⓜ kawm·pawt stewed fruit
kotlovina ① kawt·law·vee·na fried pork chops simmered in a piquant sauce containing onions, garlic, tomato, mustard,

chillies, white wine & paprika – traditionally prepared outdoors over an open fire
kozji sir ⓜ kawz·yee seer goat's milk cheese
krastavac ⓜ kra·sta·vats cucumber
krema ① kre·ma cream • filling
krempita ① krem·pee·ta layered puff pastry filled with a custard-like cream
krepka juha od mesa ① krep·ka yoo·ha awd me·sa broth • consommé
kroštule ① pl krawsh·too·le similar to Italian crostoli, these are bow-shaped pastries flavoured with lemon rind & vanilla then deep fried in oil & sprinkled with icing sugar
kruh ⓜ krooh bread
krumpir ⓜ kroom·peer potato
— **salata** sa·la·ta potato salad
kruška ① kroosh·ka pear
krvavica ① kr·va·vee·tsa blood sausage
kuglice od ruma ① pl koo·glee·tse awd roo·ma rum balls made from egg whites, ground walnuts, sugar, grated chocolate & rum – a rich treat
kuglof ⓜ koo·glawf ring-shaped sponge cake sometimes flavoured with lemon or containing raisins soaked in rum
kuhan koo·han boiled • cooked
— **na pari** na pa·ree steamed
kuhana govedina ① koo·ha·na gaw·ve·deena boiled beef
kuhana škrpina ① koo·ha·na shkr·pee·na boiled scorpion fish – a Dalmatian speciality
kuhana šunka ① koo·ha·na shoon·ka boiled ham
kuhani krumpir ① koo·ha·nee kroom·peer boiled potatoes
kukuruz ① koo·koo·rooz corn
kulen ⓜ koo·len paprika-flavoured sausage
kumin ⓜ koo·meen caraway – popular spice used in savoury dishes
kupina ① koo·pee·na blackberry
kupus ⓜ koo·poos cabbage

L

leća ① le·cha lentil
ledene kocke ① pl le·de·ne kawts·ke coffee-flavoured or chocolate-flavoured sponge cake layered with chocolate cream

lička kisela čorba ① *leech*·ka *kee*·se·la *chor*·ba 'Lika-style sour stew' – stew prepared with cubed meat, mixed vegetables & cabbage – flavoured with garlic, vinegar, sour cream & parsley

lignje ① pl *leeg*·nye calamari • squid
— **s krumpirom** s *kroom*·pee·rawm traditional Dalmatian dish consisting of squid cooked between layers of potato seasoned with mixed herbs, garlic & parsley & doused with olive oil

limun ⓜ *lee*·moon lemon

lišće maslačka ① *leesh*·che ma·*slach*·ka dandelion leaves – popular salad greens with a slightly bitter taste

losos ⓜ *law*·saws salmon

lovorov list ① *law*·vaw·rawv leest bay leaf

lubenica ① *loo*·be·nee·tsa watermelon

lubin ⓜ *loo*·been sea bass

luk ⓜ look onion

M

mađarica ① ma·*ja*·ree·tsa layers of a rich sweet baked dough interspersed with a chocolate cream filling & topped with melted chocolate

mahuna ① ma·*hoo*·na green bean

majoneza ① mai·aw·*ne*·za mayonnaise

makov kolač ① ma·*kawv* *kaw*·lach poppy-seed cake

makovnjača ① ma·*kawv*·nya·cha poppy-seed roll

makovo sjeme ⓝ ma·*kaw*·vaw *sye*·me poppy-seed – often used in pastries

malina ① ma·*lee*·na raspberry

malvazija ① mal·*va*·zee·ya white Istrian wine with a yellowy-gold colour

maneštra ① ma·*nesh*·tra vegetable & bean soup sometimes containing meat – similar to Italian minestrone
— **od bobi** awd *baw*·bee broad-bean soup with fresh maize

maraska voćna salata ① ma·*ra*·ska *vawch*·na sa·*la*·ta fruit salad containing sour & sweet cherries, pear & quince macerated in **maraskino** liqueur & dusted with sugar

maraskino ⓜ ma·ra·*skee*·naw liqueur made from Dalmatian sour cherries & flavoured with the kernels, giving it a slightly bitter aftertaste – known in English as 'maraschino'

marelica ① ma·*re*·lee·tsa apricot

mariniran ma·ree·nee·ran marinated

maslac ⓜ ma·slats butter

maslina ① ma·*slee*·na olive

maslinovo ulje ⓝ ma·slee·naw·vaw *oo*·lye olive oil

masnoća ① ma·*snaw*·cha fat

med ⓜ med honey

medovina ① me·daw·*vee*·na mead (mildly alcoholic fermented honey drink)

Međimurska salata od luka ① me·jee·*moor*·ska sa·*la*·ta awd *loo*·ka salted onions with the excess liquid removed & dressed with pumpkinseed oil – served as a side dish

Međimurski gulaš ⓜ me·jee·*moor*·skee *goo*·lash veal stewed with onion, garlic, hot peppers, pickled peppers & **ajvar**

mesna jela ① pl *me*·sna *ye*·la meat dishes

meso ⓝ *me*·saw meat

miješana salata ① mee·ye·sha·na sa·*la*·ta mixed salad

miješano meso ⓝ mee·ye·sha·naw *me*·saw mixed grill – popular menu item as Croatians love their meat

mlijeko ⓝ mlee·ye·kaw milk

mlinci ⓜ pl *mleen*·tsee pasta tatters made from flour, eggs & dripping & sometimes coated with butter, cream or cottage cheese – typical accompaniment to roasted meats or **bakalar**

mortadela ① mawr·ta·*de*·la mortadella – type of aromatic pork sausage with small squares of fat & served thinly sliced as an appetiser

moruna ① maw·*roo*·na sturgeon (fish)

musaka ① moo·*sa*·ka moussaka – layered lasagne-style dish containing meat & vegetables
— **od zelenih i crvenih paprika** awd *ze*·le·neeh ee *tsr*·ve·neeh pa·*pree*·ka moussaka made from peeled, grilled green & red capsicums layered with fried ground beef with onion & a sauce made from feta, sour cream & eggs
— **s patlidžanima i tikvicama** s pat·lee·*ja*·nee·ma ee *teek*·vee·tsa·ma eggplant & zucchini moussaka made from layered eggplant & zucchini interspersed with ground beef & a sauce made from feta, eggs & sour cream

muškatov oraščić ⓝ *moosh*·ka·tawv aw·*rash*·cheech nutmeg

N

na ražnju na *razh*·nyoo roasted on a spit
na žaru na *zha*·roo barbecued • grilled (broiled)
nabujak od riže ⓜ *na*·boo·yak awd *ree*·zhe rice pudding
nadjev ⓜ *nad*·yev stuffing
naranča ① *na*·ran·cha orange
naravni odrezak ⓜ *na*·rav·nee aw·dre·zak veal escalope
narodna jela ⓜ pl *na*·rawd·na ye·la traditional Croatian dishes
nepotpuno pečen ne·pawt·poo·naw *pe*·chen rare
noklice ① pl *naw*·klee·tse dumplings for soup made from breadcrumbs, milk-soaked bread, eggs & parsley – there are variations containing minced liver & meat

Nj

njoki ⓜ pl *nyaw*·kee gnocchi (dumplings made from semolina or potato)

O

ocat ⓜ *aw*·tsat vinegar
odojak na ražnju ⓜ *aw*·doy·ak na *razh*·nyoo suckling pig roasted on a spit
okruglice ① pl aw·kroo·glee·tse dumplings made from semolina or potato – served as a savoury accompaniment or, stuffed with plums or jam, as a dessert
omlet ⓜ *aw*·mlet omelette
  — sa sirom sa see·rawm cheese omelette
opolo ⓜ *aw*·paw·law Dalmatian red wine
orada ① aw·*ra*·da gilthead (fish)
orah ⓜ *aw*·rah walnut
orahnjača ① aw·rah·nya·cha walnut roll – ground walnut, butter, cinnamon & sugar mixture encased in a yeasty dough & then baked
oslić ⓜ *aw*·sleech hake
oštriga ① *awsh*·tree·ga oyster
ovčji sir awv·chyee seer sheep's milk cheese

P

palačinka ① pa·la·cheen·ka pancake – often served filled with jam or ground nuts then topped with chocolate, may also come with savoury fillings as a main course
  — sa sirom sa see·rawm dessert pancake filled with cottage cheese, sugar, raisins, egg & sour cream then oven baked
palenta ① pa·*len*·ta polenta
papar ⓜ *pa*·par pepper
  — od ljutih papričica awd lyoo·teeh pa·pree·chee·tsa cayenne pepper
paprika ① pa·*pree*·ka paprika
paprikaš ⓜ pa·*pree*·kash paprikash – beef or fish stew heavily flavoured with paprika
pastičada ① pa·stee·*cha*·da Dalmatian speciality consisting of beef rounds larded with smoked bacon then stewed with fried vegetables flavoured with rosemary, bay leaves & peppercorns & served with a white wine, olive, lemon juice & beef stock sauce. Another version has a sauce made from dried fruit & apples, tomato paste & red wine.
pastirska juha ① pa·*steer*·ska yoo·ha 'shepherd's soup' – soup made from cubed lamb, veal chops & pork neck also containing onion, garlic, chilli, bay leaves, paprika, tomato, potato & wine
pastrva ① *pas*·tr·va trout
paški sir ⓜ *pash*·kee seer sheep's milk cheese from the island of Pag
pašta fažol ① *pash*·ta fa·zhawl bean soup with pasta
patka ① *pat*·ka duck
  — s maslinama s ma·slee·na·ma duck rubbed with salt & garlic then marinated in a mixture of wine, lemon juice, thyme, oil & pepper & roasted in the oven
patlidžan ⓜ pat·lee·jan eggplant
pečen pe·chen baked • roasted
  — na žaru na *zha*·roo grilled
  — u tavi oo *ta*·vee pan-roasted
pečena orada s prokulicom ① pe·che·na aw·ra·da s praw·koo·lee·tsawm roast gilthead (fish) with silver beet – a Dalmatian speciality
pečena svinjetina ① pe·che·na svee·nye·tee·na roast pork

pečurka ① *pe*-choor-ka *field mushroom*

pečurke na žaru ① pl *pe*-choor-ke na *zha*-roo *grilled field mushrooms*

peršin ⓜ *per*-sheen *parsley*

pikantan pee-*kan*-tan *hot (spicy)* • *savoury*

pile na dalmatinski način ⓝ *pee*-le na dal-*ma*-teen-skee na-cheen *'Dalmatian-style chicken' – boiled chicken pieces covered with a sauce of olive oil, onion, capers, parsley & anchovies then baked in the oven*

pileća krem-juha ① *pee*-le-cha krem-*yoo*-ha *cream of chicken soup*

piletina ① *pee*-le-tee-na *chicken*

pirjan *peer*-yan *stewed*

pita sa špinatom ① *pee*-ta sa shpee-*na*-tawm *spinach pie made from flaky pastry & boiled seasoned spinach layered with cottage-style cheese*

pizza ① *pee*-tsa *pizza – often wood-fired, Croatian pizzas rival their Italian cousins as cheap delicious meals*

plavac ⓜ *pla*-vats *Dalmatian red wine*

pljeskavice od blitve ① pl *plye*-ska-vee-tse awd *bleet*-ve *patties made from silver beet, grated cheese, breadcrumbs, eggs & olive oil then seasoned with garlic & mint, fried & topped with sour cream*

podlanica ① pawd-*la*-nee-tsa *gilthead seabream (fish)*

podravski lonac ⓜ *paw*-drav-skee *law*-nats *layer of cooked dried beans, topped with pork cubes (or pork chops), a layer of cabbage, a layer of capsicum, bacon, green beans & cabbage then baked in a sealed dish*

pohan *paw*-han *fried in a breadcrumb batter*

pomfrit ⓜ pawm-*freet* *French fries* • *chips*

poriluk ⓜ *paw*-ree-look *leek*

poslastice ① pl *paw*-sla-stee-tse *desserts*

posutice ① pl *paw*-soo-tee-tse *type of pasta served with various side dishes (eg, salted pilchards)*

poširan paw-*shee*-ran *poached*

povrće ① *paw*-vr-che *vegetable(s)*

prepržen pre-*pr*-zhen *prepared au gratin*

prilozi ⓜ pl *pree*-law-zee *side dishes*

prokupac ⓜ *praw*-koo-pats *well-known red wine similar to Pinot Noir*

prošek ⓜ *praw*-shek *sweet Dalmatian dessert wine*

prstac ⓜ pr-*stats* *date mussel – popular on the Adriatic Coast*

pršut ⓜ pr-*shoot* *prized smoke-dried ham similar to Italian prosciutto*

pržen pr-*zhen* *fried*

pržen u dubokom ulju pr-zhen oo *doo*-baw-kawm oo-lyoo *deep-fried*

prženi krumpiri ⓜ pl *pr*-zhe-nee kroom-*pee*-ree *pan-fried potatoes*

pržolica s lukom ① pr-*zhaw*-lee-tsa s *loo*-kawm *pan-fried steak with onions*

pšenica ① *pshe*-nee-tsa *wheat*

puding ⓜ *poo*-deeng *pudding*

punjen *poo*-nyen *stuffed*

punjena teleća prsa ① *poo*-nye-na *te*-le-cha *pr*-sa *stuffed breast of veal*

punjene paprike ① pl *poo*-nye-ne *pa*-pree-ke *capsicums stuffed with rice, tomato paste, parsley, onion & mincemeat then oven baked*

punjene rajčice ① pl *poo*-nye-ne *rai*-chee-tse *tomatoes stuffed with breadcrumbs, garlic & herbs then oven baked*

punjene sipe ① pl *poo*-nye-ne *see*-pe *squid fried with onions & garlic, stuffed with a mixture of breadcrumbs, parsley & egg, then baked in the oven in a tomato, garlic, rosemary & wine sauce*

punjenje ⓜ *poo*-nye-nye *stuffing*

puran ⓜ *poo*-ran *turkey cock*

purica ① *poo*-ree-tsa *turkey hen*
— s mlincima s mleen-*tsee*-ma *turkey with mlinci – a Zagorje speciality often served at festive gatherings*

puževi na Vrbovečki način ⓜ pl *poo*-zhe-vee na vr-*baw*-vech-kee na-cheen *snails sautéed with onions then cooked in a sauce made from flour, paprika, meat stock & sour cream*

R

rajčica ① *rai*-chee-tsa *tomato*

rak ⓜ rak *crab*

rak (slatkovodni) ⓜ rak (*slat*-kaw-vawd-nee) *crayfish*

raž ① razh *rye*

ražanj ⓜ *ra*-zhan' *grill with a spit*

ražnjići ⓜ pl razh-*nyee*-chee *shish kebabs*

rebarca ⓜ pl re-*bar*-tsa *ribs*

repa ① *re*-pa *turnip*

restani krumpir ⓜ re·sta·nee kroom·*peer* roast potato

rezanci ⓜ pl re·*zan*·tsee pasta

riba ⓕ *ree*·ba fish

riblja juha ⓕ *reeb*·lya yoo·ha fish chowder made with freshwater fish cooked with onion, chilli, bay leaves & peppercorns to which tomato paste, paprika, vinegar & chopped parsley are added

riblji paprikaš ⓜ *reeb*·lyee pa·pree·kash carp or pike stewed in a paprika sauce & served with home-made noodles

ričet ⓜ *ree*·chet hearty winter soup containing barley, kidney beans, smoked meat & vegetables – flavoured with parsley root, bay leaf & garlic

riža ⓕ *ree*·zha rice

rižoto ⓜ ree·*zhaw*·taw risotto – cooked rice dish made from arborio rice & often served with seafood dishes
    — **od liganja** awd *lee*·ga·nya risotto containing squid, celery root, white wine, tomato paste, paprika & fish stock – topped with parmesan cheese before serving

rotkvica ⓕ rawt·*kvee*·tsa radish

rožata ⓕ *raw*·zha·ta Croatian crème caramel with the zing of lemon zest

Ruska salata ⓕ *roo*·ska sa·*la*·ta 'Russian salad' – salad of boiled potato, carrots, peas, chicken or ham, pickles & boiled eggs smothered in a sauce containing mayonnaise, lemon juice & parsley

ruzmarin ⓜ *rooz*·ma·reen rosemary

S

salama ⓕ sa·*la*·ma salami

salata ⓕ sa·*la*·ta salad
    — **od cikle i kupusa** awd *tsee*·kle ee *koo*·poo·sa beetroot & cabbage salad containing horseradish, green capsicum, onion, garlic, oil & vinegar
    — **od krastavaca** awd kra·sta·va·tsa cucumber salad
    — **od patlidžana i rajčica** awd pat·lee·*ja*·na ee *rai*·chee·tsa eggplant & tomato salad
    — **od pečenih paprika** awd pe·che·neeh pa·*pree*·ka peeled roasted red peppers sprinkled with garlic, parsley, oil & vinegar

    — **od prokulica** awd *praw*·koo·lee·tse boiled Brussels sprouts tossed with minced garlic, oil, lemon juice & vinegar
    — **od rajčica** awd *rai*·chee·tsa tomato salad

salo ⓜ sa·law lard
    — **na slavonski način** na *sla*·vawn·skee na·cheen carp pieces layered with sliced potato, sprinkled with paprika, smoked bacon & parsley then baked in the oven

sardela ⓕ sar·*de*·la pilchard

sardina ⓕ sar·*dee*·na sardine

sardine u ulju ⓕ pl sar·*dee*·ne oo oo·*lyoo* sardines in oil

sarma ⓕ *sar*·ma sour cabbage leaves stuffed with a mixture of ground meat (beef, pork & bacon), rice & garlic & flavoured with paprika, chilli & bay leaves then topped with a roux
    — **od lišća od loze** awd *leesh*·cha awd *law*·ze vine leaves wrapped around a filling of minced beef & lamb (or beef & pork), egg & rice flavoured with parsley, paprika & pepper then simmered in water, wine or beef consommé

savijača ⓕ sa·vee·*ya*·cha strudel see **štrudla**

savijena teletina ⓕ sa·*vee*·ye·na te·le·tee·na pounded veal cutlets rolled around a filling of bacon, carrot & dill pickles then coated in flour & fried

seljački ručak ⓜ se·*lyach*·kee roo·chak fried diced veal combined with eggplant, tomatoes, capsicum, mushrooms & parsley & seasoned with paprika

sendvić ⓜ *send*·veech sandwich

senf ⓜ senf mustard

silvanac ⓜ *seel*·va·nats well-known white wine from Orahovica

sipa ⓕ *see*·pa cuttlefish
    — **punjen pršutom i rižom** poo·nyen pr·*shoo*·tawm ee *ree*·zhawm cuttlefish stuffed with prosciutto & rice – a Dalmatian speciality

sipica ⓜ *see*·pee·tsa squid

sir ⓜ seer cheese

skuhan ⓜ *skoo*·han done (cooked)

skuša ⓕ *skoo*·sha mackerel

sladak *sla*·dak sweet

sladoled ⓜ *sla*·daw·led ice cream
    — **od jagoda** od ya·*gaw*·da strawberry ice cream
    — **sa šlagom** sa *shla*·gawm ice cream with whipped cream

slano ⓝ *sla·naw* salty • savoury
slanutak ⓜ *sla·noo·tak* chickpea
slastičarna ⓕ *sla·stee·char·na* cake shop
slatki kupus ⓜ *slat·kee koo·poos*
sweet cabbage
slavonska riblja salata ⓕ *sla·vawn·ska*
reeb·lya sa·la·ta Slavonian fish salad
containing a number of different types of
fish (pike, carp etc) poached with herbs &
peppercorns then combined with vegetables sautéed in oil & white wine, lemon
juice & parsley & served with sour cream
sleđ ⓜ *slej* herring
smokva ⓕ *smawk·va* fig
sok ⓜ *sawk* juice
sol ⓕ *sawl* salt
som ⓜ *sawm* catfish
— **na dunavski način** na *doo·nav·skee*
na·cheen catfish fillets flavoured with
lemon juice then rolled in flour, fried &
baked with a mixture of fried onions,
capsicum, chilli & tomato
sos ⓜ *saws* dip • gravy • sauce
srednje pečen ⓜ *sred·nye pe·chen*
medium
srnetina ⓕ *sr·ne·tee·na* venison
stolno vino ⓝ *stawl·naw vee·naw*
table wine
sušen *soo·shen* dried
sušena svinjska nožica ⓕ *soo·she·na*
sveen'·ska naw·zhee·tsa dried pork hock
svinjetina ⓕ *svee·nye·tee·na* pork
— **na Đurđevački način** na
joor·je·vach·kee na·cheen pork shanks
cooked with tomato, green capsicum,
smoked sausage, wine & sour cream &
garnished with parsley
svinjski gulaš ⓜ *sveen'·skee goo·lash*
pork goulash
svinjski kotlet ⓜ *sveen'·skee kawt·let*
pork cutlet
— **na samoborski način** na
sa·maw·bawr·skee na·cheen pork chop
served with garlic sauce & potato
svinjsko koljeno ⓝ *sveen'·skaw*
kaw·lye·naw pork knuckle
svjež *svyezh* fresh

Š

šampinjon ⓜ *sham·pee·nyawn* button
mushroom
šaran ⓜ *sha·ran* carp

šaumrole ⓕ pl *sha·oom·raw·le* puff
pastry horns baked in the oven then
filled with a mixture of whipped egg
white, sugar & lemon juice
šećer ⓜ *she·cher* sugar
škampi ⓜ pl *shkam·pee* scampi (large
prawns)
— **na buzaru** na *boo·za·roo* scampi
stew – a Dalmatian speciality
— **na gradele** na *gra·de·le* grilled
scampi – a Dalmatian speciality
školjke i rakovi ⓕ pl & ⓜ pl *shkawl'·ke*
ee ra·kaw·vee 'shellfish & crabs' –
equivalent to the collective term
'shellfish'
šljiva ⓕ *shlyee·va* plum
šljivovica ⓕ *shlyee·vaw·vee·tsa* slivovitz
(plum brandy)
špageti ⓜ pl *shpa·ge·tee* spaghetti
šparoga ⓕ *shpa·raw·ga* asparagus
špinat ⓜ *shpee·nat* spinach
štrudla ⓕ *shtroo·dla* strudel – Croatian
speciality containing a variety of sweet
or savoury fillings such as cheese, buckwheat, potato, pumpkin, walnuts, poppy
seed, nettles or fruit
— **s kupusum** s *koo·poo·sawm* savoury
strudel-like pastry filled with shredded
cabbage sautéed in oil
štrukle ⓜ pl *shtroo·kle* biscuit-sized boiled
pastry parcels containing fruit fillings
— **s jabukama** s *ya·boo·ka·ma* **štrukle**
filled with apple
— **s trešnjama** s *tresh·nya·ma* **štrukle**
filled with sour cherries
štuka ⓕ *shtoo·ka* pike
šumska jagoda ⓕ *shoom·ska ya·gaw·da*
wild strawberry
šunka ⓕ *shoon·ka* cured bacon
šunkarica ⓕ *shoon·ka·ree·tsa* type of
salami made of rolled cured offal

T

tartuf ⓜ *tar·toof* truffle – delicacy from
the region of Istria sometimes served
shaved over scrambled eggs or risotto
teleća jetra na žaru ⓕ *te·le·cha ye·tra na*
zha·roo grilled calf liver
teleća ragu-juha ⓕ *te·le·cha*
ra·goo·yoo·ha veal ragout
teleće pečenje ⓝ *te·le·che pe·che·nye*
roast veal

teletina ① *te-le-tee-na* veal

teran ⓜ *te-ran* Istrian red wine

tlačenica ① *tla-che-nee-tsa* brawn • headcheese

topljeni sir ⓜ *taw-plye-nee seer* melted soft cheese

torta od oraha ① *tawr-ta awd aw-ra-ha* walnut layer cake

traminac ⓜ *tra-mee-nats* well-known dry white wine

trapist ⓜ *tra-peest* type of tasty cheese similar to Port Salut (French cheese)

travarica ① *tra-va-ree-tsa* herbal brandy purportedly with health giving properties

trešnja ① *tresh-nya* cherry

tripice ⓟ pl *tree-pee-tse* tripe

tučeno vrhnje ⓝ *too-che-naw vrh-nye* whipped cream

tunjevina ① *too-nye-vee-na* tuna

turska kava ① *toor-ska ka-va* Turkish coffee – strong brewed coffee popular in Croatia

tvrdo kuhano jaje ⓝ *tvr-daw koo-ha-no yai-ye* hard-boiled egg

U

ukiseljena svinjetina ① *oo-kee-se-lye-na svee-nye-tee-na* pickled pork

umak ⓜ *oo-mak* dip • gravy • sauce
— **od hrena** *awd hre-na* horseradish sauce with sour cream, egg yolk, mustard & lemon juice
— **od rajčice** *awd rai-chee-tse* tomato sauce

uštipci ⓟ pl *oosh-teep-tsee* savoury doughnuts

V

voće ⓝ *vaw-che* fruit

voćna salata ① *vawch-na sa-la-ta* fruit salad

voćni sladoled ⓜ *vawch-nee sla-daw-led* fruit-flavoured ice cream

Z

začin ⓜ *za-cheen* seasoning

Zagorska pita od tikvica s makom ① *za-gawr-ska pee-ta awd teek-vee-tsa s ma-kawm* pumpkin pie with poppy seeds served in Zagorje

Zagorska svatovska juha ① *za-gawr-ska sva-tawv-ska yoo-ha* 'Zagorje-style wedding soup' – soup containing veal shanks, celery & parsley roots, kohlrabi, cabbage, onion & carrot flavoured with peppercorns & parsley, with rice, egg yolks & sour cream added

Zagorske štrukle ① pl *za-gawr-ske shtroo-kle* strudel stuffed with a mixture of cottage cheese, butter, cream & eggs – an appetiser popular in the Zagorje region

Zagorski džuveč ⓜ *za-gawr-skee joo-vech* chicken pieces baked with mixed vegetables stewed in chicken stock, parsley, celery leaves, garlic, chilli & rice

Zagorski pureći odrezak ⓜ *za-gawr-skee poo-re-chee aw-dre-zak* turkey cutlets rolled around an omelette-like filling made from fried onions, mushrooms, turkey liver & eggs then dipped in beaten eggs & breadcrumbs & fried

Zagrebački odrezak ⓜ *za-gre-bach-kee aw-dre-zak* veal stuffed with ham & cheese then fried in breadcrumbs

zec na hvarski način ⓜ *zets na hvar-skee na-cheen* from the island of Hvar, this dish contains rabbit marinated in a mixture of vinegar, oil, red wine, celery, garlic, minced onion, thyme, rosemary, peppercorns & cloves then browned & braised in port

zelena maslina ① *ze-le-na ma-slee-na* green olive

zelena paprika ① *ze-le-na pa-pree-ka* green capsicum • green bell pepper

zelena salata ① *ze-le-na sa-la-ta* green salad • lettuce

zubatac ⓜ *zoo-ba-tats* dentex (fish)

Ž

žaba ① *zha-ba* frog – frogs legs are a popular delicacy sometimes found in a **brodet** or stew with eels

žemička ① *zhe-meech-ka* type of bread roll

žgvacet od purana ⓜ *zhgva-tset awd poo-ra-na* fried cubed turkey combined with onion, garlic & tomato then simmered until tender in white wine, marjoram & basil – an Istrian specialty

emergencies

hitni slučajevi

Help!	*Upomoć!*	oo·paw·mawch
Stop!	*Stanite!*	sta·nee·te
Go away!	*Maknite se!*	mak·nee·te se
Thief!	*Lopov!*	law·pawv
Fire!	*Požar!*	paw·zhar
Watch out!	*Pazite!*	pa·zee·te

It's an emergency.
Imamo hitan slučaj.   ee·ma·maw *hee*·tan *sloo*·chai

There's been an accident.
Desila se nezgoda.   de·see·la se nez·gaw·da

Call the police.
Nazovite policiju.   na·zaw·vee·te paw·lee·tsee·yoo

Call a doctor.
Zovite liječnika.   zaw·vee·te lee·yech·nee·ka

Call an ambulance.
Zovite hitnu pomoć.   zaw·vee·te *heet*·noo *paw*·mawch

Could you please help?
Molim vas, možete li   maw·leem vas *maw*·zhe·te lee
mi pomoći?   mee *paw*·maw·chee

Can I use your phone?
Mogu li koristiti vaš   maw·goo lee kaw·ree·stee·tee vash
telefon?   te·le·fawn

I'm lost.
Izgubio/Izgubila   eez·goo·bee·aw/eez·goo·bee·la
sam se. m/f   sam se

Where are the toilets?
Gdje se nalaze nužnici?   gdye se na·la·ze noozh·nee·tsee

Is it safe at night?
Je li bezopasno noću?   ye lee bez·aw·pa·snaw naw·choo

police

Where's the police station?
Gdje se nalazi   gdye se *na*·la·zee
policijska stanica?   paw·*lee*·tseey·ska *sta*·nee·tsa

I want to report an offence.
Želim prijaviti prekršaj.   *zhe*·leem pree·*ya*·vee·tee *pre*·kr·shai

It was him.
On je to uradio.   awn ye taw oo·*ra*·dee·aw

It was her.
Ona je to uradila.   *aw*·na ye taw oo·*ra*·dee·la

I've been ...	*Ja sam*	ya sam
	bio/bila ... m/f	*bee*·aw/*bee*·la ...
He's been ...	*On je bio* ...	awn ye *bee*·aw ...
She's been ...	*Ona je bila* ...	*aw*·na ye *bee*·la ...
assaulted	*napadnut/*	*na*·pad·noot
	napadnuta m/f	*na*·pad·noo·ta
raped	*silovan/*	*see*·law·van
	silovana m/f	*see*·law·va·na
robbed	*opljačkan/*	*awp*·lyach·kan
	opljačkana m/f	*awp*·lyach·ka·na
He tried to	*On me je*	awn me ye
... me.	*pokušao* ...	*paw*·koo·sha·aw ...
She tried to	*Ona me je*	*aw*·na me ye
... me.	*pokušala* ...	*paw*·koo·sha·la ...
assault	*napasti*	*na*·pa·stee
rape	*silovati*	see·*law*·va·tee
rob	*opljačkati*	*awp*·lyach·ka·tee

174

I've lost my ...	*Izgubio/*	eez·*goo*·bee·aw/
	Izgubila sam ... m/f	eez·*goo*·bee·la sam ...
backpack	*svoj ranac*	svoy *ra*·nats
bags	*svoje torbe*	svoy·e *tawr*·be
credit card	*svoju kreditnu*	svoy·oo *kre*·deet·noo
	karticu	*kar*·tee·tsoo
jewellery	*svoj nakit*	svoy *na*·keet
money	*svoj novac*	svoy *naw*·vats
passport	*svoju*	svoy·oo
	putovnicu	poo·*tawv*·nee·tsoo
travellers	*svoje putničke*	svoy·e *poot*·neech·ke
cheques	*čekove*	*che*·kaw·ve

My ... was/were stolen.

Ukrali su mi ...	oo·kra·lee soo mee ...

essentials

175

What am I accused of?
Čime me teretite?   *chee·me me te·re·tee·te*

I'm sorry.
Žao mi je.   *zha·aw mee ye*

I (don't) understand.
Ja (ne) razumijem.   ya (ne) ra·*zoo*·mee·yem

I didn't realise I was doing anything wrong.
Nisam bio svjesan   *nee*·sam *bee*·aw *svye*·san
da radim išta krivo. m   da ra·deem *eesh*·ta *kree*·vaw
Nisam bila svjesna   *nee*·sam *bee*·la *svyes*·na
da radim išta krivo. f   da ra·deem *eesh*·ta *kree*·vaw

I didn't do it.
Ja to nisam uradio/   ya taw *nee*·sam oo·*ra*·dee·aw/
uradila. m/f   oo·*ra*·dee·la

Can I pay an on-the-spot fine?
Mogu li platiti   *maw*·goo lee *pla*·tee·tee
novčanu globu na   *nawv*·cha·noo *glaw*·boo na
licu mjesta?   *lee*·tsoo *mye*·sta

I want to contact my embassy/consulate.
Želim stupiti u   *zhe*·leem *stoo*·pee·tee oo
kontakt sa svojom   *kawn*·takt sa *svoy*·awm
ambasadom/   am·ba·*sa*·dawm/
konzulatom.   kawn·zoo·*la*·tawm

Can I make a phone call?
Mogu li obaviti   *maw*·goo lee *aw*·ba·vee·tee
telefonski poziv?   te·*le*·fawn·skee *paw*·zeev

Can I have a lawyer (who speaks English)?
Mogu li dobiti   *maw*·goo lee *daw*·bee·tee
odvjetnika (koji   *awd*·vyet·nee·ka (*koy*·ee
govori engleski)?   *gaw*·vaw·ree *en*·gle·skee)

This drug is for personal use.
Ova droga je za   *aw*·va *draw*·ga ye za
osobnu upotrebu.   *aw*·sawb·noo oo·*paw*·tre·boo

I have a prescription for this drug.
Ja imam recept   ya *ee*·mam *re*·tsept
za ovaj lijek.   za *aw*·vai *lee*·yek

doctor

liječnik

Where's the nearest ...?	*Gdje je najbliži/a ...?* m/f	gdye ye *nai*·blee·zhee/a ...
(night) chemist	*(noćna) ljekarna* f	*(nawch*·na) *lye*·kar·na
dentist	*zubar* m	*zoo*·bar
doctor	*liječnik* m	lee·*yech*·neek
emergency department	*odjel hitne pomoći* m	*aw*·dyel *heet*·ne *paw*·maw·chee
hospital	*bolnica* f	*bawl*·nee·tsa
medical centre	*medicinski centar* m	me·dee·tseen·skee *tsen*·tar
optometrist	*optičar* m	*awp*·tee·char

I need a doctor (who speaks English).
Trebam liječnika — *tre*·bam lee·*yech*·nee·ka
(koji govori engleski). — (koy·ee *gaw*·vaw·ree *en*·gle·skee)

Could I see a female doctor?
Mogu li dobiti — *maw*·goo lee *daw*·bee·tee
ženskog liječnika? — *zhen*·skawg lee·*yech*·nee·ka

Could the doctor come here?
Može li liječnik — *maw*·zhe lee lee·*yech*·neek
doći ovamo? — *daw*·chee aw·*va*·maw

Is there an after-hours emergency number?
Postoji li noćni broj — *paw*·stoy·ee lee *nawch*·nee broy
telefona za hitne — te·le·*faw*·na za *heet*·ne
slučajeve? — *sloo*·chai·e·ve

I've run out of my medication.
Nestalo mi je lijekova. ne·sta·law mee ye lee·*ye*·kaw·va

This is my usual medicine.
Ovo je moj aw·vaw ye moy
uobičajeni lijek. oo·aw·*bee*·chai·e·nee lee·*yek*

My child weighs (20 kilos).
Moje dijete teži moy·e dee·*ye*·te te·zhee
(dvadeset kila). (*dva*·de·set *kee*·la)

What's the correct dosage?
Koja je točna doza? koy·a ye *tawch*·na *daw*·za

I don't want a blood transfusion.
Ne želim transfuziju krvi. ne *zhe*·leem trans·*foo*·zee·yoo kr·vee

Please use a new syringe.
Molim upotrijebite maw·leem oo·paw·tree·*ye*·bee·te
novu špricu. naw·voo shpree·tsoo

I have my own syringe.
Ja imam svoju špricu. ya ee·mam svoy·oo shpree·tsoo

I've been vaccinated against (tetanus).
Cijepljen/Cijepljena sam tsee·*ye*·plyen/tsee·*ye*·plye·na sam
protiv (tetanusa). m/f *praw*·teev (te·ta·noo·sa)

He's been vaccinated against (hepatitis A/B/C).
On je cijepljen protiv awn ye tsee·*ye*·plyen *praw*·teev
(hepatitisa A/B/C). (he·pa·*tee*·tee·sa a/be/tse)

She's been vaccinated against (typhoid).
Ona je cijepljena aw·na ye tsee·*ye*·plye·na
protiv (tifusa). *praw*·teev tee·foo·sa

My prescription is …
Moj recept je za … moy re·tsept ye za …

How much will it cost?
Koliko će to stajati? kaw·*lee*·kaw che taw *stai*·a·tee

Can I have a receipt for my insurance?
Mogu li dobiti račun maw·goo lee daw·bee·tee ra·choon
za moje osiguranje? za moy·e aw·see·goo·ra·nye

I need new …	*Trebam nove …*	tre·bam *naw*·ve …
contact lenses	*kontakt leće*	*kawn*·takt le·che
glasses	*naočale*	na·aw·cha·le

symptoms & conditions

I'm sick.
Ja sam bolestan/
bolesna. m/f

ya sam *baw*·le·stan/
baw·le·sna

My friend is (very) sick.
Moj prijatelj
je (vrlo) bolestan. m
Moja prijateljica
je (vrlo) bolesna. f

moy *pree*·ya·tel'
ye (*vr*·law) *baw*·le·stan
moy·a *pree*·ya·te·lyee·tsa
ye (*vr*·law) *baw*·les·na

My child is (very) sick.
Moje dijete
je (vrlo) bolesno.

moy·e dee·*ye*·te
ye (*vr*·law) *baw*·le·snaw

He/She is
having a/an …

On/Ona trenutno
ima …

awn/*aw*·na tre·noot·naw
ee·ma …

  allergic
  reaction

alergičnu
reakciju

a·*ler*·geech·noo
re·*ak*·tsee·yoo

  asthma attack

napad astme

na·pad ast·me

  baby

trudove

troo·daw·ve

  epileptic fit

napad epilepsije

na·pad e·pee·*lep*·see·ye

  heart attack

srčani napad

sr·cha·nee na·pad

I've been …
Ja sam …
ya sam …

He's been …
On je …
awn ye …

She's been …
Ona je …
aw·na ye …

  injured

povrijeđen/
povrijeđena m/f

paw·vree·*ye*·jen
paw·vree·*ye*·je·na

  vomiting

povraćao/
povraćala m/f

paw·vra·cha·aw/
paw·vra·cha·la

the doctor may say ...

What's the problem?
Što nije u redu?   shtaw *nee*·ye oo *re*·doo

Where does it hurt?
Gdje vas boli?   gdye vas *baw*·lee

Do you have a temperature?
Da li imate temperaturu?   da lee *ee*·ma·te tem·pe·ra·*too*·roo

How long have you been like this?
Koliko dugo ste   kaw·*lee*·kaw *doo*·gaw ste
u ovom stanju?   oo *aw*·vawm *sta*·nyoo

Have you had this before?
Da li ste patili od   da lee ste *pa*·tee·lee awd
ovoga u prošlosti?   *aw*·vaw·ga oo *prawsh*·law·stee

Are you sexually active?
Da li ste spolno aktivni?   da lee ste *spawl*·naw *ak*·teev·nee

Have you had unprotected sex?
Da li ste imali   da lee ste *ee*·ma·lee
nezaštićeni   ne·*zash*·tee·che·nee
spolni odnos?   *spawl*·nee *awd*·naws

How long are you travelling for?
Koliko dugo ćete   kaw·*lee*·kaw *doo*·gaw *che*·te
putovati?   poo·*taw*·va·tee

You need to be admitted to hospital.
Trebate ići u   *tre*·ba·te *ee*·chee oo
bolnicu.   *bawl*·nee·tsoo

Do you ...?	Da li ...?	da lee ...
drink	*pijete*	*pee*·ye·te
smoke	*pušite*	*poo*·shee·te
take drugs	*uzimate droge*	oo·zee·ma·te *draw*·ge

Are you ...?	Jeste li ...?	*ye*·ste lee ...
allergic to	*alergični*	a·*ler*·geech·nee
anything	*na išta*	na *eesh*·ta
on medication	*na nekim*	na *ne*·keem
	lijekovima	lee·*ye*·kaw·vee·ma

the doctor may say ...

You should have it checked when you go home.

Trebate otići na	tre·ba·te aw·tee·chee na
kontrolu kada	kawn·traw·loo ka·da
odete kući.	aw·dete koo·chee

You should return home for treatment.

Trebate se vratiti	tre·ba·te se vra·tee·tee
kući na liječenje.	koo·chee na lee·ye·che·nye

You're a hypochondriac.

Vi ste hipohondar.	vee ste hee·paw·hawn·dar

I feel ...	*Osjećam se ...*	aw·sye·cham se ...
anxious	*napeto*	na·pe·taw
better	*bolje*	baw·lye
depressed	*potišteno*	paw·teesh·te·naw
dizzy	*ošamućeno*	aw·sha·moo·che·naw
hot and cold	*toplo i hladno*	taw·plaw ee hlad·naw
nauseous	*mučno u*	mooch·naw oo
	želudcu	zhe·lood·tsoo
shivery	*drhtavo*	drh·ta·vaw
strange	*čudno*	chood·naw
weak	*slabo*	sla·baw
worse	*gore*	gaw·re

It hurts here.

Boli me ovdje.   baw·lee me awv·dye

I'm dehydrated.

Ja sam dehidrirao/	ya sam de·hee·dree·ra·aw/
dehidrirala. m/f	de·hee·dree·ra·la

I can't sleep.

Ne mogu spavati.   ne maw·goo spa·va·tee

I think it's the medication I'm on.

Mislim da je to od	mee·sleem da ye taw awd
lijekova koje uzimam.	lee·ye·kaw·va koy·e oo·zee·mam

I'm on medication for ...

Ja sam na	ya sam na
lijekovima za ...	lee·ye·kaw·vee·ma za ...

health

He/She is on medication for ...
    On/Ona je na   awn/*aw*·na ye na
    lijekovima za ...   lee·*ye*·kaw·vee·ma za ...

I have (a/an) ...
    Imam ...   *ee*·mam ...

He/She has (a/an) ...
    On/Ona ima ...   awn/*aw*·na *ee*·ma ...

I've recently had (a/an) ...
    Nedavno sam   *ne*·dav·naw sam
    imao/imala ... m/f   *ee*·ma·aw/*ee*·ma·la ...

He/She has recently had (a/an) ...
    On/Ona je nedavno   awn/*aw*·na ye *ne*·dav·naw
    imao/imala ... m/f   *ee*·ma·aw/*ee*·ma·la ...

asthma	*astma* f	*ast*·ma
cold (noun)	*prehlada* f	*pre*·hla·da
constipation	*zatvorenje* n	zat·vaw·*re*·nye
cough (noun)	*kašalj* m	*ka*·shal'
dehydration	*dehidratacija* f	de·hee·dra·*ta*·tsee·ya
diabetes	*dijabetes* m	dee·ya·*be*·tes
diarrhoea	*proljev* m	*pro*·lyev
ear infection	*upala uha* f	*oo*·pa·la *oo*·ha
fever	*groznica* f	*graw*·znee·tsa
flu	*gripa* f	*gree*·pa
headache	*glavobolja* f	gla·*vaw*·baw·lya
heatstroke	*sunčanica* f	sun·*cha*·nee·tsa
hypothermia	*hipotermija* f	*hee*·paw·*ter*·mee·ya
jellyfish sting	*opeklina od*	*aw*·pe·klee·na awd
	meduze f	me·*doo*·ze
muscle cramps	*grčenje mišića* n	*gr*·che·nye mee·*shee*·cha
nausea	*mučnina* f	mooch·*nee*·na
sore throat	*grlobolja* f	gr·*law*·baw·lya
sunburn	*opekline od*	*aw*·pe·klee·ne awd
	sunca f pl	*soon*·tsa

I've been ...	Mene je ujela ...	me·ne ye oo·ye·la ...
bitten by a snake	zmija	zmee·ya
stung by a bee	pčela	pche·la
stung by a wasp	osa	aw·sa

I ...	Ja sam ...	ya sam ...
removed a tick	odstranio/ odstranila krpelja m/f	awd·stra·nee·aw/ awd·stra·nee·la kr·pe·lya
stepped on a sea urchin	stao/stala na morskog ježa m/f	sta·aw/sta·la na mawr·skawg ye·zha

women's health

(I think) I'm pregnant.
Ja (mislim da) sam trudna. ya (mee·sleem da) sam trood·na

I'm on the pill.
Ja sam na
antibaby-pilulama.
ya sam na
an·tee·bey·bee·pee·loo·la·ma

I haven't had my period for (six) weeks.
Nisam imala
mjesečnicu već
(šest) tjedana.
nee·sam ee·ma·la
mye·sech·nee·tsoo vech
(shest) tye·da·na

I've noticed a lump here.
Primjetila sam
izraslinu ovdje.
pree·mye·tee·la sam
eez·ra·slee·noo awv·dye

I need ...	Trebam ...	tre·bam ...
contraception	sredstvo za sprječavanje trudnoće	sreds·tvaw za sprye·cha·va·nye trood·naw·che
the morning-after pill	hitnu kontracepciju	heet·noo kawn·tra·tsep·tsee·yoo
a pregnancy test	test na trudnoću	test na trood·naw·choo

the doctor may say ...

Are you using contraception?

Da li koristite sredstva da lee *kaw*·ree·stee·te *sreds*·tva
za sprječavanje za sprye·*cha*·va·nye
trudnoće? trood·*naw*·che

Are you menstruating?

Da li menstruirate? da lee men·stroo·*ee*·ra·te

Are you pregnant?

Jeste li trudni? *ye*·ste lee *trood*·nee

When did you last have your period?

Kada ste zadnji put *ka*·da ste *zad*·nyee poot
imali mjesečnicu? *ee*·ma·lee *mye*·sech·nee·tsoo

You're pregnant.

Vi ste trudni. vee ste *trood*·nee

alternative treatments

alternativni oblici liječenja

I prefer ...	*Ja bih radije ...*	ya beeh *ra*·dee·ye ...
Can I see	*Mogu li*	*maw*·goo lee
someone who	*posjetiti*	*paw*·sye·tee·tee
practices ...?	*nekoga tko*	ne·*kaw*·ga tkaw
	vrši praksu ...?	vr·shee *prak*·soo ...
acupuncture	*akopunkture*	a·kaw·poonk·*too*·re
naturopathy	*naturopatije*	na·too·raw·pa·tee·ye
reflexology	*refleksologije*	re·flek·saw·*law*·gee·ye

I don't use (Western medicine).

Ja ne koristim ya ne kaw·*ree*·steem
(Zapadnjačku medicinu). (za·pad·nyach·koo me·dee·*tsee*·noo)

allergies

I'm allergic to …	*Ja sam alergičan/*	ya sam a·*ler*·gee·chan/
	alergična na … m/f	a·*ler*·geech·na na …
He/She is	*On/Ona je*	awn/*aw*·na ye
allergic to …	*alergičan/*	a·*ler*·gee·chan/
	alergična na … m/f	a·*ler*·geech·na na …
antibiotics	*antibiotike*	an·tee·bee·*aw*·tee·ke
anti-	*lijekove*	lee·*ye*·kaw·ve
inflammatories	*protiv upale*	*praw*·teev oo·pa·le
aspirin	*aspirin*	a·*spee*·reen
bees	*pčele*	*pche*·le
codeine	*kodein*	kaw·*de*·een
penicillin	*penicilin*	pe·nee·*tsee*·leen
pollen	*pelud*	*pe*·lood
sulphur-based	*lijekove koji*	lee·*ye*·kaw·ve *koy*·ee
drugs	*sadrže sumpor*	sa·dr·zhe *soom*·pawr

I have a skin allergy.
Ja imam kožnu alergiju.   ya *ee*·mam *kawzh*·noo a·*ler*·gee·yoo

I'm on a special diet.
Ja sam na posebnoj dijeti.   ya sam na *paw*·seb·noy dee·*ye*·tee

I'm allergic to (gluten).
Ja sam alergičan/   ya sam a·*ler*·gee·chan/
alergična na (gluten). m/f   a·*ler*·geech·na na (*gloo*·ten)

antihistamines	*antihistaminici* m pl	an·tee·hee·sta·*mee*·nee·tsee
inhaler	*inhalator* m	een·ha·*la*·tawr
injection	*injekcija* f	ee·*nyek*·tsee·ya

For more food-related allergies, see **vegetarian & special meals**, page 162.

parts of the body

My ... hurts.
  Moj/Moja/Moje ... boli. m/f/n   moy/moy·a/moy·e ... *baw*·lee

I can't move my ...
  Moj ... je nepomičan. m   moy ... ye ne·paw·mee·chan
  Moja ... je nepomična. f   moy·a ... ye ne·paw·meech·na
  Moje ... je nepomično. n   moy·e ... ye ne·paw·meech·naw

I have a cramp in my ...
  Grči mi se ...   gr·chee mee se ...

My ... is swollen.
  Moj ... je natekao. m   moy ... ye na·te·ka·aw
  Moja ... je natekla. f   moy·a ... ye na·te·kla
  Moje ... je nateklo. n   moy·e ... ye na·te·klaw

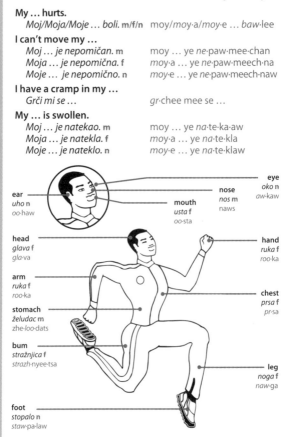

eye
oko n
aw·kaw

nose
nos m
naws

ear
uho n
oo·haw

mouth
usta f
oo·sta

head
glava f
gla·va

hand
ruka f
roo·ka

arm
ruka f
roo·ka

chest
prsa f
pr·sa

stomach
želudac m
zhe·loo·dats

bum
stražnjica f
strazh·nyee·tsa

leg
noga f
naw·ga

foot
stopalo n
staw·pa·law

chemist

I need something for (a headache).
Trebam nešto za   tre·bam *nesh*·taw za
(glavobolju).   (gla·*vaw*·baw·lyoo)

Do I need a prescription for (antihistamines)?
Da li mi treba recept   da lee mee tre·ba re·tsept
za (antihistaminike)?   za (*an*·tee·hee·sta·*mee*·nee·ke)

I have a prescription.
Ja imam recept.   ya ee·mam re·tsept

How many times a day?
Koliko puta na dan?   kaw·*lee*·kaw *poo*·ta na dan

Will it make me drowsy?
Hoće li me to napraviti   *haw*·che lee me taw na·pra·vee·tee
pospanim/pospanom? m/f   *paw*·spa·neem/*paw*·spa·nawm

antiseptic	*antiseptik* m	*an*·tee·*sep*·teek
contraceptives	*sredstva za*	*sreds*·tva za
	sprječavanje	sprye·*cha*·va·nye
	neželjene	ne·zhe·lye·ne
	trudnoće n pl	trood·*naw*·che
painkillers	*tablete protiv*	ta·*ble*·te *praw*·teev
	bolova f pl	*baw*·law·va
rehydration salts	*soli za*	*saw*·lee za
	rehidrataciju f	re·hee·dra·*ta*·tsee·yoo
thermometer	*toplomjer* m	*taw*·plaw·myer

---

listen for ...

dva *poo*·ta *dnev*·naw (ooz *hra*·noo)
    Dva puta dnevno (uz hranu).   **Twice a day (with food).**

maw·ra·te oo·ze·tee *chee*·ta·voo praw·pee·sa·noo *daw*·zoo
lee·ye·ka paw oo·*poo*·ta·ma
    Morate uzeti čitavu propisanu   **You must complete**
    dozu lijeka po uputama.   **the course.**

dentist

I have a ... *Ja imam ...* ya *ee*·mam ...
  broken tooth *razbijen zub* ra·*zbee*·yen zoob
  cavity *karijes* ka·ree·yes
  toothache *zubobolju* zoo·*baw*·baw·lyoo

I've lost a filling.
Ispala mi je plomba. ee·spa·la mee ye *plawm*·ba

My dentures are broken.
Razbilo mi se ra·zbee·law mee se
umjetno zubalo. oo·myet·naw zoo·ba·law

My gums hurt.
Bole me desni. *baw*·le me *de*·snee

I don't want it extracted.
Ne želim da ga vadite. ne *zhe*·leem da ga va·dee·te

Ouch!
Jao! ya·aw

I need (a/an) ... *Treba mi ...* tre·ba mee ...
  anaesthetic *anestetik* a·ne·ste·teek
  filling *plomba* *plawm*·ba

---

listen for ...

shee·rawm awt·*vaw*·ree·te oo·sta
  Širom otvorite usta. **Open wide.**

aw·vaw ne·che nee·ma·law baw·lye·tee
  Ovo neće nimalo boljeti. **This won't hurt a bit.**

za·*gree*·zee·te aw·vaw
  Zagrizite ovo. **Bite down on this.**

ne·*moy*·te se *mee*·tsa·tee
  Nemojte se micati. **Don't move.**

ee·*spe*·ree·te
  Isperite! **Rinse!**

A

Nouns in the dictionary have their gender indicated by ⓜ, ⓕ or ⓝ. If it's a plural noun you'll also see pl. When a word that could be either a noun or a verb has no gender indicated, it's a verb.

Nouns and adjectives are in the nominative case. You'll be understood if you just pick words out of this dictionary, but if you'd like to know more about case, see the **a–z phrasebuilder**, page 21.

Adjectives in the dictionary are given in the masculine form only. For an explanation of how to form feminine and neuter adjectives, refer to the **a–z phrasebuilder**, page 16.

Verbs are mostly given in two forms: perfective and imperfective. See the **a–z phrasebuilder**, page 17 for an explanation of these terms and when to use which form. Perfective and imperfective forms are either separated by a slash (with the perfective form given first) or consist of a root imperfective form to which a bracketed prefix is added to form the perfective. For example, the verb 'give' has the forms *dati/ davati da·*tee/*da·*va·tee with the first form being the perfective form and the second the imperfective. The verb 'call' is represented as *(po)zvati* (paw·)zva·tee which has the perfective form *pozvati* and the imperfective form *zvati*. Where two syllables are stressed in the transliteration, eg *(paw·)zva·*tee it means that once you add the prefix to form the perfective, the stress shifts to the prefix.

Where only one form of a verb is given (not all verbs have both forms) the abbreviations perf and imp have been used to identify whether they are perfective or imperfective.

A

aboard (boat, plane) *ukrcan na*
oo·kr·tsan na
aboard (train, bus) *u* oo
abortion *pobačaj* ⓜ *paw·*ba·chai
about *o · oko · u vezi · zbog* aw · *aw·*kaw ·
oo ve·zee · zbawg
above *iznad* eez·nad
abroad *u inozemstvu* oo ee·naw·*zemst·*voo
accident *nezgoda* ⓕ *nez·*gaw·da
accommodation *smještaj* ⓜ *smye·*shtai
account (bank) *račun* ⓜ *ra·*choon
across *kroz · preko* krawz · *pre·*kaw
activist *aktivist* ⓜ ak·*tee·*veest
actor *glumac* ⓜ *gloo·*mats
acupuncture *akopunktura* ⓕ
a·kaw·poonk·*too·*ra
adaptor *konverter* ⓜ kawn·*ver·*ter
addiction *ovisnost* ⓕ *aw·*vee·snawst
address *adresa* ⓕ a·*dre·*sa

administration *uprava* ⓕ oo·*pra·*va
admission (price) *ulaznica (cijena)* ⓕ
oo·*laz·*nee·tsa (tsee·*ye·*na)
admit (allow) *dozvoliti/dozvoljavati*
dawz·*vaw·*lee·tee/
dawz·vaw·*lya·*va·tee
admit (confess) *priznati/priznavati*
*pree·*zna·tee/*pree·*zna·va·tee
Adriatic Coast *Jadranska obala* ⓕ
*ya·*dran·ska aw·*ba·*la
Adriatic Sea *Jadransko more* ⓝ
*ya·*dran·skaw *maw·*re
adult *odrasla osoba* ⓕ *aw·*dra·sla
*aw·*saw·ba
advertisement *oglas* ⓜ *aw·*glas
advice *savjet* ⓜ *sa·*vyet
aerobics *aerobik* ⓕ a·e·*raw·*beek
aeroplane *zrakoplov* ⓜ *zra·*kaw·plawv
Africa *Afrika* ⓕ a·*free·*ka
after *iza · po · poslije* ee·za · paw ·
*paw·*slee·ye

(this) afternoon *(ovo) poslijepodne* ⓝ (aw-vaw) paw-slee-ye-pawd-ne

aftershave *losion za upotrebu poslije brijanja* ⓜ law-see-awn za oo-paw-tre-boo paw-slee-ye bree-ya-nya

again *opet* aw-pet

age (person) *uzrast* ⓜ ooz-rast

(three days) ago *(tri dana) prije* (tree da-na) pree-ye

agree *složiti/slagati se* slaw-zhee-tee/sla-ga-tee se

agriculture *poljodjelstvo* ⓝ paw-lyaw-dyel-stvaw

ahead *naprijed* na-pree-yed

AIDS *SIDA* ⓕ see-da

air *zrak* ⓜ zrak

air-conditioned *klimatiziran* klee-ma-tee-zee-ran

air-conditioning *klima* ⓕ klee-ma

airline *zrakoplovna tvrtka* ⓕ zra-kaw-plawv-na tvr-tka

airmail *zračna pošta* ⓕ zrach-na pawsh-ta

airplane *zrakoplov* ⓜ zra-kaw-plawv

airport *zračna luka* ⓕ zrach-na loo-ka

airport tax *porez na zračni prijevoz* ⓜ paw-rez na zrach-nee pree-ye-vawz

aisle (plane etc) *prolaz između sjedišta* ⓜ praw-laz eez-me-joo sye-deesh-ta

alarm clock *budilica* ⓕ boo-dee-lee-tsa

alcohol *alkohol* ⓜ al-kaw-hawl

all *sve* sve

allergy *alergija* ⓕ a-ler-gee-ya

alley *uska ulica* ⓕ oo-ska oo-lee-tsa

almond *badem* ⓜ ba-dem

almost *skoro* skaw-raw

alone *sam* sam

already *već* vech

also *također* ta-kaw-jer

altar *oltar* ⓜ awl-tar

altitude *visina* ⓕ vee-see-na

always *uvijek* oo-vee-yek

ambassador *veleposlanik* ⓜ ve-le-paw-sla-neek

ambulance *hitna pomoć* ⓕ heet-na paw-mawch

American football *američki nogomet* ⓜ a-me-reech-kee naw-gaw-met

amphitheatre *amfiteatar* ⓜ am-fee-te-a-tar

anaemia *anemija* ⓕ a-ne-mee-ya

anarchist *anarhist* ⓜ a-nar-heest

ancient *antički* an-teech-kee

and *i* ee

angry *ljutit* lyoo-teet

animal *životinja* ⓕ zhee-vaw-tee-nya

ankle *gležanj* ⓜ gle-zhan'

another *drugi* droo-gee

answer *odgovor* ⓜ awd-gaw-vawr

ant *mrav* ⓜ mrav

antibiotics *antibiotici* ⓜ pl an-tee-bee-aw-tee-tsee

antinuclear *antinuklearni* an-tee-noo-kle-ar-nee

antique *antikvitet* ⓜ an-tee-kvee-tet

antiseptic *antiseptik* ⓜ an-tee-sep-teek

any *bilo koji* bee-law koy-ee

apartment *stan* ⓜ stan

appendix (body) *slijepo crijevo* ⓝ slee-ye-paw tsree-ye-vaw

apple *jabuka* ⓕ ya-boo-ka

appointment *sastanak* ⓜ sa-sta-nak

apricot *kajsija* ⓕ kai-see-ya

April *travanj* ⓜ tra-van'

apse *apsida* ⓕ a-psee-da

archaeological *arheološki* ⓜ ar-he-aw-lawsh-kee

architect *arhitekt* ⓜ ar-hee-tekt

architecture *arhitektura* ⓕ ar-hee-tek-too-ra

argue *(po)svađati se* (paw-)sva-ja-tee se

arm *ruka* ⓕ roo-ka

aromatherapy *aromaterapija* ⓕ a-raw-ma-te-ra-pee-ya

arrest *uhititi* perf oo-hee-tee-tee

arrivals *dolasci* ⓜ pl daw-las-tsee

arrive *stići/stizati* stee-chee/stee-za-tee

art *umjetnost* ⓕ oo-myet-nawst

art gallery *galerija* ⓕ ga-le-ree-ya

artist *umjetnik/umjetnica* ⓜ/ⓕ oo-myet-neek/oo-myet-nee-tsa

ashtray *pepeljara* ⓕ pe-pe-lya-ra

Asia *Azija* ⓕ a-zee-ya

ask (a question) *(u)pitati* (oo-)pee-ta-tee

ask (for something) *(za)tražiti* (za-)tra-zhee-tee

asparagus *šparoga* ⓕ shpa-raw-ga

aspirin *aspirin* ⓜ a-spee-reen

asthma *astma* ⓕ ast-ma

at *kod • pri • na • u* kawd • pree • na • oo

athletics *atletika* ⓕ at-le-tee-ka

atmosphere *atmosfera* ⓕ at-maw-sfe-ra

aubergine *patlidžan* ⓜ pa-tlee-jan

August *kolovoz* ⓜ kaw-law-vawz

aunt *tetka* ⓕ tet-ka

Australia *Australija* ⓕ a-oo-stra-lee-ya

Australian Rules Football *Australski nogomet* ⓜ a-oo-stral-skee naw-gaw-met

Austria *Austrija* ① *a*-oo-stree-ya
Austro-Hungarian Empire
  Austru-Ugarsko carstvo ⓝ
  a-oo-straw-oo-gar-skaw *tsar*-stvaw
automated teller machine (ATM)
  bankovni automat ⓜ *ban*-kawv-nee
  a-oo-*taw*-mat
autumn *jesen* ① *ye*-sen
avenue *avenija* ① *a*-ve-nee-ya
awful *užasan* oo-zha-san

B

B&W (film) *crno-bijeli (film)*
  tsr-naw-bee-ye-lee (feelm)
baby *beba* ① *be*-ba
baby food *hrana za bebe* ① *hra*-na za *be*-be
baby powder *puder za bebe* ⓜ *poo*-der
  za *be*-be
baby-sitter *dadilja* ① *da*-dee-lya
back (body) *leđa* ① *le*-ja
back (position) *pozadina* ①
  paw-za-dee-na
backpack *ranac* ⓜ *ra*-nats
bacon *slanina* ① *sla*-nee-na
bad *loš* lawsh
bag *torba* ① *tawr*-ba
baggage *prtljaga* ① prt-*lya*-ga
baggage allowance *dozvoljena*
  količina prtljage ① *dawz*-vaw-lye-na
  kaw-lee-*chee*-na prt-*lya*-ge
baggage claim *šalter za podizanje*
  prtljage ⓜ *shal*-ter za paw-dee-za-nye
  prt-*lya*-ge
bakery *pekara* ① *pe*-ka-ra
balance (account) *saldo* ⓜ *sal*-daw
balcony *balkon* ⓜ *bal*-kawn
(the) Balkans *Balkan* ⓜ *bal*-kan
ball *lopta* ① *lawp*-ta
ballet *balet* ⓜ ba-*let*
banana *banana* ① *ba*-na-na
band (music) *grupa* ① *groo*-pa
bandage *zavoj* ⓜ *za*-voy
Band-aid *flaster* ⓜ *fla*-ster
bank (institution) *banka* ① *ban*-ka
bank account *bankovni račun* ⓜ
  ban-kawv-nee *ra*-choon
banknote *novčanica* ① nawv-*cha*-nee-tsa
baptism *krštenje* ① krsh-*te*-nye
bar *bar* ⓜ bar
barber *brijač* ⓜ *bree*-yach
baseball *bejzbol* ⓜ *beyz*-bawl

basket *koš* ⓜ kawsh
basketball *košarka* ① *kaw*-shar-ka
bath *kupka* ① *koop*-ka
bathing suit *kupaći kostim* ⓜ
  koo-pa-chee kaw-steem
bathroom *kupaonica* ①
  koo-pa-*aw*-nee-tsa
battery (for car) *akumulator* ⓜ
  a-koo-moo-*la*-tawr
battery (general) *baterija* ① ba-*te*-ree-ya
bay *uvala* ① oo-va-la
be *biti/bivati* bee-tee/bee-va-tee
beach *plaža* ① *pla*-zha
beach volleyball *odbojka na pjesku* ①
  awd-boy-ka na pye-skoo
bean *grah* ⓜ grah
beansprout *klica graha* ① *klee*-tsa *gra*-ha
beautiful *lijep* lee-yep
beauty salon *kozmetički salon* ⓜ
  kawz-*me*-teech-kee sa-lawn
because *zato* za-taw
bed *krevet* ⓜ *kre*-vet
bed linen *posteljina* ① paw-ste-*lyee*-na
bedding *krevetnina* ① kre-vet-*nee*-na
bedroom *spavaća soba* ① *spa*-va-cha
  saw-ba
bee *pčela* ① *pche*-la
beef *govedina* ① *gaw*-ve-dee-na
beer *pivo* ⓝ *pee*-vaw
beer hall *pivnica* ① *peev*-nee-tsa
beetroot *cikla* ① *tsee*-kla
before *prije* *pree*-ye
beggar *prosjak* ⓜ *praw*-syak
behind *iza* ee-za
Belgium *Belgija* ① *bel*-gee-ya
bell pepper *paprika* ① *pa*-pree-ka
below *ispod* ee-spawd
beside *pored • kraj • do • uz* paw-red • krai
  • daw • ooz
best *najbolji* nai-baw-lyee
bet *oklada* ① *aw*-kla-da
better *bolji* baw-lyee
between *između* ee-zme-joo
Bible *biblija* ① *bee*-blee-ya
bicycle *bicikl* ⓜ bee-*tsee*-kl
big *velik* ve-leek
bigger *veći* ve-chee
biggest *najveći* nai-ve-chee
bike *bicikl* ⓜ bee-*tsee*-kl
bike chain *lanac na biciklu* ⓜ *la*-nats na
  bee-*tsee*-kloo
bike lock *lokot na biciklu* ⓜ *law*-kawt na
  bee-*tsee*-kloo

bike path *biciklistička staza* ①
bee·tsee·*klee*·steech·ka *sta*·za

bike shop *prodavaonica bicikala* ①
praw·da·va·*aw*·nee·tsa bee·*tsee*·ka·la

bill (account) *račun* ⑩ *ra*·choon

binoculars *dalekozor* ⑪ *da*·le·kaw·zawr

bird *ptica* ① *ptee*·tsa

birth certificate *izvod iz matične knjige
rođenih* ⑪ *eez*·vawd eez *ma*·teech·ne
knyee·ge *raw*·je·neeh

birthday *rođendan* ⑪ *raw*·jen·dan

biscuit *keks* ⑪ keks

bite (dog) *ugriz* ⑪ *oo*·greez

bite (insect) *ubod* ⑪ *oo*·bawd

bitter *gorak* *gaw*·rak

black *crn* tsrn

bladder *mjehur* ⑪ *mye*·hoor

blanket *deka* ① *de*·ka

blind *slijep* slee·*yep*

blister *žulj* ⑩ zhool'

blocked *zaglavljen* za·*glav*·lyen

blood *krv* ① krv

blood group *krvna grupa* ① *krv*·na *groo*·pa

blood pressure *tlak krvi* ⑪ tlak *kr*·vee

blood test *krvne pretrage* ① pl
krv·ne *pre*·tra·ge

blue *plav* ⑩ plav

board (a plane, ship etc) *ukrcati/ukrcavati se* oo·kr·tsa·tee/oo·kr·*tsa*·va·tee se

boarding house *pansion* ⑪ pan·*see*·awn

boarding pass *zrakoplovna ulaznica* ①
zra·kaw·plawv·na oo·laz·nee·tsa

boat (ship) *brawd* brawd

boat (smaller/private) *čamac* ⑪ *cha*·mats

body *tijelo* ① *tee*·ye·law

boiled *obaren* aw·*ba*·ren

bone *kost* ① kawst

book *knjiga* ① *knyee*·ga

book (make a booking) *rezervirati* perf
re·zer·*vee*·ra·tee

booked out *popunjen* paw·*poo*·nyen

bookshop *knjižara* ① *knyee*·zha·ra

boot(s) (footwear) *čizma/e* ① sg/① pl
chee·zma/e

border *granica* ① *gra*·nee·tsa

bored *koji se dosađuje* koy·ee se
daw·*sa*·joo·ye

boring *dosadan* daw·sa·dan

borrow *posuditi/posuđivati*
paw·soo·*dee*·tee/paw·soo·*jee*·va·tee

Bosnia-Hercegovina *Bosna i
Hercegovina* ① *baw*·sna ee
her·tse·gaw·vee·na

botanic garden *botanički vrt* ⑪
baw·*ta*·neech·kee vrt

both *oba/obje* ⑪&①/① *aw*·ba/*aw*·bye

bottle *boca* ① *baw*·tsa

bottle opener *otvarač za boce* ⑪
awt·*va*·rach za *baw*·tse

bottle shop *prodavaonica alkohola* ①
praw·da·va·*aw*·nee·tsa *al*·kaw·haw·la

bottom (body) *stražnjica* ①
strazh·nyee·tsa

bottom (position) *dno* ⑪ dnaw

bowl *zdjela* ① *zdye*·la

box *kutija* ① *koo*·tee·ya

boxer shorts *bokserice* ① pl
bawk·se·ree·tse

boxing *boks* ⑪ bawks

boy *dječak* ⑩ *dye*·chak

boyfriend *dečko* ⑩ *dech*·kaw

bra *grudnjak* ⑩ *grood*·nyak

brakes *kočnice* ① pl *kawch*·nee·tse

brandy *rakija* ① *ra*·kee·ya

brave *hrabar* *hra*·bar

bread *kruh* ⑩ krooh

bread rolls *žemičke* ① pl zhe·*meech*·ke

break (s) *lomiti* (s)*law*·mee·tee

break down (po) *kvariti se*
(paw·)*kva*·ree·tee se

breakfast *doručak* ⑪ *daw*·roo·chak

breast (body) *prsa* ⑩ *pr*·sa

breathe *dahnuti/disati* dah·noo·tee/
dee·sa·tee

bribe *mito* ① *mee*·taw

bridge *most* ⑩ mawst

briefcase *aktovka* ① *ak*·tawv·ka

brilliant *briljantan* bree·*lyan*·tan

bring *donijeti/donositi* daw·nee·ye·tee/
daw·*naw*·see·tee

broccoli *brokula* ① *braw*·koo·la

brochure *brošura* ① *braw*·shoo·ra

broken *razbijen* ra·*zbee*·yen

broken down *pokvaren* paw·*kva*·ren

bronchitis *bronhitis* ⑪ *brawn*·hee·tees

brother *brat* ⑪ brat

brown *smeđ* smej

bruise *modrica* ① *maw*·dree·tsa

brush *četka* ① *chet*·ka

bucket *kanta* ① *kan*·ta

Buddhist *Budist* ⑪ *boo*·deest

budget *budžet* ⑪ *boo*·jet

buffet *bife* ⑪ bee·*fe*

bug (insect) *stjenica* ① *stye*·nee·tsa

build *(iz)graditi* (eez·)*gra*·dee·tee

builder *građevinar* ⑪ gra·je·*vee*·nar

building zgrada ① zgra-da
bumbag torbica nošena oko struka ①
tawr-bee-tsa naw-she-na aw-kaw stroo-ka
burn opeklina ① aw-pe-klee-na
burnt izgoren eez-gaw-ren
bus (city) gradski autobus ⓜ grad-skee
a-oo-taw-boos
bus (intercity) međugradski autobus ⓜ
me-joo-grad-skee a-oo-taw-boos
bus station autobuska stanica ①
a-oo-taw-boo-ska sta-nee-tsa
bus stop autobuska stanica ①
a-oo-taw-boo-ska sta-nee-tsa
business biznis ⓜ beez-nees
business class prvi razred ⓜ pr-vee ra-zred
business man/woman biznismen ⓜ&①
beez-nees-men
business person poslovna osoba ①
paw-slawv-na aw-saw-ba
business trip službeno putovanje ⓝ
sloozh-be-naw poo-taw-va-nye
busker ulični zabavljač ⓜ oo-leech-nee
za-bav-lyach
busy zauzet za-oo-zet
but osim aw-seem
butcher mesar ⓜ me-sar
butcher's shop mesnica ① me-snee-tsa
butter maslac ⓜ ma-slats
butterfly leptir ⓜ le-pteer
button dugme ⓝ doog-me
buy kupiti/kupovati koo-pee-tee/
koo-paw-va-tee

C

cabbage kupus ⓜ koo-poos
cable car uspinjača ① oo-spee-nya-cha
café kafić/kavana ⓜ/① ka-feech/ka-va-na
cake kolač ⓜ kaw-lach
cake shop slastičarnica ①
sla-stee-char-nee-tsa
calculator digitron ⓜ dee-gee-trawn
calendar kalendar ⓜ ka-len-dar
call (po)zvati (paw-)zva-tee
camera foto-aparat ⓜ faw-taw-a-pa-rat
camera shop prodavaonica foto-aparata ①
praw-da-va-aw-nee-tsa faw-taw-a-pa-ra-ta
camp kampirati imp kam-pee-ra-tee
camping ground kamp ⓜ kamp
camping store prodavaonica opreme za
kampiranje ① praw-da-va-aw-nee-tsa
aw-pre-me za kam-pee-ra-nye

campsite mjesto za kampiranje ⓜ
mye-staw za kam-pee-ra-nye
can (be able) moći imp maw-chee
can (have permission) smjeti imp smye-tee
can (tin) limenka ① lee-men-ka
can opener otvarač za limenke ⓜ
awt-va-rach za lee-men-ke
Canada Kanada ① ka-na-da
cancel poništiti/poništavati
paw-nee-shtee-tee/paw-nee-shta-va-tee
cancer rak ⓜ rak
candle svijeća ① svee-ye-cha
candy slatkiši ⓜ pl slat-kee-shee
cantaloupe dinja ① dee-nya
cape (promontory) rt ⓜ rt
capsicum paprika ① pa-pree-ka
car automobil ⓜ a-oo-taw-maw-beel
car hire najam automobila ⓜ nai-am
a-oo-taw-maw-bee-la
car owner's title potvrda vlasništva automobila ① paw-tvr-da vlas-neesh-tva
a-oo-taw-maw-bee-la
car park parkiralište ① par-kee-ra-leesh-te
car registration registracija
re-gee-stra-tsee-ya
caravan karavana ① ka-ra-va-na
cardiac arrest srčani udar ⓜ
sr-cha-nee oo-dar
cards (playing) karte za igranje ① pl
kar-te za ee-gra-nye
care (for someone) (po)brinuti se
(paw-)bree-noo-tee se
Careful! Oprez! aw-prez
carpenter tesar ⓜ te-sar
carrot mrkva ① mrk-va
carry nositi imp naw-see-tee
carton kartonska kutija ① kar-tawn-ska
koo-tee-ya
cash gotovina ① gaw-taw-vee-na
cash (a cheque) unovčiti/unovčavati
oo-nawv-chee-tee/oo-nawv-cha-va-tee
cash register blagajna ① bla-gai-na
cashier blagajnik ⓜ bla-gai-neek
casino kasino ⓜ ka-see-naw
cassette kazeta ① ka-ze-ta
castle dvorac ⓜ dvaw-rats
casual work povremeni posao ⓜ
paw-vre-me-nee paw-sa-aw
cat mačka ① mach-ka
cathedral katedrala ① ka-te-dra-la
Catholic katolik ⓜ ka-taw-leek
Catholicism Katoličanstvo ⓝ
ka-taw-lee-chan-stvaw

cauliflower cvjetača ① tsvye·ta·cha
cave spilja ① spee·lya
CD CD ⑩ tse de
celebration proslava ① praw·sla·va
cemetery groblje ⑩ graw·blye
cent cent ⑩ tsent
centimetre centimetar ⑩ tsen·tee·me·tar
centre centar ⑩ tsen·tar
ceramics keramika ① ke·ra·mee·ka
cereal žitarica ① zhee·ta·ree·tsa
certificate svjedodžba ① svye·dawj·ba
chain lanac ⑩ la·nats
chair stolica za sklapanje ① staw·lee·tsa
za skla·pa·nye
chairlift (skiing) žičara ① zhee·cha·ra
champagne šampanjac ⑩ sham·pa·nyats
championships prvenstvo ⑩ pr·vens·tvaw
chance šansa ① shan·sa
change promjena ① praw·mye·na
change (coins) kusur ⑩ koo·soor
change (money) zamijeniti/
zamijenjivati za·mee·ye·nee·tee/
za·mee·ye·nyee·va·tee
changing room kabina za
presvlačenje ① pl ka·bee·na za
pres·vla·che·nye
charming šarmantan shar·man·tan
chat up udvarati se imp do·dva·ra·tee se
cheap jeftino ⑩ yef·tee·naw
cheat varalica ① va·ra·lee·tsa
check (bill) račun ⑩ ra·choon
check provjeriti/provjeravati
praw·vye·ree·tee/praw·vye·ra·va·tee
check-in (airport) prijemni šalter ⑩
pree·yem·nee shal·ter
checkpoint mjesto kontrole ① mye·staw
kawn·traw·le
cheese sir ⑩ seer
cheese shop prodavaonica sira ①
praw·da·va·aw·nee·tsa see·ra
chef šef kuhinje ① shef koo·hee·nye
chemist (pharmacist) ljekarnik ⑩
lye·kar·neek
chemist (pharmacy) ljekarna ① lye·kar·na
cheque ček ⑩ chek
cherry trešnja ① tresh·nya
chess šah ⑩ shah
chess board šahovska ploča ①
sha·hawv·ska plaw·cha
chest (body) prsa ① pr·sa
chestnut kesten ⑩ ke·sten
chewing gum žvakača guma ①
zhva·ka·cha goo·ma

chicken (as food) piletina ① pee·le·tee·na
chickenpox vodene kozice ① pl
vaw·de·ne kaw·zee·tse
chickpea slanutak ⑩ sla·noo·tak
child dijete ⑩ dee·ye·te
child seat sjedalo za dijete ⑩ sye·da·law
za dee·ye·te
childminding čuvanje djece ⑩
choo·va·nye dye·tse
children djeca ⑩ pl dye·tsa
chilli čili ⑩ chee·lee
chilli sauce umak od čilija ⑩ oo·mak awd
chee·lee·ya
chiropractor kiropraktor ⑩
kee·raw·prak·tawr
chocolate čokolada ① chaw·kaw·la·da
choose izabrati/izabirati ee·za·bra·tee/
ee·za·bee·ra·tee
chopping board daska za sjeckanje ①
da·ska za syets·ka·nye
chopsticks štapići za jelo ① pl
shta·pee·chee za ye·law
Christian kršćanin/kršćanka ⑩/①
krsh·cha·neen/krsh·chan·ka
Christmas božić ⑩ baw·zheech
Christmas Day božićni dan ⑩
baw·zheech·nee dan
Christmas Eve badnjak ⑩ bad·nyak
church crkva ① tsr·kva
cider jabukovača ① ya·boo·kaw·va·cha
cigar cigara ① tsee·ga·ra
cigarette cigareta ① tsee·ga·re·ta
cigarette lighter upaljač ⑩ oo·pa·lyach
cinema kino ⑩ kee·naw
circle dance kolo ⑩ kaw·law
circus cirkus ⑩ tseer·koos
citizenship državljanstvo ⑩
dr·zhav·lyan·stvaw
city grad ⑩ grad
city centre gradski centar ⑩ grad·skee
tsen·tar
civil rights građanska prava ⑩ pl
gra·jan·ska pra·va
class (category) klasa ① kla·sa
classical klasičan kla·see·chan
clean čist cheest
clean (o)čistiti (aw·)chee·stee·tee
cleaning čišćenje ⑩ cheesh·che·nye
client stranka ① stran·ka
cliff litica ① lee·tee·tsa
climb popeti/penjati se paw·pe·tee/
pe·nya·tee se
cloakroom garderoba ① gar·de·raw·ba

clock *sat* ⓜ sat
close (nearby) *blizak* blee·zak
close (shut) *zatvoriti/zatvarati* zat·vaw·ree·tee/zat·va·ra·tee
closed *zatvoren* zat·vaw·ren
clothesline *konop za sušenje rublja* ⓜ kaw·nawp za soo·she·nye roob·lya
clothing *odjeća* ⓕ awd·ye·cha
clothing store *prodavaonica odjeće* ⓕ praw·da·va·aw·nee·tsa aw·dye·che
cloud *oblak* ⓜ aw·blak
cloudy *oblačan* aw·bla·chan
clutch (car) *kvačilo* ⓝ kva·chee·law
coach (sports) *trener* ⓜ tre·ner
coast *obala* ⓕ aw·ba·la
coat *kaput* ⓜ ka·poot
cocaine *kokain* ⓜ kaw·ka·een
cockroach *žohar* ⓜ zhaw·har
cocktail *koktel* ⓜ kawk·tel
cocoa *kakao* ⓝ ka·ka·aw
coffee *kava* ⓕ ka·va
coins *novčići* ⓜ pl nawv·chee·chee
cold *prehlada* ⓕ pre·hla·da
cold *hladan* hla·dan
(have a) cold *imati prehladu* imp ee·ma·tee pre·hla·doo
colleague *kolega/kolegica* ⓜ/ⓕ kaw·le·ga/kaw·le·gee·tsa
collect call *poziv na račun nazvane osobe* ⓜ paw·zeev na ra·choon naz·va·ne aw·saw·be
college *koledž* ⓜ kaw·lej
colour *boja* ⓕ boy·a
comb *češalj* ⓜ che·shal'
come *doći/dolaziti* daw·chee/ daw·la·zee·tee
comedy *komedija* ⓕ kaw·me·dee·ya
comfortable *ugodan* oo·gaw·dan
commission *komisija* ⓕ kaw·mee·see·ya
communications (profession) *komunikacije* ⓕ pl kaw·moo·nee·ka·tsee·ye
communion *pričest* ⓕ pree·chest
communism *komunizam* ⓜ kaw·moo·nee·zam
communist *komunista* ⓜ kaw·moo·nee·sta
companion *drug* ⓜ droog
company *društvo* ⓝ droosh·tvaw
compass *kompas* ⓜ kawm·pas
complain *(po)žaliti se* (paw·)zha·lee·tee se
complaint *prigovor* ⓜ pree·gaw·vawr
complimentary (free) *besplatan* be·spla·tan
computer *računalo* ⓝ ra·choo·na·law

computer game *kompjuterska igra* ⓕ kawm·pyoo·ter·ska ee·gra
concert *koncert* ⓜ kawn·tsert
concussion *potres mozga* ⓜ paw·tres maw·zga
conditioner (hair) *omekšivač (za kosu)* ⓜ aw·mek·shee·vach (za kaw·soo)
condom *prezervativ* ⓜ pre·zer·va·teev
conference (big) *konferencija* ⓕ kon·fe·ren·tsee·ya
conference (small) *vjećanje* ⓝ vye·cha·nye
confession (admission) *priznanje* ⓝ pree·zna·nye
confession (at church) *ispovijed* ⓕ ee·spaw·vee·yed
confirm (a booking) *potvrditi/potvrđivati* pawt·vr·dee·tee/pawt·vr·jee·va·tee
congratulations *čestitke* ⓕ pl che·steet·ke
conjunctivitis *konjunktivitis* ⓜ kaw·nyoonk·tee·vee·tees
connection *veza* ⓕ ve·za
conservative *konzervativan* kawn·zer·va·tee·van
constipation *zatvorenje* ⓝ zat·vaw·re·nye
consulate *konzulat* ⓜ kawn·zoo·lat
contact-lens solution *tekućina za kontakt leće* ⓕ te·koo·chee·na za kawn·takt le·che
contact lenses *kontakt leće* ⓕ pl kawn·takt le·che
contraceptives *sredstva za sprječavanje neželjene trudnoće* ⓝ pl sreds·tva za sprye·cha·va·nye ne·zhe·lye·ne trood·naw·che
contract *ugovor* ⓜ oo·gaw·vawr
convenience store *prodavaonica sa produženim radnim vremenom* ⓕ praw·da·va·aw·nee·tsa sa praw·doo·zhe·neem rad·neem vre·me·nawm
convent *samostan* ⓜ sa·maw·stan
cook *kuhar/kuharica* ⓜ/ⓕ koo·har/ koo·ha·ree·tsa
cook *(s)kuhati* (s)koo·ha·tee
cookie *keks* ⓜ keks
cooking *kuhanje* ⓝ koo·ha·nye
cool *hladan* hla·dan
coral *koralj* ⓜ kaw·ral'
corkscrew *vadičep* ⓜ va·dee·chep
corn *kukuruz* ⓜ koo·koo·rooz
corner *ugao* ⓜ oo·ga·aw
cornflakes *kukuruzne pahuljice* ⓕ pl koo·koo·rooz·ne pa·hoo·lyee·tse

corrupt *pokvaren* paw·kva·ren
cost *stajati* imp stai·a·tee
cotton *pamuk* ① pa·mook
cotton balls *kuglice vate* ① pl koo·glee·tse va·te
cotton buds *vatene čačkalice za uši* ① pl va·te·ne chach·ka·lee·tse za oo·shee
cough *(za)kašljati* (za·)kash·lya·tee
cough medicine *sirup za kašalj* ⓜ see·roop za ka·shal'
count *(iz)brojati* (eez·)broy·a·tee
counter (at bar) *šank* ⓜ shank
country (land) *zemlja* ① zem·lya
country (nation state) *država* ① dr·zha·va
countryside *seosko područje* ⓝ se·aw·skaw paw·drooch·ye
county *okrug* ⓜ aw·kroog
coupon *kupon* ⓜ koo·pawn
courgette *bučice* ① pl boo·chee·tse
court (legal) *sud* ⓜ sood
court (tennis) *igralište* ⓝ ee·gra·leesh·te
cove *dražica* ① dra·zhee·tsa
cover charge (nightclub) *cijena ulaznice* ① tsee·ye·na oo·laz·nee·tse
cow *krava* ① kra·va
crafts (handicrafts) *umjetnički obrti* ⓜ pl oo·myet·neech·kee aw·br·tee
crash *sudar* ⓜ soo·dar
crazy *lud* lood
cream (cosmetic) *krema* ① kre·ma
cream (food) *vrhnje* ⓝ vrh·nye
creche *jaslice* ① pl ya·slee·tse
credit *kredit* ⓜ kre·deet
credit card *kreditna kartica* ① kre·deet·na kar·tee·tsa
cricket (sport) *kriket* ⓜ kree·ket
Croat *Hrvat/Hrvatica* ⓜ/① hr·vat/ hr·va·tee·tsa
Croatia *Hrvatska* ① hr·vat·ska
crop *urod* ⓜ oo·rawd
cross *križ* ⓜ kreezh
crowded *prepun* pre·poon
cucumber *krastavac* ⓜ kra·sta·vats
cup *šalica* ① sha·lee·tsa
cupboard *ormar* ⓜ awr·mar
currency exchange *tečaj stranih valuta* ⓜ te·chai stra·neeh va·loo·ta
current (electricity) *struja* ① stroo·ya
current affairs *aktuelna zbivanja* ⓝ pl ak·too·el·na zbee·va·nya
custom *običaj* ⓜ aw·bee·chai
customs *carinarnica* ① tsa·ree·nar·nee·tsa

cut *(na)rezati* (na·)re·za·tee
cutlery *pribor za jelo* ⓝ pree·bawr za ye·law
CV *kratak životopis* ⓜ kra·tak zhee·vaw·taw·pees
cycle *voziti bicikl* imp vaw·zee·tee bee·tsee·kl
cycling *vožnja biciklom* ① vawzh·nya bee·tsee·klawm
cyclist *biciklist* ⓜ bee·tsee·kleest
cystitis *cistitis* ① tsee·stee·tees

D

dad *tata* ① ta·ta
daily *dnevni* dnev·nee
dance *ples* ⓜ ples
dance *(za)plesati* (za·)ple·sa·tee
dancing *plesanje* ⓝ ple·sa·nye
dangerous *opasan* aw·pa·san
dark *mračan* mra·chan
dark (of colour) *taman* ta·man
date (appointment) *spoj* ⓜ spoy
date (day) *datum* ⓜ da·toom
date (fruit) *datulja* ① da·too·lya
date (a person) *izaći/izlaziti* ee·za·chee/ ee·zla·zee·tee
date of birth *datum rođenja* ⓝ da·toom raw·je·nya
daughter *kći* ① kchee
dawn *zora* ① zaw·ra
day *dan* ⓜ dan
day after tomorrow *prekosutra* ⓝ pre·kaw·soo·tra
day before yesterday *prekjučer* ⓝ prek·yoo·cher
dead *mrtav* mr·tav
deaf *gluh* glooh
deal (cards) *(po)dijeliti* (paw·)dee·ye·lee·tee
December *prosinac* ⓜ praw·see·nats
decide *odlučiti/odlučivati* awd·loo·chee·tee/awd·loo·chee·va·tee
deck chairs *ležaljka* ① le·zhal'·ka
deep *dubok* ① doo·bawk
deforestation *krčenje šuma* ⓝ kr·che·nye shoo·ma
degrees (temperature) *stupnjevi* ⓜ pl stoop·nye·vee
delay *zakašnjenje* ① za·kash·nye·nye
delicatessen *delikatese* ① pl de·lee·ka·te·se
deliver *dostaviti/dostavljati* daw·sta·vee·tee/daw·stav·lya·tee
democracy *demokracija* ① de·maw·kra·tsee·ya

demonstration (protest) *demonstracija* ⓕ de·mawn·*stra*·tsee·ya

Denmark *Danska* ⓕ *dan*·ska

dental floss *konac za čišćenje zubi* ⓜ *kaw*·nats za *cheesh*·che·nye zoo·bee

dentist *zubar* ⓜ zoo·bar

deodorant *dezodorans* ⓜ de·zaw·*daw*·rans

depart (leave) *otići/odlaziti* aw·*tee*·chee/ *awd*·la·zee·tee

department store *robna kuća* ⓕ *rawb*·na *koo*·cha

departure *odlazak* ⓜ *awd*·la·zak

departure gate *izlaz* ⓜ *eez*·laz

deposit (bank) *depozit* ⓜ *de*·paw·zeet

deposit (surety) *jamstvo* ⓝ *yam*·stvaw

derailleur *mjenjač brzina na biciklu* ⓜ *mye*·nyach br·*zee*·na na bee·*tsee*·kloo

descendant *potomak* ⓜ *paw*·taw·mak

desert *pustinja* ⓕ *poo*·stee·nya

design *dizajn* ⓜ dee·*zain*

dessert *poslastice* ⓕ pl paw·*sla*·stee·tse

destination *odredište* ⓝ *aw*·dre·deesh·te

details *podatci* ⓝ pl paw·*dat*·tsee

diabetes *dijabetes* ⓜ dee·ya·*be*·tes

dial tone *znak slobodnog biranja na telefonu* ⓜ znak *slaw*·bawd·nawg *bee*·ra·nya na te·le·*faw*·noo

diaper *pelene* ⓕ pl pe·*le*·ne

diaphragm (body part) *dijafragma* ⓕ dee·ya·*frag*·ma

diarrhoea *proljev* ⓜ *praw*·lyev

diary *dnevnik* ⓜ *dnev*·neek

dice *kockice* ⓕ pl *kawts*·kee·tse

dictionary *rječnik* ⓜ *ryech*·neek

die *umrijeti/umirati* oo·*mree*·ye·tee/ oo·*mee*·ra·tee

diet *dijeta* ⓕ dee·*ye*·ta

different (not this one) *drugačiji* droo·*ga*·chee·yee

difficult *težak* *te*·zhak

dining car *kola za ručavanje* ⓝ *kaw*·la za roo·*cha*·va·nye

dinner *večera* ⓕ *ve*·che·ra

direct *direktan* dee·*rek*·tan

direct-dial *direktan poziv* ⓜ dee·*rek*·tan paw·zeev

direction *smjer* ⓜ smyer

director *director* ⓜ dee·*rek*·tawr

dirty *prljav* *pr*·lyav

disabled *onesposobljen* aw·ne·spaw·*sawb*·lyen

disco *disko* ⓜ *dee*·skaw

discount *popust* ⓜ *paw*·poost

discrimination *diskriminacija* ⓕ dee·skree·mee·na·*tsee*·ya

disease *bolest* ⓕ *baw*·lest

dish (food item) *jelo* ⓝ *ye*·law

dish (plate) *posuda* ⓕ *paw*·soo·da

disk (CD-ROM) *disk (CD-ROM)* ⓜ deesk (tse de rawm)

disk (floppy) *disketa* ⓕ dee·*ske*·ta

diving (underwater) *ronjenje* ⓝ *raw*·nye·nye

diving equipment *ronilačka oprema* ⓕ *raw*·nee·lach·ka *aw*·pre·ma

divorced (of man) *razveden* raz·*ve*·den

divorced (of woman) *razvedena* raz·ve·de·na

dizzy *ošamućen* aw·*sha*·moo·chen

do (u)činiti (oo·)*chee*·nee·tee

doctor (medical) *liječnik* ⓜ lee·*yech*·neek

documentary *dokumentarac* ⓜ daw·koo·men·*ta*·rats

dog *pas* ⓜ pas

dole (unemployment benefit) *potpora za nezoposlene* ⓕ *pawt*·paw·ra za ne·*za*·paw·sle·ne

doll *lutka* ⓕ *loot*·ka

dollar *dolar* ⓜ *daw*·lar

door *vrata* ⓝ *vra*·ta

dope (drugs) *trava* ⓕ *tra*·va

double *dvostruk* dvaw·strook

double bed *dupli krevet* ⓜ *doo*·plee *kre*·vet

double room *dvokrevetna soba* ⓕ *dvaw*·kre·vet·na *saw*·ba

down *dolje* *daw*·lye

downhill *nizbrdo* *neez*·br·daw

dozen *tucet* ⓜ *too*·tset

drama *drama* ⓕ *dra*·ma

dream *san* ⓜ san

dress *haljina* ⓕ *ha*·lyee·na

dried *sušeni* soo·*she*·nee

drink *piće* ⓝ *pee*·che

drink (alcoholic) *alkoholno piće* ⓝ *al*·haw·hawl·naw *pee*·che

drink (po)piti (*paw*·)*pee*·tee

drive *voziti* imp *vaw*·zee·tee

driving licence *vozačka dozvola* ⓕ *vaw*·zach·ka *dawz*·vaw·la

drug (illicit) *droga* ⓕ *draw*·ga

drug addiction *ovisnost o drogama* ⓕ aw·vee·snawst aw *draw*·ga·ma

drug dealer *trgovac drogama* ⓜ *tr*·gaw·vats *draw*·ga·ma

drug trafficking *trgovina drogama* ⓕ tr·*gaw*·vee·na *draw*·ga·ma

drug user *korisnik droga* ⓜ
kaw·ree·sneek *draw*·ga
drugs (illicit) *droge* ① pl *draw*·ge
drum (instrument) *bubanj* ⓜ *boo*·ban'
drunk *pijan* pee·yan
dry *suh* sooh
dry (o)sušiti (aw·)*soo*·shee·tee
duck *patka* ① *pa*·tka
dummy (pacifier) *duda* ① *doo*·da
DVD *DVD* ⓜ de ve de

E

each *svaki* ⓜ *sva*·kee
ear *uho* ⓝ *oo*·haw
early *rani* ra·nee
earn *zaraditi/zarađivati* za·ra·dee·tee/
za·ra·*jee*·va·tee
earplugs *čepovi za uši* ⓜ pl *che*·paw·vee
za *oo*·shee
earrings *naušnice* ① pl na·oosh·nee·tse
Earth *zemlja* ① *zem*·lya
earthquake *potres* ⓜ *paw*·tres
east *istok* ⓜ ee·stawk
Easter *uskrs* oos·krs
easy *jednostavan* yed·naw·sta·van
eat (po)jesti (paw·)ye·stee
economy class *drugi razred* ⓜ *droo*·gee
raz·red
ecstacy (drug) *ekstasi* ⓜ *ek*·sta·see
eczema *ekcem* ① ek·tsem
editor *urednik* ⓜ oo·red·neek
education *obrazovanje* ⓝ
aw·bra·zaw·*va*·nye
egg *jaje* ⓝ *yai*·e
eggplant *patlidžan* ⓜ pat·*lee*·jan
election *izbori* ⓜ pl *eez*·baw·ree
electricity *struja* ① *stroo*·ya
elevator *dizalo* ⓝ *dee*·za·law
email *e-mail* ⓝ ee·me·eel
embarrassed *posramljen* paw·sram·lyen
embassy *ambasada* ① am·ba·sa·da
emergency *hitan slučaj* ⓜ *hee*·tan *sloo*·chai
emergency department (hospital)
Odjel hitne pomoći ⓜ *aw*·dyel *heet* •ne
paw·maw·chee
emotional *emocionalan*
e·maw·tsee·aw·na·lan
employee *zaposlenik/zaposlenica* ⓜ/①
za·paw·*sle*·neek/za·paw·*sle*·nee·tsa
employer *poslodavac* ⓜ
paw·slaw·*da*·vats

empty *prazan* pra·zan
end *kraj* ⓜ krai
endangered species *ugrožene vrste* ① pl
oo·*graw*·zhe·ne *vr*·ste
engaged (marriage) *vjeren* vye·ren
engaged (phone) *zauzet* za·oo·zet
engagement *vjerenje* ⓝ *vye*·re·nye
engine *motor* ⓜ *maw*·tawr
engineer *inženjer* ⓜ een·*zhe*·nyer
engineering *inženjerstvo* ⓝ
een·zhe·*nyer*·stvaw
England *Engleska* ① en·gle·ska
English *engleski* en·gle·skee
enjoy (oneself) *provesti/provoditi se*
praw·ve·stee/praw·*vaw*·dee·tee se
enough *dosta* daw·sta
enter *ući/ulaziti* oo·chee/oo·la·*zee*·tee
entertainment guide *vodič o zbivan-
jima u svijetu razonode* ⓜ *vaw*·deech
aw *zbee*·va·nyee·ma oo svee·*sye*·too
ra·*zaw*·naw·de
entry *ulaz* ⓜ oo·laz
envelope *omotnica* ① *aw*·mawt·nee·tsa
environment *prirodna okolina* ①
pree·*rawd*·na aw·kaw·*lee*·na
epilepsy *padavica* ① pa·da·vee·tsa
equal opportunity *jednake
mogućnosti* ① pl *yed*·na·ke
maw·*gooch*·naw·stee
equality *ravnopravnost* ①
rav·naw·prav·nawst
equipment *oprema* ① *aw*·pre·ma
escalator *pokretne stepenice* ① pl
paw·kret·ne ste·pe·nee·tse
estate agency *agencija za prodaju
nekretnina* ① a·*gen*·tsee·ya za
praw·dai·oo ne·kret·*nee*·na
euro *euro* ① e·oo·raw
Europe *Europa* ① e·oo·raw·pa
evening *večer* ① ve·cher
every *svaki* ⓜ *sva*·kee
everyone *svatko* svat·kaw
everything *sve* sve
exactly *točno* tawch·naw
excellent *odličan* awd·lee·chan
excess (baggage) *višak prtljage* ⓜ
vee·shak prt·lya·ge
exchange *razmjena* ① *raz*·mye·na
exchange *razmijeniti/razmijenjivati*
raz·mee·ye·nee·tee/raz·mye·*nyee*·va·tee
exchange rate *tečaj razmjene* ⓜ te·chai
raz·mye·ne
excluded *isključen* ees·*klyoo*·chen

exhaust (car) *ispušni plinovi* ⓜ
ee-spoosh-nee plee-naw-vee
exhibition *izložba* ① eez-lawzh-ba
exit *izlaz* ⓜ eez-laz
expensive *skup* skoop
experience *iskustvo* ⓝ ees-koost-vaw
exploitation *iskorištavanje* ⓝ
ee-skaw-reesh-ta-va-nye
express *brzi* br-zee
express (mail) *ekspres pošta* ① eks-pres
pawsh-ta
express mail *poslano expres poštom* ⓜ
paw-sla-naw eks-pres pawsh-tawm
extension (visa) *produženje* ⓝ
praw-doo-zhe-nye
eye *oko* ⓝ aw-kaw
eye drops *kapi za oči* ① pl ka-pee za
aw-chee
eyes *oči* ① pl aw-chee

F

fabric *tkanina* ① tka-nee-na
face *lice* ⓝ lee-tse
face cloth *ručnik za lice* ⓜ rooch-neek
za lee-tse
factory *tvornica* ① tvawr-nee-tsa
factory worker *radnik u tvornici* ⓜ
rad-neek oo tvawr-nee-tsee
fall *pad* ⓜ pad
fall (autumn) *jesen* ① ye-sen
family *obitelj* ① aw-bee-tel'
family name *prezime* ⓝ pre-zee-me
fan (machine) *ventilator* ⓜ ven-tee-la-tawr
fan (sport, etc) *navijač* ⓜ na-vee-yach
fanbelt *remen za ventilator* ⓜ re-men za
ven-tee-la-tawr
far *daleko* da-le-kaw
fare *cijena vožnje* ① tsee-ye-na vawzh-nye
farm *farma* ① far-ma
farmer *poljodjelac* ⓜ paw-lyaw-dye-lats
fashion *moda* ① maw-da
fast *brz* brz
fat *debeo* de-be-aw
father *otac* ⓜ aw-tats
father-in-law (of husband) *punac* ⓜ
poo-nats
father-in-law (of wife) *svekar* sve-kar
faucet *slavina* ① sla-vee-na
faulty *pokvaren* pawk-va-ren
fax machine *telefaks* ⓜ te-le-faks
February *veljača* ① ve-lya-cha

feed (na)*hraniti* (na-)hra-nee-tee
feel (touch) *dirnuti/dirati* deer-noo-tee/
dee-ra-tee
feeling *osjećaj* ⓜ aw-sye-chai
feelings *osjećaji* ⓜ pl aw-sye-chai-ee
female *ženski* zhen-skee
fence *ograda* ① aw-gra-da
fencing (sport) *mačevanje* ⓝ
ma-che-va-nye
ferry *trajekt* ⓜ trai-ekt
festival *festival* ⓜ fe-stee-val
fever *groznica* ① aw-gra-znee-tsa
few *nekoliko* ne-kaw-leek-aw
fiancé *vjerenik* ⓜ vye-re-neek
fiancée *vjerenica* ① vye-re-nee-tsa
fiction (genre) *fikcija* ① feek-tsee-ya
fig *smokva* ① smaw-kva
fight (battle) *borba* ① bawr-ba
fight (fisticuffs) *tuča* ① too-cha
fill (na)*puniti* (na-)poo-nee-tee
film (cinema) *film* ⓜ feelm
film (for camera) *film za foto-aparat* ⓜ
feelm za faw-taw-a-pa-rat
film speed *brzina filma* ① br-zee-na feel-ma
filtered *filtriran* feel-tree-ran
find *naći/nalaziti* na-chee/na-la-zee-tee
fine (penalty) *novčana globa* ①
nawv-cha-na glaw-ba
fine (delicate) *sitan* see-tan
fine (weather) *vedar* ve-dar
finger *prst* ⓜ prst
finish *završiti/završavati* za-vr-shee-tee/
za-vr-sha-va-tee
Finland *Finska* ① feen-ska
fire *požar* ⓜ paw-zhar
firewood *drvo za ogrjev* ⓝ dr-vaw za
aw-gryev
first *prvi* pr-vee
first class *prvi razred* ⓜ pr-vee raz-red
first-aid kit *pribor za prvu pomoć* ⓜ
pree-bawr za pr-voo paw-mawch
fish *riba* ① ree-ba
fish shop *prodavaonica ribe* ①
praw-da-va-aw-nee-tsa ree-be
fisherman *ribar* ⓜ ree-bar
fishing *ribolov* ⓜ ree-baw-lawv
fishing village *ribarsko selo* ⓝ
ree-bar-skaw se-law
fishmonger *trgovac ribom* ⓜ tr-gaw-vats
ree-bawm
flag *zastava* ① za-sta-va
flannel *flanel* ⓜ fla-nel
flash (camera) *blic* ⓜ bleets

flashlight *(ručna) svjetiljka* ① *(rooch-*na) svye-teel'-ka
flat *plosnat* plaw-snat
flat (apartment) *stan* ⓜ stan
flea *buha* ① boo-ha
flea market *buvljak* ⓜ boov-lyak
flight *let* ⓜ let
flood *poplava* ① paw-pla-va
floor (ground) *pod* ⓜ pawd
floor (storey) *kat* ⓜ kat
florist *cvjećara* ① tsvye-cha-ra
flour *brašno* ① brash-naw
flower *cvijet* ⓜ tsvee-yet
flu *gripa* ① gree-pa
fly (po)letjeti *(paw-)let-*ye-tee
foggy *maglovit* ma-glaw-veet
follow *pratiti* imp pra-tee-tee
food *hrana* ① hra-na
food supplies *zalihe hrane* ① pl za-lee-he hra-ne
foot *stopalo* ⓜ staw-pa-law
football (soccer) *nogomet* ⓜ naw-gaw-met
footpath *pločnik* ⓜ plawch-neek
foreign *strani* stra-nee
forest *šuma* ① shoo-ma
forever *zauvijek* za-oo-vee-yek
forget *zaboraviti/zaboravljati* za-baw-ra-vee-tee/za-baw-rav-lya-tee
forgive *oprostiti/opraštati* aw-praw-stee-tee/aw-prash-ta-tee
fork *viljuška* ① vee-lyoosh-ka
fortnight *dva tjedna* ① dva tyed-na
fortune-teller *vrač* ⓜ vrach
foul *prekršaj* ⓜ pre-kr-shai
foyer *foaje* ⓜ faw-ai-e
fragile *lomljiv* lawm-lyeev
France *Francuska* ① fran-tsoo-ska
free (available) *slobodan* slaw-baw-dan
free (gratis) *besplatan* be-spla-tan
free (not bound) *nevezan* ne-ve-zan
freeze *zamrznuti/zamrzavati* za-mr-znoo-tee/za-mr-za-va-tee
fresh *svjež* svyezh
Friday *petak* ⓜ pe-tak
fridge *hladnjak* ⓜ hlad-nyak
fried *prženi* pr-zhe-nee
friend *prijatelj/prijateljica* ⓜ/① pree-ya-tel'/pree-ya-te-lyee-tsa
from *iz • od* eez • awd
frost *mraz* ⓜ mraz
frozen *zaleđen* za-le-jen
fruit *voće* ① vaw-che

fruit picking *branje voća* ① bra-nye vaw-cha
fry *(is)pržiti* (ees-)pr-zhee-tee
frying pan *tava* ① ta-va
full *pun* poon
full-time *punim radnim vremenom* poo-neem rad-neem vre-me-nawm
fun *zabavan* za-ba-van
(have) fun *uživati* imp oo-zhee-va-tee
funeral *pogreb* ⓜ paw-greb
funny *smješan* smye-shan
furniture *namještaj* ⓜ na-mye-shtai
future *budućnost* ① boo-dooch-nawst

G

game *igra* ① ee-gra
game (football) *utakmica* ① oo-tak-mee-tsa
garage *garaža* ① ga-ra-zha
garbage *smeće* ⓜ sme-che
garbage can *kanta za smeće* ① kan-ta za sme-che
garden *vrt* ⓜ vrt
gardener *vrtlar* ⓜ vrt-lar
gardening *vrtlarstvo* ① vrt-lars-tvaw
garlic *češnjak* ⓜ chesh-nyak
gas (for cooking) *plin* ⓜ pleen
gas (petrol) *benzin* ⓜ ben-zeen
gas cartridge *plinski uložak* ⓜ pleen-skee oo-law-zhak
gastroenteritis *gastroenteritis* ⓜ ga-straw-en-te-ree-tees
gate (airport, etc) *izlaz* ⓜ eez-laz
gauze *gaza* ① ga-za
gay *homoseksualan* haw-maw-sek-soo-a-lan
Germany *Njemačka* ① nye-mach-ka
get *dobiti/dobivati* daw-bee-tee/daw-bee-va-tee
get off (a train, etc) *sići/silaziti sa* see-chee/see-la-zee-tee sa
gift *dar* ⓜ dar
gig *nastup* ⓜ na-stoop
gin *džin* ⓜ jeen
girl *djevojčica* ① dye-voy-chee-tsa
girlfriend *cura* ① tsoo-ra
give *dati/davati* da-tee/da-va-tee
given name *krsno ime* ⓜ kr-snaw ee-me
glandular fever *mononukleoza* ① maw-naw-nook-le-aw-za
glass (material) *staklo* ⓜ sta-klo
glass (receptacle) *čaša* ① cha-sha

glasses (spectacles) naočale ① pl
na·aw·cha·le

glove(s) rukavica/e ① sg/① pl
roo·ka·vee·tsa/e

glue ljepilo ⓝ lye·pee·law

go ići imp ee·chee

go out izaći/izlaziti ee·za·chee/eez·la·zee·tee

go out with izaći/izlaziti sa ee·za·chee/
eez·la·zee·tee sa

goal gol ⓜ gawl

goalkeeper vratar ⓜ vra·tar

goat jarac ⓜ ya·rats

god bog ⓜ bawg

god (general) bog ⓜ bawg

goggles (skiing) naočale za skijanje ① pl
na·aw·cha·le za skee·ya·nye

goggles (swimming) zaštitne naočale za
plivanje ① pl zash·teet·ne na·aw·cha·le
za plee·va·nye

gold zlato ⓝ zla·taw

golf golf ⓜ gawlf

golf ball loptica za golf ① lawp·tee·tsa
za gawlf

golf course teren za golf ⓜ te·ren za gawlf

good dobar daw·bar

Goodbye. Zbogom. zbaw·gawm

government vlada ① vla·da

gram gram ⓜ gram

grandchild unuk/unuka ⓜ/①
oo·nook/oo·noo·ka

grandfather djed ⓜ dyed

grandmother baka ① ba·ka

grapefruit grejpfrut ⓜ greyp·froot

grapes grožđe ⓝ grawzh·je

grass (lawn) trava ① tra·va

grateful zahvalan za·hva·lan

grave (tomb) grob ⓜ grawb

gray siv ⓜ seev

great (fantastic) krasno kra·snaw

green zelen ze·len

greengrocer trgovac povrćem ⓜ
tr·gaw·vats paw·vr·chem

grey siv ⓜ seev

grocery namirnica ① na·meer·nee·tsa

groundnut kikiriki ⓜ kee·kee·ree·kee

grow (po)rasti (paw·)ra·stee

g-string g-string ⓜ ge·streeng

guaranteed garantiran ga·ran·tee·ran

guess pogoditi/pogađati
paw·gaw·dee·tee/paw·ga·ja·tee

guesthouse privatni smještaj za najam ⓜ
pree·vat·nee smyesh·tai za nai·am

guide (audio) audio vodič ⓜ a·oo·dee·aw
vaw·deech

guide (person) vodič ⓜ vaw·deech

guide dog pas vodič ⓜ pas vaw·deech

guidebook vodič ⓜ vaw·deech

guided tour ekskurzija s vodičem ①
ek·skoor·zee·ya s vaw·dee·chem

guilty kriv kreev

guitar gitara ① gee·ta·ra

gums (teeth) desni ① pl de·snee

gun puška ① poosh·ka

gym (place) teretana ① te·re·ta·na

gymnastics gimnastika ① geem·na·stee·ka

gynaecologist ginekolog ⓜ
gee·ne·kaw·lawg

H

hair (body) dlaka ① dla·ka

hair (head) kosa ① kaw·sa

hairbrush četka za kosu ① chet·ka za
kaw·soo

haircut šišanje ① shee·sha·nye

hairdresser frizer ⓜ free·zer

halal halal ha·lal

half polovina ① paw·law·vee·na

ham šunka ① shoon·ka

hammer čekić ⓜ che·keech

hammock viseća mreža za ležanje ①
vee·se·cha mre·zha za le·zha·nye

hand ruka ① roo·ka

handbag ručna torbica ① rooch·na
tawr·bee·tsa

handball rukomet ⓜ roo·kaw·met

handicrafts ručni radovi ⓜ pl rooch·nee
ra·daw·vee

handkerchief rupčić ⓜ roop·cheech

handlebars volan bicikla ⓜ vaw·lan
bee·tsee·kla

handmade ručno izrađen rooch·naw
eez·ra·jen

handsome zgodan zgaw·dan

happy sretan sre·tan

harassment uznemiravanje ⓝ
ooz·ne·mee·ra·va·nye

harbour luka ① loo·ka

hard (not easy) težak te·zhak

hard (not soft) tvrd tvrd

hardware store prodavaonica metalne i
tehničke robe ① praw·da·va·aw·nee·tsa
me·tal·ne ee teh·neech·ke raw·be

hash hašiš ⓜ ha·sheesh

hat šešir ⓜ she·sheer

have imati imp ee·ma·tee

hay fever *peludna groznica* ① pe·lood·na grawz·nee·tsa
hazelnut *ljéšnjak* ⑩ lyesh·nyak
he *on* ⑩ awn
head *glava* ① gla·va
headache *glavobolja* ① gla·vaw·baw·lya
headlights *prednje svjetlo* ⑩ pred·nye svyet·law
health *zdravlje* ⑩ zdrav·lye
hear *čuti* perf choo·tee
hearing aid *slušni aparat* ⑩ sloosh·nee a·pa·rat
heart *srce* ⑩ sr·tse
heart attack *srčani udar* ⑩ sr·cha·nee oo·dar
heart condition *poremećaj srca* ⑩ paw·re·me·chai sr·tsa
heat *vrućina* ① vroo·chee·na
heated *zagrijan* za·gree·yan
heater *grijač* ⑩ gree·yach
heating *grijanje* ⑩ gree·ya·nye
heavy *težak* te·zhak
Hello. (answering telephone) *Halo.* ha·law
Hello. (not answering telephone) *Zdravo.* zdra·vaw
helmet *kaciga* ① ka·tsee·ga
help *pomoć* ① paw·mawch
help *pomoći/pomagati* paw·maw·chee/ paw·ma·ga·tee
Help! *Upomoć!* oo·paw·mawch
hepatitis *hepatitis* ⑩ he·pa·tee·tees
her *njen/njena/njeno* ⑩/①/⑩ nyen/ nye·na/nyen·naw
herb *biljka* ① beel'·ka
herbalist *travar* ⑩ tra·var
here *ovdje* awv·dye
heroin *heroin* ⑩ he·raw·een
high *visok* vee·sawk
high school *srednja škola* ① sred·nya shkaw·la
highchair *visoka stolica za bebe* ① vee·saw·ka staw·lee·tsa za be·be
highway *autoput* ⑩ a·oo·taw·poot
hike *(pro)pješačiti* (praw·)pye·sha·chee·tee
hiking *pješačenje* ⑩ pye·sha·che·nye
hiking boots *gležnjače* ① pl glezh·nya·che
hiking route *pješački put* ⑩ pye·shach·kee poot
hill *brežuljak* ⑩ bre·zhoo·lyak
hire *iznajmiti/iznajmljivati* eez·nai·mee·tee/eez·naim·lyee·va·tee
his *njegov/njegova/negovo* ⑩/①/⑩ nye·gawv/nye·gawv·va/nye·gawv·vaw

historical *povijesni* paw·vee·ye·snee
history *povijest* ① paw·vee·yest
hitchhike *stopirati* imp staw·pee·ra·tee
HIV *HIV* ⑩ heev
hockey *hokej* ⑩ haw·key
holiday (day off) *blagdan* ⑩ blag·dan
holidays *praznici* ⑩ pl praz·nee·tsee
Holy Week *veliki tjedan* ⑩ ve·lee·kee tye·dan
home *dom* ⑩ dawm
(at) home *kući* koo·chee
homeless *koji je bez doma* ⑩ koy·ee ye bez daw·ma
homemaker *domaćica* ① daw·ma·chee·tsa
homeopathy *homeopatija* ① haw·me·aw·pa·tee·ya
homosexual *homoseksualac/ homoseksualka* ⑩/① haw·maw·sek·soo·a·lats/ haw·maw·sek·soo·al·ka
honey *med* ⑩ med
honeymoon *medeni mjesec* ⑩ me·de·nee mye·sets
horoscope *horoskop* ⑩ haw·raw·skawp
horse *konj* ⑩ kawn'
horse riding *jahanje konja* ⑩ ya·ha·nye kaw·nya
hospital *bolnica* ① bawl·nee·tsa
hospitality *gostoprimstvo* gaw·staw·preems·tvaw
hot *vruć* vrooch
hot water *topla voda* ① taw·pla vaw·da
hotel *hotel* ⑩ haw·tel
hour *sat* ⑩ sat
house *kuća* ① koo·cha
housework *kućni poslovi* ⑩ pl kooch·nee paw·slaw·vee
how *kako* ka·kaw
how much *koliko* kaw·lee·kaw
hug *(za)grliti* (za·)gr·lee·tee
huge *ogroman* aw·graw·man
human resources *ljudski resursi* ⑩ pl lyood·skee re·soor·see
human rights *ljudska prava* ⑩ pl lyood·ska pra·va
humanities *društvene znanosti* ⑩ pl droosht·ve·ne zna·naw·stee
hundred *sto* staw
Hungary *Mađarska* ① ma·jar·ska
hungry (to be) *biti gladan/gladna* ⑩/① bee·tee gla·dan/gla·dna
hunting *lov na životinje* ⑩ lawv na zhee·vaw·tee·nye

hurt (emotionally) *uvrijediti/vrijeđati*
oo-vree-*ye*-dee-tee/vree-*ye*-ja-tee
hurt (physically) *raniti/ranjavati*
ra-nee-tee/ra-*nya*-va-tee
husband *muž* ⓜ moozh

I

I *ja* ya
ice *led* ⓜ led
ice cream *sladoled* ⓜ *sla*-daw-led
ice hockey *hokej na ledu* ⓜ *haw*-key
na *le*-doo
ice-cream parlour *sladoledarna* ⓕ
sla-daw-le-*dar*-na
identification *identifikacija* ⓕ
ee-den-tee-fee-ka-*tsee*-ya
identification card (ID) *osobna iskaznica* ⓕ
aw-sawb-na ee-*skaz*-nee-tsa
idiot *budala* ⓕ boo-*da*-la
if *ako* a-kaw
ill *bolestan* baw-le-stan
Illyrians *Iliri* ⓟ pl ee-*lee*-ree
immigration *imigracija* ⓕ
ee-mee-*gra*-tsee-ya
important *važan* va-zhan
impossible *nemoguć* ne-maw-gooch
in *u · na · po · kroz* oo · na · paw · krawz
in a hurry *užurban* oo-zhoor-ban
in front of *pred* pred
included *uključen* ook-lyoo-chen
income tax *porez na dohodak* ⓜ *paw*-rez
na *daw*-haw-dak
independence *nezavisnost* ⓕ
ne-za-*vee*-snawst
India *Indija* ⓕ *een*-dee-ya
indicator (car) *žmigavac* ⓜ *zhmee*-ga-vats
indigestion *probavne smetnje* ⓕ pl
praw-bav-ne smet-nye
indoor *unutrašnji* oo-noo-trash-nyee
industry *industrija* ⓕ een-*doo*-stree-ya
infection *zaraza* ⓕ za-*ra*-za
inflammation *upala* ⓕ *oo*-pa-la
influenza *gripa* ⓕ *gree*-pa
information *informacije* ⓕ pl
een-fawr-*ma*-tsee-ye
ingredient *sastojak* ⓜ *sa*-stoy-ak
inject *ubrizgati/ubrizgavati*
oo-breez-ga-tee/oo-breez-*ga*-va-tee
injection *injekcija* ⓕ ee-*nyek*-tsee-ya
injured *povrijeđen* ⓜ paw-vree-*ye*-jen
injury *povreda* ⓕ *paw*-vre-da

inner tube *zračnica* ⓕ *zrach*-nee-tsa
innocent *nevin* ⓜ ne-veen
inside *unutra* oo-*noo*-tra
instructor *instruktor* ⓜ een-*strook*-tawr
insurance *osiguranje* ⓕ aw-see-goo-*ra*-nye
interesting *zanimljiv* za-*neem*-lyeev
intermission *prekid* ⓜ *pre*-keed
international *međunarodan*
me-joo-*na*-raw-dan
Internet *internet* ⓜ *een*-ter-net
Internet café *internet kafić* ⓜ *een*-ter-net
ka-feech
interpreter *tumač* ⓜ *too*-mach
interview *intervju* ⓜ een-ter-*vyoo*
invite *pozvati/pozivati* pawz-va-tee/
paw-*zee*-va-tee
Ireland *Irska* ⓕ *eer*-ska
iron (for clothes) *pegla* ⓕ *pe*-gla
island *otok* ⓜ *aw*-tawk
Israel *Izrael* ⓜ *ee*-zra-el
it *ovo/to* ⓜ *aw*-vaw/taw
IT *Informacijska tehnologija* ⓕ
een-fawr-*ma*-tseey-ska
teh-naw-*law*-gee-ya
Italy *Italija* ⓕ ee-*ta*-lee-ya
itch *svrbež* ⓜ svr-bezh
itemised *nabrojan* ⓜ *na*-broy-an
itinerary *plan puta* ⓜ plan *poo*-ta
IUD *spirala* ⓕ spee-*ra*-la

J

jacket *jakna* ⓕ *yak*-na
jail *zatvor* ⓜ *zat*-vawr
jam *džem* ⓜ jem
January *siječanj* ⓜ see-*ye*-chan'
Japan *Japan* ⓜ *ya*-pan
jar *staklenka* ⓕ *sta*-klen-ka
jaw *čeljust* ⓕ *che*-lyoost
jealous *ljubomoran* lyoo-baw-maw-ran
jeans *traperice* ⓕ pl *tra*-pe-ree-tse
jeep *džip* ⓜ jeep
jet lag *umor poslije dugog leta* ⓜ
oo-mawr paw-slee-ye *doo*-gawg *le*-ta
jewellery *nakit* ⓜ *na*-keet
Jewish *Židovski* zhee-dawv-skee
job *posao* ⓜ *paw*-sa-aw
jogging *trčanje* ⓝ *tr*-cha-nye
joke *šala* ⓕ *sha*-la
journalist *novinar/novinarka* ⓜ/ⓕ
naw-vee-nar/naw-vee-nar-ka
journey *putovanje* ⓝ poo-taw-*va*-nye

judge *sudac* ⓜ soo-dats
juice *sok* ⓜ sawk
July *srpanj* ⓜ sr-pan'
jump *skočiti/skakati* skaw-chee-tee/ska-ka-tee
jumper (sweater) *džemper* ⓜ jem-per
jumper leads *kablovi za punjenje akumulatora* ⓜ pl ka-blaw-vee za poo-nye-nye a-koo-moo-*la*-taw-ra
June *lipanj* ⓜ lee-pan'

K

karst *krš* ⓜ krsh
ketchup *ketchup* ⓜ ke-chap
key *ključ* ⓜ klyooch
keyboard (computer) *tastatura* ⓕ ta-sta-*too*-ra
keyboard (instrument) *klavijatura* ⓕ kla-vee-ya-*too*-ra
kick *šutnuti/šutirati shoot*-noo-tee/shoo-*tee*-ra-tee
kidney *bubreg* ⓜ boo-breg
kilo *kila* ⓕ *kee*-la
kilogram *kilogram* ⓜ kee-*law*-gram
kilometre *kilometar* ⓜ kee-*law*-me-tar
kind (nice) *prijazan* pree-ya-zan
kindergarten *vrtić za djecu* ⓜ vr-teech za dye-tsoo
king *kralj* ⓜ kral'
kiosk *kiosk* ⓜ kee-awsk
kiss *poljubac* ⓜ paw-lyoo-bats
kiss *(po)ljubiti* (paw-)lyoo-bee-tee
kitchen *kuhinja* ⓕ koo-hee-nya
knee *koljeno* ⓕ kaw-lye-naw
knife *nož* ⓜ nawzh
know *(sa)znati (sa*)-zna-tee
kosher *košer* ⓜ kaw-sher

L

labourer *radnik* ⓜ rad-neek
lace *čipka* ⓕ cheep-ka
lake *jezero* ⓕ ye-ze-raw
lamb (animal) *janje* ⓕ ya-nye
lamb (meat) *janjetina* ⓕ ya-nye-tee-na
land *zemlja* zem-lya
landlady *gazdarica* ⓕ gaz-da-ree-tsa
landlord *gazda* ⓜ gaz-da
language *jezik* ⓜ ye-zeek
laptop *prenosivi računar* ⓜ pre-*naw*-see-vee ra-choo-nar

large *krupan* kroo-pan
last (previous) *predhodni* pred-hawd-nee
last (week) *prošli* prawsh-lee
late *kasan* ka-san
later *kasnije* ka-snee-ye
laugh *(na)smijati se* (na-)smee-ya-tee se
laundrette *automatska praonica* ⓕ a-oo-*taw*-mat-ska pra-aw-nee-tsa
laundry (clothes) *pranje rublja* ⓝ pra-nye roob-lya
laundry (place) *praonica* ⓕ pra-aw-nee-tsa
laundry (room) *soba za pranje rublja* ⓕ saw-ba za pra-nye roob-lya
law *zakon* ⓜ za-kawn
law (study, professsion) *pravo* ⓝ pra-vaw
lawyer *pravnik* ⓜ prav-neek
laxative *laksativ* ⓜ lak-sa-teev
lazy *lijen* lee-yen
leader *čelnik* ⓜ chel-neek
leaf *list* ⓜ leest
learn *(na)učiti* (na-)oo-chee-tee
leather *koža* ⓕ kaw-zha
lecturer *nastavnik* ⓜ na-stav-neek
ledge *izbočina* ⓕ eez-baw-chee-na
leek *poriluk* ⓜ paw-ree-look
left (direction) *lijevi* lee-ye-vee
left luggage *odložena prtljaga* ⓕ awd-law-zhe-na prt-lya-ga
left luggage (office) *ured za odlaganje prtljage* ⓜ oo-red za awd-la-ga-nye prt-*lya*-ge
left-wing *ljevičarski* ⓜ lye-vee-char-skee
leg *noga* ⓕ naw-ga
legal *zakonit* za-kaw-neet
legislation *zakonodavstvo* ⓝ za-kaw-naw-davs-tvaw
legume *mahunar* ⓜ ma-hoo-nar
lemon *limun* ⓜ lee-moon
lemonade *limunada* ⓕ lee-moo-*na*-da
lens *leća* ⓕ le-cha
Lent *post* ⓜ pawst
lentil *leća* ⓕ le-cha
lesbian *lezbijka* ⓕ lez-beey-ka
less *manje* ma-nye
letter (mail) *pismo* ⓝ pee-smaw
lettuce *zelena salata* ⓕ ze-le-na sa-la-ta
liar *lažljivac/lažljivica* ⓜ/ⓕ lazh-lyee-vats/lazh-lyee-vee-tsa
library *knjižnica* ⓕ knyeezh-nee-tsa
lice *uši* ⓕ oo-shee
licence *dozvola* ⓕ dawz-vaw-la
licence-plate number *broj registarske tablice* ⓜ broy re-gee-star-ske ta-blee-tse

lie (not stand) *leći/ležati* le-chee/le-zha-tee
life *život* m zhee-vawt
life jacket *prsluk za spasavanje* m
   pr-slook za spa-*sa*-va-nye
lift (elevator) *dizalo* n dee-za-law
light (illumination) *svjetlost* ① svyet-lawst
light (lamp) *svjetiljka* ① svye-teel'-ka
light (not heavy) *lagan* la-gan
light (of colour) *svjetao* svye-ta-aw
light bulb *žarulja* ① zha-roo-lya
light meter *svjetlomjer* m svyet-law-myer
lighter *peniša* m pe-nee-sha
lighter (cigarette) *upaljač* m oo-pa-lyach
like (appeal to) *dopasti/dopadati se*
   daw-*pa*-stee/daw-pa-da-tee se
like (a person) *voljeti* imp vaw-lye-tee
like (want) *(po)željeti* (paw)zhe-lye-tee
linen (material) *laneno platno* n
   la-ne-naw plat-naw
linen (sheets etc) *posteljina* ①
   paw-ste-*lyee*-na
lip balm *balzam za usne* m *bal*-zam za
   oo-sne
lips *usne* ① pl oo-sne
lipstick *ruž za usne* m roozh za oo-sne
liquor store *prodavaonica alkohola* ①
   praw-da-va-*aw*-nee-tsa al-kaw-haw-la
listen (to) *(po)slušati* (paw)*sloo*-sha-tee
little *mali* ma-lee
little (not much) *malo* ma-law
live (somewhere) *stanovati* imp
   sta-*naw*-va-tee
liver *jetra* ① ye-tra
lizard *gušter* m goosh-ter
local *mjesni* mye-snee
lock *brava* ① bra-va
lock *zaključati/zaključavati*
   zak-lyoo-cha-tee/zak-lyoo-*cha*-va-tee
locked *zaključan* zak-lyoo-chan
lollies *bomboni* m pl bawm-*baw*-nee
long *dugačak* doo-ga-chak
look *(po)gledati* (paw-)gle-da-tee
look after *(po)brinuti se za*
   (paw-)bree-noo-tee se za
look for *(po)tražiti* (paw-)*tra*-zhee-tee
lookout *vidik* m vee-deek
loose *labav* ① la-bav
loose change *sitniš* m *seet*-neesh
lose (iz)gubiti (eez-)*goo*-bee-tee
lost *izgubljen* eez-goob-lyen
lost property office *ured za izgubljene
   stvari* m oo-red za eez-goob-lye-ne
   stva-ree

(a) lot *puno* n poo-naw
loud *glasan* m gla-san
love *ljubav* ① lyoo-bav
love *voljeti* imp vaw-lye-tee
lover *ljubavnik/ljubavnica* m ∕ ①
   lyoo-bav-neek/lyoo-bav-nee-tsa
low *nizak* nee-zak
lubricant *lubrikant* m loo-bree-kant
luck *sreća* ① sre-cha
lucky *sretan* sre-tan
luggage *prtljaga* ① prt-lya-ga
luggage lockers *pretinac za
   odlaganje prtljage* m pre-tee-nats za
   awd-la-ga-nye prt-lya-ge
luggage tag *etiketa za prtljagu* ①
   e-tee-*ke*-ta za prt-lya-goo
lump *grumen* m groo-men
lunch *ručak* m roo-chak
lung *pluća* n pl ploo-cha
luxury *raskošan* ra-skaw-shan

M

Macedonia *Makedonija* ①
   ma-ke-daw-nee-ya
machine *stroj* m stroy
magazine *magazin* m ma-ga-zeen
mail (letters, postal system) *pošta* ①
   pawsh-ta
mailbox *poštanski sandučić* m
   pawsh-tan-skee san-*doo*-cheech
main *glavni* glav-nee
main road *glavna ulica* ① glav-na oo-lee-tsa
make (bring about) *(na)praviti*
   (na-)pra-vee-tee
make (fabricate) *(u)činiti* (oo-)chee-nee-tee
make-up *šminka* ① shmeen-ka
mammogram *mamogram* m
   ma-maw-gram
man (human) *čovjek* m chaw-vyek
man (male person) *muškarac* m
   moosh-*ka*-rats
manager *menadžer* m me-na-jer
mandarin *mandarina* ① man-da-ree-na
mandolin *mandolina* ① man-daw-lee-na
manual worker *fizički radnik* m
   fee-zeech-kee rad-neek
many *mnogi* mnaw-gee
map (of country) *karta* ① kar-ta
map (of town) *plan grada* m plan gra-da
March *ožujak* m aw-zhoo-yak
margarine *margarin* m mar-ga-reen

marijuana *marihuana* ① ma·ree·hoo·*a*·na
marina *marina* ① ma·*ree*·na
marital status *bračno stanje* ⑩ *brach*·naw *sta*·nye
market *tržnica* ① *trzh*·nee·tsa
marmalade *marmelada* ① mar·me·*la*·da
marriage *brak* ⑩ brak
married (of man) *vjenčan* *vyen*·chan
married (of woman) *vjenčana* *vyen*·cha·na
marry *udati/udavati se* oo·*da*·va·tee/
oo·*da*·va·tee se
martial arts *borilačke vještine* ① pl
baw·ree·lach·ke vye·*shtee*·ne
mass (Catholic) *misa* ① *mee*·sa
massage *masaža* ① ma·*sa*·zha
masseur/masseuse *maser/maserka* ⑩/①
ma·*ser*/ma·*ser*·ka
mat *otirač* ⑩ aw·*tee*·rach
match (sports) *utakmica* ① oo·*tak*·mee·tsa
matches (for lighting) *šibice* ① pl
shee·bee·tse
mattress *madrac* ⑩ *mad*·rats
May *svibanj* ⑩ *svee*·ban'
maybe *možda* *mawzh*·da
mayonnaise *majoneza* ① mai·aw·*ne*·za
mayor *gradonačelnik* ⑩
gra·daw·*na*·chel·neek
me *me* mee
meal *ručak* ⑩ *roo*·chak
measles *ospice* ① pl aw·*spee*·tse
meat *meso* ⑩ *me*·saw
mechanic *automehaničar* ⑩
a·oo·taw·me·*ha*·nee·char
media *mediji* ⑩ pl *me*·dee·yee
medicine (medication) *lijekovi* ⑩ pl
lee·ye·kaw·vee
medicine (profession) *medicina* ①
me·dee·*tsee*·na
meditation *meditacija* ① me·dee·*ta*·tsee·ya
meet (for first time) *upoznati/upoznavati*
oo·*pawz*·na·tee/oo·pawz·*na*·va·tee
meet (run into) *sresti/sretati* *sre*·stee/
sre·ta·tee
melon *dinja* ① *dee*·nya
member *član/članica* ⑩/① chlan/
chlan·ee·tsa
menstruation *mjesečnica* ①
mye·sech·nee·tsa
menu *jelovnik* ⑩ *ye*·lawv·neek
message *poruka* ① *paw*·roo·ka
metal *metal* ⑩ *me*·tal
metre *metar* ⑩ *me*·tar
metro (train) *metro* ⑩ *me*·traw

metro station *metro stanica* ① *me*·traw
sta·nee·tsa
microwave (oven) *mikrovalna pećnica* ①
mee·kraw·val·na *pech*·nee·tsa
midday *podne* ⑩ *pawd*·ne
midnight *ponoć* ① *paw*·nawch
migraine *migrena* ① me·*gre*·na
military *vojska* ① *voy*·ska
military service *vojna obveza* ① *voy*·na
awb·ve·za
milk *mlijeko* ⑩ mlee·*ye*·kaw
millimetre *milimetar* ⑩ me·lee·*me*·tar
million *milijun* ⑩ mee·*lee*·yoon
mince *mljeveno meso* ⑩ *mlye*·ve·naw
me·saw
mineral water *mineralna voda* ①
mee·ne·ral·na *vaw*·da
minute *minuta* ① mee·*noo*·ta
mirror *ogledalo* ⑩ aw·*gle*·da·law
miscarriage *pobačaj* ⑩ *paw*·ba·chai
Miss *Gospođica* ① *gaw*·spaw·jee·tsa
miss (feel absence of) *nedostajati* imp
ne·*daw*·stai·a·tee
mistake *pogreška* ① *paw*·gresh·ka
mix (po)miješati (paw·)*mee*·ye·sha·tee
mobile phone *mobilni telefon* ⑩
maw·beel·nee te·*le*·fawn
modem *modem* ⑩ *maw*·dem
modern *suvremen* soo·*vre*·men
moisturiser *hidratantna krema* ①
hee·dra·*tant*·na *kre*·ma
monastery *samostan* ⑩ *sa*·maw·stan
Monday *ponedjeljak* ⑩ paw·ne·*dye*·lyak
money *novac* ⑩ *naw*·vats
monk *redovnik* ⑩ re·*dawv*·neek
Montenegro *Crna Gora* ① *tsr*·na *gaw*·ra
month *mjesec* ⑩ *mye*·sets
monument *spomenik* ⑩ *spaw*·me·neek
moon *mjesec* ⑩ *mye*·sets
more *više* *vee*·she
morning *jutro* ⑩ *yoo*·traw
morning sickness *trudnička jutarnja
mučnina* ① *trood*·neech·ka *yoo*·tar·nya
mooch·nee·na
mosque *džamija* ① *ja*·mee·ya
mosquito *komarac* ⑩ *kaw*·ma·rats
mosquito coil *zapaljivo sredstvo protiv
komaraca* ① za·*pa*·lyee·vaw *sreds*·tvaw
praw·teev kaw·*ma*·ra·tsa
mosquito net *mreža za komarce* ①
mre·zha za kaw·*mar*·tse
motel *motel* ⑩ *maw*·tel
mother *majka* ① *mai*·ka

mother-in-law (of husband) *punica* ⓕ
poo-nee-tsa
mother-in-law (of wife) *svekrva* ⓕ sve-krva
motorbike *motocikl* ⓜ maw-taw-tsee-kl
motorboat *motorni čamac* ⓜ
maw-tawr-nee cha-mats
motorcycle *motocikl* ⓜ maw-taw-tsee-kl
motorway (tollway) *autoput na kojem
se plaća cestarina* ⓜ a-oo-taw-poot na
koy-em se pla-cha tse-sta-ree-na
mountain *planina* ⓕ pla-nee-na
mountain bike *brdski bicikl* ⓜ brd-skee
bee-tsee-kl
mountain path *brdska staza* ⓕ brd-ska
sta-za
mountain range *gorski lanac* ⓜ gawr-skee
la-nats
mountaineering *alpinizam* ⓜ
al-pee-nee-zam
mouse *miš* ⓜ meesh
mouth *usta* ⓕ oo-sta
movie *film* ⓜ feelm
Mr *Gospodin* ⓜ gaw-spaw-deen
Mrs *Gospođa* ⓕ gaw-spaw-ja
Ms *G'đa* ⓕ g-ja
mud *blato* ⓝ bla-taw
muesli *muesli* ⓜ pl moo-zlee
mum *mama* ⓕ ma-ma
mumps *zaušnjaci* ⓜ pl za-oosh-nya-tsee
murder *ubojstvo* ⓝ oo-boys-tvaw
murder *ubiti/ubijati* oo-bee-tee/
oo-bee-ya-tee
muscle *mišić* ⓜ mee-sheech
museum *muzej* ⓜ moo-zey
mushroom *gljiva* ⓕ glyee-va
music *glazba* ⓕ glaz-ba
music shop *prodavaonica muzike* ⓕ
praw-da-va-aw-nee-tsa moo-zee-ke
musician *muzičar* ⓜ moo-zee-char
Muslim *musliman/muslimanka* ⓜ/ⓕ
moo-slee-man/moo-slee-man-ka
mussel *dagnja* ⓕ dag-nya
mustard *senf* ⓜ senf
mute *nijem* nee-yem
my *moj/moja/moje* ⓜ/ⓕ/ⓝ moy/moy-a/
moy-e

N

nail clippers *škarice za nokte* ⓕ pl
shka-ree-tse za nawk-te

napkin *salveta* ⓕ sal-ve-ta
nappy *pelene* ⓕ pl pe-le-ne
nappy rash *osip od pelena* ⓜ aw-seep
awd pe-le-na
national park *nacionalni park* ⓜ
na-tsee-aw-nal-nee park
nationality *nacionalnost* ⓕ
na-tsee-aw-nal-nawst
nature *priroda* ⓕ pree-raw-da
naturopathy *naturoterapije* ⓕ pl
na-too-raw-te-ra-pee-ye
nausea *mučnina* ⓕ mooch-nee-na
nave *srednja lađa crkve* ⓕ sred-nya la-ja
tsr-kve
navigation *navigacija* ⓕ na-vee-ga-tsee-ya
near *blizu* blee-zoo
nearby *obližnji* aw-bleezh-nyee
nearest *najbliži* nai-blee-zhee
necessary *potreban* paw-tre-ban
necklace *ogrlica* ⓕ aw-gr-lee-tsa
nectarine *nektarinka* ⓕ nek-ta-reen-ka
need (za)trebati* (za)-tre-ba-tee
needle (sewing) *igla za šivenje* ⓕ ee-gla
za shee-ve-nye
needle (syringe) *igla injekcije* ⓕ ee-gla
ee-nyek-tsee-ye
negative *negativan* ne-ga-tee-van
neither *niti* nee-tee
net *mreža* ⓕ mre-zha
Netherlands *Nizozemska* ⓕ
nee-zaw-zem-ska
never *nikada* nee-ka-da
new *nov* nawv
New Year's Day *novogodišnji dan* ⓜ
naw-vaw-gaw-deesh-nyee dan
New Year's Eve *doček nove godine* ⓜ
daw-chek naw-ve gaw-dee-ne
New Zealand *Novi Zeland* ⓜ naw-vee
ze-land
news *vijesti* ⓕ pl vee-ye-stee
newsstand *kiosk za prodaju novina* ⓜ
kee-awsk za praw-dai-oo naw-vee-na
newsagency *prodavaonica novina i
časopisa* ⓕ praw-da-va-aw-nee-tsa
naw-vee-na ee cha-saw-pee-sa
newspaper *novine* ⓕ pl naw-vee-ne
next (month) *slijedeći* slee-ye-de-chee
next to *pored* paw-red
nice *lijep* lee-yep
nickname *nadimak* ⓜ na-dee-mak
night *noć* ⓕ nawch
nightclub *noćni klub* ⓜ nawch-nee kloob
no (response) *ne* ne

no (absence of something) *ništa neesh*·ta
no vacancy *bez slobodnih mjesta*
  bez slaw·bawd·neeh *mye*·sta
noisy *bučan boo*·chan
none *nikakav nee*·ka·kav
nonsmoking *nepušački* ⓜ
  ne·poo·shach·kee
noodles *rezanci* ⓜ pl *re·zan*·tsee
noon *podne* ⓝ *pawd*·ne
north *sjever* ⓜ *sye*·ver
Norway *Norveška* ⓕ *nawr*·vesh·ka
nose *nos* ⓜ naws
not *ne* ne
notebook *bilježnica* ⓕ *bee*·lyezh·nee·tsa
nothing *ništa* ⓝ *neesh*·ta
November *studeni* ⓜ *stoo*·de·nee
now *sada* sa·da
nuclear energy *nuklearna energija* ⓕ
  noo·kle·ar·na e·*ner*·gee·ya
nuclear testing *nuklearna testiranja* ⓝ pl
  noo·kle·ar·na te·*stee*·ra·nya
nuclear waste *nuklearni otpad* ⓜ
  noo·kle·ar·nee *awt*·pad
number (figure) *broj* ⓜ broy
number (quantity) *količina* ⓕ
  kaw·lee·*chee*·na
numberplate *registarska tablica* ⓕ
  re·gee·*star*·ska *ta*·blee·tsa
nun *opatica* ⓕ aw·*pa*·tee·tsa
nurse *medicinska sestra* ⓕ
  me·dee·tseen·ska *se*·stra
nut *orah* ⓜ *aw*·rah

O

oats *zob* ⓕ zawb
ocean *ocean* ⓜ aw·*tse*·an
October *listopad* ⓜ *lee*·staw·pad
off (spoiled) *pokvaren pawk*·va·ren
office *ured* ⓜ oo·red
office worker *službenik/službenica* ⓜ/ⓕ
  sloozh·be·neek/*sloozh*·be·nee·tsa
often *često che*·staw
oil *ulje* ⓝ *oo*·lye
oil (petrol) *nafta* ⓕ *naf*·ta
old *star* star
olive *maslina* ⓕ *ma*·slee·na
olive oil *maslinovo ulje* ⓝ *ma*·slee·naw·vaw
  oo·lye
Olympic Games *Olimpijske igre* ⓕ pl
  aw·*leem*·peey·ske *ee*·gre
omelette *omlet* ⓜ *aw*·mlet

on *na* · *pri* · *o* · *u* na · pree · aw · oo
on time *na vrijeme* na vree·*ye*·me
once *jednom yed*·nawm
one *jedan* ⓜ *ye*·dan
one-way (ticket) *jednosmjeran*
  yed·naw·smye·ran
onion *luk* ⓜ look
only *samo* sa·maw
open *otvoren* awt·*vaw*·ren
open *otvoriti/otvarati* awt·*vaw*·ree·tee/
  awt·*va*·ra·tee
opening hours *početak radnog vremena* ⓜ
  paw·che·tak *rad*·nawg vre·me·na
opera *opera* ⓕ *aw*·pe·ra
opera house *operna dvorana* ⓕ
  aw·per·na dvaw·*ra*·na
operation *operacija* ⓕ aw·pe·*ra*·tsee·ya
operator *operator* ⓜ aw·pe·*ra*·tawr
opinion *mišljenje* ⓝ meesh·lye·nye
opposite *nasuprot* na·*soo*·prawt
optometrist *optičar* ⓜ *awp*·tee·char
or *ili* ee·lee
orange (colour) *narančast na*·ran·chast
orange (fruit) *naranča* ⓕ *na*·ran·cha
orange juice *sok od naranče* ⓜ sawk awd
  na·ran·che
orchestra *orkestar* ⓜ awr·*ke*·star
order *poredak* ⓜ *paw*·re·dak
order (demand) *narediti/naređivati*
  na·re·dee·tee/na·re·jee·va·tee
order (request) *naručiti/naručivati*
  na·roo·chee·tee/na·roo·chee·va·tee
ordinary *običan* ⓜ *aw*·bee·chan
orgasm *orgazam* ⓜ awr·*ga*·zam
original *originalan* aw·ree·gee·*na*·lan
other *drugi* droo·gee
our *naš/naša/naše* ⓜ/ⓕ/ⓝ nash/*nash*·a/
  na·she
out of order *pokvaren* ⓜ *pawk*·va·ren
outside *vani* va·nee
ovarian cyst *cista na jajniku* ⓕ *tsee*·sta na
  yai·nee·koo
ovary *jajnik* ⓜ *yai*·neek
oven *pećnica* ⓕ *pech*·nee·tsa
overcoat *zimski kaput* ⓜ *zeem*·skee *ka*·poot
overdose *prevelika doza* ⓕ *pre*·ve·leeka
  daw·za
overnight *preko noći* *pre*·kaw *naw*·chee
overseas *inostranstvo* ⓕ
  ee·naw·strans·tvaw
owe *dugovati* imp doo·*gaw*·va·tee
owner *vlasnik* ⓜ *vla*·sneek
oxygen *kisik* ⓜ *kee*·seek

oyster *oštrige* ① pl *awsh*-tree-ge
ozone layer *ozonski omotač* ⓜ *aw*-zawn-skee aw-*maw*-tach

P

pacemaker *elekronski stimulator srca* ⓜ e-*lek*-trawn-skee stee-moo-*la*-tawr sr-tsa
pacifier *duda* ① *doo*-da
package *paket* ⓜ *pa*-ket
packet (general) *kutija* ① *koo*-tee-ya
padlock *lokot* ⓜ *law*-kawt
page *stranica* ① *stra*-nee-tsa
pain *bol* ⓜ bawl
painful *bolan* *baw*-lan
painkiller *tableta protiv bolova* ① *ta*-ble-ta *praw*-teev *baw*-law-va
painter *slikar* ⓜ *slee*-kar
painting (a work) *slika* ① *slee*-ka
painting (the art) *slikarstvo* ⓜ *slee*-*kars*-tvaw
pair (couple) *par* ⓜ par
Pakistan *Pakistan* ⓜ *pa*-kee-stan
palace *palača* ① *pa*-la-cha
pan *tava* ① *ta*-va
pants (trousers) *hlače* ① pl *hla*-che
panty liners *ulošci za žensko donje rublje* ⓜ pl oo-*lawsh*-tsee za *zhen*-skaw *daw*-nye *roob*-lye
pantyhose *hulahopke* ① pl hoo-la-*hawp*-ke
pap smear *PAPA test* ⓜ *pa*-pa test
paper *papir* ⓜ *pa*-peer
paperwork *dokumentacija* ① daw-koo-men-*ta*-tsee-ya
paraplegic *paraplegičar* ⓜ pa-ra-*ple*-gee-char
parcel *paket* ⓜ *pa*-ket
parents *roditelji* ⓜ pl *raw*-dee-te-lyee
park *park* ⓜ park
park (a car) *parkirati* imp par-*kee*-ra-tee
parliament *sabor* ⓜ *sa*-bawr
part (component) *dio* ⓜ *dee*-aw
part-time *honorarni* ⓜ *haw*-naw-rar-nee
party (night out) *provod* ⓜ *praw*-vawd
party (politics) *stranka* ① *stran*-ka
pass *dobaciti/dobacivati* daw-*ba*-tsee-tee/ daw-ba-*tsee*-va-tee
passenger *putnik* ⓜ *poot*-neek
passport *putovnica* ① *poo*-tawv-nee-tsa
passport number *broj putovnice* ⓜ broy poo-*tawv*-nee-tse
past *prošlost* ① *prawsh*-lawst

pasta *tjestenina* ① tye-ste-*nee*-na
pastry *fino pecivo* ① *fee*-naw *pe*-tsee-vaw
path *staza* ① *sta*-za
pay *(u)platiti* (oo)*pla*-tee-tee
payment (by someone) *uplata* ① oo-*pla*-ta
payment (to someone) *isplata* ① ees-*pla*-ta
pea *grašak* ⓜ *gra*-shak
peace *mir* ⓜ meer
peach *breskva* ① *bresk*-va
peak (mountain) *vrh* ⓜ vrh
peanut *kikiriki* ⓜ kee-kee-*ree*-kee
pear *kruška* ① *kroosh*-ka
pedal *pedala* ① pe-*da*-la
pedestrian *pješak* ⓜ *pye*-shak
pen (ballpoint) *kemijska* ① *ke*-meey-ska
pencil *olovka* ① *aw*-lawv-ka
penis *penis* ⓜ *pe*-nees
penknife *džepni nožić* ⓜ *jep*-nee *naw*-zheech
pensioner *umirovljenik* ⓜ oo-mee-rawv-*lye*-neek
people *ljudi* ⓜ pl *lyoo*-dee
pepper *papar* ⓜ *pa*-par
pepper (bell) *paprika* ① *pa*-pree-ka
per (day) *na* na
per cent *postotak* ⓜ paw-*staw*-tak
perfect *savršen* sa-*vr*-shen
performance *priredba* ① *pree*-red-ba
perfume *parfem* ⓜ par-*fem*
period pain *menstrualni bolovi* ⓜ pl men-*straw*-al-nee *baw*-law-vee
permission *dopuštenje* ① daw-*poosh*-te-nye
permit *dozvola* ① *dawz*-vaw-la
person *osoba* ① *aw*-saw-ba
petrol *benzin* ⓜ ben-*zeen*
petrol station *benzinska stanica* ① *ben*-zeen-ska *sta*-nee-tsa
pharmacy *ljekarna* ① lye-*kar*-na
phone book *telefonski imenik* ⓜ te-*le*-fawn-skee *ee*-me-neek
phone box *telefonska govornica* ① te-*le*-fawn-ska *gaw*-vawr-nee-tsa
phonecard *telefonska kartica* ① te-*le*-fawn-ska *kar*-tee-tsa
photo *fotografija* ① faw-taw-*gra*-fee-ya
photograph *slikati* perf *slee*-ka-tee
photographer *fotograf* ⓜ faw-*taw*-graf
photography *fotografija* ① faw-taw-*gra*-fee-ya
phrasebook *zbirka fraza* ① *zbeer*-ka *fra*-za
pickaxe *pijuk* ⓜ *pee*-yook
pickles *kiseli krastavci* ⓜ pl kee-se-lee *kra*-stav-tsee

picnic *piknik* ⓜ *peek*·neek
pie *pita* ⓕ *pee*·ta
piece *komad* ⓜ *kaw*·mad
pig *svinja* ⓕ *svee*·nya
pill *tableta* ⓕ ta·*ble*·ta
(the) Pill (contraceptive) *antibaby-pilula*
  ⓕ an·tee·bey·bee·*pee*·loo·la
pillow *jastuk* ⓜ *ya*·stook
pillowcase *jastučnica* ⓕ *ya*·stooch·nee·tsa
pineapple *ananas* ⓜ *a*·na·nas
pink *ružičast* roo·zhee·chast
pistachio *trišlja* ⓕ *treesh*·lya
place *mjesto* ⓝ *mye*·staw
place of birth *mjesto rođenja* ⓝ *mye*·staw
  raw·je·nya
plaited ornamentation *pletenasti ukras* ⓜ
  ple·te·na·stee oo·kras
plane *zrakoplov* ⓜ *zra*·kaw·plawv
planet *planeta* ⓕ pla·*ne*·ta
plant *biljka* ⓕ *beel*′·ka
plastic *plastičan* pla·stee·chan
plate *tanjur* ⓜ *ta*·nyoor
plateau *plato* ⓜ pla·*taw*
platform *peron* ⓜ *pe*·rawn
play (board games) *igrati* imp ee·gra·tee
play (instrument) *(od)svirati*
  (awd)*svee*·ra·tee
play (theatre) *predstava* ⓕ *pred*·sta·va
plug (bath) *čep* ⓜ chep
plug (electricity) *utikač* ⓜ oo·tee·kach
plum *šljiva* ⓕ *shlyee*·va
poached *pošíran* paw·*shee*·ran
pocket *džep* ⓜ jep
pocket knife *džepni nožić* ⓜ *jep*·nee
  naw·zheech
poetry *poezija* ⓕ paw·e·zee·ya
point (logic) *svrha* ⓕ *svr*·ha
point *pokazati/pokazivati* paw·*ka*·za·tee/
  paw·ka·zee·va·tee
poisonous *otrovan* aw·*traw*·van
police *policija* ⓕ paw·lee·tsee·ya
police officer *policajac* ⓜ paw·lee·*tsai*·ats
police station *policijska stanica* ⓕ
  paw·*lee*·tseey·ska *sta*·nee·tsa
politician *političar* ⓜ paw·*lee*·tee·char
politics *politika* ⓕ paw·*lee*·tee·ka
pollen *pelud* ⓜ *pe*·lood
pollution *zagađenje* ⓝ za·ga·je·nye
pool (game) *bilijar* ⓜ bee·*lee*·yar
pool (swimming) *bazen za plivanje* ⓜ
  ba·zen za plee·va·nye
poor *siromašan* see·*raw*·ma·shan
popular *populáran* paw·poo·la·ran

pork *svinjetina* ⓕ svee·nye·tee·na
pork sausage *svinjska kobasica* ⓕ
  sveen′·ska kaw·*ba*·see·tsa
port (sea) *luka* ⓕ *loo*·ka
positive *pozitivan* paw·zee·tee·van
possible *moguć* maw·gooch
post office *poštanski ured* ⓜ
  pawsh·tan·skee oo·red
postage *poštarina* ⓕ pawsh·*ta*·ree·na
postcard *dopisnica* ⓕ daw·pee·snee·tsa
postcode *poštanski broj* ⓜ pawsh·tan·skee
  broy
poster *poster* ⓜ *paw*·ster
pot (ceramics) *posuda* ⓕ *paw*·soo·da
pot (dope) *trava* ⓕ tra·va
potato *krumpir* ⓜ kroom·peer
pottery *grnčarija* ⓕ grn·cha·ree·ya
pound (money, weight) *funta* ⓕ *foon*·ta
poverty *siromaštvo* ⓝ see·raw·*mash*·tvaw
powder *prah* ⓜ prah
power *snaga* ⓕ *sna*·ga
prawn *škamp* ⓜ shkamp
prayer *molitva* ⓕ maw·*leet*·va
prefer *pretpostaviti/pretpostavljati*
  pret·*paw*·sta·vee·tee/
  pret·paw·stav·lya·tee
pregnancy test kit *test na trudnoću* ⓜ
  test na trood·naw·choo
pregnant *trudna* ⓕ *trood*·na
premenstrual tension *predmenstrualna*
  napetost ⓕ pred·men·stroo·al·na
  na·pe·tawst
prepare *pripremiti/pripremati*
  pree·pre·mee·tee/pree·pre·ma·tee
prescription *recept za lijekove* ⓜ *re*·tsept
  za lee·ye·kaw·ve
present (gift) *poklon* ⓜ *paw*·klawn
present (time) *sadašnjost* ⓕ
  sa·dash·nyawst
president *predsjednik* ⓜ pred·syed·neek
pressure *pritisak* ⓜ pree·tee·sak
pretty *zgodan* zgaw·dan
price *cijena* ⓕ tsee·ye·na
priest *svećenik* ⓜ sve·che·neek
prime minister *ministar predsjednik* ⓜ
  mee·nee·star pred·syed·neek
printer (computer) *pisač* ⓜ *pee*·sach
prison *zatvor* ⓜ *zat*·vawr
prisoner *zatvorenik* ⓜ zat·vaw·re·neek
private *privatan* pree·va·tan
profit *dobitak* ⓜ daw·*bee*·tak
program *program* ⓜ *praw*·gram
projector *projektor* ⓜ proy·*ek*·tawr

promise *obećati/obećavati*
aw-be-cha-tee/aw-be-*cha*-va-tee
promontory *rt* ⓜ rt
prostitute *prostitutka* ① praw-stee-*toot*-ka
protect *(za)štititi* (za-)*shtee*-tee-tee
protected (species) *zaštićen* zash-tee-chen
protest *prosvjed* ⓜ *praws*-vyed
protest *prosvjedovati* imp
praw-svye-daw-va-tee
provisions *namirnice* ① pl *na*-meer-nee-tse
pub (bar) *gostionica* ① gaw-stee-*aw*-nee-tsa
public gardens *javni parkovi* ⓜ pl
yav-nee *par*-kaw-vee
public relations *odnosi s javnošću* ① pl
awd-naw-see s *yav*-nawsh-choo
public telephone *javni telefon* ⓜ *yav*-nee
te-*le*-fawn
public toilet *javni zahod* ⓜ *yav*-nee za-hawd
publishing *izdavanje* ① eez-*da*-va-nye
pull *(po)vući* (paw-)*voo*-chee
pump *pumpa* ① *poom*-pa
pumpkin *bundeva* ① *boon*-de-va
puncture *(pro)bušiti* (praw-)*boo*-shee-tee
pure *čist* cheest
purple *ljubičast* *lyoo*-bee-chast
purse *novčarka* ① *nawv*-char-ka
push *gurnuti/gurati* goor-noo-tee/*goo*-ra-tee
put *staviti/stavljati* sta-vee-tee/*stav*-lya-tee

Q

quadriplegic *potpuno paralizirana
osoba* ① *pawt*-poo-naw
pa-ra-*lee*-zee-ra-na *aw*-saw-ba
qualifications *kvalifikacije* ① pl
kva-lee-fee-*ka*-tsee-ye
quality *kvaliteta* ① kva-lee-*te*-ta
quarantine *karantena* ① ka-ran-*te*-na
quarter *četvrtina* ① chet-vr-*tee*-na
queen *kraljica* ① *kra*-lyee-tsa
question *pitanje* ① *pee*-ta-nye
queue *red* ⓜ red
quick *brz* brz
quiet *tih* teeh
quit *ostaviti/ostavljati* aw-sta-vee-tee/
aw-stav-lya-tee

R

rabbit *zec* ⓜ zets
race (sport) *utrka* ① *oo*-tr-ka
racetrack *trkalište* ① *tr*-ka-leesh-te

racing bike *trkaći bicikl* ⓜ *tr*-ka-chee
bee-tsee-kl
racism *rasna netrpeljivost* ① *ra*-sna
ne-tr-pe-lyee-vawst
racquet *reket* ⓜ *re*-ket
radiator *radijator* ⓜ ra-dee-*ya*-tawr
radio *radio* ⓜ *ra*-dee-aw
radish *rotkva* ① *rawt*-kva
railway station *željeznička stanica* ①
zhe-lyez-nee-chka *sta*-nee-tsa
rain *kiša* ① *kee*-sha
raincoat *kabanica* ① ka-*ba*-nee-tsa
raisin *grožđica* ① *grawzh*-jee-tsa
rape *silovanje* ① see-*law*-va-nye
rape *silovati* perf see-*law*-va-tee
rare (uncommon) *rijedak* ree-*ye*-dak
rare (meat) *nepotpuno pečen*
ne-*pawt*-poo-naw *pe*-chen
rash *osip* ⓜ *aw*-seep
raspberry *malina* ① *ma*-lee-na
rat *štakor* ⓜ *shta*-kawr
rave *rejv parti* ⓜ reyv *par*-tee
raw *sirov* ⓜ see-*law*-va-tee
razor *brijač* ⓜ *bree*-yach
razor blade *britva* ① *breet*-va
read *(pro)čitati* (praw-)*chee*-ta-tee
reading *čitanje* ① *chee*-ta-nye
ready *spreman* *spre*-man
real-estate agent *posrednik za prodaju
nekretnina* ⓜ *paw*-sred-neek za
praw-*da*-oo ne-kret-*nee*-na
rear (seat etc) *stražnji* strazh-nyee
reason *razlog* ⓜ *raz*-lawg
receipt *račun* ⓜ *ra*-choon
recently *nedavno* ne-*dav*-naw
recommend *preporučiti/preporučivati*
pre-paw-*roo*-chee-tee/
pre-paw-*roo*-chee-va-tee
record (music etc) *snimiti/snimati*
snee-mee-tee/*snee*-ma-tee
recording *snimak* ⓜ *snee*-mak
recyclable *koji se mogu reciklirati*
koy-ee se *maw*-goo re-tsee-*klee*-ra-tee
recycle *reciklirati* perf re-tsee-*klee*-ra-tee
red *crven* tsr-ven
referee *sudac* ⓜ *soo*-dats
reference *preporuka* ① pre-paw-*roo*-ka
reflexology *refleksologija* ①
re-flek-saw-*law*-gee-ya
refrigerator *hladnjak* ⓜ *hlad*-nyak
refugee *izbjeglica* ① eez-*byeg*-lee-tsa
refund *povrat novca* ⓜ *pawv*-rat
nawv-tsa

refuse *odbiti/odbijati* awd·bee·tee/ awd·bee·ya·tee
regional *područni* paw·drooch·nee
registered mail (by) *preporučenom poštom* pre·paw·roo·che·nawm pawsh·tawm
rehydration salts *soli za rehidrataciju* ① saw·lee za re·hee·dra·ta·tsee·yoo
reiki *reiki* ⑩ re·ee·kee
relationship (not family) *odnos* ⑩ awd·naws
relationship (family) *srodstvo* ⑪ srawd·stvaw
relax *opustiti/opuštati se* aw·poo·stee·tee/ aw·poosh·ta·tee se
relic *relikvija* ① re·leek·vee·ya
religion *vjera* ① vye·ra
religious (concerning religion) *vjerski* vyer·skee
religious (person) *pobožan* paw·baw·zhan
remote *udaljen* oo·da·lyen
remote control *daljinski upravljač* ⑩ da·lyeen·skee oo·prav·lyach
rent *iznajmiti/iznajmljivati* eez·nai·mee·tee/eez·naim·lyee·va·tee
repair *popraviti/popravljati* paw·pra·vee·tee/paw·prav·lya·tee
republic *republika* ① re·poo·blee·ka
reservation (booking) *rezervacija* ① re·zer·va·tsee·ya
rest *odmoriti/odmarati se* awd·maw·ree·tee/awd·ma·ra·tee se
restaurant *restoran* ⑩ re·staw·ran
restaurant (family run) *gostiona* ① gaw·stee·aw·na
résumé *rezime* ① re·zee·me
retired *umirovljen* oo·mee·rawv·lyen
return (come back) *vratiti/vraćati se* vra·tee·tee/vra·cha·tee se
return (ticket) *povratan* paw·vra·tan
reverse charge call *poziv na račun nazvane osobe* ⑩ paw·zeev na ra·choon naz·va·ne aw·saw·be
review (article) *pregled* ⑩ pre·gled
rhythm *ritam* ⑩ ree·tam
rib *rebro* ⑪ re·braw
rice *riža* ① ree·zha
rich (wealthy) *bogat* baw·gat
ride (trip) *vožnja* ① vawzh·nya
ride (horse) *jahati* imp ya·ha·tee
right (correct) *ispravan* ee·spra·van
right (direction) *desno* de·snaw
right-wing *desničarski* de·snee·char·skee

ring (on finger) *prsten* ⑩ pr·sten
ring (of phone) *nazvati/nazivati* naz·va·tee/na·zee·va·tee
rip-off *prekomjerna cijena* ① pre·kawm·yer·na tsee·ye·na
river *rijeka* ① ree·ye·ka
road *cesta* ① tse·sta
road map *putna karta* ① poot·na kar·ta
rob *(o)pljačkati* (aw)·plyach·ka·tee
rock *stijena* ① stee·ye·na
rock (music) *rock* ⑩ rawk
rock climbing *alpinističko penjanje* ⑪ al·pee·nee·steech·kaw pe·nya·nye
rock group *rock grupa* ① rawk groo·pa
rockmelon *dinja* ① dee·nya
roll (bread) *žemička* ① zhe·meech·ka
rollerblading *rošulanje* ① raw·shoo·la·nye
romantic *romantičan* raw·man·tee·chan
room *soba* ① saw·ba
room number *broj sobe* ⑩ broy saw·be
rope *uže* ① oo·zhe
round *okrugao* aw·kroo·ga·aw
roundabout *kružni tok* ⑩ kroozh·nee tawk
route *put* ⑩ poot
rowing *veslanje* ① ve·sla·nye
rubbish *smeće* ⑪ sme·che
rubbish bin *kanta za smeće* ① kan·ta za sme·che
rubella *rubeola* ① roo·be·aw·la
rug *tepih* ⑩ te·peeh
rugby *ragbi* ⑩ rag·bee
ruins *ruševine* ① pl roo·she·vee·ne
rule *pravilo* ⑪ pra·vee·law
rum *rum* ⑩ room
run *(po)trčati* (paw·)tr·cha·tee
running *trčanje* ⑪ tr·cha·nye
runny nose *šmrkav nos* ⑩ shmr·kav naws

S

sad *tužan* too·zhan
saddle *sedlo* ⑪ sed·law
safe *sef* ⑩ sef
safe *siguran* see·goo·ran
safe sex *siguran seks* ⑩ see·goo·ran seks
saint *svetac/svetica* ⑩/① sve·tats/sve·tee·tsa
salad *salata* ① sa·la·ta
salami *salama* ① sa·la·ma
salary *plaća* ① pla·cha
sale *rasprodaja* ① ra·spraw·dai·a
sales tax *porez na promet* ⑩ paw·rez na praw·met

salmon *losos* ⓜ *law*·saws
salt *sol* ⓜ sawl
same *isti* ⓜ *ee*·stee
sand *pijesak* ⓜ pee·*ye*·sak
sandal *sandala* ① san·*da*·la
sanitary napkin *higijenski uložak* ⓜ *hee*·gee·yen·skee oo·law·zhak
sardine *sardina* ① sar·*dee*·na
Saturday *subota* ① soo·*baw*·ta
sauce *umak* ⓜ *oo*·mak
saucepan *lonac* ⓜ *law*·nats
sauna *sauna* ① sa·oo·na
sausage *kobasica* ① kaw·*ba*·see·tsa
say *kazati/kazivati* ka·za·tee/ka·*zee*·va·tee
scalp *skalp* ⓜ skalp
scarf *šal* ⓜ shal
school *škola* ① *shkaw*·la
science *znanost* ① *zna*·nawst
scientist *znanstvenik* ⓜ *znanst*·ve·neek
scissors *škare* ① pl *shka*·re
score *stići/postizati* paw·*stee*·chee/ paw·*stee*·za·tee
scoreboard *semafor* ⓜ *se*·ma·fawr
Scotland *Škotska* ① *shkawt*·ska
scuba diving *ronjenje sa bocama* ⓝ *raw*·nye·nye sa baw·tsa·ma
sculpture *skulptura* ① skoolp·*too*·ra
sea *more* ⓝ *maw*·re
seasick *koji pati od morske bolesti* koy·ee *pa*·tee awd mawr·ske baw·le·stee
seaside *primorje* ⓝ *pree*·mawr·ye
season (winter etc) *godišnje doba* ⓝ *gaw*·deesh·nye daw·ba
season (for activities) *sezona* ① se·*zaw*·na
seat (place) *sjedište* ⓝ *sye*·deesh·te
seatbelt *sigornosni pojas* ⓜ *see*·goor·naw·snee poy·as
second (clock) *sekunda* ① se·*koon*·da
second *drugi* droo·gee
second class *drugi razred* ⓜ droo·gee *raz*·red
second-hand *polovni* paw·*lawv*·nee
second-hand shop *prodavaonica polovne robe* ① praw·da·va·*aw*·nee·tsa paw·*lawv*·ne *raw*·be
secretary *tajnik/tajnica* ⓜ/① *tai*·neek/ *tai*·nee·tsa
see *vidjeti/vidjati* vee·dye·tee/*vee*·ja·tee
self-service *samoposluga* ① sa·maw·*paw*·sloo·ga
self-employed *samostalno zaposlen* sa·maw·stal·naw za·*paw*·slen
selfish *sebičan* ⓜ se·*bee*·chan

sell *prodati/prodavati* praw·*da*·tee/ praw·*da*·va·tee
send *(po)slati* *(paw·)sla*·tee
sensible *razuman* ra·*zoo*·man
sensual *razbludan* raz·*bloo*·dan
separate *odvojen* awd·voy·en
September *rujan* ⓜ *roo*·yan'
Serbia *Srbija* ① *sr*·bee·ya
serious *ozbiljan* aw·zbee·lyan
service *usluga* ① oo·sloo·ga
service charge *naplata za usluge* ① *na*·pla·ta za oo·sloo·ge
service station *benziska stanica* ① *ben*·zeen·ska *sta*·nee·tsa
serviette *salveta* ① sal·*ve*·ta
several *nekoliko* ne·kaw·lee·kaw
sew *sašiti/šivati* sa·shee·tee/*shee*·va·tee
sex *seks* ⓜ seks
sexism *spolna diskriminacija* ① *spawl*·na dee·skree·mee·*na*·tsee·ya
sexy *privlačan* pree·vla·chan
shade *hladovina* ① hla·*daw*·vee·na
shadow *sjena* ① *sye*·na
shampoo *šampon* ⓜ sham·*pawn*
shape *oblik* ⓜ *aw*·bleek
share (a dorm etc) *dijeliti* imp dee·*ye*·lee·tee
share (with) *podijeliti* perf paw·dee·*ye*·lee·tee
shave *(o)brijati se* *(aw·)bree*·ya·tee se
shaving cream *pjena za brijanje* ① *pye*·na za *bree*·ya·nye
she *ona* ① *aw*·na
sheep *ovca* ① *awv*·tsa
sheet (bed) *plahta* ① *pla*·hta
shelf *polica* ① *paw*·lee·tsa
shiatsu *shiatsu* ① shee·*a*·tsoo
shingles (illness) *osip u struku* ⓜ *aw*·seep oo stroo·koo
ship *brod* ⓜ brawd
shirt *košulja* ① kaw·shoo·lya
shoe(s) *cipela/e* ① sg/① pl *tsee*·pe·la/e
shoe shop *prodavaonica cipela* ① praw·da·va·*aw*·nee·tsa *tsee*·pe·la
shoot *(u)pucati* *(oo·)poo*·tsa·tee
shop *prodavaonica* ① praw·da·va·*aw*·nee·tsa
shop *kupovati* imp koo·*paw*·va·tee
shopping *kupovina* ① koo·*paw*·vee·na
shopping centre *trgovački centar* ⓜ *tr*·gaw·vach·kee *tsen*·tar
short (duration) *kratak* kra·tak
short (height) *nizak* nee·zak
shortage *nedostatak* ① ne·daw·*sta*·tak

shorts *kratke hlače* ① pl *krat*·ke *hla*·che
shoulder *rame* ① *ra*·me
shout *viknuti/vikati* veek·noo·tee/*vee*·ka·tee
show *predstava* ① *pred*·sta·va
show *pokazati/pokazivati* paw·*ka*·za·tee/
paw·ka·*zee*·va·tee
shower (bathroom) *tuš* ⓜ toosh
shrine *moćnica* ① *mawch*·nee·tsa
shut *zatvoren* zat·*vaw*·ren
shy *stidljiv* steed·lyeev
sick *bolestan* baw·*les*·tan
side *strana* ① *stra*·na
sign *znak* ① znak
signature *potpis* ⓜ *pawt*·pees
silk *svila* ① *svee*·la
silver *srebro* ⓝ *sre*·braw
similar *sličan* slee·chan
simple *jednostavan* yed·naw·sta·van
since (May etc) *od* • *otkako* awd •
awt·ka·kaw
sing *(za)pjevati* (za·)*pye*·va·tee
Singapore *Singapur* ⓜ *seen*·ga·poor
singer *pjevač/pjevačica* ⓜ/① pye·vach/
pye·va·chee·tsa
single (man) *neoženjen* ne·*aw*·zhen·yen
single (woman) *neudata* ne·oo·da·ta
single room *jednokrevetna soba* ①
yed·naw·*kre*·vet·na *saw*·ba
singlet *potkošulja* ① *pawt*·kaw·shoo·lya
sister *sestra* ① *se*·stra
sit *sjesti/sjedati* sye·stee/sye·da·tee
size (general) *veličina* ① ve·lee·*chee*·na
skate *rošulati se* imp raw·*shoo*·la·tee se
skateboarding *vožnja na skateboardu* ①
vawzh·nya na *skeyt*·bawr·doo
ski *skijati* imp *skee*·ya·tee
skiing *skijanje* ⓝ *skee*·ya·nye
skim milk *obrano mlijeko* ⓝ aw·bra·naw
mlee·*ye*·kaw
skin *koža* ① *kaw*·zha
skirt *suknja* ① *sook*·nya
skull *lubanja* ① *loo*·ba·nya
sky *nebo* ⓝ *ne*·baw
sleep *(od)spavati* (awd·)*spa*·va·tee
sleeping bag *vreća za spavanje* ①
vre·cha za *spa*·va·nye
sleeping berth *spavaća kola* ①
spa·va·cha *kaw*·la
sleeping car *spavaći kupe* ⓜ *spa*·va·chee
koo·*pe*
sleeping pills *tableta za spavanje* ①
tab·le·ta za *spa*·va·nye
(to be) sleepy *pospan* paw·span

slice *kriška* ① *kreesh*·ka
slide (film) *dijapozitiv* ⓜ
dee·ya·paw·zee·teev
Slovakia *Slovačka* ① *slaw*·vach·ka
Slovenia *Slovenija* ① slaw·*ve*·nee·ya
slow *spor* spawr
slowly *sporo* *spaw*·raw
small *mali* ma·lee
smaller *manji* ma·nyee
smallest *najmanji* nai·ma·nyee
smell (pleasant) *miris* ⓜ *mee*·rees
smell (unpleasant) *smrad* ⓜ smrad
smile *(na)smiješiti se* (na·)smee·*ye*·shee·tee se
smoke *(is)pušiti* (ees·)*poo*·shee·tee
snack *laki obrok* ⓜ *la*·kee aw·brawk
snail *puž* ⓜ poozh
snake *zmija* ① *zmee*·ya
snorkelling *ronjenje s disalicom* ①
raw·nye·nye s *dee*·sa·lee·tsawm
snow *snijeg* ⓜ snee·*yeg*
snowboarding *daskanje na snijegu* ①
da·ska·nye na snee·*ye*·goo
soap *sapun* ⓜ *sa*·poon
soccer *nogomet* ⓜ *naw*·gaw·met
social welfare *socijalna skrb* ①
saw·tsee·yal·na skrb
socialist *socijalistički* saw·tsee·ya·*lee*·st
eech·kee
sock(s) *čarape/e* ① sg/① pl *cha*·ra·pa/e
soft drink *bezalkoholno piće* ⓝ
be·zal·kaw·hawl·naw pee·*che*
soldier *vojnik* ⓜ *voy*·neek
some *malo* ma·law
someone *netko* net·kaw
something *nešto* nesh·taw
sometimes *ponekad* paw·ne·kad
son *sin* ⓜ seen
song *pjesma* ① *pye*·sma
soon *uskoro* oo·skaw·raw
sore *bolan* baw·lan
soup *juha* ① *yoo*·ha
sour cream *kiselo vrhnje* ① *kee*·se·law
vrh·nye
south *jug* ⓜ yoog
souvenir *suvenir* ⓜ soo·ve·neer
souvenir shop *prodavaonica suvenira* ①
praw·da·va·*aw*·nee·tsa soo·ve·*nee*·ra
soy milk *sojino mlijeko* ⓝ *soy*·ee·naw
mlee·*ye*·kaw
soy sauce *soja* ① *soy*·a
spa *toplice* ① pl *taw*·plee·tse
space *prostor* ⓜ *praw*·stawr
Spain *Španjolska* ① *shpa*·nyawl·ska

sparkling wine *pjenušavo vino* ⓝ pye·noo·sha·vaw *vee*·naw

speak (pro)govoriti (praw)·gaw·vaw·ree·tee

special *poseban* ⓜ *paw*·se·ban

specialist *stručnjak* ⓜ *strooch*·nyak

speed *brzina* ⓕ *br*·zee·na

speed limit *brzinsko ograničenje* ⓝ *br*·zeen·skaw aw·gra·nee·che·nye

speedometer *brzinomjer* ⓜ *br*·zee·naw·myer

spider *pauk* ⓜ *pa*·ook

spinach *špinat* ⓜ shpee·nat

spoiled *razmažen* raz·*ma*·zhen

spoke *žbica* ⓕ *zhbee*·tsa

spoon *žlica* ⓕ *zhlee*·tsa

sport *sport* ⓜ spawrt

sports store *prodavaonica sportske robe* ⓕ praw·da·va·aw·nee·tsa *spawrt*·ske *raw*·be

sportsperson *sportaš/sportašica* ⓜ/ⓕ *spawr*·tash/spawr·*ta*·shee·tsa

sprain *uganuće* ⓝ oo·ga·noo·che

spring (coil) *opruga* ⓕ *aw*·proo·ga

spring (season) *proljeće* ⓝ *praw*·lye·che

square (town) *trg* ⓜ trg

stadium *stadion* ⓜ *sta*·dee·awn

stairway *stepenište* ⓝ ste·pe·neesh·te

stale *ustajao* oo·stai·a·aw

stamp (mail) *poštanska marka* ⓕ *pawsh*·tan·ska *mar*·ka

stand-by ticket *uvjetna karta* ⓕ oo·vyet·noo *kar*·ta

star *zvjezda* ⓕ zvyez·da

(four-)star *(sa četiri) zvjezdice* ⓕ pl (sa che·tee·ree) zvye·zdee·tse

start *početak* ⓜ *paw*·che·tak

start *započeti/započinjati* za·*paw*·che·tee/ za·*paw*·chee·nya·tee

station *stanica* ⓕ *sta*·nee·tsa

stationer's (shop) *prodavaonica uredskog materijala* ⓕ praw·da·va·*aw*·nee·tsa oo·reds·kawg ma·te·ree·*ya*·la

statue *kip* ⓜ keep

stay (at a hotel) *odsjesti/odsjedati* awd·sye·stee/awd·sye·da·tee

stay (in one place) *ostati/ostajati* imp aw·sta·tee/aw·sta·ya·tee

steak (beef) *odrezak* ⓜ *aw*·dre·zak

steal *(u)krasti* (oo·)kra·stee

steep *strm* strm

step *stepenica* ⓕ ste·*pe*·nee·tsa

stereo *linija* ⓕ *lee*·nee·ya

still water *obična voda* ⓕ *aw*·beech·na *vaw*·da

stock (food) *bujon* ⓜ boo·yawn

stockings *visoke čarape* ⓕ pl *vee*·saw·ke *cha*·ra·pe

stolen *ukraden* ⓜ oo·*kra*·den

stomach *želudac* ⓜ zhe·*loo*·dats

stomachache (to have a) *imati trbobolju* ee·ma·tee tr·baw·baw·lyoo

stone *kamen* ⓜ *ka*·men

stoned (drugged) *napljugan* nap·lyoo·gan

stop (bus, tram) *stanica* ⓕ *sta*·nee·tsa

stop (cease) *zaustaviti/zaustavljati* za·oo·sta·vee·tee/za·oo·stav·lya·tee

stop (prevent) *spriječiti/sprječavati* spree·ye·chee·tee/spree·ye·*cha*·va·tee

Stop! *Stanite/Stani!* pol/inf *sta*·nee·te/*sta*·nee

storm *oluja* ⓕ aw·loo·ya

story *priča* ⓕ *pree*·cha

stove *pećnica* ⓕ *pech*·nee·tsa

straight (not crooked) *ravan* *ra*·van

strange *neobičan* ne·aw·bee·chan

stranger *stranac* ⓜ *stra*·nats

strawberry *jagoda* ⓕ *ya*·gaw·da

stream *struja* ⓕ *stroo*·ya

street *ulica* ⓕ *oo*·lee·tsa

street market *ulična tržnica* ⓕ *oo*·leech·na *trzh*·nee·tsa

strike *štrajk* ⓜ shtraik

string *struna* ⓕ *stroo*·na

stroke (health) *moždani udar* ⓜ *mawzh*·da·nee oo·dar

stroller *dječja hodalica* ⓕ *dyech*·ya *haw*·da·lee·tsa

strong (physically) *jak* yak

stubborn *tvrdoglav* tvr·*daw*·glav

student *student* ⓜ *stoo*·dent

studio *atelje* ⓝ a·te·lye

stupid *glup* gloop

style *stil* ⓜ steel

subtitles *titlovi* ⓜ pl *teet*·law·vee

suburb *predgrađe* ⓝ *pred*·gra·je

subway *podzemna željeznica* ⓕ *pawd*·zem·na zhe·lye·znee·tsa

sugar *šećer* ⓜ *she*·cher

suitcase *kofer* ⓜ *kaw*·fer

sultana *vrsta velikih grožđica* ⓕ *vr*·sta ve·lee·keeh *grawzh*·jee·tsa

summer *ljeto* ⓝ *lye*·taw

summit *vrh* vrh

sun *sunce* ⓝ *soon*·tse

sunblock *losion za zaštitu od sunca* ⓜ *law*·see·awn za *zash*·tee·too awd *soon*·tsa

sunburn *opekline od sunca* ⓕ pl *aw*·pe·klee·ne awd *soon*·tsa

Sunday *nedjelja* ① *ne*-dye-lya
sunglasses *naočale za sunce* ① pl
  na-aw-cha-le (za *soon*-tse)
sunny *sunčan* soon-chan
sunrise *izlazak sunca* ⓜ *eez*-la-zak soon-tsa
sunset *zalazak sunca* ⓜ *za*-la-zak soon-tsa
sunstroke *sunčanica* ① soon-*cha*-nee-tsa
supermarket *supermarket* ⓜ
  soo-per-*mar*-ket
superstition *praznovjerje* ⓝ
  praz-*naw*-vyer-ye
supporter (politics) *pristaša* ⓜ *pree*-sta-sha
supporter (sport) *navijač* ⓜ na-*vee*-yach
surf *daskati na valovima* da-ska-tee na
  va-law-vee-ma
surface mail (land) *obična pošta* ①
  aw-beech-na *pawsh*-ta
surface mail (sea) *prekomorska pošta* ①
  pre-kaw-*mawr*-ska *pawsh*-ta
surfboard *daska za surfanje* ① *da*-ska za
  soor-fa-nye
surfing *daskanje na valovima* ⓝ
  da-ska-nye na *va*-law-vee-ma
surname *prezime* ⓝ *pre*-zee-me
surprise *iznenađen* ⓜ *eez*-ne-na-jen
sweater *džemper* ⓜ *jem*-per
Sweden *Švedska* ① *shved*-ska
sweet *sladak* sla-dak
sweets *bomboni* ⓜ pl bawm-*baw*-nee
swelling *oteklina* ① *aw*-te-klee-na
swim *(za)plivati* (za-)*plee*-va-tee
swimming (sport) *plivanje* ⓝ *plee*-va-nye
swimming pool *bazen za plivanje* ⓜ
  ba-zen za *plee*-va-nye
swimsuit *kupaći kostim* ⓜ *koo*-pa-chee
  kaw-steem
Switzerland *Švicarska* ① shvee-*tsar*-ska
synagogue *sinagoga* ① see-na-*gaw*-ga
synthetic *sintetičan* ⓜ seen-*te*-tee-chan
syringe *štrcaljka* ① shtr-*tsal*'-ka

T

table *stol* ⓜ stawl
table tennis *stolni tenis* ⓜ *stawl*-nee te-nees
tablecloth *stolnjak* ⓜ *stawl*-nyak
tail *rep* ⓜ rep
tailor *krojač* ⓜ *kroy*-ach
take *uzeti/uzimati* oo-ze-tee/oo-zee-ma-tee
talk *(pro)govoriti* (praw-)gaw-*vaw*-ree-tee
tall *visok* vee-sawk
tampon *tampon* ⓜ *tam*-pawn

tanning lotion *losion za dobijanje tena* ⓜ
  law-*see*-awn za daw-*bee*-ya-nye *te*-na
tap *slavina* ① sla-vee-na
tap water *obična voda* ① *aw*-beech-na
  vaw-da
tasty *ukusan* oo-koo-san
tax *porez* ⓜ *paw*-rez
taxi *taksi* ⓜ *tak*-see
taxi stand *taksi stanica* ① *tak*-see
  sta-nee-tsa
tea *čaj* ⓜ chai
teacher *učitelj* ⓜ oo-chee-tel'
team *momčad* ① *mawm*-chad
teaspoon *žličica* ① *zhle*-chee-tsa
technique *tehnika* ① *teh*-nee-ka
teeth *zubi* ⓜ pl zoo-bee
telegram *telegram* ⓜ *te*-le-gram
telephone *telefon* ⓜ *te*-le-fawn
telephone *telefonirati* imp
  te-le-faw-*nee*-ra-tee
telephone box *telefonska govornica* ①
  te-*le*-fawn-ska gaw-*vawr*-nee-tsa
telephone centre *telefonska centrala* ①
  te-*le*-fawn-ska tsen-*tra*-la
telescope *teleskop* ⓜ *te*-le-skawp
television (general) *televizija* ①
  te-le-*vee*-zee-ya
television set *televizor* ⓜ te-le-*vee*-zawr
tell *reći* perf re-chee
temperature (fever) *groznica* ①
  grawz-nee-tsa
temperature (weather) *temperatura* ①
  tem-pe-ra-*too*-ra
temple *hram* ⓜ hram
tennis *tenis* ⓜ *te*-nees
tennis court *tenisko igralište* ①
  te-nee-skaw *ee*-gra-leesh-te
tent *šator* ⓜ *sha*-tawr
tent peg *šatorski kolčić* ⓜ *sha*-tawr-skee
  kawl-cheech
terrible *strašan* stra-shan
test *test* ⓜ test
thank *zahvaliti/zahvaljivati*
  za-*hva*-lee-tee/za-hva-*lyee*-va-tee
thank you *hvala vam/ti* pol/inf *hva*-la
  vam/tee
that (one) *ono* ① *aw*-naw
theatre *kazalište* ① *ka*-za-leesh-te
their *njihov/njihova/njihovo* ⓜ/①/ⓝ
  nyee-hawv/nyee-haw-va/nyee-haw-vaw
there *tamo* ta-maw
they *oni/one/ona* ⓜ/①/ⓝ *aw*-nee/
  aw-ne/aw-na

thick (liquid) *gust* goost
thick (object) *debeo* de·be·aw
thief *lopov* law·pawv
thin *tanak* @ ta·nak
think *(po)misliti (paw·)mee·slee·tee*
third *treći* tre·chee
(to be) thirsty *žedan* zhe·dan
this *ovaj/ova/ovo* @/①/@ aw·vai/aw·va/
aw·vaw
this (one) *ovo* @ aw·vaw
thread *konac* @ kaw·nats
throat *grlo* @ gr·law
thrush (illness) *infekcija kandide* ①
een·fek·tsee·ya kan·dee·de
thunderstorm *grmljavina* ① grm·lya·vee·na
Thursday *četvrtak* @ chet·vr·tak
ticket *karta* ① kar·ta
ticket collector *osoblje koje uzima
odrezak karte* ① aw·sawb·lye koy·e
oo·zee·ma aw·dre·zak kar·te
ticket machine *automat za prodaju
karata* a·oo·taw·mat za praw·dai·oo
ka·ra·ta
ticket office *šalter* @ shal·ter
tide *plima i oseka* ① plee·ma e aw·se·ka
tight *tijesan* tee·ye·san
time *vrijeme* @ vree·ye·me
time difference *razlika u vremenu* ①
raz·lee·ka oo vre·me·noo
timetable *vozni red* @ vawz·nee red
tin (can) *limenka* ① lee·men·ka
tin opener *otvarač za limenke* @
awt·va·rach za lee·men·ke
tiny *sićušan* @ see·choo·shan
tip (gratuity) *bakšiš* bak·sheesh
tire (car) *guma na automobile* ① goo·ma
na a·oo·taw·maw·bee·le
tire (general) *guma* ① goo·ma
tired *umoran* oo·maw·ran
tissues *papirnati rupčići* @ pl
pa·peer·na·tee roop·chee·chee
to *do · na · prema · u · za* daw · nad ·
pre·ma · oo · za
toast *tost* @ tawst
toaster *toster* @ taw·ster
tobacco *duhan* @ doo·han
tobacconist *prodavač duhana* @
praw·da·vach doo·ha·na
tobogganing *sanjkanje* @ san'·ka·nye
today *danas* da·nas
toe *nožni prst* @ nawzh·nee prst
together *zajedno* zai·ed·naw
toilet *zahod* @ za·hawd

toilet paper *toaletni papir* @
taw·a·let·nee pa·peer
tomato *rajčica* ① rai·chee·tsa
tomato sauce *umak od rajčica* @ oo·mak
awd rai·chee·tsa
tomorrow *sutra* soo·tra
tomorrow afternoon *sutra popodne*
soo·tra paw·pawd·ne
tomorrow evening *sutra uvečer* soo·tra
oo·ve·cher
tomorrow morning *sutra ujutro* soo·tra
oo·yoo·traw
tonight *večeras* ve·che·ras
too (expensive etc) *suviše* soo·vee·she
tooth *zub* @ zoob
toothache *zubobolja* ① zoo·baw·baw·lya
toothbrush *četkica za zube* ① chet·kee·tsa
za zoo·be
toothpaste *pasta za zube* ① pa·sta za
zoo·be
toothpick *čačkalica* ① chach·ka·lee·tsa
torch (flashlight) *(ručna) svjetiljka* ①
(rooch·na) svye·teel'·ka
touch (sense) *dirnuti/dirati* deer·noo·tee/
dee·ra·tee
tour *ekskurzija* ① ek·skoor·zee·ya
tourist *turist* @ too·reest
tourist office *turistička agencija* ①
too·ree·steech·ka a·gen·tsee·ya
towards (direction) *prema* pre·ma
towel *ručnik* @ rooch·neek
tower *toranj* @ taw·ran'
toxic waste *toksični otpad* @
tawk·seech·nee awt·pad
toy shop *prodavaonica igračaka* ①
praw·da·va·aw·nee·tsa ee·gra·cha·ka
track (path) *put* @ poot
track (sport) *staza* ① sta·za
trade *trgovina* ① tr·gaw·vee·na
tradesperson *obrtnik* @ aw·brt·neek
traffic *promet* @ praw·met
traffic light *semafor* @ se·ma·fawr
trail *put* @ poot
train *vlak* @ vlak
train station *željeznička stanica* ①
zhe·lyez·neech·ka sta·nee·tsa
tram *tramvaj* @ tram·vai
transit lounge *tranzitna čekaonica* ①
tran·zeet·na che·ka·aw·nee·tsa
translate *prevesti/prevoditi* pre·ve·stee/
pre·vaw·dee·tee
transport *prijevoz* @ pree·ye·vawz
travel *(pro)putovati* (praw·)poo·taw·va·tee

T

english–croatian

217

travel agency *putna agencija* ① *poot*·na a·*gen*·tsee·ya

travel sickness *mučnina od vožnje* ① mooch·*nee*·na awd *vawzh*·nye

travellers cheque *putnički čekovi* ⓜ pl *poot*·neech·kee *che*·kaw·vee

tree *stablo* ① *sta*·blaw

trip (journey) *izlet* ⓜ *eez*·let

trolley *kolica za prtljagu* ① kaw·*lee*·tsa za prt·*lya*·goo

trousers *hlače* ① pl *hla*·che

truck *kamion* ⓜ ka·*mee*·awn

trust *(po)vjerovati (paw)*·vye·*raw*·va·tee

try *probati/probavati praw*·ba·tee/ *praw*·ba·va·tee

try (attempt) *pokušati/pokušavati paw*·koo·sha·tee/*paw*·koo·*sha*·va·tee

T-shirt *majica* ① *mai*·ee·tsa

tube (tyre) *zračnica* ① *zrach*·nee·tsa

Tuesday *utorak* ⓜ *oo*·taw·rak

tumour *tumor* ⓜ *too*·mawr

tuna (as food) *tunjevina* ① *too*·nye·vee·na

tuna (fish) *tuna* ① *too*·na

tune *melodija* ① *me*·law·dee·ya

turkey *puran* ⓜ *poo*·ran

turn *okrenuti/okretati* aw·*kre*·noo·tee/ aw·kre·ta·tee

TV (set) *televizor* ⓜ te·le·*vee*·zawr

tweezers *pinceta* ① peen·*tse*·ta

twice *dvaput* dva·poot

twin room *dvokrevetna soba* ① dvaw·kre·vet·na *saw*·ba

twins *blizanci* ⓜ pl blee·*zan*·tsee

two *dva* dva

type *vrsta* ① *vr*·sta

typical *tipičan* tee·*pee*·chan

tyre (car) *guma na automobile* ① *goo*·ma na a·oo·taw·maw·*bee*·le

tyre (general) *guma* ① *goo*·ma

U

ultrasound *ultrazvuk* ① *ool*·tra·zvook

umbrella *suncobran* ⓜ soon·tsaw·bran

uncomfortable *neudoban* ne·oo·daw·ban

underground railway *podzemna željeznica* ① *pawd*·zem·na zhe·lye·znee·tsa

understand *razumjeti/razumijevati* ra·*zoo*·mye·tee/ra·zoo·mee·ye·va·tee

underwear *donje rublje* ⓝ *daw*·nye roob·lye

unemployed *nezaposlen* ne·za·paw·slen

unfair *nepravedan* ne·pra·ve·dan

uniform *uniforma* ① oo·nee·fawr·ma

universe *svemir* ⓜ *sve*·meer

university *sveučilište* ⓝ sve·oo·chee·leesh·te

unleaded *bezolovni be·*zaw·lawv·nee

unsafe *nesiguran* ne·see·goo·ran

until (Friday, etc) *do* daw

unusual *neobičan* ne·aw·bee·chan

up *gore* gaw·re

urgent *hitan* hee·tan

urinary infection *infekcija mokraćnih kanala* ① een·fek·tsee·ya maw·krach·neeh ka·*na*·la

USA *SAD* ① pl es a de

useful *koristan* kaw·ree·stan

V

vacancy *slobodno mjesto* ⓝ slaw·bawd·naw *mye*·staw

vacant *prazan* pra·zan

vacation *praznici* ⓜ pl *praz*·nee·tsee

vaccination *cijepljenje* ⓝ tsee·*yep*·lye·nye

vagina *vagina* ① va·*gee*·na

validate *potvrditi/potvrđivati* pawt·*vr*·dee·tee/pawt·vr·*jee*·va·tee

valley *dolina* ① daw·lee·na

valuable *dragocjen* dra·*gaw*·tsyen

value (price) *vrijednost* ① vree·*yed*·nawst

van *kombi* ⓜ *kawm*·bee

veal *teletina* ① te·le·tee·na

vegetable *povrće* ⓝ *paw*·vr·che

vegetarian *vegetarijanac* ⓜ ve·ge·ta·ree·*ya*·nats

vein *vena* ① *ve*·na

venereal disease *spolna bolesta* ① spawl·na baw·les·ta

Venetian *venecijanski* ve·ne·*tsee*·yan·skee

Venice *Venecija* ① *ve*·ne·tsee·ya

venue *lokal* ⓜ *law*·kal

very *vrlo* vr·law

video recorder *video rekorder* ① *vee*·de·aw re·*kawr*·der

video tape *video kazeta* ① *vee*·de·aw ka·*ze*·ta

view *prizor* ⓜ *pree*·zawr

village *selo* ⓝ *se*·law

vine *vinova loza* ① *vee*·naw·va *law*·za

vinegar *ocat* ⓜ *aw*·tsat

vineyard *vinograd* ⓜ *vee*·naw·grad

virus *virus* ⓜ *vee*·roos

visa *viza* ① *vee*·za

visit *posjetiti/posjećivati* paw·sye·tee·tee/ paw·sye·chee·va·tee
vitamins *vitamini* ⓟ pl vee·ta·mee·nee
vodka *vodka* ⓕ vawd·ka
voice *glas* ⓜ glas
volleyball (sport) *odbojka* ⓕ awd·boy·ka
volume *ton* ⓜ tawn
vote *glasovati* imp gla·saw·va·tee

W

wage *plaća* ⓕ pla·cha
wait (for) *(pri)čekati nekoga* (pree·)che·ka·tee ne·kaw·ga
waiter *konobar* ⓜ kaw·naw·bar
waiting room *čekaonica* ⓕ che·ka·aw·nee·tsa
wake (someone) up *(pro)buditi nekoga* (praw·)boo·dee·tee ne·kaw·ga
walk *hodati* imp haw·da·tee
walkway *hodnik* ⓜ hawd·neek
wall (outer) *zid* ⓜ zeed
walled city *citadela* ⓕ tsee·ta·de·la
want *(po)željeti* (paw·)zhe·lye·tee
war *rat* ⓜ rat
wardrobe *ormar za odjeću* ⓜ awr·mar za aw·dye·choo
warm *topao* ⓜ taw·pa·aw
warn *upozoriti/upozoravati* oo·paw·zaw·ree·tee/ oo·paw·zaw·ra·va·tee
wash (oneself) *(o)prati se* (aw·)pra·tee se
wash (something) *(o)prati* (aw·)pra·tee
wash cloth (flannel) *ručnik* ⓜ rooch·neek
washing machine *stroj za pranje rublja* ⓜ stroy za pra·nye roob·lya
watch *(po)gledati* (paw·)gle·da·tee
watch *sat* ⓜ sat
water *voda* ⓕ vaw·da
water bottle *boca za vodu* ⓕ baw·tsa za vaw·doo
water bottle (hot) *termofor* ⓜ ter·maw·fawr
water taxi *taksi na vodi* ⓜ tak·see na vaw·dee
waterfall *vodopad* ⓜ vaw·daw·pad
waterfront *riva* ⓕ ree·va
watermelon *lubenica* ⓕ loo·be·nee·tsa
waterproof *nepromočiv* ne·praw·maw·cheev
water-skiing *skijanje na vodi* ⓕ skee·ya·nye na vaw·dee
wave *val* ⓜ val

way (manner) *način* ⓜ na·cheen
we *mi* mee
weak *slab* slab
wealthy *bogat* baw·gat
wear *nositi* imp naw·see·tee
weather *vremenski uvjeti* ⓜ pl vre·men·skee oo·vye·tee
wedding *vjenčanje* ⓝ vyen·cha·nye
wedding cake *svadbena torta* ⓕ svad·be·na tawr·ta
wedding present *svadbeni dar* ⓜ svad·be·nee dar
Wednesday *srijeda* ⓕ sree·ye·da
week *tjedan* ⓜ tye·dan
(this) week *(ovaj) tjedan* ⓜ (aw·vai) tye·dan
weekend *vikend* ⓜ veek·end
weigh *(iz)vagati* (eez·)va·ga·tee
weight *težina* ⓕ te·zhee·na
weights *tegovi* ⓜ pl te·gaw·vee
welcome *dočekati/dočekivati* daw·che·ka·tee/daw·che·kee·va·tee
welfare *socijalna skrb* ⓕ saw·tsee·yal·na skrb
well *dobro* daw·braw
west *zapad* ⓜ za·pad
wet *mokar* ⓜ maw·kar
what *koji/koja/koje* ⓜ/ⓕ/ⓝ koy·ee/koy·a/koy·e
wheel *kotač* ⓜ kaw·tach
wheelchair *invalidska kolica* ⓕ pl een·va·leed·ska kaw·lee·tsa
when *kada* ka·da
where *gdje* gdye
which *koji* koy·ee
whisky *viski* ⓜ vee·skee
white *bijel* bee·yel
who *tko* tkaw
wholemeal bread *crni kruh* ⓜ tsr·nee krooh
why *zašto* zash·taw
wide *širok* shee·rawk
wife *žena* ⓕ zhe·na
win *pobijediti/pobjeđivati* paw·bee·ye·dee·tee/paw·bye·jee·va·tee
wind *vjetar* ⓜ vye·tar
window *prozor* ⓜ praw·zawr
windscreen *vjetrobran* ⓜ vye·traw·bran
windsurfing *jedrenje na dasci* ⓝ ye·dre·nye na das·tsee
wine *vino* ⓝ vee·naw
wings *krila* ⓝ pl kree·la
winner *pobjednik* ⓜ paw·byed·neek
winter *zima* ⓕ zee·ma

wire *žica* ① *zhee*·tsa
wish *(po)željeti* (paw·)*zhe*·lye·tee
with *kod · od · sa · za* kawd · awd · sa · za
within (an hour) *u roku od* oo *raw*·koo awd
without *bez* bez
wok *duboka posuda za prženje* ①
  doo·baw·ka paw·soo·da za pr·zhe·nye
woman *žena* ① *zhe*·na
wonderful *divan* dee·van
wood *drvo* ⑩ *dr*·vaw
wool *vuna* ① *voo*·na
word *riječ* ① ree·*yech*
work *rad* ⑩ rad
work *raditi* imp ra·dee·tee
work experience *radno iskustvo* ⑩
  rad·naw ee·skoos·tvaw
work permit *radna dozvola* ① *rad*·na
  dawz·vaw·la
workout *tjelovježba* ① tye·law·vyezh·ba
workshop *radionica* ① ra·dee·*aw*·nee·tsa
world *svijet* ⑩ svee·yet
World Cup *svjetski kup* ⑩ *svyet*·skee koop
worried *zabrinut* ⑩ za·bree·noot
worship *(po)moliti se* (paw·)*maw*·lee·tee
  (se)
wrist *ručni zglob* ⑩ *rooch*·nee zglawb
write *(na)pisati* (na·)*pee*·sa·tee
writer *pisac* ⑩ *pee*·sats
wrong *kriv* kreev

yacht *jahta* ① *yah*·ta
year *godina* ① *gaw*·dee·na
(this) year *(ova) godina* ① (*aw*·va)
  gaw·dee·na
yellow *žut* ⑩ zhoot
yes *da* da
yesterday *jučer* yoo·cher
(not) yet *(ne) još* (ne) yawsh
yoga *joga* ① *yaw*·ga
yogurt *jogurt* ⑩ *yaw*·goort
you inf *ti* tee
you pol sg & pl *vi* vee
young *mlad* mlad
your *tvoj/tvoja/tvoje* ⑩/①/⑩ tvoy/
  tvoy·a/*tvoy*·e
youth hostel *prenoćište za mladež* ⑩
  pre·naw·cheesh·te za *mla*·dezh
Yugoslavia *Jugoslavija* ①
  yoo·gaw·*sla*·vee·ya

zip/zipper *šlic* ⑩ shleets
zodiac *zodijak* ⑩ *zaw*·dee·yak
zoo *zološki vrt* ⑩ *zaw*·lawsh·kee vrt
zucchini *bučice* ① pl *boo*·chee·tse

Nouns in the dictionary have their gender indicated by ⓜ, ⓕ or ⓝ. If it's a plural noun you'll also see pl. When a word that could be either a noun or a verb has no gender indicated, it's a verb.

Nouns and adjectives are in the nominative case. You'll be understood if you just pick words out of this dictionary, but if you'd like to know more about case, see the **a–z phrasebuilder,** page 21.

Adjectives in the dictionary are given in the masculine form only. For an explanation of how to form feminine and neuter adjectives, refer to the **a–z phrasebuilder,** page 16.

Verbs are mostly given in two forms: perfective and imperfective. See the **a–z phrasebuilder,** page 17 for an explanation of these terms and when to use which form. Perfective and imperfective forms are either separated by a slash (with the perfective form given first) or consist of a root imperfective form to which a bracketed prefix is added to form the perfective. For example, the verb 'give' has the forms *dati/ davati da*·tee/*da*·va·tee with the first form being the perfective form and the second the imperfective. The verb 'call' is represented as *(po)zvati (paw·)zva*·tee which has the perfective form *pozvati* and the imperfective form *zvati*. Where two syllables are stressed in the transliteration, eg *(paw·)zva*·tee it means that once you add the prefix to form the perfective, the stress shifts to the prefix. Verbs are listed alphabetically according to their root (unprefixed) form.

Where only one form of a verb is given (not all verbs have both forms) the abbreviations perf and imp have been used to identify whether they are perfective or imperfective.

A

adresa ⓕ a·*dre*·sa *address*
aerobik ⓜ a·e·*raw*·beek *aerobics*
Afrika ⓕ a·free·ka *Africa*
agencija za prodaju nekretnina ⓕ
a·*gen*·tsee·ya za *praw*·dai·oo
ne·kret·*nee*·na *estate agency*
ako a·kaw *if*
akopunktura ⓕ a·kaw·poonk·*too*·ra
acupuncture
aktivist ⓜ ak·*tee*·veest *activist*
aktovka ⓕ ak·*tawv*·ka *briefcase*
aktuelna zbivanja ⓝ pl ak·too·el·na
zbee·va·nya *current affairs*
akumulator ⓜ a·koo·moo·*la*·tawr
battery (for car)
alcohol ⓜ *al*·kaw·hawl *alcohol*
alergija ⓕ a·*ler*·gee·ya *allergy*
alkoholno piće ⓝ *al*·kaw·hawl·naw
pee·che *drink (alcoholic)*

alpinističko penjanje ⓝ
al·pee·*nee*·steech·kaw *pe*·nya·nye *rock
climbing*
alpinizam ⓜ al·pee·*nee*·zam
mountaineering
ambasada ⓕ am·ba·*sa*·da *embassy*
amfiteatar ⓜ am·fee·te·*a*·tar
amphitheatre
amfora ⓕ *am*·faw·ra *amphora*
ananas ⓜ a·na·nas *pineapple*
anarhist ⓜ a·*nar*·heest *anarchist*
anemija ⓕ a·*ne*·mee·ya *anaemia*
antibaby-pilula ⓕ an·tee·bey·bee·pee·
loo·la *the Pill (contraceptive)*
antibiotici ⓜ pl an·tee·bee·*aw*·tee·tsee
antibiotics
antički an·*teech*·kee *ancient*
antikvitet ⓜ an·tee·*kvee*·tet *antique*
antinuklearni an·tee·*noo*·kle·ar·nee
antinuclear
antiseptik ⓜ an·tee·*sep*·teek *antiseptic*

arheološki ⓜ ar·he·*aw*·lawsh·kee *archaeological*
arhitekt ⓜ ar·hee·*tekt* *architect*
arhitektura ⓕ ar·hee·tek·*too*·ra *architecture*
aromaterapija ⓕ a·raw·ma·te·ra·*pe*·ya *aromatherapy*
aspirin ⓜ a·*spee*·reen *aspirin*
astma ⓕ *ast*·ma *asthma*
atelje ⓜ a·te·*lye* *studio*
atletika ⓕ at·*le*·tee·ka *athletics*
atmosfera ⓕ at·*maw*·sfe·ra *atmosphere*
audio vodič ⓜ a·oo·dee·aw *vaw*·deech *guide (audio)*
Australija ⓕ a·oo·*stra*·lee·ya *Australia*
Austrija ⓕ a·oo·*stree*·ya *Austria*
Austru-Ugarsko carstvo ⓝ a·oo·straw·oo·gar·skaw *tsar*·stvaw *Austro-Hungarian Empire*
autobus a·oo·*taw*·boos *bus*
autobuska stanica ⓕ a·oo·*taw*·boo·ska *sta*·nee·tsa *bus station • bus stop*
automat za prodaju karata ⓜ a·oo·*taw*·mat za *praw*·dai·oo *ka*·ra·ta *ticket machine*
automatska praonica ⓕ a·oo·*taw*·mat·ska pra·*aw*·nee·tsa *launderette*
automehaničar ⓜ a·oo·*taw*·me·*ha*·nee·char *mechanic*
automobil ⓜ a·oo·*taw*·*maw*·beel *car*
autoput ⓜ a·oo·*taw*·*poot* *highway*
avenija ⓕ a·ve·*ne*·ya *avenue*
Azija ⓕ a·*zee*·ya *Asia*

B

badem ⓜ *ba*·dem *almond*
badnjak ⓜ *bad*·nyak *Christmas Eve*
baka ⓕ *ba*·ka *grandmother*
bakšiš *bak*·sheesh *tip (gratuity)*
balet ⓜ *ba*·*let* *ballet*
Balkan ⓜ *bal*·kan *the Balkans*
balkon ⓜ *bal*·kawn *balcony*
banana ⓕ ba·*na*·na *banana*
banka ⓕ *ban*·ka *bank (institution)*
bankovni automat ⓜ *ban*·kawv·nee a·oo·*taw*·mat *automated teller machine (ATM)*
bankovni račun ⓜ *ban*·kawv·nee *ra*·choon *bank account*
bar ⓜ bar *bar*

baterija ⓕ ba·te·*ree*·ya *battery (general)*
bazen za plivanje ⓜ *ba*·zen za *plee*·va·nye *swimming pool*
beba ⓕ *be*·ba *baby*
bejzbol ⓜ *beyz*·bawl *baseball*
Belgija ⓕ *bel*·gee·ya *Belgium*
benzin ⓜ ben·*zeen* *gasoline • petrol*
benziska stanica ⓕ ben·*zeen*·ska *sta*·nee·tsa *gas station • petrol station*
besplatan be·*spla*·tan *free (gratis)*
bez bez *without*
— **slobodnih mjesta** *slaw*·bawd·neeh *mye*·sta *no vacancy*
bezalkoholno piće ⓝ be·zal·kaw·hawl·naw *pee*·che *soft drink*
bezolovni be·zaw·lawv·nee *unleaded*
biblija ⓕ *bee*·blee·ya *Bible*
bicikl ⓜ *bee*·tsee·kl *bicycle*
biciklist ⓜ bee·tsee·*kleest* *cyclist*
bife ⓝ *bee*·fe *buffet*
bijel *be*·yel *white*
bilijar ⓜ bee·*lee*·yar *pool (game)*
bilježnica ⓕ bee·*lyezh*·nee·tsa *notebook*
biljka ⓕ *beel*·ka *herb • plant*
biti/bivati bee·tee/bee·*va*·tee *be*
biznis ⓜ *beez*·nees *business*
biznismen ⓜ&ⓕ *beez*·nees·men *business man/woman*
blagajna ⓕ bla·*gai*·na *cash register*
blagajnik ⓜ bla·*gai*·neek *cashier*
blagdan ⓜ *blag*·dan *holiday (day off)*
blato ⓝ *bla*·taw *mud*
blic ⓜ bleets *flash (camera)*
blizak *blee*·zak *close (nearby)*
blizanci ⓜ pl blee·*zan*·tsee *twins*
blizu *blee*·zoo *near*
boca ⓕ *baw*·tsa *bottle*
— **za vodu** za *vaw*·doo *water bottle*
bog ⓜ bawg *god (general)*
bogat *baw*·gat *wealthy*
boja ⓕ *boy*·a *a colour*
boks ⓜ bawks *boxing*
bokserice ⓕ pl bawk·se·ree·tse *boxer shorts*
bol ⓕ bawl *pain*
bolan *baw*·lan *painful*
bolest ⓕ *baw*·lest *disease*
bolestan *baw*·les·tan *sick*
bolji *baw*·lyee *better*
bolnica ⓕ *bawl*·nee·tsa *hospital*
bomboni ⓜ pl bawm·*baw*·nee *candy • lollies • sweets*
borba ⓕ *bawr*·ba *fight (battle)*

borilačke vještine ① pl baw·ree·lach·ke vye·shtee·ne *martial arts*
Bosna i Hercegovina ① baw·sna ee her·tse·gaw·vee·na *Bosnia-Hercegovina*
botanički vrt ⓜ baw·ta·neech·kee vrt *botanic garden*
božić ⓜ baw·zheech *Christmas*
božićni dan ⓜ baw·zheech·nee dan *Christmas Day*
bračno stanje ⓝ brach·naw sta·nye *marital status*
brak ⓜ brak *marriage*
brašno ⓝ brash·naw *flour*
brat ⓜ brat *brother*
brava ① bra·va *lock*
brdska staza ① brd·ska sta·za *mountain path*
brdski bicikl ⓜ brd·skee bee·tsee·kl *mountain bike*
breskva ① bresk·va *peach*
brežuljak ⓜ bre·zhoo·lyak *hill*
brijač ⓜ bree·yach *barber • razor*
(o)brijati se (aw·)bree·ya·tee se *shave*
briljantan bree·lyan·tan *brilliant*
(po)brinuti se (paw·)bree·noo·tee se *care (for someone)*
(po)brinuti se za (paw·)bree·noo·tee se za *look after*
britva ① breet·va *razor blade*
brod ⓜ brawd *ship*
broj ⓜ broy *number (figure)*
  — **putovnice** poo·tawv·nee·tse *passport number*
  — **registarske tablice** re·gee·star·ske ta·blee·tse *licence-plate number*
  — **sobe** saw·be *room number*
(iz)brojati (eez·)broy·a·tee *count*
brokula ① braw·koo·la *broccoli*
bronhitis ⓜ brawn·hee·tees *bronchitis*
brošura ① braw·shoo·ra *brochure*
brz brz *fast*
brzi br·zee *express*
brzina ① br·zee·na *speed*
  — **filma** feel·ma *film speed*
brzinomjer ⓜ br·zee·naw·myer *speedometer*
brzinsko ograničenje ⓝ br·zeen·skaw aw·gra·nee·che·nye *speed limit*
bučan boo·chan *noisy*
bučice ① pl boo·chee·tse *courgette • zucchini*
budala ① boo·da·la *idiot*
budilica ① boo·dee·lee·tsa *alarm clock*

Budist ⓜ boo·deest *Buddhist*
(pro)buditi nekoga (praw·)boo·dee·tee ne·kaw·ga *wake (someone) up*
budućnost ① boo·dooch·nawst *future*
budžet ⓜ boo·jet *budget*
buha ① boo·ha *flea*
bundeva ① boon·de·va *pumpkin*
(pro)bušiti (praw·)boo·shee·tee *puncture*
buvljak ⓜ boov·lyak *flea market*

C

carinarnica ① tsa·ree·nar·nee·tsa *customs*
CD ⓜ tse de *CD*
cent ⓜ tsent *cent*
centar ⓜ tsen·tar *centre*
centimetar ⓜ tsen·tee·me·tar *centimetre*
cesta ① tse·sta *road*
cigara ① tsee·ga·ra *cigar*
cigareta ① tsee·ga·re·ta *cigarette*
cijena ① tsee·ye·na *price*
  — **ulaznice** oo·laz·nee·tse *cover charge (nightclub etc)*
  — **vožnje** vawzh·nye *fare*
cijepljenje ⓝ tsee·yep·lye·nye *vaccination*
cipela/e ① sg/① pl tsee·pe·la/e *shoe(s)*
cirkus ⓜ tseer·koos *circus*
cistitis ⓜ tsee·stee·tees *cystitis*
citadela ① tsee·ta·de·la *walled city*
crkva ① tsr·kva *church*
crn tsrn *black*
Crna Gora ① tsr·na gaw·ra *Montenegro*
crno-bijeli (film) tsr·naw·bee·ye·lee (feelm) *B&W (film)*
crven tsr·ven *red*
crvi ⓜ pl tsr·vee *worms*
cura ① tsoo·ra *girlfriend*
cvijet ⓜ tsvee·yet *flower*
cvjećara ① tsvye·cha·ra *florist*

Č

čačkalica ① chach·ka·lee·tsa *toothpick*
čaj ⓜ chai *tea*
čamac ⓜ cha·mats *boat*
čarapa/e ① sg/① pl cha·ra·pa/e *sock(s)*
čaša ① cha·sha *glass (receptacle)*
ček ⓜ chek *cheque*
čekaonica ① che·ka·aw·nee·tsa *waiting room*

(pri)čekati nekoga (pree-)che·ka·tee ne·kaw·ga wait (for)

čekić ⓜ che·keech hammer

čeljust ⓕ che·lyoost jaw

čelnik ⓜ chel·neek leader

čep ⓜ chep plug (bath)

čepovi za uši ⓜ pl che·paw·vee za oo·shee earplugs

čestitke ⓕ pl che·steet·ke congratulations

često che·staw often

češalj ⓜ che·shal' comb

češnjak ⓜ chesh·nyak garlic

četka ⓕ chet·ka brush
— **za kosu** za kaw·soo hairbrush

četkica za zube ⓕ chet·kee·tsa za zoo·be toothbrush

četvrtak ⓜ chet·vr·tak Thursday

četvrtina ⓕ chet·vr·tee·na quarter

(u)činiti (oo·)chee·nee·tee do · make

čipka ⓕ cheep·ka lace

čist cheest clean · pure

(o)čistiti (aw·)chee·stee·tee clean

čišćenje ⓝ cheesh·che·nye cleaning

čitanje ⓝ chee·ta·nye reading

(pro)čitati (praw·)chee·ta·tee read

čizma/e sg/ⓕ pl chee·zma/e boot(s) (footwear)

član(ica) ⓜ/ⓕ chlan(·ee·tsa) member

čokolada ⓕ chaw·kaw·la·da chocolate

čovjek ⓜ chaw·vyek man (human)

čuti perf choo·tee hear

čuvanje djece ⓝ choo·va·nye dye·tse childminding

D

da da yes

dadilja ⓕ da·dee·lya baby-sitter

dahnuti/disati dah·noo·tee/dee·sa·tee breathe

daleko da·le·kaw far

dalekozor ⓜ da·le·kaw·zawr binoculars

daljinski upravljač ⓜ da·lyeen·skee oo·prav·lyach remote control

dan ⓜ dan day

danas da·nas today

Danska ⓕ dan·ska Denmark

dar ⓜ dar gift

daska ⓕ da·ska board
— **za surfanje** za soor·fa·nye surfboard

daskanje na snijegu ⓝ da·ska·nye na snee·ye·goo snowboarding

daskanje na valovima ⓝ da·ska·nye na va·law·vee·ma surfing

dati/davati da·tee/da·va·tee give

datulja ⓕ da·too·lya date (fruit)

datum ⓜ da·toom date (day)
— **rođenja** raw·je·nya date of birth

debeo de·be·aw fat · thick (object)

dečko ⓜ dech·kaw boyfriend

deka ⓕ de·ka blanket

delikatese ⓕ pl de·lee·ka·te·se delicatessen

demokracija ⓕ de·maw·kra·tsee·ya democracy

demonstracija ⓕ de·mawn·stra·tsee·ya demonstration (protest)

depozit ⓜ de·paw·zeet deposit (bank)

desni ⓜ pl de·snee gum (teeth)

desničarski de·snee·char·skee right-wing

desno de·snaw right (direction)

dezodorans ⓜ de·zaw·daw·rans deodorant

digitron ⓜ dee·gee·trawn calculator

dijabetes ⓜ dee·ya·be·tes diabetes

dijafragma ⓕ dee·ya·frag·ma diaphragm (body part)

dijapozitiv ⓜ dee·ya·paw·zee·teev slide (film)

dijeliti imp dee·ye·lee·tee share (a dorm etc)

(po)dijeliti (paw·)dee·ye·lee·tee deal (cards)

dijeta ⓕ dee·ye·ta diet

dijete ⓝ dee·ye·te child

dinja ⓕ dee·nya cantaloupe · melon · rockmelon

dio ⓜ dee·aw part (component)

director ⓜ dee·rek·tawr director

direktan dee·rek·tan direct
— **poziv** paw·zeev direct-dial

dirnuti/dirati deer·noo·tee/dee·ra·tee feel · touch

disk (CD-ROM) ⓜ deesk (tse de rawm) disk (CD-ROM)

disketa ⓕ dee·ske·ta disk (floppy)

disko ⓜ dee·skaw disco

diskriminacija ⓕ dee·skree·mee·na·tsee·ya discrimination

divan dee·van wonderful

dizajn ⓜ dee·zain design

dizalo ⓝ dee·za·law elevator · lift

djeca ⓝ pl *dye*-tsa *children*

dječak ⓜ *dye*-chak *boy*

dječja hodalica ⓕ *dyech*-ya *haw*-da-lee-tsa *stroller*

djed ⓜ dyed *grandfather*

djevojčica ⓕ dye-*voy*-chee-tsa *girl*

dlaka ⓕ *dla*-ka *hair (body)*

dnevni *dnev*-nee *daily*

dnevnik ⓜ *dnev*-neek *diary*

dno ⓝ dnaw *bottom (position)*

do daw *beside • to*

dobaciti/dobacivati daw-*ba*-tsee-tee/ daw-ba-*tsee*-va-tee *pass*

dobar *daw*-bar *good*

dobitak ⓜ daw-*bee*-tak *profit*

dobiti/dobivati daw-bee-tee/ daw-*bee*-va-tee *get*

dobro *daw*-braw *well*

doček nove godine ⓜ *daw*-chek *naw*-ve gaw-dee-ne *New Year's Eve*

dočekati/dočekivati daw-che-ka-tee/ daw-che-*kee*-va-tee *welcome*

doći/dolaziti daw-chee/daw-la-zee-tee *come*

dokumentacija ⓕ daw-koo-men-*ta*-tsee-ya *paperwork*

dokumentarac ⓜ daw-koo-men-*ta*-rats *documentary*

dolar ⓜ *daw*-lar *dollar*

dolasci ⓜ pl daw-*las*-tsee *arrivals*

dolina ⓕ daw-*lee*-na *valley*

dolje *daw*-lye *down*

dom ⓜ dawm *home*

donijeti/donositi daw-*nee*-ye-tee/ daw-*naw*-see-tee *bring*

donje rublje ⓝ *daw*-nye *roob*-lye *underwear*

dopasti/dopadati se daw-pa-stee/ daw-*pa*-da-tee se *like (appeal to)*

dopisnica ⓕ daw-*pee*-snee-tsa *postcard*

dopuštenje ⓝ daw-poosh-*te*-nye *permission*

doručak ⓜ daw-*roo*-chak *breakfast*

dosadan daw-sa-dan *boring*

dosta *daw*-sta *enough*

dostaviti/dostavljati daw-sta-vee-tee/ daw-*stav*-lya-tee *deliver*

dozvola ⓕ dawz-*vaw*-la *licence • permit*

dozvoliti/dozvoljavati dawz-vaw-lee-tee/ dawz-vaw-*lya*-va-tee *admit (allow)*

dozvoljena količina prtljage ⓕ dawz-vaw-*lye*-na kaw-lee-*chee*-na prt-*lya*-ge *baggage allowance*

dragocjen dra-*gaw*-tsyen *valuable*

drama ⓕ *dra*-ma *drama*

dražica ⓕ dra-*zhee*-tsa *cove*

droga/e ⓕ sg/ⓕ pl *draw*-ga/e *drug(s) (illicit)*

drug droog *companion*

drugačiji droo-*ga*-chee-yee *different (another)*

drugi *droo*-gee *another • other • second*
— **razred** raz-red *economy class • second class*

društvene znanosti ⓕ pl *droosht*-ve-ne zna-naw-stee *humanities*

društvo ⓝ *droosh*-tvaw *company*

drvo ⓝ *dr*-vaw *wood*
— **za ogrjev** za *aw*-gryev *firewood*

država ⓕ *dr*-zha-va *country (nation state)*

državljanstvo ⓝ dr-zhav-*lyan*-stvaw *citizenship*

dubok ⓜ doo-*bawk* *deep*

dugačak doo-ga-chak *long*

dugme ⓝ *doog*-me *button*

dugovati imp doo-*gaw*-va-tee *owe*

duhan ⓜ *doo*-han *tobacco*

dupli krevet ⓜ doo-plee *kre*-vet *double bed*

dva dva *two*
— **tjedna** ⓝ *tyed*-na *fortnight*

dvaput *dva*-poot *twice*

DVD ⓜ de ve de *DVD*

dvokrevetna soba ⓕ *dvaw*-kre-vet-na *saw*-ba *double room • twin room*

dvorac ⓜ *dvaw*-rats *castle*

dvostruk *dvaw*-strook *double*

Dž

džamija ⓕ *ja*-mee-ya *mosque*

džem ⓜ jem *jam*

džemper ⓜ *jem*-per *jumper • sweater*

džep ⓜ jep *pocket*

džepni nožić ⓜ *jep*-nee *naw*-zheech *pocket knife*

džin ⓜ jeen *gin*

džip ⓜ jeep *jeep*

E

ekcem ⓜ ek-*tsem* *eczema*

ekskurzija ⓕ ek-*skoor*-zee-ya *tour*
— **s vodičem** s vaw-*dee*-chem *guided tour*

ekspres pošta ① *eks*·pres *pawsh*·ta express (mail)

ekstasi ① *ek*·sta·see ecstasy (drug)

e-mail ① ee·*me*·eel email

emocionalan e·maw·tsee·aw·na·lan emotional

Engleska ① *en*·gle·ska England

engleski *en*·gle·skee English

euro ① e·oo·raw euro

Europa ① e·oo·*raw*·pa Europe

farma ① *far*·ma farm

festival ⓜ fe·*stee*·val festival

fikcija ① *feek*·tsee·ya fiction (genre)

film ⓜ feelm film • movie
— **za foto-aparat** za *faw*·taw·a·*pa*·rat film (for camera)

filtriran feel·*tree*·ran filtered

fino pecivo ⓝ fee·naw pe·tsee·vaw pastry

Finska ① *feen*·ska Finland

fizički radnik ① fee·zeech·kee *rad*·neek manual worker

flanel ⓜ fla·*nel* flannel

flaster ① *fla*·ster Band-aid

foaje ⓜ faw·*a*·e foyer

foto-aparat ⓜ *faw*·taw·a·*pa*·rat camera

fotograf ⓜ faw·taw·graf photographer

fotografija ① faw·taw·*gra*·fee·ya photo • photography

Francuska ① *fran*·tsoo·ska France

frizer ⓜ *free*·zer hairdresser

funta ① *foon*·ta pound (money, weight)

galerija ① ga·*le*·ree·ya art gallery

garantiran ga·ran·*tee*·ran guaranteed

garaža ① ga·*ra*·zha garage

garderoba ① gar·de·*raw*·ba cloakroom

gastroenteritis ⓜ *ga*·straw·en·te·*ree*·tees gastroenteritis

gazda ⓜ *gaz*·da landlord

gazdarica ① *gaz*·da·ree·tsa landlady

gdje *gdye* where

G'da *g*·ja Ms

gimnastika ① geem·*na*·stee·ka gymnastics

ginekolog ⓜ gee·ne·*kaw*·lawg gynaecologist

gitara ① gee·*ta*·ra guitar

gladan/gladna ⓜ/① *gla*·dan/*gla*·dna hungry

glas ⓜ glas voice

glasan ⓜ *gla*·san loud

glasovati imp *gla*·saw·va·tee vote

glava ① *gla*·va head
— **ulica** *oo*·lee·tsa main road

glavni *glav*·nee main

glavobolja ① gla·*vaw*·baw·lya headache

glazba ① *glaz*·ba music

(po)gledati (*paw*)*gle*·da·tee look • watch

gležanj ⓜ *gle*·zhan' ankle

gležnjače ① pl glezh·nya·che hiking boots

gljiva ① *glyee*·va mushroom

gluh glooh deaf

glumac ⓜ *gloo*·mats actor

glup gloop stupid

godišnje doba ⓝ *gaw*·deesh·nye *daw*·ba season (winter etc)

gol ⓜ gawl goal

golf ⓜ gawlf golf

gorak *gaw*·rak bitter

gore *gaw*·re up

gorski lanac ⓜ *gawr*·skee *la*·nats mountain range

Gospodin ⓜ gaw·*spaw*·deen Mr

Gospođa ① *gaw*·spaw·ja Mrs

Gospođica ① *gaw*·spaw·jee·tsa Miss

gostiona ① gaw·stee·*aw*·na restaurant (family run)

gostionica ① gaw·stee·*aw*·nee·tsa pub (bar)

gostoprimstvo gaw·staw·*preems*·tvaw hospitality

gotovina ① gaw·taw·*vee*·na cash

govedina ① *gaw*·ve·dee·na beef

(pro)govoriti (praw)gaw·*vaw*·ree·tee speak • talk

grad ⓜ grad city

(iz)graditi (eez·)*gra*·dee·tee build

gradski autobus ⓜ *grad*·skee a·oo·*taw*·boos bus (city)

gradski centar ⓜ *grad*·skee *tsen*·tar city centre

građanska prava ⓝ pl *gra*·jan·ska *pra*·va civil rights

građevinar ⓜ gra·je·*vee*·nar builder

gram ⓜ gram gram

granica ① *gra*·nee·tsa border

grijač ⓜ *gree*·yach heater

grijanje ⓝ *gree*·ya·nye heating

gripa ① *gree*·pa influenza

(za)grliti (za-)gr·lee·tee *hug*
grlo ⑩ gr·law *throat*
grmljavina ① grm·lya·vee·na *thunderstorm*
grnčarija ① grn·cha·ree·ya *pottery*
grob ⑩ grawb *grave (tomb)*
groblje ① graw·blye *cemetery*
groznica ① grawz·nee·tsa *fever*
grožđica ① grawzh·jee·tsa *raisin*
grudnjak ⑩ grood·nyak *bra*
grumen ⑩ groo·men *lump*
grupa ① groo·pa *band (music)*
g-string ① ge·streeng *g-string*
guma ① goo·ma *gum (substance)* •
  tire • *tyre*
  — na automobile na
  a·oo·taw·maw·bee·le *tire (car)*
gurnuti/gurati goor·noo·tee/goo·ra·tee
  push
gust goost *thick (liquid)*
gušter ⑩ goosh·ter *lizard*

H

halal ha·lal *halal*
haljina ① ha·lyee·na *dress*
Halo. ha·law *Hello. (answering telephone)*
halucinacija ① ha·loo·tsee·na·tsee·ya
  hallucination
hašiš ⑩ ha·sheesh *hash*
hepatitis ⑩ he·pa·tee·tees *hepatitis*
heroin ⑩ he·raw·een *heroin*
hidratantna krema ① hee·dra·tant·na
  kre·ma *moisturiser*
higijenski uložak ⑩ hee·gee·yen·skee
  oo·law·zhak *sanitary napkin*
Hinduist ⑩ heen·doo·eest *Hindu*
hitan hee·tan *urgent*
  — slučaj sloo·chai *emergency*
hitna pomoć ① heet·na paw·mawch
  ambulance
HIV ⑩ heev *HIV*
hlače ① pl hla·che *trousers*
hladan hla·dan *cold* • *cool*
hladnjak ⑩ hlad·nyak *refrigerator*
hladovina ① hla·daw·vee·na *shade*
hodati imp haw·da·tee *walk*
hodnik ⑩ hawd·neek *walkway*
hokej ⑩ haw·key *hockey*
  — na ledu na le·doo *ice hockey*
homeopatija ① haw·me·aw·pa·tee·ya
  homeopathy

homoseksualac/homoseksualka ⑩/①
  haw·maw·sek·soo·a·lats/
  haw·maw·sek·soo·al·ka *homosexual*
homoseksualan haw·maw·sek·soo·a·lan *gay*
honorarni ⑩ haw·naw·rar·nee *part-time*
horoskop ⑩ haw·raw·skawp *horoscope*
hotel ⑩ haw·tel *hotel*
hrabar hra·bar *brave*
hram ⑩ hram *temple*
hrana ① hra·na *food*
  — za bebe za be·be *baby food*
(na)hraniti (na·)hra·nee·tee *feed*
Hrvat/Hrvatica ⑩/① hr·vat/hr·va·tee·tsa
  Croat
Hrvatska ① hr·vat·ska *Croatia*
hvala vam/ti pol/inf hva·la vam/tee
  thank you

I

i ee *and*
ići imp ee·chee *go*
  — u kupovinu imp oo
  koo·paw·vee·noo *go shopping*
identifikacija ① ee·den·tee·fee·ka·tsee·ya
  identification
igla injekcije ① ee·gla ee·nyek·tsee·ye
  syringe
igla za šivenje ① ee·gla za shee·ve·nye
  sewing needle
igra ① ee·gra *game*
igralište ⑩ ee·gra·leesh·te *court (tennis)*
igrati imp ee·gra·tee *play (board games)*
ili ee·lee *or*
Iliri ⑩ pl ee·lee·ree *Illyrians*
imati imp ee·ma·tee *have*
ime ⑩ ee·me *name (given)*
imigracija ① ee·mee·gra·tsee·ya
  immigration
Indija ① een·dee·ya *India*
indijski oraščić ⑩ een·deey·skee
  aw·rash·cheech *cashew*
industrija ① een·doo·stree·ya *industry*
infekcija ① een·fek·tsee·ya *infection*
  — kandide kan·dee·de *thrush (illness)*
  — mokraćnih kanala maw·krach·neeh
  ka·na·la *urinary infection*
informacije ① pl een·fawr·ma·tsee·ye
  information
Informacijska tehnologija ①
  een·fawr·ma·tseey·ska
  teh·naw·law·gee·ya *IT*

injekcija ① ee-*nyek*-tsee-ya *injection*
inostranstvo ⑩ ee-naw-*strans*-tvaw
 overseas
instruktor ⑩ een-*strook*-tawr
 instructor
internet ⑩ een-ter-net *Internet*
 — kafić ka-feech *Internet café*
intervju ⑩ een-ter-*vyoo* *interview*
invalidska kolica ① pl een-*va*-leed-ska
 kaw-*lee*-tsa *wheelchair*
inženjer ⑩ een-*zhe*-nyer *engineer*
inženjerstvo ⑩ een-zhe-*nyer*-stvaw
 engineering
Irska ① *eer*-ska *Ireland*
isključen ees-*klyoo*-chen *excluded*
iskustvo ⑩ ees-*koost*-vaw *experience*
isplata ① ees-*pla*-ta *payment*
 (to someone)
ispod ee-spawd *below*
ispovijed ① ee-*spaw*-vee-yed *confession*
 (at church)
ispravan ee-*spra*-van *right (correct)*
isti ⑩ ee-stee *same*
istok ⑩ ee-stawk *east*
Italija ① ee-*ta*-lee-ya *Italy*
iz eez *from*
iza ee-za *after* • *behind*
izabrati/izabirati ee-*za*-bra-tee/
 ee-za-bee-ra-tee *choose*
izaći/izlaziti ee-za-chee/ee-zla-zee-tee
 go out
izaći/izlaziti sa ee-za-chee/
 eez-la-zee-tee sa *go out with
 (date) a person*
izbjeglica ① eez-byeg-lee-tsa *refugee*
izbočina ① eez-*baw*-chee-na *ledge*
izbori ⑩ pl eez-baw-ree *election*
izdavanje ⑩ eez-*da*-va-nye *publishing*
izgoren eez-gaw-ren *burnt*
(iz)gubiti (eez-)*goo*-bee-tee *lose*
izgubljen eez-goob-lyen *lost*
izlaz ⑩ eez-laz *departure gate* • *exit*
izlazak ⑩ eez-*la*-zak *night out*
izlazak sunca ⑩ eez-*la*-zak *soon*-tsa
 sunrise
izlet ⑩ eez-let *trip (journey)*
izložba ① eez-*lawzh*-ba *exhibition*
između eez-zme-joo *between*
iznad eez-nad *above*
iznajmiti/iznajmljivati eez-*nai*-mee-tee/
 eez-naim-lye-va-tee *hire* • *rent*
iznenađen ⑩ eez-*ne*-na-jen *surprise*
Izrael ⑩ ee-zra-el *Israel*

ja ya *I*
jabuka ① ya-*boo*-ka *apple*
jabukovača ① ya-boo-kaw-va-cha *cider*
Jadranska obala ① ya-dran-ska *aw*-ba-la
 Adriatic Coast
Jadransko more ① ya-dran-skaw *maw*-re
 Adriatic Sea
jagoda ① ya-*gaw*-da *strawberry*
jahanje konja ① ya-ha-nye *kaw*-nya
 horse riding
jahati imp ya-ha-tee *ride (horse)*
jahta ① *yah*-ta *yacht*
jaje ① yai-e *egg*
jajnik ⑩ *yai*-neek *ovary*
jak yak *strong (physically)*
jakna ① *yak*-na *jacket*
janje ① ya-nye *lamb (animal)*
janjetina ① ya-*nye*-tee-na *lamb (meat)*
Japan ⑩ ya-pan *Japan*
jarac ⑩ ya-rats *goat*
jaslice ① pl ya-slee-tse *creche*
jastučnica ① ya-stooch-nee-tsa
 pillowcase
jastuk ⑩ ya-stook *pillow*
javni yav-nee *public*
 — parkovi ⑩ pl par-kaw-vee *public
 gardens*
 — telefon ⑩ te-le-fawn *public telephone*
 — zahod ⑩ za-hawd *public toilet*
je ① ye *her*
jedan ① ye-dan *one*
jednake mogućnosti ① pl yed-na-ke
 maw-gooch-naw-stee *equal opportunity*
jednokrevetna soba ①
 yed-naw-*kre*-vet-na *saw*-ba *single room*
jednom yed-nawm *once*
jednosmjeran yed-naw-*smye*-ran
 one-way (ticket)
jednostavan yed-naw-sta-van *easy*
jedrenje na dasci ⑩ ye-dre-nye na
 das-tsee *windsurfing*
jeftino ⑩ yef-tee-naw *cheap*
jelo ① ye-law *dish (food item)*
jelovnik ⑩ ye-*lawv*-neek *menu*
jesen ① ye-sen *autumn* • *fall*
(po)jesti (paw-)ye-stee *eat*
jetra ① ye-tra *liver*
jezero ① ye-ze-raw *lake*
jezik ⑩ ye-zeek *language*
joga ① yaw-ga *yoga*

jogurt ⓜ *yaw*-goort *yogurt*
(ne) još (ne) yawsh *(not) yet*
jučer yoo-cher *yesterday*
jug ⓜ yoog *south*
Jugoslavija ⓕ *yoo-gaw-sla-*vee-ya *Yugoslavia*
juha ⓕ *yoo*-ha *soup*
jutro ⓝ *yoo*-traw *morning*

K

kabanica ⓕ ka-*ba*-nee-tsa *raincoat*
kabina za presvlačenje ⓕ pl ka-*bee*-na za pres-*vla*-che-nye *changing room*
kablovi za punjenje akumulatora ⓜ pl *ka*-blaw-vee za *poo*-nye-nye a-koo-moo-*la*-taw-ra *jumper leads*
kaciga ⓕ *ka*-tsee-ga *helmet*
kada *ka*-da *when*
kafić ⓜ *ka*-feech *café*
kajsija ⓕ *kai*-see-ya *apricot*
kakao ⓜ *ka*-ka-aw *cocoa*
kako *ka*-kaw *how*
kalendar ⓜ ka-*len*-dar *calendar*
kamen ⓜ *ka*-men *stone*
kamion ⓜ *ka*-mee-awn *truck*
kamp ⓜ kamp *camping ground*
kampirati imp kam-*pee*-ra-tee *camp*
Kanada ⓕ *ka*-na-da *Canada*
kanta ⓕ *kan*-ta *bucket*
— **za smeće** za *sme*-che *garbage can*
kapi za oči ⓕ pl *ka*-pee za *aw*-chee *eye drops*
kaput ⓜ *ka*-poot *coat*
karantena ⓕ ka-ran-*te*-na *quarantine*
karavana ⓕ ka-ra-*va*-na *caravan*
karta ⓕ *kar*-ta *map (of country)* • *ticket*
karte za igranje ⓕ pl *kar*-te za ee-*gra*-nye *cards (playing)*
kartonska kutija ⓕ *kar*-tawn-ska koo-*tee*-ya *carton*
kasan *ka*-san *late*
kasino ⓜ ka-*see*-naw *casino*
kasnije *ka*-snee-ye *later*
(za)kašljati (za-)*kash*-lya-tee *cough*
kat ⓜ kat *floor (storey)*
katedrala ⓕ ka-te-*dra*-la *cathedral*
Katoličanstvo ⓝ ka-taw-lee-*chan*-stvaw *Catholicism*
katolik ⓜ *ka*-taw-leek *Catholic*
kava ⓕ *ka*-va *coffee*
kazalište ⓝ *ka*-za-leesh-te *theatre*

kazati/kazivati *ka*-za-tee/ka-*zee*-va-tee *say*
kazeta ⓕ ka-*ze*-ta *cassette*
kći ⓕ kchee *daughter*
keks ⓜ keks *biscuit*
kemijska ⓕ *ke*-meey-ska *pen (ballpoint)*
keramika ⓕ ke-*ra*-mee-ka *ceramics*
kikiriki ⓜ *kee*-kee-ree-kee *groundnut* • *peanut*
kila ⓕ *kee*-la *kilo*
kilogram ⓜ *kee*-law-gram *kilogram*
kilometar ⓜ *kee*-law-me-tar *kilometre*
kino ⓝ *kee*-naw *cinema*
kiosk ⓜ *kee*-awsk *kiosk*
— **za prodaju novina** za *praw*-dai-oo *naw*-vee-na *newsstand*
kip ⓜ keep *statue*
kiropraktor ⓜ *kee*-raw-prak-tawr *chiropractor*
kiseli krastavci ⓜ pl *kee*-se-lee *kra*-stav-tsee *pickles*
kiselo vrhnje ⓝ *kee*-se-law *vrh*-nye *sour cream*
kisik ⓜ *kee*-seek *oxygen*
kiša ⓕ *kee*-sha *rain*
kivi ⓜ *kee*-vee *kiwifruit*
klasa ⓕ *kla*-sa *class (category)*
klasičan *kla*-see-chan *classical*
klasni sistem ⓜ *kla*-snee *see*-stem *class system*
klavijatura ⓕ kla-vee-ya-*too*-ra *keyboard (instrument)*
klima ⓕ *klee*-ma *air-conditioning*
klimatiziran klee-ma-*tee*-zee-ran *air-conditioned*
ključ ⓜ klyooch *key*
knjiga ⓕ *knyee*-ga *book*
knjižara ⓕ *knyee*-zha-ra *bookshop*
knjižnica ⓕ *knyeezh*-nee-tsa *library*
kockice ⓕ pl *kawts*-kee-tse *dice*
kočnice ⓕ pl *kawch*-nee-tse *brakes*
kod kawd *at* • *with*
kofer ⓜ *kaw*-fer *suitcase*
koji *koy*-ee *which*
koji/koja/koje ⓜ/ⓕ/ⓝ *koy*-ee/koy-a/ *koy*-e *what*
kokain ⓜ kaw-*ka*-een *cocaine*
kokos ⓜ *kaw*-kaws *coconut*
koktel ⓜ kawk-*tel* *cocktail*
kola za ručavanje ⓝ *kaw*-la za roo-*cha*-va-nye *dining car*
kolač ⓜ *kaw*-lach *cake*
kolačić ⓜ kaw-*la*-cheech *biscuit* • *cookie*

koledž ⓜ *kaw*·lej *college*

kolega/kolegica ⓜ/ⓕ kaw·*le*·ga/ kaw·*le*·gee·tsa *colleague*

koliba ⓕ *kaw*·lee·ba *lodge*

kolica za prtljagu ⓕ kaw·*lee*·tsa za prt·*lya*·goo *trolley*

količina ⓕ kaw·lee·*chee*·na *number (quantity)*

koliko kaw·*lee*·kaw *how much*

koljeno ⓝ *kaw*·lye·naw *knee*

kolo ⓝ *kaw*·law *circle dance*

kolovoz ⓜ *kaw*·law·vawz *August*

komad ⓜ *kaw*·mad *piece*

komarac ⓜ *kaw*·ma·rats *mosquito*

kombi ⓜ *kawm*·bee *van*

komedija ⓕ kaw·*me*·dee·ya *comedy*

komisija ⓕ kaw·*mee*·see·ya *commission*

kompas ⓜ *kawm*·pas *compass*

kompjuterska igra ⓕ kawm·*pyoo*·ter·ska ee·gra *computer game*

komunikacije ⓕ pl kaw·moo·nee·*ka*·tsee·ye *communications (profession)*

komunista ⓜ kaw·moo·*nee*·sta *communist*

komunizam ⓜ kaw·moo·*nee*·zam *communism*

konac ⓜ *kaw*·nats *thread*
— **za čišćenje zubi** ⓝ za *cheesh*·che·nye zoo·bee *dental floss*

koncert ⓜ *kawn*·tsert *concert*

konferencija ⓕ kon·fe·*ren*·tsee·ya *conference (big)*

konj ⓜ kawny *horse*

konjunktivitis ⓜ kaw·nyoonk·tee·*vee*·tees *conjunctivitis*

konobar ⓜ *kaw*·naw·bar *waiter*

konop za sušenje rublja ⓜ *kaw*·nawp za soo·she·nye roob·lya *clothesline*

kontakt leće ⓕ pl *kawn*·takt *le*·che *contact lenses*

konverter ⓜ kawn·*ver*·ter *adaptor*

konzervativan kawn·zer·va·tee·van *conservative*

konzulat ⓜ kawn·*zoo*·lat *consulate*

koralj ⓜ *kaw*·ral' *coral*

korisnik droga ⓜ *kaw*·ree·sneek *drug user*

koristan kaw·*ree*·stan *useful*

kosa ⓕ *kaw*·sa *hair (head)*

kost ⓕ kawst *bone*

koš ⓜ kawsh *basket*

košarka ⓕ kaw·*shar*·ka *basketball*

košer ⓜ *kaw*·sher *kosher*

košulja ⓕ *kaw*·shoo·lya *shirt*

kotač ⓜ *kaw*·tach *wheel*

kozmetički salon ⓜ kawz·*me*·teech·kee *sa*·lawn *beauty salon*

koža ⓕ *kaw*·zha *leather • skin*

kraj ⓜ krai *end*

kraj krai *beside*

kralj ⓜ kral' *king*

kraljica ⓕ *kra*·lyee·tsa *queen*

krasno kra·snaw *great (fantastic)*

(u)krasti (oo·)kra·stee *steal*

kratak *kra*·tak *short*
— **životopis** ⓜ zhee·vaw·taw·pees *CV*

kratke hlače ⓕ pl *krat*·ke *hla*·che *shorts*

krava ⓕ *kra*·va *cow*

krčenje šuma ⓝ kr·che·nye shoo·ma *deforestation*

kredit ⓜ kre·deet *credit*

kreditna kartica ⓕ kre·deet·na *kar*·tee·tsa *credit card*

kreker ⓜ *kre*·ker *cracker*

krema ⓕ *kre*·ma *cream (cosmetic)*

krevet ⓜ *kre*·vet *bed*

krevetnina ⓕ kre·vet·*nee*·na *bedding*

kriket ⓜ *kree*·ket *cricket (sport)*

krila ⓝ pl *kree*·la *wings*

kriška ⓕ *kreesh*·ka *slice*

kriv kreev *guilty • wrong*

krivnja ⓕ *kreev*·nya *fault (someone's)*

križ ⓜ kreezh *cross*

krojač ⓜ *kroy*·ach *tailor*

kroz krawz *across • in*

krsno ime ⓝ *kr*·snaw ee·me *given name*

krš ⓜ krsh *karst*

kršćanin/kršćanka ⓜ/ⓕ krsh·cha·neen/ krsh·chan·ka *Christian*

krštenje ⓝ krsh·*te*·nye *baptism*

kruh ⓜ krooh *bread*

krumpir ⓜ *kroom*·peer *potato*

krupan *kroo*·pan *large*

kruška ⓕ *kroosh*·ka *pear*

kružni tok ⓜ *kroozh*·nee tawk *roundabout*

krv ⓕ krv *blood*

krvna grupa ⓕ *krv*·na groo·pa *blood group*

krvne pretrage ⓕ pl *krv*·ne *pre*·tra·ge *blood test*

kuća ⓕ *koo*·cha *house*

kući koo·chee *(at) home*

kućni poslovi ⓜ pl *kooch*·nee *paw*·slaw·vee *housework*

kuglice vate ① pl koo-glee-tse va-te *cotton balls*
kuhanje ⓝ koo-ha-nye *cooking*
kuhar/kuharica ⓜ/① koo-har/koo-ha-ree-tsa *cook*
(s)kuhati (s)koo-ha-tee *cook*
kuhinja ① koo-hee-nya *kitchen*
kukuruz ⓜ koo-koo-rooz *corn*
kukuruzne pahuljice ① pl koo-koo-rooz-ne pa-hoo-lyee-tse *cornflakes*
kupaći kostim ⓜ koo-pa-chee kaw-steem *bathing suit • swimsuit*
kupaonica ① koo-pa-aw-nee-tsa *bathroom*
kupiti/kupovati koo-pee-tee/koo-paw-va-tee *buy*
kupka ① koop-ka *bath*
kupon ⓜ koo-pawn *coupon*
kupovati imp koo-paw-va-tee *shop*
kupovina ① koo-paw-vee-na *shopping*
kupus ⓜ koo-poos *cabbage*
kusur ⓜ koo-soor *change (coins)*
kutija ① koo-tee-ya *box • packet*
kvačilo ⓝ kva-chee-law *clutch (car)*
kvalifikacije ① pl kva-lee-fee-ka-tsee-ye *qualifications*
kvaliteta ① kva-lee-te-ta *quality*
(po)kvariti se (paw-)kva-ree-tee se *break down*

L

labav la-bav *loose*
lagan la-gan *light (not heavy)*
laki obrok ⓜ la-kee aw-brawk *snack*
laksativ ⓜ lak-sa-teev *laxative*
lanac la-nats *chain*
laneno platno ⓝ la-ne-naw plat-naw *linen (material)*
lažljivac/lažljivica ⓜ/① lazh-lyee-vats/lazh-lyee-vee-tsa *liar*
leća ① le-cha *lens • lentil*
leći/ležati le-chee/le-zha-tee *lie (not stand)*
led ⓜ led *ice*
leđa ① le-ja *back (body)*
leptir ⓜ le-pteer *butterfly*
let ⓜ let *flight*
(po)letjeti (paw-)let-ye-tee *fly*
lezbijka ① lez-beey-ka *lesbian*
ležaljka ① le-zhal'-ka *deck chairs*
lice ⓝ lee-tse *face*
liječnik ⓜ lee-yech-neek *doctor (medical)*

lijekovi ⓜ pl lee-ye-kaw-vee *medicine (medication)*
lijen lee-yen *lazy*
lijep lee-yep *beautiful • nice*
lijevi lee-ye-vee *left (direction)*
limenka ① lee-men-ka *can (tin)*
limun ⓜ lee-moon *lemon*
limunada ① lee-moo-na-da *lemonade*
linija ① lee-nee-ya *stereo*
lipanj ⓜ lee-pan' *June*
list ⓜ leest *leaf*
listopad ⓜ lee-staw-pad *October*
litica ① lee-tee-tsa *cliff*
lokal ⓜ law-kal *venue*
lokot ⓜ law-kawt *padlock*
(s)lomiti (s)law-mee-tee *break*
lomljiv lawm-lyeev *fragile*
lonac ⓜ law-nats *saucepan*
lopov ⓜ law-pawv *thief*
lopta ① lawp-ta *ball*
loptica za golf ① lawp-tee-tsa za gawlf *golf ball*
losion law-see-awn *lotion*
— za dobijanje tena za daw-bee-ya-nye te-na *tanning lotion*
— za upotrebu poslije brijanja za oo-paw-tre-boo paw-slee-ye bree-ya-nya *aftershave*
— za zaštitu od sunca za zash-tee-too awd soon-tsa *sunblock*
losos ⓜ law-saws *salmon*
loš lawsh *bad*
lov na životinje ⓜ lawv na zhe-vaw-tee-nye *hunting*
lubanja ① loo-ba-nya *skull*
lubenica ① loo-be-nee-tsa *watermelon*
lubrikant ⓜ loo-bree-kant *lubricant*
lud lood *crazy*
luk ⓜ look *onion*
luka ① loo-ka *harbour • port (sea)*
lutka ① loot-ka *doll*

Lj

(po)ljubiti (paw-)lyoo-bee-tee *kiss*
ljubomoran lyoo-baw-maw-ran *jealous*
ljudi ⓜ pl lyoo-dee *people*
ljudska prava ⓝ pl lyood-ska pra-va *human rights*
ljudski resursi ⓜ pl lyood-skee re-soor-see *human resources*
ljutit lyoo-teet *angry*

M

mačevanje ⓜ ma·che·va·nye
fencing (sport)
mačka ⓕ mach·ka *cat*
madrac ⓜ mad·rats *mattress*
Mađarska ⓕ ma·jar·ska *Hungary*
magazin ⓜ ma·ga·zeen *magazine*
maglovit ma·glaw·veet *foggy*
majica ⓕ mai·ee·tsa *T-shirt*
majka ⓕ mai·ka *mother*
Makedonija ⓕ ma·ke·daw·nee·ya
Macedonia
mali ma·lee *small*
malo ma·law *little (not much)* • *some*
mama ⓕ ma·ma *mum*
mandarina ⓕ man·da·ree·na *mandarin*
mandolina ⓕ man·daw·lee·na *mandolin*
mango ⓜ man·gaw *mango*
manje ma·nye *less*
manji ma·nyee *smaller*
marakuja ⓕ ma·ra·koo·ya *passionfruit*
margarin ⓜ mar·ga·reen *margarine*
marihuana ⓕ ma·ree·hoo·a·na
marijuana
marina ⓕ ma·ree·na *marina*
marmelada ⓕ mar·me·la·da *marmalade*
masaža ⓕ ma·sa·zha *massage*
maser/maserka ⓜ/ⓕ ma·ser/ma·ser·ka
masseur/masseuse
maslac ⓜ ma·slats *butter*
maslina ⓕ ma·slee·na *olive*
maslinovo ulje ⓝ ma·slee·naw·vaw
oo·lye *olive oil*
me(ne) me(·ne) *me*
med ⓜ med *honey*
medeni mjesec ⓜ me·de·ne mye·sets
honeymoon
medicina ⓕ me·dee·tsee·na *medicine
(profession)*
medicinska sestra ⓕ me·dee·tseen·ska
se·stra *nurse*
mediji ⓜ pl me·dee·yee *media*
meditacija ⓕ me·dee·ta·tsee·ya
meditation
međugradski autobus ⓜ
me·joo·grad·skee a·oo·taw·boos
bus (intercity)
međunarodan me·joo·na·raw·dan
international
melodija ⓕ me·law·dee·ya *tune*
menadžer ⓜ me·na·jer *manager*

menstrualni bolovi ⓜ pl
men·stroo·al·nee baw·law·vee
period pain
mesar ⓜ me·sar *butcher*
mesnica ⓕ me·snee·tsa *butcher's shop*
meso ⓝ me·saw *meat*
metal ⓜ me·tal *metal*
metar ⓜ me·tar *metre*
metro ⓜ me·traw *metro (train)*
— stanica ⓕ sta·nee·tsa *metro station*
mi mee *we*
migrena ⓕ mee·gre·na *migraine*
(po)miješati (paw·)mye·ya·sha·tee *mix*
mikrovalna pećnica ⓕ mee·kraw·val·na
pech·nee·tsa *microwave (oven)*
milijun ⓜ mee·lee·yoon *million*
milimetar ⓜ mee·lee·me·tar *millimetre*
mineralna voda ⓕ mee·ne·ral·na vaw·da
mineral water
ministar predsjednik ⓜ mee·nee·star
pred·syed·neek *prime minister*
minuta ⓕ mee·noo·ta *minute*
mir ⓜ meer *peace*
miris ⓜ mee·rees *smell (pleasant)*
misa ⓕ mee·sa *mass (Catholic)*
(po)misliti (paw·)mee·slee·tee *think*
miš ⓜ meesh *mouse*
mišić ⓜ mee·sheech *muscle*
mišljenje ⓝ meesh·lye·nye *opinion*
mito ⓝ mee·taw *bribe*
mjehur ⓜ mye·hoor *bladder*
mjesec ⓜ mye·sets *month* • *moon*
mjesečnica ⓕ mye·sech·nee·tsa
menstruation
mjesni mye·snee *local*
mjesto ⓝ mye·staw *place*
— kontrole kawn·traw·le *checkpoint*
— rođenja raw·je·nya *place of birth*
— za kampiranje za kam·pee·ra·nye
camp site
mlad mlad *young*
mlijeko ⓝ mlee·ye·kaw *milk*
mljeveno meso ⓝ mlye·ve·naw me·saw
mince
mnogi mnaw·gee *many*
mobilni telefon ⓜ maw·beel·nee
te·le·fawn *mobile phone*
moći imp maw·chee *can (be able)*
moćnica ⓕ mawch·nee·tsa *shrine*
moda ⓕ maw·da *fashion*
modem ⓜ maw·dem *modem*
modrica ⓕ maw·dree·tsa *bruise*
moguć maw·gooch *possible*

moj ⓜ moy *my*
moja ⓕ moy·a *my*
moje ⓝ moy·e *my*
mokar ⓜ maw·kar *wet*
(po)moliti se (paw·)maw·lee·tee (se) *worship*
molitva ⓕ maw·leet·va *prayer*
molitvenik ⓜ maw·leet·ve·neek *prayer book*
momčad ⓕ mawm·chad *team*
mononukleoza ⓕ maw·naw·nook·le·aw·za *glandular fever*
more ⓝ maw·re *sea*
most ⓜ mawst *bridge*
motel ⓜ maw·tel *motel*
motocikl ⓜ maw·taw·tsee·kl *motorbike*
motor ⓜ maw·tawr *engine*
motorni čamac ⓜ maw·tawr·nee cha·mats *motorboat*
možda mawzh·da *maybe*
moždani udar ⓜ mawzh·da·nee oo·dar *stroke (health)*
mračan mra·chan *dark*
mrav ⓜ mrav *ant*
mraz ⓜ mraz *frost*
mreža ⓕ mre·zha *net*
— za komarce za kaw·mar·tse *mosquito net*
mrkva ⓕ mrk·va *carrot*
mrtav mr·tav *dead*
mučnina ⓕ mooch·nee·na *nausea*
— od vožnje awd vawzh·nye *travel sickness*
muesli ⓜ pl moo·zlee *muesli*
musliman/muslimanka ⓜ/ⓕ moo·slee·man/moo·slee·man·ka *Muslim*
muškarac ⓜ moosh·ka·rats *man (male person)*
muzej ⓜ moo·zey *museum*
muzičar ⓜ moo·zee·char *musician*
muž ⓜ moozh *husband*

N

na na *at • in • on • per (day)*
— vrijeme vree·ye·me *on time*
nabrojan ⓜ na·broy·an *itemised*
nacionalni park ⓜ na·tsee·aw·nal·nee park *national park*
nacionalnost ⓕ na·tsee·aw·nal·nawst *nationality*
način ⓜ na·cheen *way (manner)*

naći/nalaziti na·chee/na·la·zee·tee *find*
nad nad *to*
nadimak ⓜ na·dee·mak *nickname*
nafta ⓕ naf·ta *oil (petrol)*
najam automobila ⓜ nai·am a·oo·taw·maw·bee·la *car hire*
najbliži nai·blee·zhee *nearest*
najbolji nai·baw·lyee *best*
najmanji nai·ma·nyee *smallest*
najveći nai·ve·chee *biggest*
nakit ⓜ na·keet *jewellery*
namirnice ⓕ pl na·meer·nee·tse *groceries*
namještaj ⓜ na·mye·shtai *furniture*
naočale ⓕ pl na·aw·cha·le *glasses (spectacles)*
— za skijanje za skee·ya·nye *goggles (skiing)*
— za sunce (za soon·tse) *sunglasses*
naplata za usluge ⓕ na·pla·ta za oo·sloo·ge *service charge*
(na)praviti (na·)pra·vee·tee *make (bring about)*
naprijed na·pree·yed *ahead*
naranča ⓕ na·ran·cha *orange (fruit)*
narančast na·ran·chast *orange (colour)*
narediti/naređivati na·re·dee·tee/na·re·jee·va·tee *order (demand)*
naručiti/naručivati na·roo·chee·tee/na·roo·chee·va·tee *order (request)*
nastavnik ⓜ na·stav·neek *lecturer*
nastup ⓜ na·stoop *gig*
nasuprot na·soo·prawt *opposite*
naš ⓜ nash *our*
naša ⓕ nash·a *our*
naše ⓝ nash·e *our*
naturoterapije ⓕ pl na·too·raw·te·ra·pee·ye *naturopathy*
naušnice ⓕ pl na·oosh·nee·tse *earrings*
navigacija ⓕ na·vee·ga·tsee·ya *navigation*
navijač ⓜ na·vee·yach *supporter (sport, etc)*
nazvati/nazivati naz·va·tee/na·zee·va·tee *ring (of phone)*
ne ne *no • not*
nebo ⓝ ne·baw *sky*
nedavno ne·dav·naw *recently*
nedjelja ⓕ ne·dye·lya *Sunday*
nedostajati imp ne·daw·stai·a·tee *miss (feel absence of)*
nedostatak ⓜ ne·daw·sta·tak *shortage*
negativan ne·ga·tee·van *negative*

nekoliko *ne*·kaw·leek·aw • *few* • *several*
nektarinka ① *nek*·ta·reen·ka *nectarine*
nemoguć *ne*·maw·gooch *impossible*
neobičan *ne*·aw·bee·chan *strange* • *unusual*
neoženjen ne·*aw*·zhen·yen *single (man)*
nepotpuno pečen *ne*·pawt·poo·naw pe·chen *rare (meat)*
nepravedan *ne*·pra·ve·dan *unfair*
nepromočiv ne·*praw*·maw·cheev *waterproof*
nepušački ⓜ *ne*·poo·shach·kee *nonsmoking*
nesiguran *ne*·see·goo·ran *unsafe*
nešto *nesh*·taw *something*
netko *net*·kaw *someone*
neudata *ne*·oo·da·ta *single (woman)*
neudoban *ne*·oo·daw·ban *uncomfortable*
nevezan *ne*·vez·an *free (not bound)*
nevin ⓜ *ne*·veen *innocent*
nezaposlen *ne*·za·paw·slen *unemployed*
nezavisnost ① *ne*·za·*vee*·snawst *independence*
nezgoda ① *nez*·gaw·da *accident*
nijem nee·*yem* *mute*
nikada *nee*·ka·da *never*
nikakav *nee*·ka·kav *none*
ništa *neesh*·ta *no* • *nothing*
niti *nee*·tee *neither*
nizak *nee*·zak *low* • *short (height)*
nizbrdo *neez*·br·daw *downhill*
Nizozemska ① *nee*·zaw·zem·ska *Netherlands*
noć ① *nawch* *night*
noćni klub ⓜ *nawch*·nee kloob *nightclub*
noga ① *naw*·ga *leg*
nogomet ⓜ *naw*·gaw·met *football (soccer)*
Norveška ① *nawr*·vesh·ka *Norway*
nos ⓜ *naws* *nose*
nositi imp *naw*·see·tee *carry* • *wear*
nov nawv *new*
novac ⓜ *naw*·vats *money*
novčana globa ① *navv*·cha·na *glaw*·ba *fine (penalty)*
novčanica ① navv·*cha*·nee·tsa *banknote*
novčarka ① *navv*·char·ka *purse*
novčići ⓜ pl *navv*·chee·chee *coins*
Novi Zeland ⓜ *naw*·vee ze·land *New Zealand*
novinar(ka) ⓜ/① *naw*·vee·nar(·ka) *journalist*
novine ① pl *naw*·vee·ne *newspaper*

novogodišnji dan ⓜ naw·vaw·*gaw*·deesh·nyee dan *New Year's Day*
nož ⓜ *nawzh* *knife*
nožni prst ⓜ *nawzh*·nee prst *toe*
nuklearna energija ① *noo*·kle·ar·na e·*ner*·gee·ya *nuclear energy*
nuklearna testiranja ① pl *noo*·kle·ar·na te·*stee*·ra·nya *nuclear testing*
nuklearni otpad ⓜ *noo*·kle·ar·nee *awt*·pad *nuclear waste*

Nj

njegov ⓜ *nye*·gawv *his*
njegova ① *nye*·gaw·va *his*
njegovo ① *nye*·gaw·vaw *his*
njen ⓜ nyen *his*
njena ① *nye*·na *his*
njeno ① *nye*·naw *his*
Njemačka ① *nye*·mach·ka *Germany*
njihov ⓜ *nyee*·hawv *their*
njihova ① *nyee*·haw·va *their*
njihovo ① *nyee*·haw·vaw *their*

O

o oo *about* • *on*
oba ⓜ&ⓜ *aw*·ba *both*
obala ① *aw*·ba·la *coast*
obaren aw·*ba*·ren *boiled*
obećati/obećavati aw·be·cha·tee/ aw·be·*cha*·va·tee *promise*
običaj ⓜ *aw*·bee·chai *custom*
običan ⓜ *aw*·bee·chan *ordinary*
obična pošta ① *aw*·beech·na *pawsh*·ta *surface mail (land)*
obična voda ① *aw*·beech·na *vaw*·da *still water* • *tap water*
obitelj ① *aw*·bee·tel' *family*
obje ① *aw*·bye *both*
oblačan aw·*bla*·chan *cloudy*
oblak ⓜ *aw*·blak *cloud*
oblik ⓜ *aw*·bleek *shape*
obližnji *aw*·bleezh·nyee *nearby*
obrano mlijeko ① *aw*·bra·naw mlee·*ye*·kaw *skim milk*
obrazovanje ⓝ aw·bra·zaw·*va*·nye *education*
obrtnik ⓜ *aw*·brt·neek *tradesperson*
ocat ⓜ *aw*·tsat *vinegar*
ocean ⓜ aw·*tse*·an *ocean*

oči ① pl *aw*·chee *eyes*
od awd *from • since (May etc) • with*
odbiti/odbijati awd·bee·tee/
    awd·*bee*·ya·tee *refuse*
odbojka ① *awd*·boy·ka *volleyball (sport)*
    — na pjesku na *pye*·skoo
    beach volleyball
odgovor ⓜ awd·gaw·vawr *answer*
odjeća ① *awd*·ye·cha *clothing*
odlazak ⓜ awd·la·zak *departure*
odličan awd·lee·chan *excellent*
odložena prtljaga ① awd·law·zhe·na
    prt·*lya*·ga *left luggage*
odlučiti/odlučivati awd·loo·chee·tee/
    awd·loo·chee·va·tee *decide*
odmoriti/odmarati se awd·*maw*·ree·tee/
    awd·*ma*·ra·tee·se *rest*
odnos ⓜ awd·naws *relationship (not
    family)*
odnosi s javnošću ⓜ pl awd·naw·see s
    yav·nawsh·choo *public relations*
odrasla osoba ① aw·dra·sla *aw·saw·ba
    adult*
odredište ⓝ aw·dre·deesh·te *destination*
odrezak ⓜ aw·dre·zak *fillet • steak*
odsjesti/odsjedati awd·sye·stee/
    awd·*sye*·da·tee *stay (at a hotel)*
odvojen awd·voy·en *separate*
oglas ⓜ aw·glas *advertisement*
ogledalo ⓜ aw·gle·*da*·law *mirror*
ograda ① aw·gra·da *fence*
ogrlica ① aw·gr·lee·tsa *necklace*
ogroman aw·graw·man *huge*
ogrtač ⓜ aw·gr·tach *cape (cloak)*
oklada ① aw·kla·da *bet*
oko ⓝ aw·kaw *eye*
oko aw·kaw *about*
okrenuti/okretati aw·kre·noo·tee/
    aw·kre·ta·tee *turn*
okrug ⓜ aw·kroog *county*
okrugao aw·kroo·ga·aw *round*
Olimpijske igre ① pl aw·*leem*·peey·ske
    ee·gre *Olympic Games*
olovka ① aw·lawv·ka *pencil*
oltar ⓜ awl·tar *altar*
oluja ① aw·loo·ya *storm*
omekšivač (za kosu) ⓜ
    aw·mek·*shee*·vach (za *kaw*·soo)
    conditioner (hair)
omlet ⓜ aw·mlet *omelette*
omotnica ① aw·mawt·nee·tsa *envelope*
on ⓜ awn *he*
ona ① & ⓝ aw·na *she • they* ⓝ

one ① aw·nee *they* ①
onesposobljen aw·ne·*spaw*·sawb·lyen
    disabled
oni ⓜ aw·nee *they* ⓜ
ono ⓝ aw·naw *it • that (one)*
opasan aw·pa·san *dangerous*
opatica ① aw·*pa*·tee·tsa *nun*
opeklina ① aw·pe·klee·na *burn*
opekline od sunca ① pl aw·pe·klee·ne
    awd soon·tsa *sunburn*
opera ① aw·pe·ra *opera*
operacija ① aw·pe·*ra*·tsee·ya *operation*
operator ⓜ aw·pe·*ra*·tawr *operator*
operna dvorana ① aw·per·na dvaw·*ra*·na
    opera house
opet aw·pet *again*
(o)prati (aw·)*pra*·tee *wash (something)*
(o)prati se (aw·)*pra*·tee se *wash (oneself)*
oprema ① aw·*pre*·ma *equipment*
Oprez! aw·prez *Careful!*
oprostiti/opraštati aw·*praw*·stee·tee/
    aw·*prash*·ta·tee *forgive*
opruga ① aw·proo·ga *spring (coil)*
optičar ⓜ awp·tee·char *optometrist*
opustiti/opuštati se aw·*poo*·stee·tee/
    aw·*poosh*·ta·tee se *relax*
orah ⓜ aw·rah *nut*
orgazam ⓜ awr·*ga*·zam *orgasm*
originalan aw·ree·gee·*na*·lan *original*
orkestar ⓜ awr·*ke*·star *orchestra*
ormar ⓜ awr·mar *cupboard*
    — za odjeću za *aw*·dye·choo *wardrobe*
osiguranje ⓝ aw·see·goo·*ra*·nye
    insurance
osim aw·seem *but*
osip ⓜ aw·seep *rash*
    — od pelena awd *pe*·le·na *nappy rash*
    — u struku aw·seep oo *stroo*·koo
    shingles (illness)
osjećaj ⓜ aw·sye·chai *feeling*
osjećaji ⓜ pl aw·sye·chai·ee *feelings*
osoba ① aw·saw·ba *person*
osobna iskaznica ① aw·*sawb*·na
    ee·skaz·nee·tsa *identification card (ID)*
ospice ① pl aw·spee·tse *measles*
ostati/ostajati aw·sta·tee/aw·sta·ya·tee
    stay (in one place)
ostaviti/ostavljati aw·sta·vee·tee/
    aw·stav·lya·tee *quit*
suh sooh *dry*
ošamućen aw·sha·moo·chen *dizzy*
oštrige ① pl awsh·tree·ge *oyster*
otac ⓜ aw·tats *father*

oteklina ① *aw*-te-klee-na *swelling*
otići/odlaziti aw-*tee*-chee/aw-*dla*-zee-tee *depart (leave)*
otirač ⓜ aw-*tee*-rach *mat*
otkako awt-ka-kaw *from • since (May etc)*
otok ⓜ aw-*tawk* *island*
otrovan aw-*traw*-van *poisonous*
otvarač awt-*va*-rach *opener*
— za boce za *baw*-tse *bottle opener*
— za limenke za lee-*men*-ke *can opener*
otvoren awt-*vaw*-ren *open*
otvoriti/otvarati awt-*vaw*-ree-tee/ awt-*va*-ra-tee *open*
ova ① *aw*-va *this*
ovaj ⓜ *aw*-vai *this*
ovca ① *awv*-tsa *sheep*
ovdje *awv*-dye *here*
ovisnost ① *aw*-vee-snawst *addiction*
— o drogama aw *draw*-ga-ma *drug addiction*
ovo ⓝ *aw*-vaw *it • this (one)*
ozbiljan *aw*-zbee-lyan *serious*
ozonski omotač ⓜ *aw*-zawn-skee aw-*maw*-tach *ozone layer*
ožujak ⓜ *aw*-zhoo-yak *March*

P

pad ⓜ pad *fall*
padavica ① *pa*-da-vee-tsa *epilepsy*
paket ⓜ *pa*-ket *package • parcel*
Pakistan ⓜ *pa*-kee-stan *Pakistan*
palača ① *pa*-la-cha *palace*
pamuk ⓜ *pa*-mook *cotton*
pansion ⓜ pan-*see*-awn *boarding house*
PAPA test ⓜ *pa*-pa test *pap smear*
papar ⓜ *pa*-par *pepper*
papir ⓜ *pa*-peer *paper*
papirnati rupčići ⓜ pl *pa*-peer-na-te roop-chee-chee *tissues*
paprika ① *pa*-pree-ka *bell pepper • capsicum*
par ⓜ par *pair (couple)*
paraplegičar ⓜ pa-ra-*ple*-gee-char *paraplegic*
parfem ⓜ par-*fem* *perfume*
park ⓜ park *park*
parkiralište ① par-*kee*-ra-leesh-te *car park*
parkirati imp par-*kee*-ra-tee *park (a car)*
pas ⓜ pas *dog*
— vodič *vaw*-deech *guide dog*

pasta za zube ① *pa*-sta za *zoo*-be *toothpaste*
patka ① *pa*-tka *duck*
patlidžan ⓜ pa-*tlee*-jan *aubergine • eggplant*
pauk ⓜ *pa*-ook *spider*
pčela ① *pche*-la *bee*
pećnica ① *pech*-nee-tsa *oven • stove*
pedala ① pe-*da*-la *pedal*
pegla ① *pe*-gla *iron (for clothes)*
pekara ① *pe*-ka-ra *bakery*
pelene ① pl *pe*-le-ne *diaper • nappy*
pelud ⓜ *pe*-lood *pollen*
peludna groznica ① *pe*-lood-na *grawz*-nee-tsa *hay fever*
penis ⓜ *pe*-nees *penis*
peniša ① pe-*nee*-sha *lighter*
pepeljara ① pe-*pe*-lya-ra *ashtray*
peron ⓜ *pe*-rawn *platform*
petak ⓜ *pe*-tak *Friday*
peticija ① pe-*tee*-tsee-ya *petition*
piće ⓝ *pee*-che *drink*
pijan *pee*-yan *drunk*
pijesak ⓜ *pee*-ye-sak *sand*
piknik ⓜ *peek*-neek *picnic*
piletina ① *pee*-le-tee-na *chicken (as food)*
pinceta ① *peen*-tse-ta *tweezers*
pisac ⓜ *pee*-sats *writer*
pisač ⓜ *pee*-sach *printer (computer)*
(na)pisati (na-)*pee*-sa-tee *write*
pismo ⓝ *pee*-smaw *letter (mail)*
pita ① *pee*-ta *pie*
pitanje ⓝ *pee*-ta-nye *question*
(u)pitati (oo-)*pee*-ta-tee *ask (a question)*
(po)piti (*paw*-)*pee*-tee *drink*
pivnica ① *peev*-nee-tsa *beer hall*
pivo ⓝ *pee*-vaw *beer*
pjena za brijanje ① *pye*-na za *bree*-ya-nye *shaving cream*
pjenušavo vino ① pye-*noo*-sha-vaw *vee*-naw *sparkling wine*
pjesma ① *pye*-sma *song*
(pro)pješačiti (praw-)pye-*sha*-chee-tee *hike*
pješačenje ⓝ pye-*sha*-che-nye *hiking*
pješački put ⓜ *pye*-shach-kee poot *hiking route*
pješak ⓜ *pye*-shak *pedestrian*
pjevač/pjevačica ⓜ/① *pye*-vach/ *pye*-va-chee-tsa *singer*
(za)pjevati (za-)*pye*-va-tee *sing*
plaća ① *pla*-cha *salary • wage*
plahta ① *pla*-hta *sheet (bed)*

plan grada ⓜ plan *gra*·da *map (of town)*
plan puta ⓜ plan *poo*·ta *itinerary*
planeta ⓕ pla·*ne*·ta *planet*
planina ⓕ pla·*nee*·na *mountain*
plastičan *pla*·stee·chan *plastic*
(u)platiti (oo·)*pla*·tee·tee *pay*
plato ⓜ pla·*taw plateau*
plav ⓜ plav *blue*
plaža ⓕ *pla*·zha *beach*
plesanje ⓜ *ple*·sa·nye *dancing*
(za)plesati (za·)*ple*·sa·tee *dance*
pletenasti ukras ⓜ *ple*·te·na·stee oo·kras *plaited ornamentation*
plima i oseka ⓕ *plee*·ma ee aw·se·ka *tide*
plin ⓜ pleen *gas (for cooking)*
plinski uložak ⓜ *pleen*·skee oo·law·zhak *gas cartridge*
plivanje ⓜ *plee*·va·nye *swimming (sport)*
(za)plivati (za·)*plee*·va·tee *swim*
(o)pljačkati (aw·)*plyach*·ka·tee *rob*
pločnik ⓜ *plawch*·neek *footpath*
plosnat *plaw*·snat *flat*
pluća ⓕ pl *ploo*·cha *lung*
po paw *after • per*
pobačaj ⓜ *paw*·ba·chai *abortion • miscarriage*
pobijediti/pobjeđivati paw·bee·*ye*·dee·tee/paw·bye·*jee*·va·tee *win*
pobjednik ⓜ *paw*·byed·neek *winner*
pobožan paw·*baw*·zhan *religious (person)*
početak ⓜ paw·*che*·tak *start*
  — radnog vremena *rad*·nawg *vre*·me·na *opening hours*
pod ⓜ pawd *floor (ground)*
podatci ⓜ pl paw·*dat*·tsee *details*
podijeliti perf paw·dee·*ye*·lee·tee *share (with)*
podne ⓜ *pawd*·ne *midday*
područni paw·*drooch*·nee *regional*
podzemna željeznica ⓕ pawd·*zem*·na zhe·lye·znee·tsa *subway • underground railway*
poezija ⓕ paw·e·*zee*·ya *poetry*
pogoditi/pogađati paw·*gaw*·dee·tee/paw·*ga*·ja·tee *guess*
pogreb ⓜ *paw*·greb *funeral*
pogreška ⓕ paw·*gresh*·ka *mistake*
pokazati/pokazivati paw·*ka*·za·tee/paw·ka·*zee*·va·tee *point • show*
poklon ⓜ *paw*·klawn *present (gift)*
pokretne stepenice ⓕ pl *paw*·kret·ne ste·*pe*·nee·tse *escalator*

pokušati/pokušavati paw·koo·sha·tee/paw·koo·*sha*·va·tee *try (attempt)*
pokvaren paw·*kva*·ren *broken down • corrupt • faulty • spoiled*
polica ⓕ *paw*·lee·tsa *shelf*
policajac ⓜ paw·lee·*tsai*·ats *police officer*
policija ⓕ paw·lee·*tsee*·ya *police*
policijska stanica ⓕ paw·*lee*·tseey·ska *sta*·nee·tsa *police station*
političar ⓜ paw·*lee*·tee·char *politician*
politika ⓕ paw·*lee*·tee·ka *politics*
poljodjelac ⓜ paw·lyaw·*dye*·lats *farmer*
poljodjelstvo ⓜ paw·lyaw·*dyel*·stvaw *agriculture*
poljubac ⓜ paw·*lyoo*·bats *kiss*
polovina ⓕ paw·law·*vee*·na *half*
polovni paw·lawv·nee *second-hand*
pomoć ⓕ *paw*·mawch *help*
pomoći/pomagati paw·*maw*·chee/paw·*ma*·ga·tee *help*
ponedjeljak ⓜ paw·ne·*dye*·lyak *Monday*
ponekad paw·ne·kad *sometimes*
poništiti/poništavati paw·*nee*·shtee·tee/paw·nee·*shta*·va·tee *cancel*
ponoć ⓕ *paw*·nawch *midnight*
popeti/penjati se paw·*pe*·tee/*pe*·nya·tee se *climb*
poplava ⓕ paw·*pla*·va *flood*
popraviti/popravljati paw·*pra*·vee·tee/paw·prav·*lya*·tee *repair*
popularan paw·poo·la·ran *popular*
popunjen paw·poo·nyen *booked out*
popust ⓜ paw·poost *discount*
pored paw·red *beside • next to*
poredak ⓜ paw·re·dak *order*
poremećaj srca ⓜ paw·re·me·chai *sr*·tsa *heart condition*
porez ⓜ paw·rez *tax*
  — na dohodak na *daw*·haw·dak *income tax*
  — na promet na *praw*·met *sales tax*
  — na zračni prijevoz na zrach·nee pree·*ye*·vawz *airport tax*
poriluk ⓜ paw·ree·look *leek*
poruka ⓕ paw·roo·ka *message*
posao ⓜ paw·sa·aw *job*
poseban ⓜ paw·se·ban *special*
poširan paw·shee·ran *poached*
posjetiti/posjećivati paw·sye·tee·tee/paw·sye·*che*·va·tee *visit*
poslano expres poštom paw·sla·naw eks·pres pawsh·tawm *by express mail*
poslastice ⓕ pl paw·sla·stee·tse *dessert*

poslije *paw*-slee-ye *after*

(ovo) poslijepodne ⓝ *(aw*-vaw)
paw-slee-ye-*pawd*-ne *(this) afternoon*

poslodavac ⓜ *paw*-slaw-*da*-vats *employer*

poslovna osoba ⓕ *paw*-slawv-na
aw-saw-ba *business person*

pospan *paw*-span *(to be) sleepy*

posramljen paw-*sram*-lyen *embarrassed*

post ⓜ pawst *Lent*

posteljina ⓕ paw-ste-*lyee*-na *bed linen*

poster ⓜ *paw*-ster *poster*

postići/postizati paw-stee-*chee*/
paw-*stee*-za-tee *score*

postotak ⓜ paw-*staw*-tak *per cent*

posuda ⓕ paw-*soo*-da *dish (plate)* • *pot (ceramics)*

posuditi/posuđivati paw-soo-dee-tee/
paw-soo-*jee*-va-tee *borrow*

pošta ⓕ *pawsh*-ta *mail (letters)* • *postal system*

poštanska marka ⓕ *pawsh*-tan-ska
mar-ka *stamp (mail)*

poštanski broj ⓜ *pawsh*-tan-skee broy
postcode

poštanski sandučić ⓜ *pawsh*-tan-skee
san-*doo*-cheech *mailbox*

poštanski ured ⓜ *pawsh*-tan-skee oo-red
post office

poštarina ⓕ pawsh-*ta*-ree-na *postage*

potkošulja ⓕ pawt-*kaw*-shoo-lya *singlet*

potomak ⓜ *paw*-taw-mak *descendant*

potpis ⓜ *pawt*-pees *signature*

potpuno paralizirana osoba ⓕ
pawt-poo-naw pa-ra-lee-*zee*-ra-na
aw-saw-ba *quadriplegic*

potreban *paw*-tre-ban *necessary*

potres ⓜ *paw*-tres *earthquake*

— mozga *maw*-zga *concussion*

potvrda vlasništva automobila
ⓕ *paw*-tvr-da *vlas*-neesh-tva
a-oo-taw-maw-*bee*-la *car owner's title*

potvrditi/potvrđivati pawt-*vr*-dee-tee/
pawt-vr-*jee*-va-tee
confirm (a booking) • *validate*

povijesni *paw*-vee-ye-snee *historical*

povijest ⓕ *paw*-vee-yest *history*

povrat novca ⓜ *pawv*-rat *nawv*-tsa
refund

povratan *paw*-vra-tan *return (ticket)*

povrće ⓝ *paw*-vr-che *vegetable*

povreda ⓕ *paw*-vre-da *injury*

povremeni posao ⓜ *paw*-vre-me-nee
paw-sa-aw *casual work*

povrijeđen ⓜ paw-*vree*-ye-jen *injured*

pozadina ⓕ *paw*-za-dee-na *back (position)*

pozitivan *paw*-zee-tee-van *positive*

poziv na račun nazvane osobe ⓜ
paw-zeev na ra-choon *naz*-va-ne
aw-saw-be *collect call* • *reverse charge call*

pozvati/pozivati pawz-va-tee/
paw-*zee*-va-tee *invite*

požar ⓜ *paw*-zhar *fire*

prah ⓜ prah *powder*

pranje rublja ⓕ pra-nye *roob*-lya *laundry (clothes)*

praonica ⓕ pra-*aw*-nee-tsa *laundry (place)*

pratiti imp pra-*tee*-tee *follow*

pravilo ⓝ pra-*vee*-law *rule*

pravnik ⓜ *prav*-neek *lawyer*

pravo ⓝ pra-*vaw* *law (study, professsion)*

prazan pra-zan *empty* • *vacant*

praznici ⓜ pl *praz*-nee-tsee *holidays* • *vacation*

praznovjerje ⓝ praz-*naw*-vyer-ye
superstition

pred pred *in front of*

predgrađe ⓝ *pred*-gra-je *suburb*

predmenstrualna napetost ⓕ
pred-*men*-stroo-al-na *na*-pe-tawst
premenstrual tension

prednje svjetlo ⓝ *pred*-nye *svyet*-law
headlights

predsjednik ⓜ *pred*-syed-neek *president*

predstava ⓕ *pred*-sta-va *play (theatre)* • *show*

pregled ⓜ *pre*-gled *review (article)*

prehlada ⓕ *pre*-hla-da *cold*

prekid ⓜ *pre*-keed *intermission*

prekjučer ⓜ *prek*-yoo-cher *day before yesterday*

preko *pre*-kaw *across*

— noći *naw*-chee *overnight*

prekomjerna cijena ⓕ *pre*-kawm-yer-na
tsee-*ye*-na *rip-off*

prekomorska pošta ⓕ *pre*-kaw-mawr-ska
pawsh-ta *surface mail (sea)*

prekosutra ⓜ *pre*-kaw-soo-tra *day after tomorrow*

prekršaj ⓜ *pre*-kr-shai *foul*

prema *pre*-ma *to* • *towards (direction)*

prenočište za mladež ⓝ
pre-naw-cheesh-te za *mla*-dezh
youth hostel

prenosivi računar ⑩ pre·*naw*·see·vee ra·*choo*·nar *laptop*

preporučenom poštom pre·*paw*·roo·che·nawm *pawsh*·tawm *registered mail (by)*

preporučiti/preporučivati pre·paw·roo·*chee*·tee/ pre·paw·roo·*chee*·va·tee *recommend*

preporuka ① pre·*paw*·rooka *reference*

prepun pre·*poon crowded*

prethodni *pred*·hawd·nee *last (previous)*

pretinac za odlaganje prtljage ⑩ *pre*·tee·nats za awd·*la*·ga·nye prt·*lya*·ge *luggage lockers*

pretpostaviti/pretpostavljati pret·*paw*·sta·vee·tee/ pret·*paw*·stav·lya·tee *prefer*

prevelika doza ① pre·ve·leeka *daw*·za *overdose*

prevesti/prevoditi pre·ve·stee/ pre·*vaw*·dee·tee *translate*

prezervativ pre·zer·va·*teev condom*

prezime ① pre·*zee*·me *surname*

pri pree *at · on*

pribor za jelo ⑩ *pree*·bawr za ye·law *cutlery*

pribor za prvu pomoć ⑩ *pree*·bawr za pr·voo paw·mawch *first-aid kit*

priča ① *pree*·cha *story*

pričest ① *pree*·chest *communion*

prigovor ⑩ *pree*·gaw·vawr *complaint*

prijatelj/prijateljica ⑩/① pree·ya·*tel*'/ pree·ya·*te*·lyee·tsa *friend*

prijazan pree·ya·zan *kind (nice)*

prije pree·ye *ago · before*

prijemni šalter ⑩ pree·*yem*·nee *shal*·ter *check-in (airport)*

prijevoz ⑩ pree·ye·vawz *transport*

primjer ⑩ *pree*·myer *example*

primorje ⑩ pree·*mawr*·ye *seaside*

pripremiti/pripremati pree·pre·mee·tee/ pree·pre·ma·tee *prepare*

priredba ① pree·*red*·ba *performance*

priroda ① *pree*·raw·da *nature*

prirodna okolina ① *pree*·rawd·na aw·kaw·lee·na *environment*

pristaša ① pree·sta·sha *supporter (politics)*

pritisak ① pree·*tee*·sak *pressure*

privatan pree·va·tan *private*

privatni smještaj za najam pree·vat·nee smyesh·tai za *nai*·am *guesthouse*

privlačan pree·vla·chan *sexy*

priznanje ⑩ pree·zna·nye *confession (admission)*

priznati/priznavati pree·zna·tee/ pree·zna·va·tee *admit (confess)*

prizor ⑩ *pree*·zawr *view*

prljav pr·lyav *dirty*

probati/probavati praw·ba·tee/ praw·ba·va·tee *try*

probavne smetnje ① pl praw·bav·ne smet·nye *indigestion*

prodati/prodavati praw·da·tee/ praw·da·va·tee *sell*

prodavač droga ⑩ praw·*da*·vach draw·ga *drug dealer*

prodavač duhana ① praw·*da*·vach doo·ha·na *tobacconist*

prodavaonica ① praw·da·va·*aw*·nee·tsa *shop*

— **alkohola** al·kaw·haw·la *bottle shop · liquor store*
— **bicikala** bee·*tsee*·ka·la *bike shop*
— **cipela** *tsee*·pela *shoe shop*
— **električne robe** e·*lek*·treech·ne raw·be *electrical store*
— **foto-aparata** faw·taw·a·pa·*ra*·ta *camera shop*
— **igračaka** ee·gra·cha·ka *toy shop*
— **metalne i tehničke robe** me·tal·ne ee teh·neech·ke raw·be *hardware store*
— **muzike** moo·zee·ke *music shop*
— **novina i časopisa** naw·vee·na ee cha·saw·pee·sa *newsagency*
— **odjeće** aw·dye·che *clothing store*
— **opreme za kampiranje** aw·pre·me za kam·pee·ra·nye *camping store*
— **polovne robe** paw·lawv·ne raw·be *second-hand shop*
— **ribe** ree·be *fish shop*
— **sa produženim radnim vremenom** sa praw·doo·zhe·neem rad·neem vre·me·nawm *convenience store*
— **sira** see·ra *cheese shop*
— **sportske robe** spawrt·ske raw·be *sports store*
— **suvenira** soo·ve·nee·ra *souvenir shop*
— **uredskog materijala** oo·reds·kawg ma·te·ree·*ya*·la *stationer's (shop)*

produženje ⑩ praw·doo·zhe·nye *extension (visa)*

program ⑩ *praw*·gram *program*

proizvesti/proizvoditi praw·*eez*·ve·stee/ praw·eez·*vaw*·dee·tee *produce*

projektor ⓜ proy-*ek*-tawr *projector*
prokulica ⓕ praw-koo-lee-tsa *Brussels sprout*
prolaz između sjedišta ⓜ *praw*-laz eez-me-joo sye-*deesh*-ta *aisle (plane etc)*
proljeće ⓜ praw-*lye*-che *spring (season)*
proljev ⓜ praw-*lyev diarrhoea*
promet ⓜ praw-met *traffic*
promjena ⓕ praw-*mye*-na *change*
prosinac ⓜ praw-*see*-nats *December*
prosjak ⓜ praw-syak *beggar*
proslava ⓕ praw-*sla*-va *celebration*
prostitutka ⓕ praw-stee-*toot*-ka *prostitute*
prostor ⓜ praw-stawr *space*
prosvjed ⓜ praws-vyed *protest*
prosvjedovati imp praw-svye-daw-*va*-tee *protest*
prošli prawsh-lee *last (week)*
prošlost ⓕ prawsh-lawst *past*
provesti/provoditi se praw-ve-stee/praw-*vaw*-dee-tee se *enjoy (oneself)*
provjeriti/provjeravati praw-vye-ree-tee/praw-vye-*ra*-va-tee *check*
provod ⓜ praw-vawd *party (night out)*
prozor ⓜ praw-zawr *window*
prsa ⓕ pr-sa *breast (body)* · *chest (body)*
prsluk za spasavanje ⓜ pr-slook za spa-*sa*-va-nye *life jacket*
prst ⓜ prst *finger*
prsten ⓜ pr-sten *ring (on finger)*
prtljaga ⓕ prt-*lya*-ga *luggage*
prvenstvo ⓝ pr-*vens*-tvaw *championships*
prvi pr-vee *first*
— razred ⓜ *ra*-zred *business class* · *first class*
prženi pr-zhe-nee *fried*
(is)pržiti (ees-)pr-zhee-tee *fry*
ptica ⓕ ptee-tsa *bird*
puder za bebe ⓜ poo-der za be-be *baby powder*
pumpa ⓕ poom-pa *pump*
pun poon *full*
punac ⓜ poo-nats *father-in-law (of husband)*
punica ⓕ poo-nee-tsa *mother-in-law (of husband)*
punim radnim vremenom poo-neem rad-neem vre-me-nawm *full-time*
(na)puniti (na-)poo-nee-tee *fill*
puno ⓝ poo-naw *(a) lot*
puran ⓜ poo-ran *turkey*

pustinja ⓕ poo-stee-nya *desert*
(is)pušiti (ees-)poo-shee-tee *smoke*
puška ⓕ poosh-ka *gun*
put ⓜ poot *route* · *track* · *trail*
(u)pucati (oo-)poo-tsa-tee *shoot*
putna agencija ⓕ *poot*-na a-*gen*-tsee-ya *travel agency*
putna karta ⓕ *poot*-na *kar*-ta *road map*
putnički čekovi ⓜ pl *poot*-neech-kee che-kaw-vee *travellers cheque*
putnik ⓜ *poot*-neek *passenger*
putovanje ⓝ poo-taw-*va*-nye *journey*
(pro)putovati (praw-)poo-*taw*-va-tee *travel*
putovnica ⓕ poo-*tawv*-nee-tsa *passport*
puž ⓜ poozh *snail*

R

račun ⓜ *ra*-choon *account (bank)* · *bill (account)* · *check* · *receipt*
računalo ⓝ *ra*-choo-na-law *computer*
rad ⓜ rad *work*
— za barom za *ba*-rawm *bar work*
radijator ⓜ ra-dee-*ya*-tawr *radiator*
radio ⓜ *ra*-dee-aw *radio*
radionica ⓕ ra-dee-aw-*nee*-tsa *workshop*
raditi imp *ra*-dee-tee *work*
radna dozvola ⓕ *rad*-na *dawz*-vaw-la *work permit*
radnik ⓜ *rad*-neek *labourer*
— u tvornici oo *tvawr*-nee-tsee *factory worker*
radno iskustvo ⓝ *rad*-naw ee-*skoos*-tvaw *work experience*
ragbi ⓜ *rag*-bee-ee *rugby*
rajčica ⓕ *rai*-chee-tsa *tomato*
rak ⓜ rak *cancer*
rakija ⓕ *ra*-kee-ya *brandy*
rame ⓝ *ra*-me *shoulder*
rani *ra*-nee *early*
raniti/ranjavati *ra*-nee-tee/*ra*-*nya*-va-tee *hurt (physically)*
raskošan *ra*-skaw-shan *luxury*
rasna netrpeljivost ⓕ *ra*-sna ne-tr-pe-lyee-vawst *racism*
rasprodaja ⓕ *ra*-spraw-dai-a *sale*
(po)rasti (paw-)*ra*-stee *grow*
rat ⓜ rat *war*
ravan *ra*-van *straight (not crooked)*
ravnopravnost ⓕ *rav*-naw-*prav*-nawst *equality*

razbijen ra·zbee·yen *broken*

razlika u vremenu ① *raz·*lee·ka oo vre·me·noo *time difference*

razlog ⓜ *raz·*lawg *reason*

razmažen raz·*ma·*zhen *spoiled*

razmijeniti/razmjenjivati raz·mee·ye·nee·tee/raz·mye·nyee·va·tee *exchange*

razmjena ① *raz·*mye·na *exchange*

razuman *raz·*zoo·man *sensible*

razumjeti/razumijevati ra·zoo·mye·tee/ra·zoo·mee·ye·va·tee *understand*

razveden raz·ve·den *divorced (of man)*

razvedena raz·ve·de·na *divorced (of woman)*

realan *re·*a·lan *realistic*

rebro ⓝ *re·*braw *rib*

recept za lijekove ⓜ *re·*tsept za lee·ye·kaw·ve *prescription*

reciklirati perf re·tsee·klee·ra·tee *recycle*

reći perf *re·*chee *tell*

red ⓜ red *queue*

redovnik ⓜ re·*dawv·*neek *monk*

refleksologija ① re·flek·saw·*law·*gee·ya *reflexology*

registarska tablica ① re·gee·star·ska ta·blee·tsa *numberplate*

registracija re·gee·*stra·*tsee·ya *car registration*

rejv parti ⓜ reyv par·tee *rave*

reket ⓜ *re·*ket *racquet*

relikvija ① re·*leek·*vee·ya *relic*

rep ⓜ rep *tail*

republika ① re·poo·blee·ka *republic*

restoran ⓜ re·*staw·*ran *restaurant*

rezanci ⓜ pl re·*zan·*tsee *noodles*

(na)rezati (na·)re·za·tee *cut*

rezervacija ① re·zer·*va·*tsee·ya *reservation (booking)*

rezervirati perf re·zer·vee·ra·tee *book (make a booking)*

rezime ⓜ re·zee·*me* *résumé*

riba ① *ree·*ba *fish*

ribar ⓜ *ree·*bar *fisherman*

ribarsko selo ⓝ *ree·*bar·skaw se·law *fishing village*

ribolov ⓜ *ree·*baw·lawv *fishing*

riječ ① *ree·*yech *word*

rijedak ree·ye·dak *rare (uncommon)*

rijeka ① *ree·*ye·ka *river*

ritam ⓜ *ree·*tam *rhythm*

riva ① *ree·*va *waterfront*

rizik ⓜ *ree·*zeek *risk*

riža ① *ree·*zha *rice*

rječnik ⓜ *ryech·*neek *dictionary*

robna kuća ① *rawb·*na koo·cha *department store*

rock grupa ① rawk *groo·*pa *rock group*

rock ⓜ rawk *rock (music)*

roditelji ⓜ pl *raw·*dee·te·lyee *parents*

rođendan ⓜ *raw·*jen·dan *birthday*

romantičan raw·man·tee·chan *romantic*

ronilačka oprema ① *raw·*nee·lach·ka aw·pre·ma *diving equipment*

ronjenje ⓝ *raw·*nye·nye *diving (underwater)*
— **s disalicom** s dee·sa·lee·tsawm *snorkelling*
— **sa bocama** sa *baw·*tsa·ma *scuba diving*

rošulanje ⓝ *raw·*shoo·la·nye *rollerblading*

rošulati se imp raw·shoo·la·tee se *skate*

rotkva ① *rawt·*kva *radish*

rt ⓜ rt *cape • promontory*

rubeola ① roo·be·aw·la *rubella*

ručak ⓜ *roo·*chak *lunch • meal*

ručna svjetiljka ① *rooch·*na svye·teel'·ka *flashlight • torch*

ručna torbica ① *rooch·*na tawr·bee·tsa *handbag*

ručni radovi ⓜ pl *rooch·*nee ra·daw·vee *handicrafts*

ručni zglob ⓜ *rooch·*nee zglawb *wrist*

ručnik ⓜ *rooch·*neek *towel • wash cloth*
— **za lice** za lee·tse *face cloth*

ručno izrađen *rooch·*naw eez·ra·jen *handmade*

rujan ⓜ *roo·*yan *September*

ruka ① *roo·*ka *arm • hand*

rukavica/e ① sg/ⓜ pl roo·*ka·*vee·tsa/e *glove(s)*

rukomet ⓜ *roo·*kaw·met *handball*

ruksak ⓜ *rook·*sak *backpack*

rum ⓜ room *rum*

rupčić ⓜ *roop·*cheech *handkerchief*

ruševine ① pl *roo·*she·vee·ne *ruins*

ruž za usne ⓜ roozh za oo·sne *lipstick*

ružičast roo·*zhee·*chast *pink*

S

sa sa *with*

sabor ⓜ *sa·*bawr *parliament*

SAD ⓜ pl es a de *USA*

sada *sa·*da *now*

sadašnjost ① *sa*·dash·nyawst *present (time)*

salama ① sa·*la*·ma *salami*

salata ① sa·*la*·ta *salad*

saldo ⑩ *sal*·daw *balance (account)*

salveta ① sal·*ve*·ta *serviette*

sam sam *alone*

samo *sa*·maw *only*

samoposluga ① sa·maw·*paw*·sloo·ga *self-service*

samostalno zaposlen sa·maw·stal·naw za·*paw*·slen *self-employed*

samostan ⑩ *sa*·maw·stan *convent · monastery*

san ⑩ san *dream*

sandala ① san·*da*·la *sandal*

sanjkanje san'·ka·nye *tobogganing*

sapun ⑩ *sa*·poon *soap*

sardina ① sar·*dee*·na *sardine*

sastanak ⑩ *sa*·sta·nak *appointment*

sastojak ⑩ *sa*·stoy·ak *ingredient*

sašiti/šivati *sa*·shee·tee/*shee*·va·tee *sew*

sat ⑩ sat *clock · hour · watch*

sauna ① *sa*·oo·na *sauna*

savjet *sa*·vyet *advice*

savršen *sa*·vr·shen *perfect*

sebičan *se*·be·chan *selfish*

sedlo ⑪ *sed*·law *saddle*

seks ⑩ seks *sex*

sekunda ① se·*koon*·da *second (clock)*

selo ① *se*·law *village*

semafor ⑩ *se*·ma·fawr *scoreboard · traffic light*

senf ⑩ senf *mustard*

seosko područje ⑪ *se*·aw·skaw paw·drooch·ye *countryside*

sestra ① *se*·stra *sister*

sezona ① se·*zaw*·na *season (for activities)*

shiatsu ① shee·*a*·tsoo *shiatsu*

sići/silaziti sa *see*·chee/see·*la*·zee·tee sa *get off (a train, etc)*

sićušan ⑩ *see*·choo·shan *tiny*

SIDA ① *see*·da *AIDS*

sigornosni pojas ⑩ *see*·goor·naw·snee poy·as *seatbelt*

sef ⑩ sef *safe*

siguran *see*·goo·ran *safe*
— **seks** seks *safe sex*

siječanj ⑩ *see*·ye·chan' *January*

silovanje ⑩ *see*·la·va·nye *rape*

silovati perf *see*·*law*·va·tee *rape*

sin ⑩ seen *son*

sinagoga ① *see*·na·*gaw*·ga *synagogue*

Singapur ⑩ *seen*·ga·poor *Singapore*

sintetičan ⑩ *seen*·*te*·tee·chan *synthetic*

sir ⑩ seer *cheese*

siromašan *see*·*raw*·ma·shan *poor*

siromaštvo ⑪ *see*·raw·*mash*·tvaw *poverty*

sirov ⑩ *see*·rawv *raw*

sirup za kašalj ⑩ *see*·roop za *ka*·shal' *cough medicine*

sitan *see*·tan *fine (delicate)*

siv ⑩ seev *gray · grey*

sjedalo za dijete ⑪ sye·*da*·law za dee·ye·te *child seat*

sjedište ⑪ sye·deesh·te *seat (place)*

sjekira za razbijanje leda ① sye·*kee*·ra za raz·*bee*·ya·nye *le*·da *ice axe*

sjena ① sye·na *shadow*

sjesti/sjedati sye·stee/sye·*da*·tee *sit*

sjever ⑩ sye·ver *north*

skalp ⑩ skalp *scalp*

skijanje ⑪ *skee*·ya·nye *skiing*
— **na vodi** na *vaw*·dee *water-skiing*

skijati imp *skee*·ya·tee *ski*

skočiti/skakati *skaw*·chee·tee/*ska*·ka·tee *jump*

skoro *skaw*·raw *almost*

skulptura ① skoolp·*too*·ra *sculpture*

skup ⑩ skoop *rally*

skup *skoop* *expensive*

slab slab *weak*

sladak *sla*·dak *sweet*

sladoled ⑩ *sla*·daw·led *ice cream*

sladoledarna ① sla·daw·le·*dar*·na *ice-cream parlour*

slanina ① *sla*·nee·na *bacon*

slanutak ⑩ sla·*noo*·tak *chickpea*

slastičarnica ① sla·stee·*char*·nee·tsa *cake shop*

(po)slati (paw·)*sla*·tee *send*

slavan *sla*·van *famous*

slavina ① *sla*·vee·na *faucet · tap*

sled ⑩ slej *herring*

sličan *slee*·chan *similar*

slijedeći slee·ye·de·chee *next (month)*

slijep slee·*yep* *blind*

slijepo crijevo ⑪ slee·ye·paw tsree·ye·yaw *appendix (body)*

slika ① *slee*·ka *painting (a work)*

slikar ⑩ *slee*·kar *painter*

slikarstvo ① slee·*kars*·tvaw *painting (the art)*

slikati perf *slee*·ka·tee *photograph*

slobodan slaw·*baw*·dan *free (available)*

---

slobodno mjesto ⓝ *slaw*-bawd-naw *mye*-staw vacancy

Slovačka ⓕ *slaw*-vach-ka Slovakia

Slovenija ⓕ slaw-*ve*-nee-ya Slovenia

složiti/slagati se *slaw*-zhee-tee/*sla*-ga-tee se agree

(po)slušati (paw-)*sloo*-sha-tee listen (to)

slušni aparat ⓜ *sloosh*-nee a-*pa*-rat hearing aid

službenik/službenica ⓜ/ⓕ *sloozh*-be-neek/*sloozh*-be-nee-tsa office worker

službeno putovanje ⓝ *sloozh*-be-naw poo-taw-*va*-nye business trip

smeće ⓝ *sme*-che garbage

smeđ ⓜ smej brown

(na)smijati se (na-)smee-*ya*-tee se laugh

(na)smiješiti se (na-)smee-*ye*-shee-tee se smile

smjer ⓜ smyer direction

smiješan *smye*-shan funny

smještaj ⓜ *smye*-shtai accommodation

smjeti imp *smye*-tee can (have permission)

smokva ⓕ *smaw*-kva fig

smrad ⓜ smrad smell (unpleasant)

snaga ⓕ *sna*-ga power

snijeg ⓜ snee-*yeg* snow

snimak ⓜ *snee*-mak recording

snimiti/snimati snee-mee-tee/ snee-ma-tee record (music etc)

soba ⓕ *saw*-ba room

soba za pranje rublja ⓕ *saw*-ba za *pra*-nye roob-lya laundry (room)

socijalistički saw-tsee-ya-*lee*-steech-kee socialist

socijalna skrb ⓕ *saw*-tsee-yal-na skrb social welfare

soja ⓕ *soy*-a soy sauce

sojino mlijeko ⓝ *soy*-ee-naw mlee-*ye*-kaw soy milk

sok ⓜ sawk juice
— **od naranče** awd *na*-ran-che orange juice

sol ⓕ sawl salt

soli za rehidrataciju ⓕ *saw*-lee za re-hee-dra-*ta*-tsee-yoo rehydration salts

spavaća kola ⓕ *spa*-va-cha *kaw*-la sleeping berth

spavaća soba ⓕ *spa*-va-cha *saw*-ba bedroom

spavaći kupe ⓜ *spa*-va-chee koo-*pe* sleeping car

(od)spavati (awd-)*spa*-va-tee sleep

spilja ⓕ *spee*-lya cave

spirala ⓕ spee-*ra*-la IUD

spoj ⓜ spoy date (appointment)

spolna bolesta ⓕ *spawl*-na baw-*les*-ta venereal disease

spolna diskriminacija ⓕ *spawl*-na dee-skree-mee-*na*-tsee-ya sexism

spomenik ⓜ *spaw*-me-neek monument

spor spawr slow

sporo *spaw*-raw slowly

sport ⓜ spawrt sport

sportaš/sportašica ⓜ/ⓕ *spawr*-tash/ spawr-*ta*-shee-tsa sportsperson

spreman *spre*-man ready

spriječiti/sprječavati spree-*ye*-chee-tee/ spree-ye-*cha*-va-tee stop (prevent)

Srbija ⓕ *sr*-bee-ya Serbia

srčani udar ⓜ *sr*-cha-nee oo-dar heart attack

srce ⓝ *sr*-tse heart

srebro ⓝ *sre*-braw silver

sreća ⓕ *sre*-cha luck

srednja škola ⓕ *sred*-nya shkaw-la high school

sredstva za sprječavanje neželjene trudnoće ⓝ pl *sreds*-tva za spr-*cha*-va-nye ne-zhe-lye-ne trood-*naw*-che contraceptives

sresti/sretati *sre*-stee/*sre*-ta-tee meet (run into)

sretan *sre*-tan happy • lucky

srijeda ⓕ sree-*ye*-da Wednesday

srodstvo ⓝ *srawd*-stvaw relationship (family)

srpanj ⓜ *sr*-pan' July

stablo ⓝ *sta*-blaw tree

stadion ⓜ *sta*-dee-awn stadium

stajati imp *stai*-a-tee cost

staklenka ⓕ *sta*-klen-ka jar

staklo ⓝ *sta*-klo glass (material)

stan ⓜ stan apartment

stanica ⓕ *sta*-nee-tsa station • stop (bus etc)

Stanite/Stani! pol/inf *sta*-nee-te/*sta*-nee Stop!

stanovati imp sta-*naw*-va-tee live (somewhere)

star star old

staviti/stavljati sta-vee-tee/*stav*-lya-tee put

staza ⓕ *sta*-za path • track (sport)

stepenica ⓕ ste-*pe*-nee-tsa step

stepenište ⓝ *ste·pe·neesh·te stairway*

stići/stizati *stee·chee/stee·za·tee arrive*

stidljiv *steed·lyeev shy*

stijena ⓕ *stee·ye·na rock*

stil ⓜ *steel style*

stjenica ⓕ *stye·nee·tsa bug (insect)*

sto *staw hundred*

stol ⓜ *stawl table*

stolica za sklapanje ⓕ *staw·lee·tsa za skla·pa·nye chair*

stolni tenis ⓜ *stawl·nee te·nees table tennis*

stolnjak ⓜ *stawl·nyak tablecloth*

stopalo ⓝ *staw·pa·law foot*

stopirati imp *staw·pee·ra·tee hitchhike*

strana ⓕ *stra·na side*

stranac ⓜ *stra·nats stranger*

strani *stra·nee foreign*

stranica ⓕ *stra·nee·tsa page*

stranka ⓕ *stran·ka client · party (politics)*

strašan *stra·shan terrible*

stražnji *strazh·nyee rear (seat etc)*

stražnjica ⓕ *strazh·nyee·tsa bottom (body)*

strm *strm steep*

stroj ⓜ *stroy machine*

   — **za pranje rublja** za *pra·nye roob·lya washing machine*

stručnjak ⓜ *strooch·nyak specialist*

struja ⓕ *stroo·ya current (electricity) · stream*

struna ⓕ *stroo·na string*

studeni ⓜ *stoo·de·nee November*

student ⓜ *stoo·dent student*

stupnjevi ⓜ pl *stoop·nye·vee degrees (temperature)*

subota ⓕ *soo·baw·ta Saturday*

sud ⓜ *sood court (legal)*

sudac ⓜ *soo·dats judge · referee*

sudar ⓜ *soo·dar crash*

suknja ⓕ *sook·nya skirt*

sunčan *soon·chan sunny*

sunčanica ⓕ *soon·cha·nee·tsa sunstroke*

sunce ⓝ *soon·tse sun*

suncobran ⓜ *soon·tsaw·bran umbrella*

supermarket ⓜ *soo·per·mar·ket supermarket*

sušeni *soo·she·nee dried*

(o)sušiti (aw·)*soo·shee·tee dry*

sutra *soo·tra tomorrow*

   — **popodne** paw·*pawd·ne tomorrow afternoon*

   — **ujutro** oo·yoo·traw *tomorrow morning*

   — **uvečer** oo·ve·cher *tomorrow evening*

suvenir ⓜ *soo·ve·neer souvenir*

suviše *soo·vee·she too (expensive etc)*

suvremen *soo·vre·men modern*

svadbena torta ⓕ *svad·be·na tawr·ta wedding cake*

svadbeni dar ⓜ *svad·be·nee dar wedding present*

(po)svađati se (paw·)*sva·ja·tee se argue*

svaki ⓜ *sva·kee each · every*

svatko *svat·kaw everyone*

sve *sve all · everything*

svećenik ⓜ *sve·che·neek priest*

svekar ⓜ *sve·kar father-in-law (of wife)*

svekrva ⓕ *sve·kr·va mother-in-law (of wife)*

svemir ⓜ *sve·meer universe*

svetac/svetica ⓜ/ⓕ *sve·tats/sve·tee·tsa saint*

sveučilište ⓝ *sve·oo·chee·leesh·te university*

svi *svee all · everything*

svibanj ⓜ *svee·ban' May*

svijeća ⓕ *svee·ye·cha candle*

svijet ⓜ *svee·yet world*

svila ⓕ *svee·la silk*

svinja ⓕ *svee·nya pig*

svinjetina ⓕ *svee·nye·tee·na pork*

svinjska kobasica ⓕ *sveen'·ska kaw·ba·see·tsa pork sausage*

(od)svirati (awd·)*svee·ra·tee play (instrument)*

svjedodžba ⓕ *svye·dawj·ba certificate*

svjetao *svye·ta·aw light (of colour)*

svjetiljka ⓕ *svye·teel'·ka light (lamp) · flashlight · torch*

svjetlomjer ⓜ *svyet·law·myer light meter*

svjetlost ⓕ *svyet·lawst light (illumination)*

svjetski kup ⓜ *svyet·skee koop World Cup*

svjež *svyezh fresh*

svrbež ⓜ *svr·bezh itch*

svrha ⓕ *svr·ha point (logic)*

Š

šah ⓜ *shah chess*

šahovska ploča ⓕ *sha·hawv·ska plaw·cha chess board*

šal ⓜ *shal scarf*

šala ⓕ *sha·la joke*

šalica ⓕ *sha·lee·tsa cup*

šalter ⓜ *shal*-ter *ticket office*
— **za podizanje prtljage** za *paw*-dee-za-nye prt-*lya*-ge *baggage claim*
šampanjac ⓜ sham-*pa*-nyats *champagne*
šampon ⓜ sham-*pawn* *shampoo*
šank ⓜ shank *counter (at bar)*
šansa ⓕ *shan*-sa *chance*
šator ⓜ *sha*-tawr *tent*
šatorski kolčić ⓜ *sha*-tawr-skee *kawl*-cheech *tent peg*
šarmantan shar-*man*-tan *charming*
šećer ⓜ *she*-cher *sugar*
šef kuhinje ⓜ shef koo-hee-nye *chef*
šešir ⓜ *she*-sheer *hat*
šibice ⓕ pl *shee*-bee-tse *matches (for lighting)*
širok *shee*-rawk *wide*
šišanje ⓝ *shee*-sha-nye *haircut*
škamp ⓜ shkamp *prawn*
škare ⓕ pl *shka*-re *scissors*
škarice za nokte ⓕ pl *shka*-ree-tse za *nawk*-te *nail clippers*
škola ⓕ *shkaw*-la *school*
Škotska ⓕ *shkawt*-ska *Scotland*
šlic ⓜ shleets *zip • zipper*
šljiva ⓕ *shlyee*-va *plum*
šminka ⓕ *shmeen*-ka *make-up*
šmrkav nos ⓜ shmr-kav naws *runny nose*
Španjolska ⓕ shpa-*nyawl*-ska *Spain*
šparoga ⓕ shpa-*raw*-ga *asparagus*
špinat ⓜ *shpee*-nat *spinach*
štakor ⓜ *shta*-kawr *rat*
štapići za jelo ⓜ pl shta-*pee*-chee za *ye*-law *chopsticks*
štrajk ⓜ shtraik *strike*
štrcaljka ⓕ *shtr*-tsal'-ka *syringe*
šuma ⓕ *shoo*-ma *forest*
šunka ⓕ *shoon*-ka *ham*
šutnuti/šutirati *shoot*-noo-tee/ shoo-*tee*-ra-tee *kick*
Švedska ⓕ *shved*-ska *Sweden*
Švicarska ⓕ shvee-*tsar*-ska *Switzerland*

T

tableta ⓕ ta-*ble*-ta *pill*
— **protiv bolova** *praw*-teev *baw*-law-va *painkiller*
— **za spavanje** za *spa*-va-nye *sleeping pills*
tajnik/tajnica ⓜ/ⓕ *tai*-neek/*tai*-nee-tsa *secretary*

također ta-*kaw*-jer *also*
taksi ⓜ *tak*-see *taxi*
— **na vodi** na *vaw*-dee *water taxi*
— **stanica** ⓕ *sta*-nee-tsa *taxi stand*
taman ta-*man* *dark (of colour)*
tamo ta-*maw* *there*
tampon ⓜ *tam*-pawn *tampon*
tanak ⓜ ta-*nak* *thin*
tanjur ⓜ ta-*nyoor* *plate*
tastatura ⓕ ta-sta-*too*-ra *keyboard (computer)*
tata ⓜ *ta*-ta *dad*
tava ⓕ *ta*-va *frying pan • pan*
tečaj razmjene ⓜ *te*-chai *raz*-mye-ne *exchange rate*
tečaj stranih valuta ⓜ *te*-chai stra-neeh va-*loo*-ta *currency exchange*
tegovi ⓜ pl *te*-gaw-vee *weights*
tehnika ⓕ *teh*-nee-ka *technique*
tekućina za kontakt leće ⓕ te-*koo*-chee-na za *kawn*-takt *le*-che *contact-lens solution*
telefaks ⓜ *te*-le-faks *fax machine*
telefon ⓜ *te*-le-fawn *telephone*
telefonirati imp te-le-faw-*nee*-ra-tee *telephone*
telefonska centrala ⓕ te-*le*-fawn-ska tsen-*tra*-la *telephone centre*
telefonska govornica ⓕ te-*le*-fawn-ska gaw-vawr-nee-tsa *phone box*
telefonska kartica ⓕ te-*le*-fawn-ska *kar*-tee-tsa *phonecard*
telefonski imenik ⓜ te-*le*-fawn-skee ee-me-neek *phone book*
telegram ⓜ *te*-le-gram *telegram*
teleskop ⓜ *te*-le-skawp *telescope*
teletina ⓕ *te*-le-tee-na *veal*
televizija ⓕ te-le-*vee*-zee-ya *television (general)*
televizor ⓜ te-le-*vee*-zawr *television set*
temperatura ⓕ tem-pe-ra-*too*-ra *temperature (weather)*
tenis ⓜ *te*-nees *tennis*
tenisko igralište ⓝ *te*-nee-skaw ee-*gra*-leesh-te *tennis court*
tepih ⓜ *te*-peeh *rug*
teren za golf ⓜ *te*-ren za *gawlf* *golf course*
teretana ⓕ te-re-*ta*-na *gym (place)*
termofor ⓜ *ter*-maw-fawr *water bottle (hot)*
tesar *te*-sar *carpenter*
test ⓜ test *test*
— **na trudnoću** na trood-*naw*-choo *pregnancy test kit*

tetka ① *tet*·ka *aunt*
težak *te*·zhak *difficult • heavy*
težina ① *te*·zhee·na *weight*
ti tee *you inf*
tih teeh *quiet*
tijelo ① tee·*ye*·law *body*
tijesan tee·*ye*·san *tight*
tipičan *tee*·pee·chan *typical*
titlovi ⓜ pl *teet*·law·vee *subtitles*
(ovaj) tjedan ① (aw·vai) tye·dan *(this) week*
tjelovježba ① tye·law·*vyezh*·ba *workout*
tjestenina ① tye·ste·nee·na *pasta*
tkanina ① *tka*·nee·na *fabric*
tko tkaw *who*
tlak krvi ⓜ tlak *kr*·vee *blood pressure*
to ⓞ taw *it*
toaletni papir ① taw·a·*let*·nee pa·*peer* *toilet paper*
točno *tawch*·naw *exactly*
toksični otpad ⓜ *tawk*·seech·nee *awt*·pad *toxic waste*
ton ⓜ tawn *volume*
topao ① *taw*·pa·aw *warm*
topla voda ① *taw*·pla *vaw*·da *hot water*
toplice ① pl *taw*·plee·tse *spa*
toranj ⓜ *taw*·ran' *tower*
torba ① *tawr*·ba *bag*
tost ⓜ tawst *toast*
toster ⓜ *taw*·ster *toaster*
trajekt ⓜ trai·ekt *ferry*
tramvaj ⓜ tram·vai *tram*
tranzitna čekaonica ① *tran*·zeet·na che·ka·*aw*·nee·tsa *transit lounge*
traperice ① pl *tra*·pe·ree·tse *jeans*
trava ① *tra*·va *grass (lawn) • pot (dope)*
travanj ⓜ tra·van' *April*
(po)tražiti (paw)*tra*·zhee·tee *look for*
(za)tražiti (za)*tra*·zhee·tee *ask (for something)*
trčanje ① *tr*·cha·nye *running*
(po)trčati (paw)*tr*·cha·tee *run*
(za)trebati (za)*tre*·ba·tee *need*
treći *tre*·chee *third*
trener ⓜ *tre*·ner *coach (sports)*
trešnja ① *tresh*·nya *cherry*
trg ⓜ trg *square (town)*
trgovac ⓜ *tr*·gaw·vats *trader*
 — drogama *draw*·ga·ma *drug dealer*
 — povrćem *paw*·vr·chem *greengrocer*
 — ribom *ree*·bawm *fishmonger*
trgovački centar ⓜ *tr*·gaw·vach·kee *tsen*·tar *shopping centre*

trgovina ① tr·*gaw*·vee·na *trade*
 — drogama ① *draw*·ga·ma *drug trafficking*
trišlja ① *treesh*·lya *pistachio*
trkaći bicikl ⓜ *tr*·ka·chee bee·*tsee*·kl *racing bike*
trkalište ① *tr*·ka·leesh·te *racetrack*
trudna ① *trood*·na *pregnant*
trudnička jutarnja mučnina ① *trood*·neech·ka yoo·*tar*·nya mooch·*nee*·na *morning sickness*
tržnica ① *trzh*·nee·tsa *market*
tucet ⓜ *too*·tset *dozen*
tuča ① *too*·cha *fight (fisticuffs)*
tumač ⓜ *too*·mach *interpreter*
tumor ⓜ *too*·mawr *tumour*
tuna ① *too*·na *tuna (fish)*
tunjevina ① *too*·nye·vee·na *tuna (as food)*
turist ⓜ *too*·reest *tourist*
turistička agencija ① too·*ree*·steech·ka a·*gen*·tsee·ya *tourist office*
tuš ⓜ toosh *shower (bathroom)*
tužan *too*·zhan *sad*
tvoj *tvoy* *your*
tvoja ① *tvoy*·a *your*
tvoje ① *tvoy*·e *your*
tvornica ① *tvawr*·nee·tsa *factory*
tvrd tvrd *hard (not soft)*
tvrdo kuhan tvr·daw *koo*·han *hard-boiled*
tvrdoglav tvr·*daw*·glav *stubborn*

u oo *aboard (train, bus) • at • in • on • to*
 — inozemstvu ee·naw·*zemst*·voo *abroad*
 — vezi ve·zee *about • to do with*
ubiti/ubijati oo·bee·tee/oo·*bee*·ya·tee *murder*
ubod ⓜ oo·bawd *bite (insect)*
ubojstvo ① oo·*boys*·tvaw *murder*
ubrizgati/ubrizgavati oo·breez·ga·tee/ oo·breez·*ga*·va·tee *inject*
učitelj ⓜ oo·chee·*tel'* *teacher*
(na)učiti (na·)oo·chee·tee *learn*
ući/ulaziti oo·chee/oo·la·zee·tee *enter*
udaljen oo·da·lyen *remote*
udati/udavati se oo·da·tee/oo·*da*·va·tee se *marry*
udvarati se imp oo·*dva*·ra·tee se *chat up*
uganuće ① oo·ga·*noo*·che *sprain*

ugao ⓜ *oo-ga-aw corner*
ugodan *oo-gaw-dan comfortable*
ugovor ⓜ *oo-gaw-vawr contract*
ugriz ⓜ *oo-greez bite (dog)*
ugrožene vrste ① pl *oo-graw-zhe-ne vr-ste endangered species*
uhititi perf *oo-hee-tee-tee arrest*
uho ⓝ *oo-haw ear*
uključen *ook-lyoo-chen included*
ukraden ⓜ *oo-kra-den stolen*
ukrcan na *oo-kr-tsan na aboard (boat, plane)*
ukrcati/ukrcavati se *oo-kr-tsa-tee / oo-kr-tsa-va-tee se board (a plane, ship etc)*
ukusan *oo-koo-san tasty*
ulaz ⓜ *oo-laz entry*
ulaznica (cijena) ① *oo-laz-nee-tsa (tsee-ye-na) admission (price)*
ulica ① *oo-lee-tsa street*
ulična tržnica ① *oo-leech-na trzh-nee-tsa street market*
ulični zabavljač ⓜ *oo-leech-nee za-bav-lyach busker*
ulje ⓝ *oo-lye oil*
ultrazvuk ⓜ *ool-tra-zvook ultrasound*
umak ⓜ *oo-mak sauce*
umirovljen *oo-mee-rawv-lyen retired*
umirovljenik ⓜ *oo-mee-rawv-lye-neek pensioner*
umjetnički obrti ⓜ pl *oo-myet-neech-kee aw-br-tee crafts (handicrafts)*
umjetnik/umjetnica ⓜ/①
oo-myet-neek/oo-myet-nee-tsa artist
umjetnost ① *oo-myet-nawst art*
umoran *oo-maw-ran tired*
umrijeti/umirati *oo-mree-ye-tee/ oo-mee-ra-tee die*
uniforma ① *oo-nee-fawr-ma uniform*
unovčiti/unovčavati *oo-nawv-chee-tee/ oo-nawv-cha-va-tee cash (a cheque)*
unuk/unuka ⓜ/① *oo-nook/oo-noo-ka grandchild*
unutra *oo-noo-tra inside*
unutrašnji *oo-noo-trash-nyee indoor*
upala ① *oo-pa-la inflammation*
upaljač ⓜ *oo-pa-lyach cigarette lighter*
uplata ① *oo-pla-ta payment (by someone)*
Upomoć! *oo-paw-mawch Help!*
upoznati/upoznavati *oo-pawz-na-tee/ oo-pawz-na-va-tee meet (for first time)*
upozoriti/upozoravati
oo-paw-zaw-ree-tee/ oo-paw-zaw-ra-va-tee warn

uprava ① *oo-pra-va administration*
ured ⓜ *oo-red office*
　— za izgubljene stvari
　za eez-goob-lye-ne stva-ree lost property office
　— za odlaganje prtljage
　za awd-la-ga-nye prt-lya-ge left luggage (office)
urednik ⓜ *oo-red-neek editor*
urod ⓜ *oo-rawd crop*
uska ulica ① *oo-ska oo-lee-tsa alley*
uskoro *oo-skaw-raw soon*
uskrs *oos-krs Easter*
usluga ① *oo-sloo-ga service*
usne ① pl *oo-sne lips*
uspinjača ① *oo-spee-nya-cha cable car*
usta ① *oo-sta mouth*
ustajao *oo-stai-a-aw stale*
uši ① pl *oo-shee lice*
utakmica ① *oo-tak-mee-tsa match (sports)*
utikač ⓜ *oo-tee-kach plug (electricity)*
utorak ⓜ *oo-taw-rak Tuesday*
utrka ① *oo-tr-ka race (sport)*
uvala ① *oo-va-la bay*
uvijek *oo-vee-yek always*
uvjetna karta ① *oo-vyet-noo kar-ta stand-by ticket*
uz *ooz beside*
uzbrdo *ooz-br-daw uphill (to go)*
uzeti/uzimati *oo-ze-tee/oo-zee-ma-tee take*
uznemiravanje ⓝ *ooz-ne-mee-ra-va-nye harassment*
uzrast ⓜ *ooz-rast age (person)*
užasan *oo-zha-san awful*
uže ⓝ *oo-zhe rope*
uživati imp *oo-zhee-va-tee (have) fun*
užurban *oo-zhoor-ban in a hurry*

V

vadičep ⓜ *va-dee-chep corkscrew*
(iz)vagati *(eez-)va-ga-tee weigh*
vagina ① *va-gee-na vagina*
val ⓜ *val wave*
vani *va-nee outside*
važan *va-zhan important*
večer ⓜ *ve-cher evening*
večera ① *ve-che-ra dinner*
večeras *ve-che-ras tonight*
već *vech already*

veći *ve*-chee *bigger*

vedar *ve*-dar *fine (weather)*

vegetarijanac ⓜ ve-ge-ta-ree-*ya*-nats *vegetarian*

veličina ① ve-lee-*chee*-na *size (general)*

velik *ve*-leek *big*

veliki tjedan ① *ve*-lee-kee *tye*-dan *Holy Week*

veljača ① *ve*-lya-cha *February*

vena ① *ve*-na *vein*

Venecija ① ve-*ne*-tsee-ya *Venice*

venecijanski ve-ne-*tsee*-yan-skee *Venetian*

ventilator ⓜ ven-tee-*la*-tawr *fan (machine)*

veslanje ⓝ ve-*sla*-nye *rowing*

veza ① *ve*-za *connection*

vi vee *you* pol sg & pl

video kazeta ① *vee*-de-aw ka-*ze*-ta *video tape*

video rekorder ⓜ *vee*-de-aw re-*kawr*-der *video recorder*

vidik ⓜ *vee*-deek *lookout*

vidjeti/viđati *vee*-dye-tee/*vee*-ja-tee *see*

vijesti ① pl *vee*-ye-stee *news*

vikend ⓜ *veek*-end *weekend*

viknuti/vikati *veek*-noo-tee/*vee*-ka-tee *shout*

viljuška ① vee-*lyoosh*-ka *fork*

vino ⓝ *vee*-naw *wine*

vinograd ⓜ *vee*-naw-grad *vineyard*

vinova loza ① *vee*-naw-va *law*-za *vine*

virus ⓜ *vee*-roos *virus*

visina ① vee-*see*-na *altitude*

viski ⓜ *vee*-skee *whisky*

visok vee-*sawk* *high* • *tall*

visoka stolica za bebe ① *vee*-saw-ka *staw*-lee-tsa za *be*-be *highchair*

višak prtljage ⓜ *vee*-shak prt-*lya*-ge *excess (baggage)*

više *vee*-she *more*

vitamini ⓜ pl vee-ta-*mee*-nee *vitamins*

viza ① *vee*-za *visa*

vjećanje ⓝ *vye*-cha-nye *conference (small)*

vjenčan *vyen*-chan *married (of man)*

vjenčana *vyen*-cha-na *married (of woman)*

vjenčanje ⓝ *vyen-cha*-nye *wedding*

vjera ① *vye*-ra *religion*

vjeren *vye*-ren *engaged (marriage)*

vjerenica ① *vye*-re-nee-tsa *fiancée*

vjerenik ⓜ *vye*-re-neek *fiancé*

vjerenje ⓝ *vye*-re-nye *engagement*

(po)vjerovati (paw-)*vye*-raw-va-tee *trust*

vjerski *vyer*-skee *religious (concerning religion)*

vjetar ⓜ *vye*-tar *wind*

vjetrobran ⓜ *vye*-traw-bran *windscreen*

vlada ① *vla*-da *government*

vlak ⓜ vlak *train*

vlasnik ⓜ *vla*-sneek *owner*

voće ⓝ *vaw*-che *fruit*

voda ① *vaw*-da *water*

vodene kozice ① pl *vaw*-de-ne *kaw*-zee-tse *chickenpox*

vodič ⓜ *vaw*-deech *guide (person)* • *guidebook*

vodka ① *vawd*-ka *vodka*

vodopad ⓜ *vaw*-daw-pad *waterfall*

vojna obveza ① *voy*-na *awb*-ve-za *military service*

vojnik ⓜ *voy*-neek *soldier*

vojska ① *voy*-ska *military*

volan bicikla ⓜ *vaw*-lan bee-*tsee*-kla *handlebars*

voljeti imp *vaw*-lye-tee *like (a person)* • *love*

vozačka dozvola ① *vaw*-zach-ka *dawz*-vaw-la *driving licence*

voziti imp *vaw*-zee-tee *drive*
— **bicikl** imp bee-*tsee*-kl *cycle*

vozni red ⓜ *vawz*-nee red *timetable*

vožnja ① *vawzh*-nya *ride (trip)*
— **biciklom** bee-*tsee*-klawm *cycling*
— **na skateboardu** na *skeyt*-bawr-doo *skateboarding*

vrač ⓜ vrach *fortune-teller*

vrata ① *vra*-ta *door*

vratar ⓜ *vra*-tar *goalkeeper*

vratiti/vraćati se *vra*-tee-tee/*vra*-cha-tee se *return (come back)*

vreća za spavanje ① *vre*-cha za *spa*-va-nye *sleeping bag*

vremenski uvjeti ⓜ pl *vre*-men-skee *oo*-vye-tee *weather*

vrh ⓜ vrh *summit*

vrhnje ⓝ *vrh*-nye *cream (food)*

vrijednost ① *vree*-yed-nawst *value (price)*

vrijeme ⓝ *vree*-ye-me *time*

vrlo *vr*-law *very*

vrsta ① *vr*-sta *type*

vrt ⓜ vrt *garden*

vrtić za djecu ⓜ vr·teech za dye·tsoo kindergarten
vrtlar ⓜ vrt·lar gardener
vrtlarstvo ⓝ vrt·lars·tvaw gardening
vruć vrooch hot
vrućina ⓕ vroo·chee·na heat
(po)vući (paw·)voo·chee pull
vuna ⓕ voo·na wool

Z

za za to · with
zabavan za·ba·van fun
zaboraviti/zaboravljati za·baw·ra·vee·tee/za·baw·rav·lya·tee forget
zabrinut ⓜ za·bree·noot worried
zagađenje ⓝ za·ga·je·nye pollution
zaglavljen za·glav·lyen blocked
zagrijan za·gree·yan heated
zahod ⓜ za·hawd toilet
zahvalan za·hva·lan grateful
zahvaliti/zahvaljivati za·hva·lee·tee/za·hva·lyee·va·tee thank
zajedno zai·ed·naw together
zakašnjenje ⓝ za·kash·nye·nye delay
zaključan zak·lyoo·chan locked
zaključati/zaključavati zak·lyoo·cha·tee/zak·lyoo·cha·va·tee lock
zakon ⓜ za·kawn law
zakonit za·kaw·neet legal
zakonodavstvo ⓝ za·kaw·naw·davs·tvaw legislation
zalazak sunca ⓜ za·la·zak soon·tsa sunset
zaleđen za·le·jen frozen
zalihe hrane ⓕ pl za·lee·he hra·ne food supplies
zamijeniti/zamjenjivati za·mee·ye·nee·tee/za·mee·ye·nyee·va·tee change (money)
zamrznuti/zamrzavati za·mr·znoo·tee/za·mr·za·va·tee freeze
zanimljiv za·neem·lyeev interesting
zapad ⓜ za·pad west
započeti/započinjati za·paw·che·tee/za·paw·chee·nya·tee start
zaposlenik/zaposlenica ⓜ/ⓕ za·paw·sle·neek/za·paw·sle·nee·tsa employee
zaraditi/zarađivati za·ra·dee·tee/za·ra·jee·va·tee earn
zaraza ⓕ za·ra·za infection
zastava ⓕ za·sta·va flag
zaštićen zash·tee·chen protected (species)
(za)štititi (za·)shtee·tee·tee protect
zašto zash·taw why
zato za·taw because
zatvor ⓜ zat·vawr gaol · jail
zatvoren zat·vaw·ren closed
zatvorenik ⓜ zat·vaw·re·neek prisoner
zatvorenje ⓝ zat·vaw·re·nye constipation
zatvoriti/zatvarati zat·vaw·ree·tee/zat·va·ra·tee close (shut)
zaušnjaci ⓜ pl za·oosh·nya·tsee mumps
zaustaviti/zaustavljati za·oo·sta·vee·tee/za·oo·stav·lya·tee stop (cease)
zauvijek za·oo·vee·yek forever
zauzet za·oo·zet busy · engaged (phone)
zavoj ⓜ za·voy bandage
završiti/završavati za·vr·shee·tee/za·vr·sha·va·tee finish
zbirka fraza ⓕ zbeer·ka fra·za phrasebook
zbog zbawg about
Zbogom. zbaw·gawm Goodbye.
zdjela ⓕ zdye·la bowl
zdravlje ⓝ zdrav·lye health
Zdravo. zdra·vaw Hello. (not answering telephone)
zec ⓜ zets rabbit
zelen ze·len green
zelena salata ⓕ ze·le·na sa·la·ta lettuce
zemlja zem·lya country · Earth · land · soil
zgodan zgaw·dan handsome
zgrada ⓕ zgra·da building
zid ⓜ zeed wall (outer)
zima ⓕ zee·ma winter
zimski kaput ⓜ zeem·skee ka·poot overcoat
zlato ⓝ zla·taw gold
zmija ⓕ zmee·ya snake
znak ⓜ znak sign
znanost ⓕ zna·nawst science
znanstvenik ⓜ znanst·ve·neek scientist
(sa)znati (sa·)zna·tee know
zob ⓕ zawb oats
zodijak ⓜ zaw·dee·yak zodiac
zološki vrt ⓜ zaw·lawsh·kee vrt zoo
zora ⓕ zaw·ra dawn
zračna luka ⓕ zrach·na loo·ka airport
zračna pošta ⓕ zrach·na pawsh·ta airmail
zračnica ⓕ zrach·nee·tsa tube (tyre)
zrak ⓜ zrak air
zrakoplov ⓜ zra·kaw·plawv airplane
zrakoplovna tvrtka ⓕ zra·kaw·plawv·na tvr·tka airline

zrakoplovna ulaznica ① *zra*·kaw·plawv·na *oo*·laz·nee·tsa *boarding pass*
zub ⓜ zoob *tooth*
zubar ⓜ *zoo*·bar *dentist*
zubi ⓜ pl *zoo*·bee *teeth*
zubobolja ① zoo·*baw*·baw·lya *toothache*
(po)zvati (*paw*·)*zva*·tee *call*
zvjezda ① *zvyez*·da *star*
(sa četiri) zvjezdice pl (sa *che*·tee·ree) *zvye*·zdee·tse *(four-)star*

Ž

žal ⓜ zhal *beach*
(po)žaliti se (*paw*·)*zha*·lee·tee se *complain*
žarulja ① *zha*·roo·lya *light bulb*
žbica ① *zhbee*·tsa *spoke*
žedan *zhe*·dan *(to be) thirsty*

(po)željeti (paw·)*zhe*·lye·tee *like • want • wish*
željeznička stanica ① zhe·lyez·nee·chka *sta*·nee·tsa *railway station*
želudac ⓜ zhe·*loo*·dats *stomach*
žemička ① zhe·*meech*·ka *roll (bread)*
žena ① *zhe*·na *wife • woman*
ženski *zhen*·skee *female*
žica ① *zhee*·tsa *wire*
žičara ① *zhee*·cha·ra *chairlift (skiing)*
Židovski *zhee*·dawv·skee *Jewish*
žitarica ① zhee·*ta*·ree·tsa *cereal*
život ⓜ *zhee*·vawt *life*
životinja ① zhee·*vaw*·tee·nya *animal*
žlica ① *zhlee*·tsa *spoon*
žličica ① *zhlee*·chee·tsa *teaspoon*
žmigavac ⓜ *zhmee*·ga·vats *indicator (car)*
žohar ⓜ *zhaw*·har *cockroach*
žulj ⓜ zhool' *blister*
žut ⓜ zhoot *yellow*
žvakača guma ① *zhva*·ka·cha *goo*·ma *chewing gum*